"My God and My All"

A PRAYER
For Those Who Live Alone

I live alone, dear Lord,
Stay by my side,
In all my daily needs
Be Thou my guide.
Grant me good health,
For that indeed, I pray,
To carry on my work
from day to day.
Keep pure my mind,
My thoughts, my every deed,
Let me be kind, unselfish
In my neighbor's need.
Spare me from fire, from flood,
Malicious tongues,
From thieves, from fear,
And evil ones.
If sickness or an accident befall,
Then humbly, Lord, I pray,
Hear Thou my call.
And when I'm feeling low,
Or in despair,
Lift up my heart
And help me in my prayer.
I live alone, dear Lord,
Yet have no fear,
Because I feel Your Presence
Ever near. Amen.

Joe Kotcka

⟫⟫⟫⟩⟩⟩ *With Ecclesiastical Approval* ⟩⟩⟩⟩⟫⟫

A PICTURE HISTORY OF RUSSIA

A PICTURE HISTORY

OF RUSSIA

EDITED BY JOHN STUART MARTIN

Revised and Augmented Third Edition

CROWN PUBLISHERS, INC.
NEW YORK

REVISED AND AUGMENTED THIRD EDITION

© 1945, 1956, 1968, by Crown Publishers, Inc.

Printed in the United States of America

Published simultaneously in Canada by

General Publishing Company Limited

Designed by Robert Josephy

CONTENTS

ACKNOWLEDGMENTS

It would have been impossible to collate this book without the understanding and assistance of many people. To bring the work into focus, to give it depth and dependability, not only the thoughtful advice of scholars steeped in the subject was essential, but also the aid of persons well acquainted with the whole range of Russian archives, art, and iconography.

To all those who contributed to this work in one or other of these ways, the Editor wishes here to express sincere thanks.

In preparing the present, enlarged edition, prime assistance has been rendered by Professor Ellsworth L. Raymond, head of Russian area studies at New York University. After serving at the U.S. Embassy in Moscow (1938–1943) as a research analyst, Dr. Raymond brought home a talented Russian wife, and by recent tours of Russia, he and she have kept in touch with Soviet life. He worked with the U.S. Army General Staff (1944–1946), and has held fellowships from the Rockefeller Foundation, Ford Foundation, and New York State Government. The author of two books (*Soviet Economic Progress* and *The Soviet State*), Dr. Raymond has also taught at the Graduate Institute of International Studies in Switzerland.

In collecting and articulating the original volume (Chapters I through XII), consultation was generously given by members of the faculty of the Intensive Study of Contemporary Russian Civilization held in 1944 at Cornell University. Frederick L. Schuman, Woodrow Wilson Professor of Government at Williams College, cast a helpfully critical eye upon many of the picture selections for those chapters and most of the captions.

Dr. Franz Weidenreich, disinguished guest anthropologist at The American Museum of Natural History, contributed the chart and discussion of the dispersal of mankind, through the kind offices of his colleague, Dr. William Gregory. Their assistant, Miss D. F. Levett Bradley, supplied fine charts and maps. The museum's library staff fetched and carried countless heavy books. At the American Geographical Society, John Philip functioned as the book's chief map-maker, with A.G.S. staff members standing by to do research. From the unrivaled collection of Dr. Alfred Salmony of the Institute of Fine Arts of New York University came many a picture of the artifacts by which pre-Slavic history is traced.

Dr. Corliss Lamont kindly made available his definitive tabulations of the Soviet Union's national composition.

In The New York Public Library, Avram Yarmolinsky and Mrs. Anna Heifetz of the Slavonic Division, and Miss Ramona Jawitz in the Picture Collection were infallibly patient and productive. So were certain staff experts in The Metropolitan Museum of Art.

Officials of the Library of Congress were kind and attentive.

Miss Lee T. Dixon, secretary to Dr. Frank E. Adair, president of the American Cancer Society, came up cheerfully with certain elusive facts about Russian medicine.

The list below accords credit due to the sources of picture material used in the book, and another page affords the reader a bibliography of collateral studies compiled by Prof. Raymond.

J.S.M.

PREFACES

There was a time when a man named Napoleon overran most of continental Europe and even penetrated into the Nile valley. He did this at first in the name of Republicanism, which was the product of mankind's greatest revolution since the Renaissance. Later he did it in his own name; for success and power made of him a megalomaniac and he thought he could never fail. In due course he came up against the Russian people, whose tsar at that time was the first one called Alexander. The Russians, not wishing to become the helots of any ruler save their own, and responding to their leaders' strategy of retreat-and-conquer, beat Napoleon on their own soil and then chased him across Europe. The British polished him off. Thereafter, for over a century, the Tsars of Russia and the Crown of England regarded themselves as the arbiters of the Old World.

The final battles of World War II have taken place as this book goes to press. The man called Hitler, who overran most of continental Europe in the name of national socialism, but actually out of a peculiar mass megalomania of the German ("Master") Race, has suffered Napoleon's precise fate. With strategy and fortitude as great as those of their ancestors in 1812, the Russians grappled with Hitler's armies, stopped them and hurled them back, thus saving the British and American people vast amounts of blood, sweat and treasure. There can be no suggestion today that the Russians fought Hitler to save Europe and the British Empire and America, any more than when they beat Napoleon. They fought, now as then, to save their own skins. And now as then, in victory they give themselves full credit for making Europe safer for themselves.

American might in the Pacific Theatre, culminating in the atomic bomb, put an end to Japan's pretensions as a world power before the U.S.S.R. got more than started to help toward that end. But Russia's interests in the Far East are considerable and must be regarded with respect commensurate to her new position in Europe.

In other words, in the world to which peace has returned, Russia will consider her stake and authority are second to none.

In this war the Russians were headed, not by a tsar, but by the tsarlike head of a political system which is supposed to be an antithesis of tsarism. The government of Stalin differs from all other great governments, and it is still changing its form. Here arises a fact of profound importance: no matter how much or how little of an arbiter in world affairs Joseph Stalin's nation now seeks to be, it is essential that non-Russians make an earnest attempt to understand the Soviet peoples and the transition they are going through. The great majority of human beings dislike or scorn those things which they do not understand. At this juncture in the world's history, it would be catastrophic for non-Russians and Russians to take this attitude toward each other. A mutuality of live-and-let-live, with respect on both sides, would appear to recommend itself as the most sensible and profitable attitude. As Eric Johnston, president of the U. S. Chamber of Commerce, said to the trade leaders of Moscow:

"Each of our two countries should be allowed to pursue its own unique economic experiment unimpeded by the other. Here we stand, we Americans. There you stand, you peoples of the Soviet Union, on the other side of the gulf. Let us admit and tolerate the gulf...."

The basic difference between the Soviets of today and most other people is that the Soviet state denounces the profit system; regards as state property — the property of all — every means of producing wealth and all the country's capital. This is offensive to most other nations, where concepts of private property and personal gain seem ageless and unchangeable. What most people forget is that this anti-capitalist system, which sprang from the ratiocinations of a European wanderer named Marx, took root and flowered in a country where, to start with at the time of its Revolution, very few people had anything in the way of capital. For centuries the Russian masses had been Have-Nots who needed only leaders and discipline to teach them to overthrow the extremely few Haves who ruled and exploited them.

But even if Soviet Russia today should be viewed as a menace to capitalism, as a world proselytizer for Communism as well as a home practitioner thereof, still it would be wisest for the people of other countries to study the Soviet Russian peoples; to find out just "how they got that way" and what, perhaps, to expect from them now that they have proven their potency in world affairs. Foolish indeed is the person who says that anyone who exhibits interest in Russia nowadays is an incipient Communist, or that to read Russian history is to expose oneself to the Red contagion.

August, 1945   John Stuart Martin

This augmented edition of A PICTURE HISTORY OF RUSSIA, after eleven years have passed, endeavors to retain the objective viewpoint of the original edition while clarifying the latter in the light of later, more complete information about Soviet Russia's formative and World War II years. In view of the postwar strides made by the U.S.S.R. toward "world supremacy" and the retrogression of other great powers as a result of World War II and of the rise of nationalism and self-determination of colonial peoples, some understanding of what modern Russia is and how it evolved seems more important than ever.

April, 1956   J.S.M.

A third edition of this book seemed obligatory when, after less than ten years in the saddle, Nikita Khrushchev was unhorsed in 1964 by a team of bureaucrats whose very tameness seemed a new portent in Soviet history, and therefore perhaps new handwriting on the wall of the world's future. And what years the ones between 1956 (the year of our second edition) and 1967, the U.S.S.R.'s golden anniversary, had been! Forty new pages are a lot to add to a book with the broad scope and long-range focus of this one. Yet even that number has seemed insufficient, and the updating accounts all too cursory, to cover so eventful a period.

In extenuation, let it be realized that the speed of mankind's evolution — in all directions — appears (like the population) to be increasing geometrically. Yesterday's astounding Sputnik is today's sophisticated vehicle to the moon. The "agrarian reform" of 1949 in China has resulted in a Communist monster-state threatening even to the gigantic U.S.S.R. And the latter, long a landlocked leviathan, now ranges the globe with a huge new navy and merchant marine as well as with superplanes, megarockets, and all-sensing sidereal satellites.

The more things change nowadays the more different they get, not the more same. If these new pages give some sense of this, then even in their brevity they will do their job. For in the next Soviet era, as in all mankind's, the changes doubtless will be even more rapid and radical. To expatiate too much here on "just yesterday" might obscure some amazing "only tomorrows."

1968   J.S.M.

A SHORT BIBLIOGRAPHY OF BOOKS ON RUSSIA

Note: Out-of-print books and those believed to be not easily available to the general public have been omitted.

BRUMBERG, ABRAHAM. *Communism After Stalin* (New York: Praeger, 1960).

BRZEZINSKI, ZBIGNIEW K. *The Soviet Bloc: Unity and Conflict* (Cambridge: Harvard University Press, 1967).

CAMPBELL, ROBERT. *Soviet Economic Power* (Boston: Houghton Mifflin, 1966).

CARR, EDWARD H. *The Bolshevik Revolution, 1917–1923* (New York: Macmillan, 1953)

—— *The Interregnum, 1923–1924* (New York: Macmillan, 1954).

—— *Socialism in One Country, 1924–1926* (New York: Macmillan, 1960).

CRESSEY, GEORGE B. *Soviet Potentials: A Geographic Appraisal* (Syracuse: Syracuse University Press, 1962).

DEUTSCHER, ISAAC. *Stalin, a Political Biography* (New York: Oxford University Press, 1967).

FAINSOD, MERLE. *How Russia Is Ruled* (Cambridge: Harvard University Press, 1963).

FLORINSKY, MICHAEL T. *Russia: A Short History* (New York: Macmillan, 1964).

GARTHOFF, RAYMOND L. *Soviet Military Policy* (New York: Praeger, 1966).

GOLDMAN, MARSHALL I. *Soviet Foreign Aid* (New York: Praeger, 1967).

KERENSKY, ALEXANDER. *Russia and History's Turning Point* (New York: Duell, Sloan and Pearce, 1965).

LAQUEUR, WALTER. *Russia and Germany: A Century of Conflict* (Boston: Little Brown, 1965).

LASERSON, MAX M. *The American Impact on Russia—Diplomatic and Ideological—1784–1917* (New York: Macmillan, 1950).

LINDEN, CARL A. *Khrushchev and the Soviet Leadership, 1957–1964* (Baltimore: Johns Hopkins University Press, 1966).

MASSIE, ROBERT K. *Nicholas and Alexandra* (New York: Atheneum, 1967).

McNEAL, ROBERT H. *International Relations Among Communists* (Englewood Cliffs, N. J.: Prentice-Hall, 1967).

McNEILL, WILLIAM H. *America, Britain and Russia, Their Cooperation and Conflict, 1941–1946* (New York: Oxford University Press, 1954).

MORTON, HENRY W. *Soviet Sport: Mirror of Soviet Society* (New York: Collier Books, 1963).

MOSELY, PHILIP E., ed. *The Soviet Union, 1922–1962* (New York: Praeger, 1963).

Outline History of the USSR (Moscow: Foreign Languages Publishing House, 1960).

PAGE, STANLEY W. *Lenin and World Revolution* (New York: New York University Press, 1959).

RAYMOND, ELLSWORTH. *The Soviet State* (New York: Macmillan, 1968).

RIGBY, T. H., *Stalin* (Englewood Cliffs, N. J.: Prentice-Hall, 1966).

RUBINSTEIN, ALVIN Z. *The Foreign Policy of the Soviet Union* (New York: Random House, 1966).

SCHAPIRO, LEONARD. *The Government and Politics of the Soviet Union* (New York: Random House, 1966).

SHULMAN, MARSHALL D. *Beyond the Cold War* (New Haven: Yale University Press, 1966).

SPINKA, MATHEW. *The Church in Soviet Russia* (New York: Oxford University Press, 1956).

STALIN, JOSEPH. *Foundations of Leninism* (New York: International, 1939).

The State of Soviet Science (Cambridge: Massachusetts Institute of Technology Press, 1965).

SWEARINGEN, RODGER, ed. *Soviet and Chinese Communist Power in the World Today* (New York: Basic Books, 1966).

TOMASIC, DINKO. *The Impact of Russian Culture on Soviet Communism* (Glencoe, Ill.: The Free Press, 1953).

TREADGOLD, DONALD W. *The Great Siberian Migration, 1861–1913* (Princeton: Princeton University Press, 1957).

—— *Twentieth Century Russia* (Chicago: Rand McNally, 1964).

TROTSKY, LEON. *The Russian Revolution* (Garden City, N.Y.: Doubleday, 1959).

WREN, MELVIN C. *The Course of Russian History* (New York: Macmillan, 1968).

I. PREHISTORIC RUSSIA

Many anthropologists — students of the origin and evolution of man — are by now persuaded that the vast reaches of Asia, Mother of Continents, contained the prime spawning grounds of mankind. The species *homo sapiens* may also have been generated independently, in Africa. But the chief garden or gardens of Eden were probably in the enormous land mass to which India, on the southeast, and Europe on the extreme west, are mere geologic appendages.

This likelihood is interesting not only in itself, but in any historical contemplation of the society which today, as a union of sixteen nations and twelve autonomous republics, inhabits and controls a bulk of the Eurasian land mass aggregating one-sixth of the earth's inhabitable surface, about 9,000,000 square miles, or roughly thrice the area of the United States. This country still commonly called Russia, but more properly the Union of Soviet Socialist Republics, actually represents a huge synthesis of earth's most ancient peoples. Whatever it may now be or in future become as a "country" or a "power," the U.S.S.R. of today stands in history as the greatest of all those human mergers which nature evolved several millennia after the series of racial explosions which dispersed throughout the world the original, nascent portions of the human family.

Any study of the Russian people from their earliest polyglot emergence to their present unified state calls, therefore, for a glance at the nature of the land mass which brought them forth. From the Bering Strait to the Baltic and from the Arctic Ocean to the borders of Turkey, Iran (Persia), India, Thibet and China, the U.S.S.R. is one gigantic plain framed on the south and southeast by mountains. Except in its far northeastern corner, this plain is interrupted only once by a north-south mountain chain and that one, the Urals, is little more forbidding than the Adirondacks or the Ozarks. The southerly barriers of the plain are some of the earth's mightiest mountains — the Caucasus, the Hindu Kush, the Pamirs, the Tien Shan, the Altai.

The drainage of this plain is extraordinary. In the European part, all the main streams originate around a slight central elevation, where Moscow is now, and from there wind their way to five seas: the White and the Baltic in the north; the Black, Azov and Caspian in the south. In the Asian part, five great river systems cross the continent from south to north, flowing from the heart of Asia into the Arctic.

All along the Arctic Ocean there is a tundra (marshy) belt, flowered in summer, frozen in winter, precisely like northern Canada. Then comes the forest area, comprising about one-third of the world's lumber supply. Southward as the forest thins out there begin the great black-soil plains followed, farther south, by deserts, and finally by strips of sub-tropics. Thus from north to south one encounters practically all types of climate, vegetation and animal life. The territory of the Union is greater than all of South America, and no other single country knows such distances within its borders. As night begins to fall along its western borders, day is breaking on its Pacific coast.

In so wide and deep a land mass, it is not surprising to find every resource of nature in bountiful quantities — coal, oil, all the metals, all the minerals.

Long before the dawn of history, man inhabited this living space, hunting beasts like the wooly mammoth, whose carcasses are still preserved in the frozen soil of Siberia. Various tribes of the Ural-Altai family, including the Finnish, Turk and Mongol, inhabited the North. In the South, over the great plains, peoples of the Indo-European family swarmed in succession from Asia into Europe. From the northwest came two other strains, the Germanic Goths and the Norsemen. Probably about eight centuries before Christ the Scythians out of Persia began to roam the South Russian steppes. The cities of ancient Greece started to colonize the coasts of the Black Sea in the next century. Flourishing Greek city states dotted the coastline and traded with the Scythians. In the fourth century B.C. the Sarmatians took the place of the Scythians. With the rise of Rome the South of Russia became a part of the empire of the Caesars. When Rome began to weaken, the Goths reached the shores of the Black Sea. But the main drive of peoples was from the East. In the fifth century A.D. the Huns swept into Europe under Attila, the "scourge of God." Then in the sixth century came the Avars, eliminating what remained of the Huns. All the way from the Altai Mountains the Turks drove into southern Russia about a century later. On the Volga a Bulgar kingdom flourished; now only the name is preserved in Balkan Bulgaria, but by an entirely different people. In the eighth century the Khazars ruled South Russia, fought with the Arabs and the Greeks, and adopted Judaism as their faith.

What is now the Asiatic part of the Soviet Union had, from ancient times, peoples and cultures, prehistoric and historic, too numerous to mention here, at times forming part of great Mongolian empires that centered in China. In the West, in Transcaucasia, the ancient Urartd culture flourished long before our era, even before the Scythians. The Persian King Darius I, whose armies later fought the Greeks at Marathon, tried to invade South Russia, but the Scythians so harassed his army while retreating that he had to withdraw. One of the generals of Alexander the Great attempted to go east north of the Black Sea while the Macedonian conqueror marched southeast through the Persian Empire, but failed to get through.

But where are the Russians, or rather, their ancestors, the early Slavs? They came from somewhere around the Carpathian mountains, some going northwest, others northeast. Probably in about the sixth century A.D. the Slavs began penetrating north along the rivers of Russia. With the Finnish tribes they seem to have had no conflicts; the land is vast, the forest dense, and the interpenetration of the Slavs was peaceful. The steppes in the South were a constant source of trouble. There powerful armies of horsemen appeared, as if from nowhere, amid the tall boundless grass. The forests provided lumber and a good place to hide; but they were also full of wild beasts and spooks. The rivers were the real sanctuary: they provided fishing and easy avenues for communication. The Slavs began to dot the rivers with their settlements, forming highways from the Vikings of Scandinavia to the Greeks in Byzantium (later Constantinople). Soon the Slavs began to develop trade as well as hunting and fishing, and some of their settlements became towns: Staraya Russa, Novgorod, Kiev.

Empires fought over parts of what later became Russia. Various civilizations colonized its edges. Nomadic peoples like the Hungarians rode its steppes. Other nomads settled and stayed for a few centuries, only to be dislodged by the next wave from the East. But it was the Slavs who gradually penetrated and populated the entire area. They came, multiplied, and made it their permanent home.

In the 9th Century, the Vikings began to descend south from Scandinavia. They ravaged the coasts of western and southern Europe, established "Norman" states as far down as Sicily and in 1066 under William, Duke of Normandy, conquered England. In the east of Europe the Slavs used to refer to them as the Varangians. These invaders came over the Baltic Sea, went up the rivers, then dragged their boats across the narrow strips of land separating the sources of the rivers and launched their boats once more to go down the rivers flowing south into the Black and Caspian seas. The Norse warriors quickly subjugated the Slavs, but they were few in numbers and they also were soon absorbed by the Slavs.

The first ruler of Russia was a Viking adventurer named Rurik who, according to legend, settled in Novgorod in 862 and died probably around 873. What remains of Russia's prehistory now fills museums. On the bones of these ancient civilizations the Slavs slowly created their state, and it is with these efforts of the Slavs that the history of Russia proper really begins.

THE LIVING SPACE CALLED "RUSSIA"

UNION OF SOVIET SOCIALIST REPUBLICS

Length: N to S — 2,880 miles

Breadth: E to W — 7,000 miles

Area: 8,600,000 square miles (1968)

Population: 238,000,000 (est. 1968)

Ethnic Groups: 177

Nationalities having own administrative divisions: 53

Languages: 80 approx.   (*See table* pp. 244-5).

THE LAND MASS

THE MIDNIGHT SUN shines on 9,000 miles of Russian coastline all summer.

CAPE CHELASKOE. A northernmost point of the U.S.S.R. mainland is Cape Chelaskoe at 70°13′ N. The cross was erected in 1821 by Lieut. Wrangell of the Russian Army, later Governor of Alaska. (The extra bar on the Russian Orthodox cross represents the mocking legend placed over Christ's head. The bottom bar is slanted to recall Christ's pressing down with his foot in anguish.)

LAND STRUCTURE NORTH OF LENINGRAD (*left*), air view made from the *Graf Zeppelin*.

MOUNT ELBRUS. Dawn on Mt. Elbrus, highest peak (5,630 metres) in the Caucasus. The Germans planted their flag here in 1942 — but got little farther.

EARLY MEN AND BEASTS

Natural historians and artists have tried to picture earliest man in north Europe and Asia. Top and bottom of this page are American versions of a parade of mammoths and reindeer. and of a family of Baltic staghunters. They were painted for the American Museum of Natural History in New York City by Artist Charles R. Knight. The other three pictures are Russian: cave men stoning a mammoth in a pitfall, a cave clan at home; later Stone Age settlement with barns, fences, kine, cooking utensils, arrows spears. All such pictures are imaginary but not wholly so. They are based on objects found in graves, camp sites, and on rock carvings like those on page 8. Few people are so interested in their pre-history as the Russians, who are constantly searching and digging for relics all over their living space.

Mammoth carcasses have been found in Russia's frozen tundra so well preserved that the flesh could be eaten.

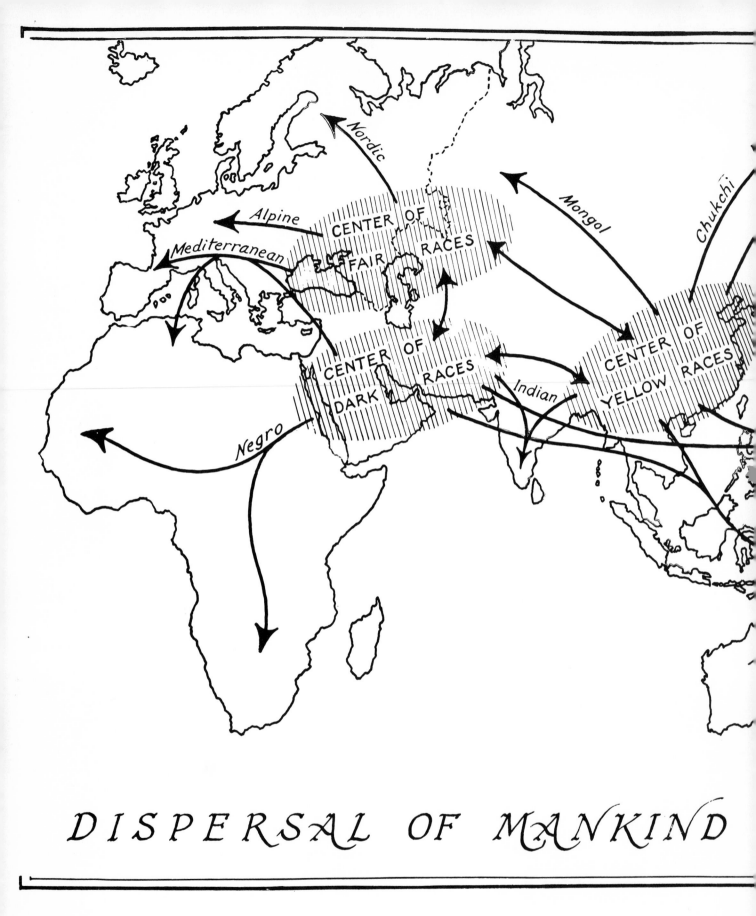

DISPERSAL OF MANKIND

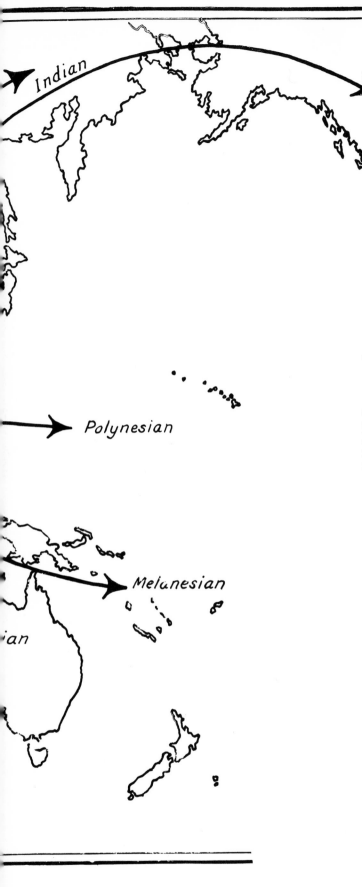

Indian

Polynesian

Melanesian

ian

"THE GARDENS OF EDEN"

In 1926 the late great Dr. Henry Fairfield Osborn, president of the American Museum of Natural History (New York), summarized and expanded the theory (1911) of the late Dr. William D. Matthew, that the higher mammals in general, and mankind in particular, had their origin in Central Asia. Findings in the Gobi desert of human traces contemporary with all but the very oldest (Eolithic) of Europe, led Dr. Osborn to prophesy "that the Dawn Man will be found in the high Asiatic plateau region and not in the forested lowlands of Asia." Soon after, in 1929, the so-called Peking Man, oldest of *homo sapiens* yet known, was indeed exhumed in an Asian highland, though farther east than Dr. Osborn had predicted.

With his 1926 writing, Dr. Osborn published a chart by his colleague Dr. William K. Gregory, schematizing the dispersal areas of the basic branches of the human family from around the Central Asian plateau, with the Himalaya Mountains as a vortex. This chart has not been revised since that time.

For the record and to bring this *Picture History of Russia* down to 1945, the editor invited Dr. Franz Weidenreich, then an honored guest at the late Dr. Osborn's institution and the world's leading student of ancient man, to refine and redraw the chart of the Dispersal of Mankind. The accompanying chart is the result. Without going into such detail as the Gregory chart, the Weidenreich version defines clearly not just one big "Garden of Eden" in Central Asia, but three of them, far flung on Asia's edges.

The one for the dark races stretches from western India to northeast Africa. This, believed the oldest, includes the presumed Biblical site of *"the"* Garden of Eden somewhere in Mesopotamia and should give satisfaction to Fundamentalists. The center for the yellow races is put where the layman would expect to find it: where the yellow races are thickest today. And the center for the fair races, covering the Caucasus, reconfirms the white man in his use of the term Caucasian.

Dr. Weidenreich's arrows indicate the major migrations and interminglings of the world's basic human stocks. They show clearly why the living space now called "Russia" inevitably became the cradle of so many kinds of men.

STONE AGE MEN

After the last Ice Age, man wandered northward from his lower Asian birthplace. Man also strayed westward and eastward until all of Europe and even America (via the Aleutian land bridge or island chain) became thinly populated with men who had fire, skin garments and stone weapons but no metals. What is now Russia contained early people not very different from those found in Spain, Cornwall and China. They mostly followed ocean coast lines and river valleys.

With flints they "carved" on rocks the birds and beasts they saw around them. The Neolithic (late stone age) artist of these scratchings near the White Sea tried duplicating his own kind of bear-like footprint (*see left below*).

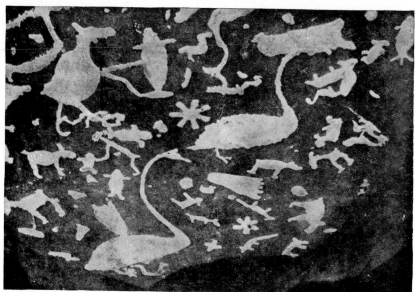

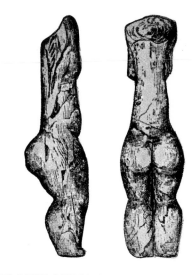

THIS NOT VERY PRETTY Neolithic lady from near Kiev reveals late Stone Age effort to sculpt in three dimensions.

Though mostly they wandered in the open, sheltering in caves only if the weather was rough, when Stone Age people died they were buried in style. **"DOLMEN"** is the name for these burial houses of 3,000 B.C. or so in the Caucasus. Massive slab structures like them are found all around the Mediterranean and in Britain. The hole (sometimes plugged with a stone) was for inserting added corpses. Whole colonies of dolmens have been found, usually on a bluff commanding a sea view. In flat inland country, the dolmens are sunk in the ground. The side view (*below, right*) shows how ponderous were the roof slabs.

METAL-USING MEN

By 1,000 B.C., the earliest "Russians" (like men in other countries) had learned to carve stone really well. The wing-shaped deity on the far right, a monolith six feet high, stands near Minusinsk in the southern Urals and reminds one of an Eskimo totem, from which it is not far removed. It is contemporary with the spidery, impolite "sun god" figure in copper (*left, below*), also from the Ural region where the people were hunters and trappers sooner than artisans.

The pair of branching horns (probably oxen) with bells below (*right*) was hung near a spring as an offering to the god thereof, near Kazbek in the Caucasus. Interesting to archaeologists is the evident influence of Mesopotamian culture from far over the mountains to the south.

Mesopotamian influence is strongly visible in a silver urn found at Maikop in the Caucasus, dated by archaeologists about 2,000 B.C. The peoples of the Tigris and Euphrates valleys penetrated northwards to get furs, taking with them their skills in metal work which developed in Sumeria and Ur as early as 4,000 B.C. To see the whole design of this urn, look below.

The picture unfolded is that of the World as the Caucasians conceived it. Above are the forests and mountains of the north, with a bear in the woods. The rivers flow south into the sea and the animals of the earth parade: ox, horse, lion, goat, pig. A duck swims in one river, a wading bird emerges from the other. The holes were for handles.

THE SCYTHIANS

Earliest inhabitants of Russia proper of whom any real history is known were the Scythians, a nomadic people of the same stock as the Iranians (Persians) with a strong Turko-Mongol admixture. The western Scythians were fat, indolent, agricultural. The eastern ones were nomads who lived on and with their horses; even ate them and drank their milk. They wore long snug trousers and stout boots of soft leather. Their weapons, with which they made very free, were a short javelin and a bow-and-arrow carried in one case.

The Scythians appeared on the South Russian steppe about 700 B.C. out of the east. They fought and traded with the Greeks who soon colonized on the shores of the Black Sea. Of them, the Greek historian Herodotus wrote: "Having neither cities nor forts, and carrying their dwellings with them wherever they go; accustomed, one and all, to shoot from horseback; and living not by husbandry but on their cattle, their wagons the only houses that they possess, how can they fail of being unconquerable?"

GREEK INFLUENCE upon the Scythians is seen in the handle on the mirror at the right. Strictly Scythian mirrors had no handles, but the lion at the end identifies this one as Scythian because the Scythians invariably introduced animals in their art. The nostrils of the horse's head (*far right*) are, fancifully, two rabbits.

This magnificent Scythian stag is solid gold, actual size. It had blue glass-paste eyes. It was found in what is now Hungary.

In the urn frieze above can be seen Scythians stringing a bow, inspecting a toothache, wrapping up a leg wound. The detail on the right shows a Scythian hobbling his extremely well-drawn horse. The Scyths had their horses buried with them.

THE SARMATIANS

By the 3rd Century B.C. the Black Sea coasts had been occupied and the Scythians driven out by another fierce Iranian-Mongol people, the Sarmatians. Their weapons were a long lance and a sword and they wore union suits of finely woven bronze chain-mail. As the Greeks had known the Scyths, so did the Romans know the Sarmatians: to their grief.

The figure at the left is from Trajan's column in Rome: a Sarmatian warrior as he looked to the Roman Legions. Next below is the best that one Sarmatian artist could do with a horse. Below that is a more gracefully wrought lion eating a horse.

Most potent of the Sarmatian tribes were the Alans. The Caucasian clan called the Rukh-as, meaning "light" or "brilliant" Alans, was (according to some authorities) the progenitor of the Ros or Rus clan ("Russian").

Herodotus relates that the Sarmatians were descendants of young Scythian warriors who intermarried with the Amazons, from whom they learned to let their women have great freedom and influence, even to joining in battle.

AND THEIR EASTERN COUSINS. In the Altai Mountains and further east, in Mongolia, the Sarmatians had contemporary cousins. Their remains are found, as are the Sarmatians' proper, in burial places to which these nomads would ride back with their dead chiefs from their farthest wanderings. The only textile characteristic of nomads is felt, made from the hair of horses and cattle. The felt rug (*right*) and felt saddle blanket above it are typically Sarmatian though found in the Altai. The Sarmatians were supreme across South Russia until about A.D. 150. The Romans built Sevastopol as a port for the Sarmatian trade.

SOME PEOPLE WHO KNEW EARLY RUSSIA

GREEKS AND PERSIANS. As early as the 6th Century B.C. the Persians knew of the early peoples of South Russia. In 512 B.C. the great King Darius sent a column around through the Bosphorus to take the Scyths from the west. This expedition petered out in the vastnesses of the steppe.

In 339 B.C. King Philip II of Macedonia punished the Scyths severely at the Danube, to secure his northern flank for his conquest of all the Balkans. His son Alexander the Great (*right, above*) failed to include Scythia in the "world" that he conquered. While he was chasing Darius III of Persia (*far right*) out of Asia Minor, he sent a column under his general Zopyrion up across the Danube to subjugate the northern coast of the Black Sea. But this expedition met the same fate as the earlier Persian one. The Scyths so harried and discouraged Zopyrion that he got no farther than Olbia (331 B.C.), returned to Thrace.

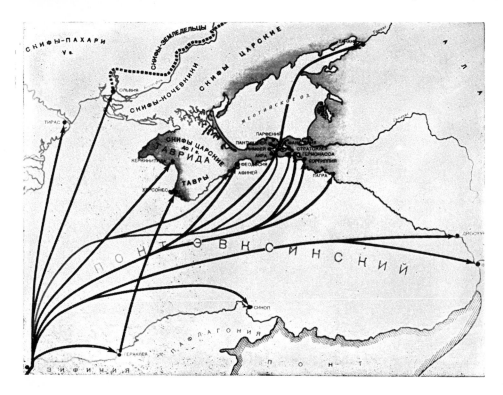

THE MAIN OBJECT: TRADE.

At Olbia (near modern Odessa) was one of the main Greek settlements with forts (*left, above*) and fine mansions of slave-owning merchants (*above*). Settlements like Olbia dotted the Black Sea coast clear to the Caucasus. On the modern Russian map at left, the principal routes and stations of the Greeks are delineated fanning out from Byzantium, together with the overland route (dotted line) described by Herodotus, leading to Tartary and the China trade.

Furs, honey and slaves were the chief trade goods of the northern peoples, who fought many a war to keep open their river routes to the Greek market, where they obtained ornaments and utensils of precious metal; also fabrics, perfumes, weapons and, often, tribute.

THE GOTHS

Interrupting the migrations from Asia and putting a quietus on the Sarmatians, in the 2nd Century A.D. the Teutonic Goths swarmed down Russia's rivers to the Black Sea. Wherever they were buried are found the inevitable *fibula* or shoulder clasp for a tunic (*right*). The Goths divided into the Ostrogoths, who settled in central Europe, and the Visigoths who swept westward into Spain.

But tough though the Goths were, they did not leave Russia willingly. Russia might have become a predominantly Teuton country but for one more of those swirling migrations from Asia which swept across in A.D. 375 — the Huns under Attila.

THE HUNS

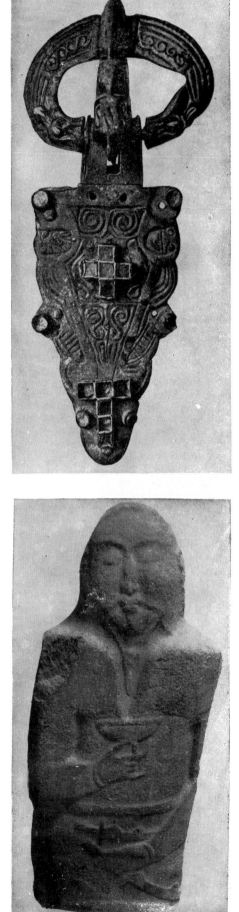

These Turko Mongols from north central Asia were closely akin, racially, to the Hordes that were to follow them a millennium later. Attila was the precursor of Genghiz and Tamerlane, except that his predilection was for butchery and rapine while the later Mongols were more interested in tribute. Their racial center of gravity came to rest in the Crimea. (*Right*): a Hunnish ornament of gold with semi-precious stones *Essential point:* in Hunnish art, all the animals so beloved by other Asian peoples completely disappear.

THE TURKS

Because they have so long lived in the Middle East as Turks, people are prone to forget that this warlike breed originated in the Altai region and came charging into the west in the 6th Century A.D., propelled by the Tang of China. They swept a lot more Avars (Sarmatians) before them. They helped subdue the Huns with whom, after the fighting subsided, they united (and also with the Bulgars of the steppes) to create the Khazar mixture.

With the Turks as with all Asian migrants, the horse was primary. The mounted archer (*above, center*) and cavalrymen resting under a tree (*lower left*) are typical Turkish artifacts.

The Turks (eastern branch) left the country dotted with their towering stone gods and funerary figures (*right*). No archaeologist has yet explained what looks like a wine glass that was often placed in the hand of the dead chief's statue.

SOME OTHER TRIBES OF EARLY RUSSIA

THE KHAZARS. Compounded of Turk, Hun and local ingredients, the Khazars of the lower Volga dominated South Russia peacefully except for defensive action against the Persians and the Arabs. They traded with Byzantium, adopted the Jewish religion. Their capital was Itil (Astrakhan) at the Volga's mouth. (*Left*): A Khazar mirror-back.

THE KIRGHIZ. Far to the East of the Khazars were the Kirghiz: a wild, remote people whose penchant for death masks was interesting. The mascaraed lady at the right looked just so in life.

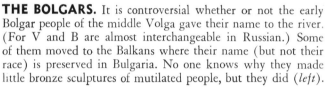

THE BOLGARS. It is controversial whether or not the early Bolgar people of the middle Volga gave their name to the river. (For V and B are almost interchangeable in Russian.) Some of them moved to the Balkans where their name (but not their race) is preserved in Bulgaria. No one knows why they made little bronze sculptures of mutilated people, but they did (*left*).

URAL TRAPPERS. Strange forest people lived by hunting and trapping in the Urals. Their "shaman" religion, of animal ancestorships and animal powers enjoyed by human descendants, is mirrored exactly among the Amerindians. (*Right*): A typical animal-headed shaman piece. The figure below (*left*) is a Ural Trapper with his arrow.

THE FINNS. The hardy, fleet-footed Finns of today are descended from a branch of the Ural-Altai trappers (an Asian stock) who left the mountains for the more arable plain to the west. Art was not much in the Finns. About the only thing found in their graves is a pendant ornament (*bottom left*).

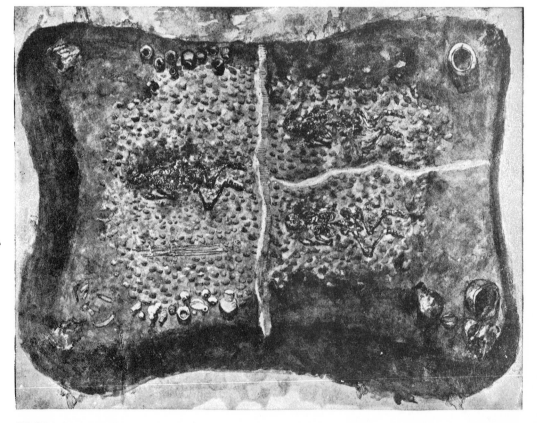

FROM DIGGINGS LIKE THIS (*above*) the story of prehistoric Russia is deciphered. From burial sites, camping spots, old villages, the bones and artifacts of early men are recovered for examination and interpretation by scholars of today. The burial site pictured here (drawn by N. K. Roerich in 1897) was the mound at Maikop whence came the bowl shown on page 9. Three skeletons of 2000 B.C. Caucasians are seen, each with knees crooked to the right, head pointed south. The corpses had been covered with some kind of red pigment, probably as a preservative.

14

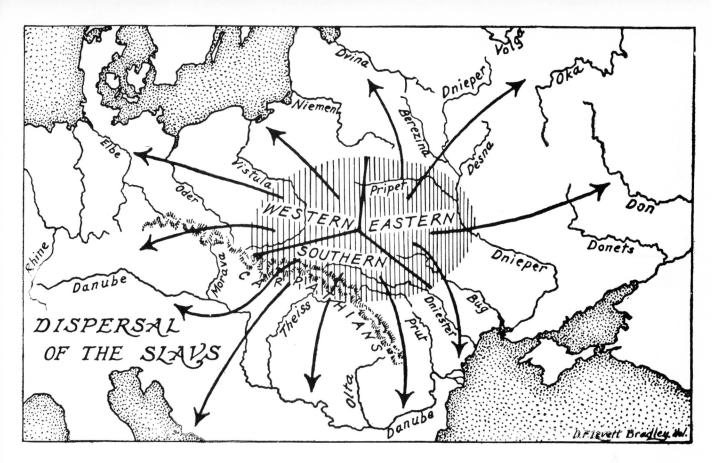

DISPERSAL OF THE SLAVS

D. Flevett Bradley. del.

FINALLY, THE SLAVS

Of the breed that was to become the master race in the Russian living space, the prime things to realize are: (1) *They were peaceful.* Living beside broad rivers on fertile plains, they tilled the soil, lived as clans and villages ("inhabited places") and were not organized militarily. (2) *They were prolific.* While other peoples rampaged hither and yon, getting killed off and spread out thin, the Slavs were home-bodies who just kept on multiplying, spreading out slowly, filling up their world's vast vacant places. (3) *Their language survived their migrations and interminglings.* The Slavic tongue can be recognized wherever the Slavs' descendants are found today.

The Slavs originated northeast of the Carpathians (*see chart, above*) in the area that gives rise to five great rivers: the Vistula, Pripet-Dnieper, Bug, Dniester and Prut. When the Goths moved out, the Slavs spread west to the Elbe, north to the Dvina, northeast to the Oka, east to the Don, southeast to the Black Sea, south to the Danube, southwest to the Adriatic. The Western Slavs mingled with other tribes. The Eastern ones grew and grew, followed the rivers, swallowed up all conquerors until they, with Norse and Finnish and Mongol and Turkish and Hunnish admixtures of varying degrees, became the Russian people. Russia's rivers were the arteries of Slavic migration north and south, and defense lines against invaders from the east.

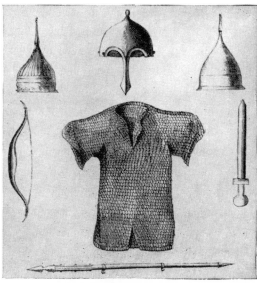

WEAPONS. When fighting was necessary, the early Slavs did it with bow, javelin, short-sword, helmet and mail shirt (*left*) which all seem derivative from neighbors who paid more attention to war.

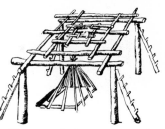

Framework for underground granary

Cultivator

LIVING EQUIPMENT. More interesting than his weapons are the early Slav's tools and contrivances for living. Items pictured here were still to be found in rural Russia in the present century.

Footpowered grain mill (modern operator)

How to descend a frozen waterfall

Friction fire-maker

15

THE NORSE, BY INVITATION

Quite as well known in the Russia of their day as in Gaul and Britain were the wing-helmed Vikings or Varangians, ancestors of all present day Scandinavians. Often they sailed up the broad Russian rivers and the Slavs welcomed them locally as mercenaries against their foes. The Vikings had settlements on the Oka and the Don, even on the lower Volga, and exacted tribute from those whom they protected. The Vikings called the gregarious Slavs' country "Gardarisk" (land of stockade towns). In the 7th century, the Slavs were pushed back from the Don and up the Dnieper to a high-banked spot where their chieftain Kiy founded the wood-walled town of Kiev. Further north, their main trading posts were Smolensk and Novgorod ("new town"), founded by primitive Slavs who probably never left their primordial marshes. According to legend, in the 9th Century the Slavs, seeing the decadence of their Khazar protectors against the Turks, and aware of new threats from the southeast in the form of the Magyars (who soon went on through to Hungary) and the Pechenegs (one more Mongol horde), sent an embassy to the leader of a company of Vikings who had visited their land before (*left*). This leader's name was Rurik. They asked him to be their protector. The year of his landing (A.D. 862) is often accepted as the year of Russia's founding as a nation. Rurik settled on Lake Ladoga to keep open an avenue of retreat since he did not trust "the savage habits of the people." He posted deputies in outlying villages to protect his flanks.

"Russ" was another name for the Vikings or Varangians and seems most likely the origin of "Russian."

RURIK'S LANDING at Novgorod is a classic scene in Russian painting (*above, left*). Another is the Viking funeral (*above*), perhaps Rurik's in 873, when he was succeeded by his kinsman Oleg. The hardy Norse incinerated their chiefs in their own ships, usually with great fiery sacrificing of live slaves, captives, favorite animals.

THREE HEROES. Legendary in Russian history are a trio of heroes of these early times: Dobrynia Nikitich, Ilya Murometz, Aliosha Popovich. The Russian painter Vasnetsov has drawn them (*left*) in character: Dobrynia, the simple, honest soldier; Ilya, giant of strength, the leader; Aliosha, a priest's son, the sly one, relying on his fleet wits and arrows.

II. THE KIEV STATE

When Rurik died, his successor, Oleg, established himself in the city of Kiev on the Dnieper. Mixed detachments of Vikings and Slavs began to raid the Greek coast of the Black Sea and the Persian coast of the Caspian. The Byzantine Greeks referred in their chronicles to "Russians" or to "Varangians" interchangeably. Oleg attacked Constantinople, the seat of the emperor of Byzantium, but failed to capture the city.

Soon the emperor found it to his advantage to negotiate with these raiders from the North and to sign treaties with them, even to hire them as guards and to fight the Turks. Russian "guests" were allowed into certain quarters of Constantinople to exchange their furs, honey, slaves and amber for the wares of the much higher Greek civilization. The Greeks even allowed these guests to go sightseeing in Constantinople. But the emperor took no chances and made the sightseers check their arms, bathe and not move around in groups exceeding fifty people.

Serving as a link between the Byzantine empire and the distant North, Kiev began to flourish. One of the Kiev princes, Svyatoslav, dominated the entire South and attempted to extend his realm into the Balkans. However, the Kiev state could not as yet oppose the Byzantine empire either militarily or diplomatically. In A.D. 971 Svyatoslav had to give in and withdraw from the Balkans. On his way home he was ambushed and murdered by nomadic tribesmen.

The Kiev Russians were heathens. They had primitive religion, worshiping large wooden idols which personified the various forces of nature. In spite of that, they seem to have had a fairly tolerant attitude toward all religions. Olga, the wife of Prince Igor (son of Rurik) and mother of Svyatoslav, became a Christian. She visited Constantinople and was received by the emperor. Among the early Russian warriors there are reported to have been many Christians. In A.D. 988, Vladimir I, the ruler of Kiev, became a Christian. The emperor was hard pressed by rebellion in the Balkans. He wanted an alliance with Vladimir against the rebels. Vladimir demanded in exchange the hand of the emperor's sister. After some negotiations Vladimir helped the emperor to crush the rebellion, became a Christian, married the sister and by her had two sons.

The old wooden idols of the Slavs were tied to horses' tails and dragged into the Dnieper. The inhabitants were driven into the Dnieper and baptized wholesale by Greek priests. Only in Novgorod did the people stand up for their old gods. Vladimir's warriors had to suppress a rebellion and baptize the people of Novgorod by force.

The adoption of Christianity from the Byzantine empire produced deep changes in the Kiev state. With the Greek priests there came the alphabet, an adaptation of the Greek script for the use of the Slavs that had been devised some years previously for use in the Balkans. There also came artisans and stonemasons. Imitations of Greek churches were erected in both Kiev and Novgorod. The emperor sent a bishop to Kiev and expected to rule Kiev Russia through the church. But the Russian princes continued strengthening their commercial and cultural ties with the Byzantine empire without submitting to domination. Soon the bishop of Kiev was a Russian approved by the patriarch at Constantinople.

A regular court, after the Greek model, was established in Kiev. The Russian people, however, remained on a double religious standard for a long time, very much like the people of Mexico or Ireland. The old gods simply moved away to the basement or the attic, becoming spirits and spooks that were revered and feared no less than the church and the Christian saints. It must also be noted that about the same time the western Slavs — the Czechs and the Poles — also became Christians, but adopted Christianity from Rome, thus laying the basis for no end of quarreling among the Slavs in succeeding centuries.

Kiev Russia grew and prospered. Prince Yaroslav the Wise promulgated the first Russian code of laws, known as the "Russian Truth." Yaroslav also seems to have been skilled in statecraft. He got his sister, son and daughters married off to important kings and princesses. Kiev Russia became a state known throughout Europe, playing no mean role in the diplomacy of the times. Why then, we may ask, did it collapse?

One of the reasons for the downfall of Kiev Russia was the system of succession to the throne. The ruling houses regarded the country as a private estate. When the prince died the oldest son would get Kiev, the next Novgorod, and so on. They did not, however, "get" those cities in the full sense of the word. They "sat" in them. If the older brother died, everyone had to move, to change their "seats." With the appearance of the third and fourth generations this arrangement led to endless trouble. A bearded nephew would be asked to vacate a good "seat" to an uncle still in the cradle. If the bearded one had a strong army and a loyal following, he would fight. Thus the entire realm was split by endless feuds of princes fighting over cities, over the question of who was going to sit where. To make matters worse, the contesting princes would invite nomads from the steppes to assist them in doing away with this or that obstreperous cousin. The country not only suffered from constant civil war but was finally overrun by the nomads who burned and pillaged. The Mongols captured and burned Kiev in 1240.

Thus the road to Byzantium down the Dnieper became impassable. The nomads were in control. An able prince, Vladimir Monomach, whose mother was the daughter of a Greek emperor, tried to reassemble the realm. For a time he succeeded. His sister married the German emperor, and Monomach himself took as his wife the daughter of an English king. But after his death in 1125 the disintegration continued. Trade declined and general impoverishment ensued. The population began to flee, some west, others north.

Those who fled north from Kiev had to go through thick forests. They settled beyond these forests through which the nomads could not ride. Thus around present-day Moscow there arose a new centre, the Vladimir-Suzdal principality. In 1147 one of its princes entertained his ally in an estate built on the Moscow River. This is the first mention of the city of Moscow in Russian history. The capital of this principality was the city of Vladimir. The head of the Russian church moved there from devastated Kiev. Andrei Bogolubsky ("God-loving"), a most energetic prince of Vladimir, tried to assemble all of Russia again, do away with feudal strife, and re-establish one-man rule. The absence of any real economic ties between the various now disjointed parts of Russia prevented this. Andrei was murdered by the nobility in 1174.

In spite of all this, the Vladimir princes managed to build a beautiful capital, to create a new type of church architecture, the Vladimir-Suzdal style, monuments of which still stand. The famous queen Tamara of Georgia was married to one of the sons of a Vladimir prince.

In the distant North there flourished the "republic" of Novgorod. It was a city of landowners and merchants which constantly had to suppress revolts of artisans and peasants. It was ruled by an assembly that met on the square in front of St. Sophia and decided matters by voice vote. Frequently the contesting parties settled matters through a fist fight on the bridge across the river Volkhov. Novgorod and its "young brother" republic Pskov were members of the Hanseatic League that included several dozen trading cities in northern and western Europe all the way down to Lisbon in Portugal. The enterprising merchantmen of Novgorod went down the Volga and established the city of Nizhny-Novgorod (now Gorky). They also went north and reached the White Sea and the Arctic. Thus did the Russians penetrate into some of the most distant corners of Europe.

In the 13th Century the splintering of the country received its final blow. From the East, all the way from distant Mongolia, there came a new conqueror: the Tartar invasion began.

"ON TO BYZANTIUM!"

THE RIVER ROAD. When Prince Oleg took over from Rurik at Novgorod (to continue the legend), he knew that the latter's comrades, Askold and Dir, had descended the Dnieper river road to trade at Byzantium, occupying Kiev on their way (A.D. 865). Trade with Byzantium being the main object and duty of the reigning princes, Oleg (*upper left*) followed Rurik's friends, slew them at Kiev as traitors to Rurik's son Igor, and proceeded to Byzantium himself. This expedition, and Oleg's settling at Kiev, definitely transferred the main stream of early Russian history from the Don and Volga basins to the Dnieper. Legend says Oleg took 2,000 ships to Byzantium, which were probably not so fancy as the artist's conception (*above, right*), but merely big dugouts. However, he had enough to enter and nail his shield to the city's wall (*right*) and obtain a trade treaty in 907.

DEATH OF OLEG. Setting out for a campaign against the Khazars, Oleg met a soothsayer in the forest who, in Poet Pushkin's 1822 version of the legend, told him:

"*Thy death-wound shall come from thy good battle steed.*"

Oleg pooh-poohed this notion. But the prophet was right. To be on the safe side, Oleg turned the horse, Destrer, his favorite, out to pasture. Returning from the wars, he found the animal had died. He went to see the skeleton, and:

From the skull of the charger a snake, with a hiss
Crept forth as the hero was speaking:
Round his legs, like a ribbon, it twined its black ring;
And the Prince shrieked aloud as he felt the keen sting.

TRADE

The trade treaties provided for the northerners' well-being while among the Greeks, but specified they must go home each autumn. So the Prince and his deputies spent the winter and early spring collecting tribute from their vassal tribes and villages: furs, wax, honey (*upper left*). From Scandinavia they obtained fine swords which the Greeks prized. Captives they took south to sell as slaves, mostly to the Arabs (*upper right*).

SANCTIONS

The northerners often raided Greek settlements, putting prisoners cruelly to the sword for discipline or as heathen sacrifices (*see below*). But at least one such raid, by Rurik's son Igor in 941, backfired. The Byzantines attacked and destroyed his fleet with "Greek Fire" —a varying mixture of petroleum, coal, saltpeter, sulphur or pitch, fired by slaking quicklime and pumping the blaze through a bronze pipe (*left*).

SVYATOSLAV THE GREAT

Igor's widow, Olga, ruled Kiev after him as regent for their young son Svyatoslav, but when the latter came of age, he proved himself not only the first prince with a Slavonic name but Russia's first great expansionist. He was a hearty campaigner whose saddle was his pillow. "I come against you," he would warn his enemies, scorning surprise. His druzhina (warrior band) was the first really potent Slav fighting force, with only a few Norsemen in it (*above*). Ever vigilant, Svyatoslav retained the Volga and Don trade routes. He roved south westward to the Danube, and headquartered at Pereyaslavets rather than Kiev because he found trade better there.

SVYATOSLAV'S MOTHER became a Christian (*see next page*) but her warlike son declined, saying his warriors would laugh at him. He continued to consecrate his sword before the old Norse gods (*above*) and the burials of his chieftains (*bottom, left*) were conducted with old-time Norse and Slavic rites: drinking, feasting and mourning around the grave mound, in which scores of horses and servants were strangled and buried.

THE HARD-RIDING PECHENEGS (*left*) who followed the Magyars as the dominant Mongolic nomads of the steppe, were Svyatoslav's chief domestic plague. His chief foreign rival was Emperor John Zimisces of Byzantium, whom he visited as a friend (*below, right*), later attacked at Adrianople (*right*). John was not sorry (and perhaps not guiltless) when some Pechenegs surprised Svyatoslav and murdered him in the 12th year of his reign (972).

Not all Scotsmen realize that their patron St. Andrew is Russia's patron, too. Andrew was Simon Peter's brother, born near the Sea of Galilee. Pious Russians believe that the north coast of the Black Sea and east to the Volga was his early mission ground. He preached to Scythians, Sarmatians and Slavs on the hills of Kiev (*left*) before going to Britain. Two later saints, Cyril and Methodius (*below*), were Greeks who in the 10th Century preached in Moravia (Czecho-Slovakia) by invitation and there, to translate the Scriptures, invented a Slavonic alphabet which found its way eastward into Russia. But for the migrations of the Pechenegs and Magyars, who disrupted the Moravian kingdom, Slavonic Europe might thus have evolved in unison, but as things turned out the Southern, Western and Eastern Slavs became separated.

THE GROUND of Russia had been prepared for Christianity by the missionaries when Rurik's daughter-in-law, Olga, went to Constantinople and was baptized in 957, late in her life (*left*). Emperor Constantine Porphyrogenitus stood godfather for her and wanted to marry her, but she returned to Kiev, where her heathen son Svyatoslav did not mind breaking sod for one of Russia's first churches (*above, left*).

While her son was growing up, shrewd, energetic Olga ruled Russia with the cunning and daring required in that barbaric day. She avenged the slaying of Igor, her husband, by exacting a tribute of pigeons and sparrows from the guilty tribe (Drevlyane, on the Pripet River), then tying torches to the birds which flew back into the town and burned it up.

VLADIMIR I and ORTHODOXY

The sons of Svyatoslav were, like most heirs of their day, quarrelsome and murderous. The youngest, Vladimir, was fleeing to Sweden for his health when he found, at Novgorod, the backing that enabled him to return and wrest Kiev from his brother Yaropolk.

Vladimir was a thoroughgoing heathen who celebrated his victories with much sacrificial bloodshed. At Kiev he erected statues of all the old Slav pantheon: Svarog, father of the gods; Dazhd-Bog, the sun god; Veles, the god of cattle; Stribog, the wind god; Perun, god of thunder and battle. Perhaps it was his sense of economy, to save needed manpower from the sacrificial slaughter block, that persuaded him to investigate other religions. He passed up Judaism because its followers could eat no pork and had to wander homeless "for their sins." Islam he rejected because it forbade strong drink, which he believed indispensable in chilly Russia. He chose Greek rather than Roman Catholicism be-

cause the former meant tying to rich Byzantium rather than to barbaric Germany, and because the Roman Pope assumed supremacy over the temporal power. Also, his emissaries to St. Sophia, the majestic mother church at Byzantium, said they scarcely knew "whether they were on earth or in heaven" in the great cathedral.

Old banners like the one above represent Vladimir as a strong-willed oldster. He ordered the mass baptism of all Kiev's people (*below*). Force was necessary to convert cities like Novgorod, and he applied it. He captured the Greek colony of Kherson in Crimea, obliged Emperor Constantine VIII to send his sister Anne as wife.

YAROSLAV AND THE FIRST RUSSIAN LAW

By various wives, Vladimir had twelve sons. When the betraying and murdering were over after the old man's death, again it was the son with Novgorod's backing who won out: Yaroslav. Two sons by Anne, named Boris and Gleb, were later canonized for their martyrdom by Brother Svyatopolk, "The Accursed." Yaroslav was never canonized but his fame as a soldier-statesman is memorialized by many a bust (*left*) and statue. His headgear (*right*) is preserved among Russian national treasures, though he fought little in it.

FOR 35 YEARS (1019-1054) Yaroslav "The Wise" ruled Russia. He built churches, finally quelled the Pechenegs, still further extended the realm left by Vladimir in which North and South were joined (see map, page 26). But his greatest work was in collecting and codifying Russian law, civil and canonical. The former covered matters from murder to minute trade regulations. The latter strengthened church jurisdiction over domestic relations, greatly improving woman's status. It gave the church care of all its own servants and of doctors, nurses, beggars and disinherited persons (*izgoi*, "excluded") with whom Russia then abounded after centuries of complex succession customs. Under Yaroslav was installed the first Russian-born metropolitan of the Russian church. (*Right*): Yaroslav's laws being promulgated. Yaroslav brought to its peak the grand-prince system of government, which fell apart so soon after his demise. He saw the system's weaknesses, tried to correct them by making his several sons promise to behave — which of course, they didn't.

FOREIGN RELATIONS. Yaroslav married off his sister Mary to King Kazimir I of Poland, his daughters to the Kings of Hungary, France and Norway. Anne, who went tearfully but dutifully to France (*left*), bore Philip I (*above*), thus putting Yaroslav among the ancestors of England's royal family. Yaroslav's son Vsevold married a daughter of the Byzantine emperor Constantine Monomachus. Thus for the first time was Russia widely allied abroad.

MONASTERIES AND HISTORY

Hilarion, who became Russia's first native primate, used to meditate in a cave near Kiev. Prince Yaroslav encouraged the development of this retreat and others into the first Russian monasteries. They were important not only as training grounds for the clergy but as repositories of learning and the homes of men who now began to chronicle Russian history. Reputed first chronicler was Nestor (*left*), who lived and wrote between 1056 and 1114 at the Pechersky Monastery near Kiev.

Old pictures of the chroniclers (*right*) represent them as sitting up in high chairs, above and aloof from the world. Writing the Russian Chronicles was regarded as sacred work and great pains were exerted to ensure accuracy, as well as moral and spiritual emphasis. This resulted in surprisingly detailed and revealing accounts of Russia's early history, town by town, district by district. Besides encouraging the Chronicles, Yaroslav had many Greek books copied and translated, and in effect founded Russia's first library in one of the churches built by him.

EXCERPT FROM NESTOR: "...God in his wrath causes foreigners to attack a nation, and then, when its inhabitants are thus crushed by the invaders, they remember God."

POLITICAL AS WELL AS SPIRITUAL sanctuary was afforded by the monasteries, and even the tsars sometimes took refuge in them from their enemies. Monks learned to fight as well as pray. (*Below*): a siege at the Troitza-Sergieva monastery.

VLADIMIR MONOMACH, OLD KIEV'S LAST GREAT MAN

Yaroslav tried to unscramble the princely succession of Russia by having his heirs move up toward the top spot, Kiev, through other seats arranged by their commercial importance, with Chernigov second only to Kiev; then Pereaslavl, Smolensk, Rostov, etc., etc. Fraternal feuds boiled until Vladimir II, an able grandson of Yaroslav with the Greek surname of Monomach (*right*), convened a family council to hold Russia together.

The Kievans would gladly have elected Vladimir II before his turn came but he adhered rigidly to his grandfather's rules and did not accept power until 1113, by which time he had united the princes, imported a British wife, Gyseth, daughter of England's King Harold I, and led three great crusades against the heathen.

(*Far right*): Gyseth's arrival from England to marry Vladimir Monomach.

THE FUR-TRIMMED CROWN of Vladimir Monomach (*above*) which set the Russian imperial style thereafter, is revered not only because its wearer united Russia but because he was as brave as he was good. Sometimes called the King Alfred of Russia, he charged his children: "Fear neither battle nor beast. Play the man. Nothing can hurt you unless God wills it."

IN THE FORESTS Vladimir Monomach, a great hunter (*right, above*), was "thrown by a bull, butted by a stag, trampled by an elk, bitten by a bear, borne to the ground by a wolf." His and Russia's worst enemies were the Cumans or Polovtsy, one more steppe tribe even fiercer than the Pechenegs (*right*). Vladimir Monomach led the princes victoriously into the Cumans' eastern home in 1103, and his rule from 1113 to 1125 was comparatively free from danger. His stout son Mstislav added another seven years of peace. But then Kievan Russia fell apart again, never to rise as the country's chief city.

OCCUPATION OF RUSSIA BY THE RUSSIANS, I *from Rurik through Yaroslav*

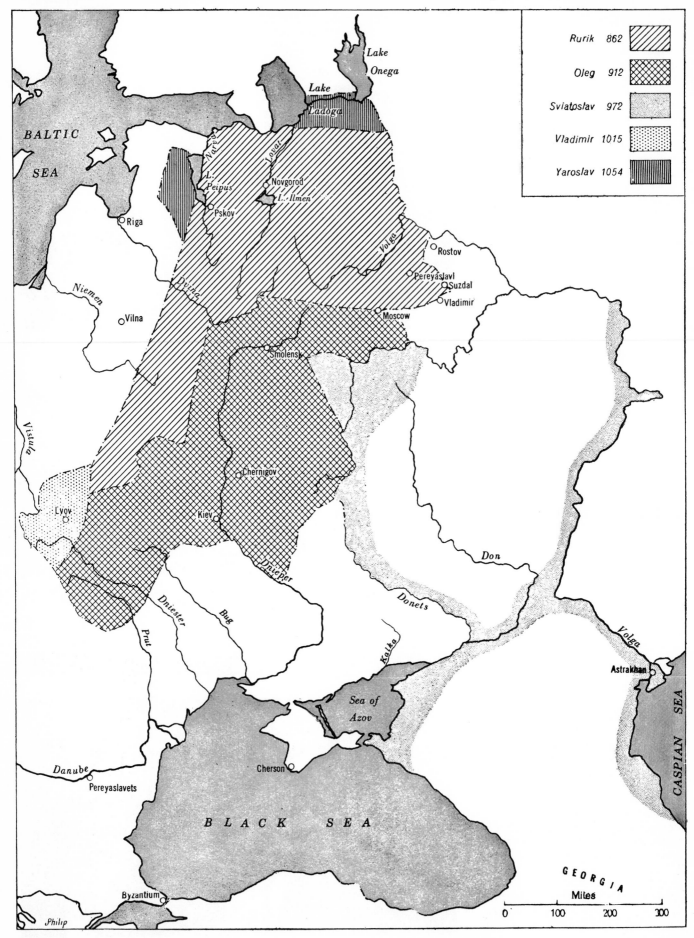

Legend:
- Rurik 862
- Oleg 912
- Sviatoslav 972
- Vladimir 1015
- Yaroslav 1054

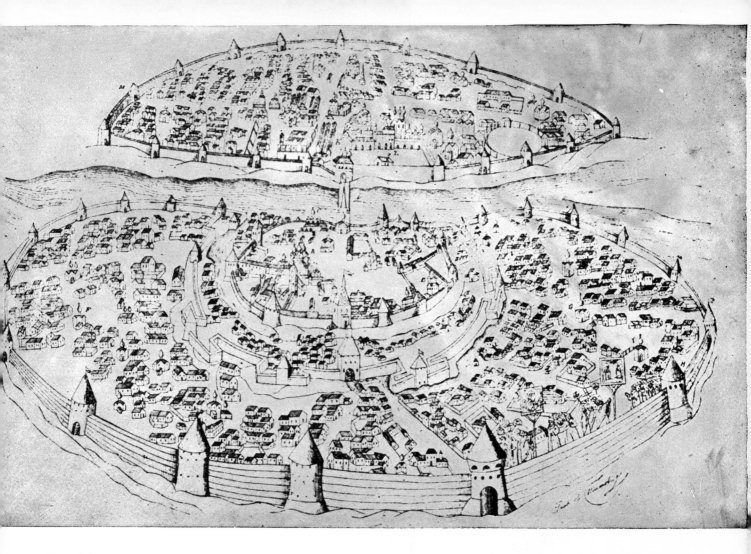

KIEV'S RIVALS

The decline of Kiev was due not solely to quarreling princes and barbarian invasions. The prolific Russians themselves were multiplying. Other towns besides Kiev were growing large, and trade with Mesopotamia and the Orient, down the Don and Volga, rivalled that with Byzantium down the Dnieper. Novgorod was a member of the Hanseatic League (witness its Latin-lettered seal *below*), and traded with all of Europe.

THE STRENGTH OF NOVGOROD and Chernigov, chief rivals of Kiev, was so often proven that more and more prestige attached to their sturdy walls than to the precarious spires of Kiev. (*Above*): An early view of Novgorod, showing the log fortifications and division of the city into two parts by the river Volkhov.

THE CHURCH GROWS. As population waxed at the northern end of the river road in the 12th Century, so did the Russian Church. Cathedral cupolas arose in Vladimir (1158) and Pereyaslavl (1152)—(*left*). One of Russia's holiest ikons was brought from Byzantium to Vladimir in 1155: the famed Virgin of Vladimir (*right*), now at Moscow.

27

KIEV FADES OUT

The actual end of Kiev's supremacy did not come until 1169 when Andrei Bogolubsky (god-loving), son of Vladimir Monomach's youngest son (Yury of the Long Arms), capped a career of frontier warfare based on the towns of Rostov and Suzdal by storming the capital, ousting his cousin Isaslav II and cutting down the Kievites as though they were foreigners.

Andrei (*right, bearded*) did not stay in Kiev but took the premier prince's title away to Vladimir, near Moscow, as his new capital, which he built up to rival Kiev in magnificence. He attempted to subjugate Novgorod as well (*below*), but failed. Old ikons (*below, right*) show Andrei building churches and distributing alms; but his fellow princes regarded him as a high-handed dictator. They combined against him in 1174.

TRIAL BY FIRE. Despite the law code handed down by Yaroslav, and the spread of Christianity, heathenish justice was meted out by Russia's princes through the 11th and even into the 12th Century. Where there was no evidence and a large sum was involved, the accused was obliged to thrust his hand into flame to attest his story (*below*). Flinching attested guilt. In cases of smaller sums, the trial was by water (ducking).

LYRIC INTERLUDE

Between Andrei I of Vladimir and the dark chapters of the next two centuries, a lyric interlude enters Russia's history. One of Andrei's kinsmen married Tamara, Queen of Georgia, one of those fabulously beautiful creatures without whom no country's history is complete. She, who had her portrait done with her father and children, but minus her husband (*below*), commanded her court poet, Shotan Rustavelli, to write an epic extolling her beauty and wisdom. His opus, "The Knight and the Tiger Skin," is one of the classics of feudal poesy, with a strong Persian influence. During Stalin's day the Soviets revived Tamara's fame, for Stalin came from mountainous Georgia (*left*).

POET RUSTAVELLI. He had no trouble extolling Queen Tamara because he himself deeply loved the great lady and was not obliged to conceal the fact.

THE KNIGHT AND THE TIGER SKIN. The plot of Rustavelli's poem, wandering and confused, is secondary to the excuses it gives the poet to rhapsodize about his heroine, Queen Tinatin, heiress to the throne of Arabia. She is loved by Prince Avantil, who joins with a mysterious knight, Tariel, who appears from the mountains with the skin of a tiger he has killed there. Tariel is love-lorn for an Indian princess, Nestan. The two share many exploits, are finally united with their ladies.

YELLOW PERIL

Suddenly in the early 13th Century, from across the Volga and from over the mountains of Queen Tamara's country, out of Persia which they had conquered, swept a phenomenon which Russia would not soon forget, and barely survive: the advance columns of the Tartar Mongol Hordes of Genghiz Khan. Russia's old enemies, the nomad Cumans, cried for help. Russian princes rushed southward. Their scouts met the invaders at the River Kalka near the Sea of Azov. Outgeneraled, they were badly beaten. The Tartars laid planks on their captives and feasted and danced upon them while the prisoners were crushed to death (*above*). The Tartars proceeded north from the Kalka but, upon bumping into the Bulgars on the middle Volga, mysteriously disappeared whence they had come. But after thirteen years they reappeared (*see next chapter*).

III. THE TARTAR YOKE AND RUSSIA'S REBIRTH

Through Central Asia and the Caucasus the Tartar horde of Genghiz Khan (1155-1227) moved into the South Russian steppes After their first visit in 1223 and mysterious withdrawal, the Tartars reappeared in 1236, destroyed the Volga Bulgars completely, and moved into Central Russia. In a single month they captured and burned fourteen cities, among them Moscow. Next they descended on Kiev, which they also captured and burned (1240). The invasion then proceeded into Galicia and through the Carpathian Mountains into Hungary and what is now Czechoslovakia.

Russia was crushed and all resistance seemed hopeless. In vain did the prince of Galicia appeal to western Europe and to the Pope; he even became a Catholic. Neither the Pope nor Western Europe came to his aid when the danger of the Tartars moving farther west abated. Instead, a crusade was begun to Catholicize prostrate Russia. From the north the Swedes attempted to move in, but were defeated in 1240 by Alexander, an able prince of Novgorod. The German Teutonic Knights besieged Pskov and began moving toward Novgorod. Alexander armed the peasants and in 1242 whipped the Teutonic Knights on frozen Lake Peipus.

Though repulsed, the Swedes and the Germans did manage to cut off access to the Baltic Sea from the Russians. Kiev being destroyed, the old link with the Byzantine empire became very weak In the west, Poland and Lithuania united in 1386 into one state This was a Roman Catholic state unfriendly to the Greek Orthodox Russians In the face of the German danger all the Slavs did occasionally unite, as in 1410 when near Tannenberg a combined Russian, Lithuanian and Polish force inflicted a crushing defeat on the German knights On the whole, however Catholic Poland was interested in keeping the Russians out of Europe. Thus the Swedes, the Germans, the Poles, and two centuries later the Turks, formed a cordon all along Russia's western border, cutting the country off from Europe for several centuries.

The Tartars devastated all of Russia with the exception of Novgorod. The road to Novgorod was marshy and the city-republic, realizing resistance was hopeless, sent emissaries pledging submission. The Russian princes now had to travel to distant Mongolia and obtain confirmation of their rank from the Great Khan himself. Later such confirmation was issued by a subsidiary Tartar regime, the Golden Horde, which established itself on the lower Volga not far from the present site of Stalingrad.

The Tartars were willing to let the Russian princes alone provided they delivered the necessary tribute. The princes preferred to collect the tribute themselves, because Tartar tribute collectors were often murdered by the populace and such murders brought terrible revenge from the Tartars. In order to collect tribute, one had to have some kind of administrative order. Although the role of a tribute collector for the oppressors was a highly unpopular one, some of the more farsighted princes realized that, for the time being, this was the only method of preventing a new and even more devastating invasion.

The church was even more farsighted. The bishops realized that the only hope for the future lay in somehow reuniting the country and at the same time keeping the Tartar armies out. The church tried its best to prevent the princes from quarreling and fighting among themselves It forgave their sin, which they had to commit when visiting the Tartar horde, of passing between heathen fires to be purified before facing the Khan.

Ivan, prince of Moscow, who reigned from 1328 to 1341, was nicknamed Kalita (Moneybag). Ivan Kalita used all means, honorable and dishonorable, to increase his realm and at the same time not to annoy the Tartars. The church seems to have blessed every move he made, and Moscow Russia began to grow.

In 1378 Prince Dmitry decided to challenge the Tartars. Two years later in September, 1380 on the Kulikovo field near the river Don a decisive battle took place. The Tartars fled, and Dmitry of the Don, as he now became known, was victorious. One victory, however, did not eliminate the Tartar yoke. The invaders returned once more, and the Russians continued to pay tribute. But the great Tartar empire began to disintegrate and split up into numerous kingdoms.

Toward the very end of the 14th Century the Tartars reunited under Tamerlane. With an enormous horde, said to be around a million and a half strong, the new conqueror appeared in South Russia. For reasons of their own this army turned around upon reaching the city of Oskol and went south through Persia into India — burning, devastating, building pyramids out of human skulls. The princes of Moscow continued to pay tribute, but increased their army and expanded their territory.

In 1453 Constantinople was captured by the Turks, and the last link that Russia had with the West was severed. The Moscow prince, Ivan III (now called Grand Duke) married Sophia Paleolog, the niece of the slain Byzantine emperor. With her there came to Moscow a number of well-educated Greek emigrants. The Grand Duke adopted the Byzantine doubleheaded eagle as a symbol of his power. The mantle of empire moved to Moscow, and so did the center of eastern Christianity. In 1480 Ivan III discontinued tribute payments to the Tartars, by now badly split and quarreling among themselves, and the Tartar yoke came officially to an end.

The new situation demanded a new ideology, and such an ideology was soon found. Ancient Rome, it was said, succumbed to the barbarians for its heresies. Constantinople, the "second Rome," fell to the Turks because of its sins. But Moscow, the "third Rome," was going to remain righteous, and there never would be a fourth Rome. The Grand Duke of Moscow was not only the ruler of all the Russias, but also the protector of the only remaining true Christian faith. Who devised this theory it is hard to say, but the idea appealed to Ivan III, and emigré Greek scholars skillfully substantiated this notion with all kinds of quotations and citations from lay and ecclesiastical history. Moscow was now the center of the world, the last remaining bastion of Christianity against the infidels of the South and East and the papist heretics of the West. The Grand Duke of Moscow now had not only a kingdom but a cause.

The grandson of Ivan III was a most remarkable, tempestuous, energetic man. Ivan IV, the Terrible, proclaimed himself Tsar (Caesar), developing further the notion first expressed by his grandfather. In 1552 Ivan captured Kazan and became ruler of this Tartar kingdom. Four years later he conquered the Tartar kingdom of Astrakhan. The Cossack Yermak penetrated into Siberia and the rule of Ivan extended across the Urals. Thus Russia suddenly acquired population of other than the Russian nationality. What up to that point was a uni-national country now became a multi-national state. This is a point to remember well in contemplating Russian history from the reign of Ivan IV to date.

In the West, Ivan was less successful. He fought the Swedes and the Poles, trying to break through to the sea. But western European military technique proved superior. Russia remained isolated from the West, and only a hundred years later, under Peter the Great, was Ivan's idea of establishing a direct passage to Europe accomplished. Ivan did, however, start trade relations with the West. Through the Arctic and the White Sea, English merchants rediscovered Russia, appeared in Moscow, and were received by Ivan.

Ivan was an educated man and a firm believer in the principle of autocracy. His courtiers, the descendants of feudal princes who once were rulers in their own right, had different ideas. The high nobility, or *boyars* as they were then known, wanted an oligarchy. His ruthless extermination of these remnants of feudalism earned for Ivan his sobriquet "Terrible." The people, however, were on the side of the Tsar; to them he was Ivan the Severe. The Tsar's bodyguard, recruited from the petty nobility and even artisans, spread terror among the boyars.

Ivan tried to beautify Moscow. St. Basil's on the Red Square was built in his reign. He encouraged printing and the manufacture of cannon, in general tried to strengthen the state. A strong state meant higher taxes. Under Ivan occurred the first rebellions of the city poor and uprisings of tribes other than Russians.

The Tsar had a terrific temper, approaching madness in his later years. In one tantrum he smote his son and heir on the head, killing him. Thereafter Ivan sought consolation in public penitence and prayer. He died a lonely and feared man, leaving the throne to a son more suited to be a monk than a tsar.

RUSSIAN MONK v. MONGOL CHIEFTAIN

IN RUSSIA'S STRUGGLE FOR SURVIVAL against the Tartar hordes, the church played a militant part. Monks were trained to warfare to help the state and to protect their monasteries. At the Battle of Kulikovo, the Metropolitan Sergius "loaned" two cowled champions to Prince Dmitry. Artist Victor Vasnetzov here pictures one of them, Monk Peresviet, in single combat with Mongol Chief Chelibey. The monk is generally supposed to have won.

THE MONGOL HORDES

In A.D. 1206 at the headwaters of the River Orkhon in far Mongolia (*see map below*), a monster war council of the Ta-Ta tribes was held. Bursting with population and energy, they had organized armies to conquer the world. Elected as their generalissimo was one Temuchin whom they called Genghiz Khan ("Heavenly Emperor"), a man of far vision and iron will (*left* and *above*). He marched east first and conquered China (1215), then southwest to conquer the vast kingdom of Khorezm (Turkestan, Afghanistan, Persia). Some of his advance columns crossed the Caucasus and the Don steppes but the Battle of Kalka in 1223 seems to have been unpremeditated, a scouting encounter. Genghiz Khan died in 1227 before the real Tartar invasion of Europe was mounted with 300,000 men. This expedition aimed at the new north Volga towns before Kiev, and quickly levelled them — Vladimir, Ryazan, Yaroslavl, Moscow and ten others.

GENGHIZ KHAN'S SON Ogodai gave command of the European invasion to Batu (*below*), his nephew, whose field chief was the brilliant general Subutai. To their original forces the Tartars added scores of thousands of subject Turks from Khorezm who were almost their equals as cavalry. Speed, surprise and tactics were Batu's and Subutai's specialties. With subject forces in the center, they rode the flanks with picked men (*right*). A favorite trick was having the center retire, then closing the flanks with murderous archery crossfire. To their bows and arrows, with which they were deadly accurate from the saddle, they added long spears and swords or cutlasses and various mechanical aids for sieges (*see next page*). In victory they carried off one-tenth of all remaining population and property.

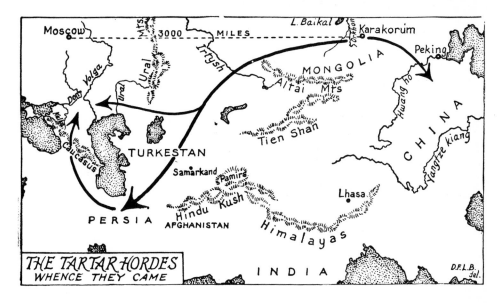

THE TARTAR HORDES
WHENCE THEY CAME

D.F.L.B. del.

33

MECHANIZED WARFARE

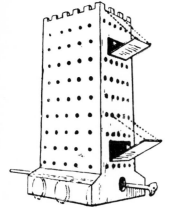

From China the Tartars enlisted many able advisers especially Ye-liu Chiu tsai who, after Genghiz Khan's death, amounted to chief of staff. The Chinese, after centuries of warfare among their own brick-walled cities, furnished the Tartars with a variety of mechanical siege devices new to Russia, whose cities' wooden walls they pierced like so much cheese. Some of these devices are pictured on this page.

Assault tower on wheels with archery loop-holes, drop-gates, low-level battering ram.

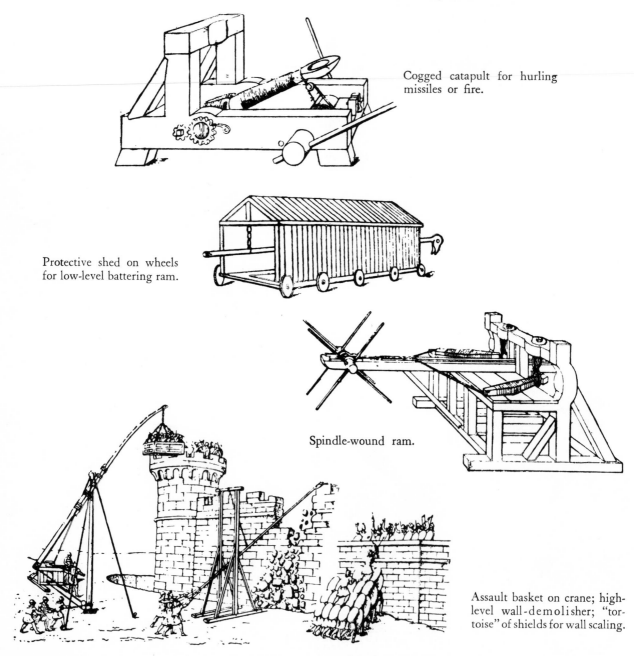

Cogged catapult for hurling missiles or fire.

Protective shed on wheels for low-level battering ram.

Spindle-wound ram.

Assault basket on crane; high-level wall-demolisher; "tortoise" of shields for wall scaling.

MOBILE INVASION

Being nomads, the Mongols had the utmost mobility. Two days in the saddle were nothing. A week afield with nothing to eat but mare's milk and blood was standard practice. And the far-ranging mounted warriors, each of whom used a dozen or more horses in relays, had their radius of action further extended by the fact that their armies' entire bases were mobile, too. Their villages and towns were of *yerts* (felt tents) which travelled collapsed or erected on wheels, drawn by draft cattle, sometimes camels. (*Left*): Mongols pitching a yert camp. (*Below*): Interior of a smith's or armorer's yert.

THE WORD "HORDE" meant not just a fighting force of Mongols but an entire administrative and social segment of the tribes, including civil officials, priests, living quarters, livestock. After Batu and Subutai had conquered Russia, Poland and the Balkans, penetrating as far as Vienna and the Adriatic, they heard that Ogodai had died (1241). Batu had to return for the election of the new khan. Meantime he set up the mobile capital of his own "Golden" (rich) Horde at Sarai on the lower Volga. The chief's huge yert (perhaps twenty feet between wheels) looked something like the illustration below out of *Marco Polo's Travels*.

THE YOKE

After the Tartar battering rams and torches levelled Kiev in 1240 (*left*), the Tartars overran Galicia, Poland, the Carpathians and Hungary. These conquests, added to what the far eastern and southern Mongol armies had taken, put the Mongols in control of the entire Eurasian land mass except for Scandinavia, western Europe, India and South China. The tribute collectible from such a realm is incalculable but an inkling of what the Tartar yoke on Russia alone brought in was Batu's demand for beaver, sable, fox, bear and marten furs, plus one son from every family which had three.

THE CZECHS under King Vaclav and the **GERMANS** under Frederick II (*right*) arrested the Tartars' westward push. How long they would have held if Batu had not gone home to vote is debatable.

DANIEL OF GALICIA (*far left, with helmet off*) was the last Slav prince beaten by the Tartars. He had fought them at the Kalka in 1223 and would not take his loss of Galisch lying down. He begged the kings of Western Europe and Pope Innocent IV (*left*) to crusade against the heathen scourge. He even became a Catholic to get the Pope's support. But with the danger abated, no one bothered to join Daniel. All his efforts did was broaden the base for centuries of strife between Polish Catholicism and Russian Orthodoxy.

36

BEGINNINGS OF MOSCOW

In contrast to Daniel of Galicia and other irreconcilables was Alexander, brave but prudent prince of Novgorod. Seeing how futile resistance was, he paid homage and tribute to the Tartar Khan at the distant home capital of Karakorum though refusing to worship the Khan's gods (*left*). His idea: to preserve his city and use the Tartar power against his western enemies, the Swedes, Germans, Poles, Lithuanians. The Tartars admired Alexander, named him Grand Prince, spared Novgorod.

ALEXANDER'S SON DANIEL took as his portion the forest fortress town of Moscow, on rising ground near (but not on) the sources of the Volga, Oka, Don and Dnieper rivers. This comparatively remote place became a refuge for survivors of the Tartar scourge of other towns. Its princes after Daniel, the first two Basils and the first two Ivans (*below*), followed Daniel's and Alexander's policy of appeasing the Tartars and building up their realm. This they did by buying, ransoming or attracting labor and, acting as the Tartars' tax collectors, amassing wealth. Example: Ivan I, "The Moneybag," commanded a force of 50,000 Tartars to collect from the neighboring city of Tver. He got his share, and in due time Moscow annexed proud Tver. (*Above*): Building Moscow's first Kremlin (citadel). (*Left*): Early Moscow. (*Bottom*): Tartar tribute collector.

Ivan I   Ivan II

ALEXANDER NEVSKY, NATIONAL HERO

Despite his truckling to the Tartars, Alexander of Novgorod became one of Russia's national heroes and was canonized. This was because in 1236, just before the Tartars came, he rode with a little band of warriors against the Swede Jarl Birger who was crusading against Orthodox Russia at the Pope's instigation. Alexander whipped the Swedes at the Neva (*above*), sinking some of their ships, and was thereafter called Nevsky (of the Neva).

To emissaries of the Pope who sought to convert him to Catholicism, Alexander remained adamant (*right*).

But Alexander's resistance to the Swedes and the Pope was outdone by his victory over the German knights, one of Russia's great sagas (*see next page*).

ALEXANDER NEVSKY'S FATHER, Yaroslav II, was poisoned at the court of the Great Khan in Karakorum when he went there in 1246. Alexander had to make four trips to Tartar headquarters to keep his domain intact because frequently Tartar tax collectors were defied or even murdered and Alexander had then to explain matters, make amends. Returning from the last trip in 1263, he died at St. Fedor Monastery on the Volga (*left*). The bishop at Vladimir who had to announce his death to the people said feelingly: "My dear children, know that the sun of Russia has set."

In 1938, the celebrated Soviet cinema impresario, Sergei Mikhailovich Eisenstein, produced a screen epic about Alexander Nevsky with Actor Nicholai Cherkasov in the lead. "My subject is patriotism," said Producer Eisenstein, who received the Order of Lenin for his work. He wove his plot about one other exploit of Alexander: his repulse of the German Knights in Livonia.

Various orders of Teutonic Knights were formed in the late 12th Century to participate in liberating the Holy Land. When the English and French crusaders had accomplished that and by 1204 had captured and sacked Constantinople, the Germans followed their merchants and priests to the east shores of the Baltic. Their "crusade" there became as much a hunt for plunder and lands as a holy war to subjugate Orthodoxy.

Just after Alexander had beaten off the Swedes, German Knights besieged Novgorod's "younger brother" city of Pskov. Alexander roused and hastily armed a force of peasants and rushed to the rescue. The Germans had a cavalry wedge formation which reminded Impresario Eisenstein of the panzer formations of a later German oppressor. On the ice of Lake Peipus, Alexander outmaneuvered even this armored threat and drove off the invaders. (*Below*): Details of the battle à la Eisenstein.

I. Hearing that the Germans have burned Pskov and hanged its Governor, the people of Novgorod send for Alexander Nevsky to lead them. Their "Liberty Bell" assembles the town meeting.

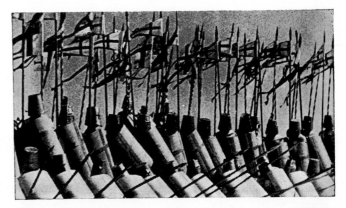

IV. The Germans form a defensive wall of massed shields and spears, whence arrows and swordsmen issue to decimate the attacking Russians. But brave Alexander is not dismayed.

II. For Russia and her "little people," not for Novgorod's selfish rich merchants, Nevsky agrees. He arms the peasants, appoints two Novgorod men his lieutenants, picks his battle ground at Raven Rock on frozen Lake Peipus.

III. After the Germans' flying wedge has struck deep into the Russian center, Nevsky leads his mounted troops in a flank charge. The peasant mob attacks from the other flank.

V. Nevsky crashes through the wall, challenges the Grand Master of the Teutonic Order to single combat, unhorses him. The Russians charge again. The Germans flee, are engulfed when the ice breaks, in a fine victory of Right over Wrong.

VI. In triumph afterwards, Nevsky liberates the Germans' serfs, lets the chief Fifth Columnist (*below*) be slaughtered, warns the world to visit Russia peacefully or beware her sword.

DMITRY OF THE DON

Dmitry, the son of Ivan II, was only eleven years old when he came to the succession in 1359. An older Dmitry, the prince of Suzdal, challenged the child's right and got himself appointed Grand Prince by the Khan. Whereupon the *boyars* (propertied aristocrats) of Moscow put the boy on horseback and rode up to put things right.

Significance of this episode: Moscow was now a city not only of substance but of determination, with men in it who would fight for their rights. The young Prince Dmitry lived up to this spirit when, to discipline Nizhny-Novgorod, he sent the ruling bishop, Sergius, to close all the churches there until the city came to heel. He sought and obtained implicit loyalty from all his neighbor princes. In this he often disregarded gradations of seniority granted by the Khan.

Not only was Moscow now feeling its oats but the Khanate was divided within itself. Several cities risked skirmishes with the Tartar tribute collectors and Dmitry backed them up with an army in 1378. He also reduced Moscow's tribute.

In late 1378, when Mamai Khan demanded the old tribute from Moscow, Dmitry flatly refused it (*below*). He was ready to fight, with more than 150,000 men behind him and all the princes except two or three. With the blessing of Bishop Sergius (*bottom, left*), Dmitry went south to meet Mamai and, in the Meadow of Kulikovo beside the Don, he won a bloody battle (*bottom, right*) which earned him the honorary tag "Donskoi" (of the Don).

Dmitry Donskoi's temerity might have brought great grief upon Moscow, for there had arisen among the Tartars a new, ambitious great Khan named Timur the Lame, whose name has come down to us contracted into Tamerlane. By 1371, Timur controlled everything from the Caspian to Manchuria. This mighty man set out for Russia in the 1390's and Dmitry's son Basil went trembling to meet him, sending meanwhile for the potent Virgin of Vladimir icon to protect him in the coming battle. For some reason Timur turned south and east through Russia to India, leaving Russia to the Golden Horde, which Moscow could handle. Timur is best remembered by the Persians, who represented him as very grandiose (*left*). His tomb (*right*) and palace (*below*) at Samarkand are still objects of wonder.

The withdrawal of **TIMUR**, who is often shown sitting on one edge of his throne to accommodate his game leg (*above*), marked the virtual end of the Tartar yoke. Remnant hordes in Kazan and Crimea had yet to be dealt with, but by the time of Basil (1425-1462) many Tartar chiefs were actually in Moscow's service and intermarrying.

MARK OF THE MONGOL

Artist Vereschagin's grisly painting of a pile of rotting skulls, with scavenger birds flocking to it, is a classic and not wholly unjustified epitome for the mark the Mongols left on Russia. It is true that they left just such horrid pyramids behind them, besides fire-gutted cities, slaughtered herds, wasted forests. But historians find a few constructive things to say for the Tartar hordes. They tolerated all religions, until they chose Islam for their own. They taught Russia how to fight. They clarified Russian taxation, finance and justice. They gave Russia a postal system. And if the absolutism of their khans gave Russia's rulers a taste for autocracy, so did their discipline give the Russian people, of all classes, an understanding of the individual's duty to his state. Universal service, by the highest as well as the low, was a concept forced upon Russians in their struggle to survive the Tartars, who had accepted that concept long before setting out from east Asia to conquer the world.

MOSCOW QUARRELS BUT SURVIVES

With the subsidence of the Tartar menace and the steady growth of Moscow's territory and riches (see p. 37), there was plenty of time and cause for interminable quarrels and intrigue among the nobility and princes of Muscovy. The painting above, of a grand duchess crying bloody murder at court, typifies the period between Dmitry Donskoi (died 1389) and Russia's next great ruler, Ivan III (1462). (*Below*): 15th Century Moscow, showing the stone wall (*Kremlin*) built by Dmitry.

IVAN III "THE GREAT"

The blinding of Basil II in 1443 by a jealous, usurping cousin was characteristic of rowdy, post-Tartar Moscow. But Basil survived backed by Moscow's men of substance and by the church. He enlarged the realm and passed it on intact to his son, Ivan III (right). Under him Moscow got its own Metropolitan, independent of the bishop at Kiev who now controlled only the Lithuanian church. And the wild Muscovy territory to the northeast was pioneered by monks, much as Spanish America was to be a century later.

When Ivan III came to power, the stage was set for his "greatness." He was a slow-going, confident character who accomplished more by planning and waiting than by direct action. The relatively bloodless absorption of neighboring Novgorod with its northeast territory far vaster than Moscow's, was his first major performance. This he accomplished not by pitched battles but by playing upon Novgorod's strategic weakness. Situated in a marsh, it could be, and was, starved out.

BEING A "REPUBLIC," whose affairs had to be settled by unanimous vote of the city council, Novgorod experienced frequent factional brawls which its Bishop had to break up (above). Ivan III simply placed his army athwart the city's supply lines, made his demands, and let the starving Novgorodians fight it out. When they capitulated he took away from them, to their deep sorrow (left, above), the big bell which summoned their public meetings and symbolized their freedom.

Being a maritime city, Novgorod's wharfs (left) were busy with foreign trade. This was one reason Ivan III wanted it. Also, it was a springboard for expeditions to conquer and colonize the northeast wilderness. For Novgorod controlled all north Russia from Lapland to the Urals, and this now became part of Muscovy. (Left): An early Muscovite expedition, on skis, heading northward for exploration.

"THIRD ROME"

Constantinople, home of the Mother Church, fell to the Turks in 1453. The consequences of this to Russia were considerable. Ivan III, a widower, was offered by Rome in 1472, and he accepted, Zoe (*left*), niece of Emperor Constantine Paleolog (who had died fighting in his capital's walls), as his wife. She took the Slav name Sophia and brought to Ivan an ivory throne (*right*) with the double-headed eagle of Byzantium (facing east and west). Ivan adopted this insignium as Russia's coat-of-arms in place of the old St. George & Dragon (*below*) which had come in with Christianity.

SOPHIA WAS STRONG-MINDED. She encouraged Ivan to refuse the last vestiges of Tartar tribute (*below*). Her thinking also set in motion the whole procedure leading up to Moscow calling itself the "Third Rome" and Rurik a relative of Emperor Augustus!

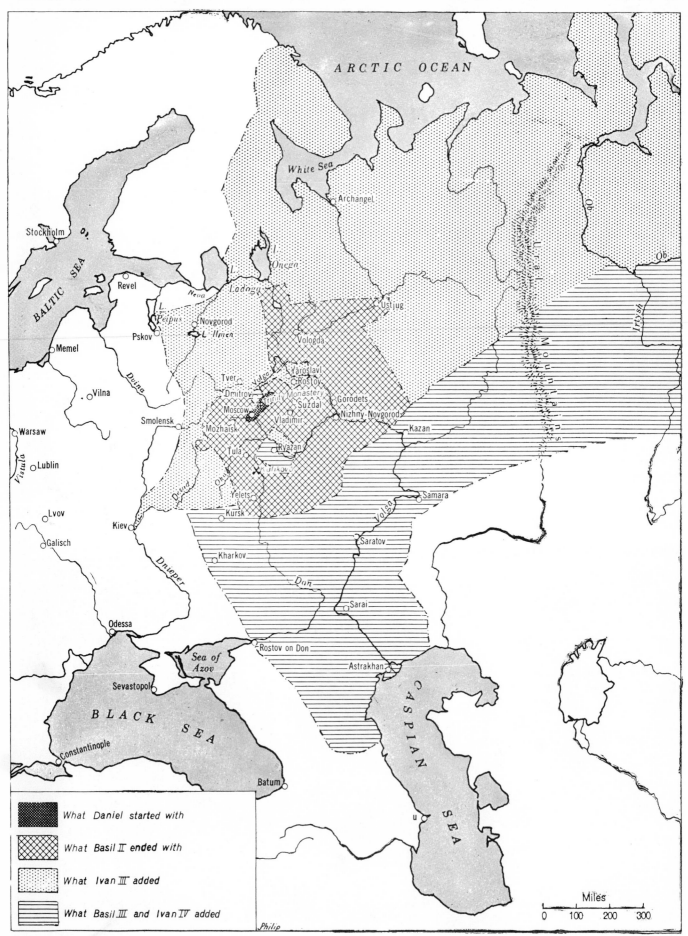

ARCTIC OCEAN

White Sea

Stockholm

Archangel

L. Onega

L. Ladoga

BALTIC SEA

Revel

Neva

Ustjug

L. Peipus

Novgorod

Pskov

L. Ilmen

Vologda

Memel

Duina

Yaroslavl

Tver

Rostov

Vilna

Volga

Dmitrov

Trinity Monastery

Gorodets

Smolensk

Moscow

Suzdal

Nizhny-Novgorod

Mozhaisk

Vladimir

Warsaw

Kazan

Vistula

Tula

Ryazan

Lublin

Desna

Oka

Yelets

Samara

Lvov

Kursk

Volga

Kiev

Galisch

Kharkov

Saratov

Dnieper

Don

Ural Mountains

Irtysh

Ob

Ob

Sarai

Odessa

Rostov on Don

Sea of Azov

Astrakhan

Sevastopol

BLACK SEA

CASPIAN SEA

Constantinople

Batum

Philip

What Daniel started with

What Basil II **ended** with

What Ivan III added

What Basil III and Ivan IV added

Miles
0   100   200   300

IVAN IV, "SEVERE" OR "TERRIBLE"

Ivan III's third son, Basil III, even more autocratic than his father, reigned for twenty-eight years (1505-1533) and added Ryazan and Smolensk to Muscovy. His second wife, Helen Glinsky of Lithuania, bore him a son, Ivan, who was three years old when Basil died. Her regency, advised by her lover Prince Obolensky, was unpopular with the boyars who promptly dispatched Obolensky after her death which may have been by poison. The Shuisky family then won a tussle for the regency and their treatment of the gloomy young prince undoubtedly affected his character and life. They kept him cooped up, half starved, ill clad, trotting him out only on state occasions, when their fawning to impress foreigners was evilly ironic. He was allowed no nurse, tutor or friend, but managed to get hold of some history books, which he devoured with special attention to the behavior of caesars, khans and other autocrats. (*Left*): Ivan IV.

WHEN IVAN WAS 13 he suddenly turned Andrei Shuisky, his chief tormentor, over to an executioner and took charge of matters for himself. He picked three comparatively low-born men for his Chosen Council: the Metropolitan Makary, the court chaplain Sylvester (*right*) and the chamberlain, Adashev. From the Shuiskys and other boyars he had learned that he must look to the people, not the nobles, for his throne's support. Gratefully (at first) he accepted the advice of his councillors.

In 1547, when Ivan was 17, Moscow burned to the ground. The boyars said it was witchcraft and brutally slew Ivan's uncle Yury for it. When they came to threaten him, Ivan boldly set his soldiers on the boyars, beginning a long series of executions which was to last for years and earn for him a reputation of blood and fury.

RUSSIA'S FIRST "TSAR"

When he was 16, Ivan IV startled Moscow by announcing that he would be crowned not just as Grand Prince but as Tsar of All the Russias. Further, he would marry Anastasia, daughter of a suburban family named Romanov who were popular among the common folk but no great aristocrats. Further, he wished the boyars to know that, while he was a miserable sinner, so were they. Let them repent and mend their ways. At a special meeting of all classes (*right*), Ivan issued new rules for local justice, taxation and government. He made it possible for humble folk to petition the Tsar, and saw to it that Adashev appointed a lot of good new judges.

SIGISMUND AUGUSTUS (*above*), king of the joined states of Lithuania and Poland, was Ivan's chief antagonist on the west. Ivan did the boyars the honor of assembling them again to decide on peace or war with Sigismund. War was chosen, and long and bitter were Ivan's western campaigns. In the end he lost more there than he gained.

In the east, Ivan did better. With an army of 100,000 men, German engineers, and 150 cannon he subdued the Tartar kingdom of Kazan between Moscow and the Urals in 1552. In 1554 he added Astrakhan and all the lower Volga country. His return from Kazan (*right*) was his greatest military triumph.

FOREIGN AFFAIRS

Ivan IV's third big addition to Muscovy was the work of a Cossack named Yermak who, condemned to death for rebellion, sallied beyond the Urals in 1581 with a handful of adventurers (*upper left*), and overcame the reigning Siberian prince, Kuchum. Yermak laid his spoils at Ivan's feet, was pardoned, and the colonization of Siberia began. This eastward march, mostly peaceful, was not to end until the Russians reached the Pacific.

An English seafarer named Richard Chancellor appeared at Ivan's court in 1553 (*left*). He had rediscovered the Arctic route into the White Sea. Through him Ivan made trade treaties with Queen Mary, and later, Elizabeth (*above*). Ivan sent Osip Nepey as his ambassador to London, imported mining and medical specialists, anticipated Peter the Great in his efforts to establish contact with western Europe.

Ivan negotiated for the hand of Queen Elizabeth's kinswoman, Mary Hastings (*left, below*), to be his sixth wife, to strengthen his English alliance. The emissary (Nikita Romanov) who inspected and married Mary as proxy for the Tsar, complicated things by falling in love and trying to keep her for himself. Sir Jerome Bowes, ambassador from Elizabeth, had his hands full straightening out this mess which included a wild chase through Ivan's palace. Legend says that on the last day of his life, Ivan busied himself by (1) displaying his wealth to impress Sir Jerome (*below*); (2) playing a chess game to decide whether he or Nikita Romanov should have Mary.

GOOD . . .

Well **aware** of his own proclivities for savagery and evil, Ivan ascribed this side of his nature to his upbringing and the wickedness of the boyars who had controlled him. The higher side of his nature was inspired by his vision of himself as the Tsar, the protector and benefactor of his people and his country. This duality is not hard to understand and is clearly reflected in the deeds and works of Ivan.

In 1547 (when he was 17) he sent to Western Europe for scholars and artisans to elevate his realm from its near barbarism. He encouraged Ivan Federov (*right*) to become Russia's first printer (1563), and books in Greek, Italian, German were produced on a crude press (*left*) set up in the Greek Church. Sylvester, the court chaplain, published an extraordinary code for the conduct of life, called the *Domostroy*. The legal code was revised and submitted to a great church assembly.

Printer Federov had a partner, Peter Mstislavtsev, and both were hounded out of Russia into Lithuania by religious purists who objected to their printed version of the Gospels (1565). In 1574 they were invited to Ostrog where they produced the first complete Slavonic Bible.

. . . AND EVIL

The early death of Ivan's young wife — he believed by poisoning — deeply embittered him and was a turning point toward the excesses and cruelties of his later life. As a youth he had enjoyed torturing animals. He took pleasure in the old Russian sport of setting bears on unarmed muzhiks (*left, below*). Now, in his fear and suspicion of the boyars, he had them tortured and slaughtered by scores, keeping long lists of their names over which he alternately gloated and repented. In his punishment of Novgorod for a "conspiracy" in 1570, he had batches of the population, of every class, systematically butchered every day for five weeks.

He broke with his trusted advisers and drove them away from him into monasteries or exile. **THE METROPOLITAN PHILIP** bravely protested the rule of terror. This worried Ivan and in 1568 he had Philip sequestered in a monastery at Tver. Later he felt he needed Philip's blessing for his attack on Novgorod. Philip replied: "Only the good are blessed." Ivan had him brutally strangled in his monastery cell (*above*).

MADNESS
AND DEATH

Midway in his rule, Ivan was beside himself with hatred and suspicion of the boyars. He left Moscow for a monastery where he alternated between wildest debauchery, violent executions and abject, pious remorse. He returned to Moscow only when the boyars consented to his dividing the realm half as state property, half his own, with his own private police. He grew increasingly irascible. In one fit of frenzy he struck his eldest and favorite son Ivan with his steel-tipped staff, killing him (*right*). This deed resulted, incidentally, in the succession passing to a younger son, Fedor, who was weak in mind and body.

IVAN'S CLOSEST ADVISERS and bishops remonstrated with him. He had them exiled or executed. Some Finnish magicians (*left, above*) predicted his early demise, and were exquisitely tortured for their pains.

Ivan tried to atone for his savageries, especially the insensate butcheries at Novgorod, by reading the Bible and praying. But he was haunted by his victims (*above*), his hair fell out, he could not sleep, he howled all night.

Death came to Ivan IV in 1584, of a stroke suffered (some say) during the famed chess game for Mary Hastings (*left*). Before expiring he assumed a cowl and died as the monk Jonah. The aristocracy whom he had terrorized called him "Terrible"; the People, whom he had befriended, called him "Severe." On balance, his 51-year reign did vastly more to build up Russia than to tear it apart (*see map* p. 46). Good or bad, he was great.

BORIS GODUNOV

Weak sons of strong Tsars were Russia's curse and the boyars' natural prey. Ivan IV's remaining sons (after he killed his favorite and eldest) were Fedor, a simple soul, shown here in his 30's (*above*) and Dmitry, an infant. Fedor was crowned with Nikita Romanov to look after him. When Nikita died, the regency passed to a schemer of Tartar origin who had only lately become a boyar by betrothing his sister Irene to Fedor.

This man, Boris Godunov, soon squelched all other boyars, including the potent Shuisky family whom he scattered to the far corners of Russia. When the infant Dmitry had been mysteriously disposed of, and Fedor had died, Boris made an elaborate pretense of indifference until the people and the boyars and the new Russian patriarch, Job, all came begging him to be Tsar (*right*). He did not refuse.

TSAR BORIS lived in perpetual fear — perhaps of his own guilty conscience. In 1601 he dispersed the Romanov family as he had the Shuiskys. Nikita's eldest son, Fedor Romanov, landed in a monastery as the monk Philaret (*right*). His wife became a nun (Martha) and their small son Michael was exiled all alone. Perhaps this was lucky for Michael, keeping him from harm's way until his day came.

IV. TROUBLED TIMES AND OLD MUSCOVY

Tsar Fedor (1584-1598) prayed a lot. He inherited from his father, Ivan IV, not only a great realm but also a good deal of trouble. The peasants who used to till the land that belonged to the nobility had the right to move on to another nobleman's land on one day in the year, St. George's Day. In 1581 Ivan IV deprived them of this privilege. Thus the peasant became permanently attached to one nobleman's land and serfdom was officially established in Russia.

Since Tsar Fedor really could not reign, the actual ruler was his brother-in-law, **Boris Godunov.** With the death of Fedor the old house of Rurik expired. Crafty Boris skillfully engineered his own proclamation as tsar by popular acclaim. The new tsar feared the old nobility, in whose eyes he was but an upstart, with obscure Tartar ancestry. Famine was sweeping the country. Hunger riots took place in Moscow, the serfs were revolting against the nobility. In 1603 the tsar's troops defeated with difficulty a large mass of peasants in revolt, who marched right up to Moscow. Tsar Boris had to fight both the upper and lower classes.

Here one of the most interesting and confusing episodes in Russian history took place. One of the several wives of Ivan IV had an infant son, who was murdered by parties unknown. In the general unrest that prevailed in the country the rumor arose that Boris, then not yet tsar, had instigated the murder in order to clear his own way to the throne. The Polish nobility managed to produce a young man purported to be the tsarevich Dmitry who had miraculously escaped assassination. In 1604 this "Dmitry" became active in Poland, claiming the throne of Russia. Tsar Boris proclaimed that Dmitry was no other than Gregory Otrepev, a rebellious monk who had escaped to Poland. The real identity of the pretender remains unknown to the present day. Poland supported Dmitry's claim. Dmitry invaded Russia with a mixed Russian-Polish army, which absorbed as it went along numerous rebellious serfs and Cossacks.

In April, 1605, Tsar Boris suddenly died, and the people interpreted this as a sign of divine wrath. In June of the same year the Pretender entered Moscow, accompanied by large detachments of Polish troops. He married the daughter of a Polish nobleman, Marina Mniszek. After this marriage the court in Moscow became openly Polish. In May, 1606, Moscow revolted against the Poles and the Pretender was killed. Basil Shuisky, a member of the old nobility against which Ivan IV fought so hard, became tsar. Instead of a Polish tsar one now had a boyar tsar, and the lower classes were in revolt. The "Troubled Times" that began because of the expiration of the old Rurik dynasty now became a country-wide social and class struggle.

In 1609 a large Polish army invaded Russia and besieged Smolensk. A revolt against the tsar was brewing in Moscow. A group of noblemen deposed Tsar Basil in 1610, but soon the Poles were admitted into Moscow by those of the nobility who preferred foreign rule to a peasant revolution. The first attempt to free the capital failed. The second attempt originated in the rich commercial city of Nizhny-Novgorod (now Gorky). The butcher Minin and the nobleman Prince Pozharsky raised a large popular army, which included many peasants. In 1612 this army approached Moscow. The capital was besieged, a relief army sent from Poland was defeated, and on October 26, 1612, Moscow was freed.

In 1613 a popular assembly elected as tsar a young man not particularly distinguished, but on whose candidacy the various quarreling factions did finally agree. Thus, Michael, first of the Romanovs, came to the Russian throne. Russia's troubles were, however, far from over. In 1615 near Pskov the

Russians managed to inflict a defeat on the famous warrior king of Sweden, Gustavus Adolphus. As a result, Moscow was able to obtain peace with Sweden at the price of losing access to the Baltic for another hundred years.

Michael Romanov ruled with the aid of his father, who was the patriarch of the Greek Orthodox church. The union of church and state seemed complete. The country was slowly recovering from civil war and foreign intervention. Taxes were high, but government expenditures were higher. The government tried to encourage foreign trade, but the Swedes and the Poles effectively barred all roads to the west.

The second Romanov was Alexis (1645-1676), called "the most quiet one," but who had a turbulent reign. At the beginning of his reign unbearable living conditions provoked revolts in a number of cities, which had to be suppressed. The head of the church was now Patriarch Nikon, an original thinker and a very ambitious man. He decided to clean the ecclesiastical books of no end of mistakes that had crept in through centuries of copying. What seemed a technical matter became an issue of dogma. A large section of the faithful decided to stick to the old texts and the old ritual. Nikon was ruthless in his reforms, and what amounted to civil war inside the church resulted. The anti-Nikon faction, or Old Believers as they called themselves, fought back just as strongly. The tsar was on Nikon's side, but the split in the church was not altogether distasteful to the court, because it weakened the church and strengthened the throne. In 1666 a congress of bishops, with two visiting patriarchs from the Near East present, approved Nikon's canonical reforms, but condemned him to exile. The church was thus both weakened and split.

Alexis the Most Quiet One was bothered not only by revolts in the cities. There were revolts of subjugated nationalities on the upper Volga and even in Siberia. In 1667 a large Cossack revolt under Stepan Razin took place. Three years later Razin began to besiege Astrakhan. The revolt spread all the way up the Volga. What began as a Cossack expedition was now a full-fledged peasant war against the tsar and the nobility. With great difficulty Moscow suppressed the revolt, captured Razin, brought him to Moscow, and had him executed on the Red Square in 1671. Thus ended the first large-scale peasant war against tsardom, to be repeated almost exactly one hundred years later under Empress Catherine.

One must remember that all this time Poland dominated not only Smolensk and Byelorussia, but also the Ukraine. The Cossacks in the Ukraine repeatedly revolted and were suppressed by the Poles. The leader of the Ukrainians was Bogdan Khmelnitsky, chief of the Zaporog Cossacks. To fight the Poles more effectively the Ukrainians entered into alliances with their old enemy, the Tartar Khan of the Crimea, while the Holy Father in Rome absolved the Polish troops of all sins in their war against the Ukrainians. In 1653 Moscow decided to support the Ukrainians. Bogdan Khmelnitsky and 60,000 Cossacks voted to be under the "eastern tsar," the tsar of Muscovy. Thus what centuries earlier used to be Kiev Russia, now the Ukraine, joined hands with Russia again. But only in 1686 did Poland consent to give up Kiev, the ancient capital of Russia.

Tsar Alexis was a man of considerable culture. He was keenly aware of Russia's backwardness. In his reign foreigners were encouraged to settle in Moscow, the army was being trained by foreign officers. Alexis himself liked to dabble in dangerous foreign cultural matters. At court one had even foreign theatricals, and some of the courtiers occasionally even dressed in European clothes. All this, of course, was done behind closed doors. Neither the tsar nor the court could definitely make up their minds whether they really wanted a break with the past. Alexis fought the Swedes, once more trying to get through to the Baltic, but lost. Russia was ripe for reform and modernization, but Alexis the Most Quiet One never could make up his mind altogether. A much more energetic and decisive sovereign tackled the job eventually. This was Alexis' son, the great Peter.

MARK OF IVAN

Outstanding monument to Ivan IV is majestic, multicolored St. Basil's Cathedral in Moscow, named for St. Basil of Caesarea (4th Century) whose asceticism appealed strongly to one side of Ivan's nature. An epitome of Ivan's life and character is the legend (apocryphal) that, after the finished drawings were accepted, he had the architect blinded so he could never create anything like it. Later tsars added to the original pile (*above*).

FAMINE struck at Moscow repeatedly under Boris. Throngs of the hungry fled to the wilderness and to the Cossack bands, whose plundering raids grew bolder and bolder.

REVOLT by the peasants, the Cossacks and angry refugees from crushed boyar households (*below*), plagued the reign of Tsar Boris and made him increasingly unpopular. His chief weakness was that his title was not inherited from Ivan IV, and he knew it. His efforts to quell the uprisings only aggravated them.

A STRONG POLAND

While Russia weakened in Ivan IV's last years and under Boris Godunov, Poland had grown strong. In 1569 she had signed the Union of Lublin with Lithuania (*above*), agreeing to elect a king jointly with that potent neighbor. In 1586 the death of King Stepan Batory (*left*) made the Polish-Lith throne vacant and Sigismund of Sweden was chosen (*below*). He was a Catholic, and Protestant Sweden soon replaced him on her own throne with his uncle, Charles IX. But Sigismund III continued as king of Poland and the restless condition of Russia very nearly placed that country in his hands as well.

Because of losing his Swedish throne, Sigismund made cause against Sweden with Boris Godunov, who was able to regain some of Russia's lost territory on the Baltic. But neither man made the most of his great political opportunities.

RUSSIA'S IRELAND is a term sometimes applied to Poland. Like Ireland it is situated on the western flank of its large neighbor and being likewise Roman Catholic it is definitely different in religious ties and outlook. From the days of Daniel of Galicia who first allied Poland with Rome, Poland has always been a troublesome and often a threatening factor interposed between Russia and Europe.

PRETENDER DMITRY

Among the refugees from Boris Godunov's boyar purge was a youth whose real name may have been Gregory Otrepev, son of a Romanov retainer. After a brief monkhood and a stay among the Dnieper Cossacks, he entered the service of a Polish tycoon, Adam Wisniowiecki, to whom he made a deathbed "confession" (*below, left*). He said he was Dmitry, a last son of Ivan IV who was supposed to have been murdered in 1591 (*left*). Recovering, "Dmitry" was taken before Governor Mniszek of Crakow, with whose daughter Marina (*below*) he promptly fell in love. Governor Mniszek showed his find to King Sigismund, who subsidized "Dmitry," let him build up a Polish following and waited to see what would happen in Russia. Boris Godunov was furious, denounced the Pretender roundly, but soon had to fight him on Russian soil.

After Godunov's army had beaten the Pretender's, some 40,000 Cossacks joined the latter, and a lot of influential Muscovites. Just then Boris Godunov died, his son was murdered and Patriarch Job was deposed. The Pretender's way into Moscow lay wide open.

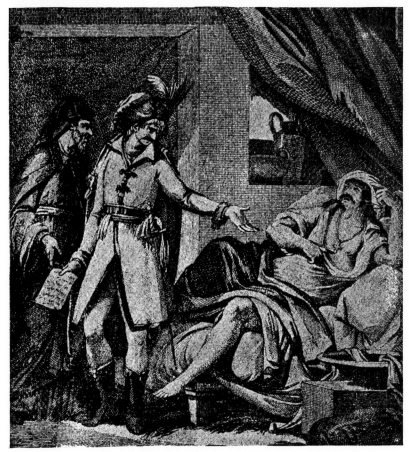

MARINA IN MOSCOW

Pretender Dmitry was homely, awkward, red-headed, but not without courage and ability. Moscow's populace, quite as willing as he to pretend or really believe he was of royal blood and therefore divinely entitled to be Tsar, received him warmly when he entered with his army in 1604. He staged a meeting (in a tent) with Ivan IV's widow, Martha, who thereafter gave public demonstrations of motherly love. This woman and Marina Mniszek, whose father took her to Moscow when all seemed safe (*above*) and who was there married to Dmitry and crowned with much ceremony (*below*), are interesting. After this Dmitry's death, they cheerfully accepted another "real" Dmitry, Marina even bearing the second one a child (*See* p. 61).

BASIL IV
v. "DMITRY"

One aspirant to Russia's throne who refused to accept "Dmitry" as real was Prince Basil Shuisky (*below, left*). Within a year he rallied the boyars. This was not difficult because, though he was not truckling to the Poles who had helped crown him, "Dmitry" was flouting the old stiff Russian court etiquette, ridiculing the boyars for their ignorance, letting Marina and her father ride roughshod over high Muscovite society. One fine day in May, 1606, Basil Shuisky and his fellows galloped into the Kremlin bent on murder.

Seeing his staunchest supporter, General Basmanov, who had been one of Boris Godunov's mainstays, cut down in the courtyard by Basil Shuisky's men, Dmitry became panicky. He leaped from a window into a paved courtyard (*left*).

Dmitry was badly hurt by his fall, but even then sympathetic palace guards might have saved him had not Shuisky & Co. spread the word that the Widow Martha now disowned her "son," branded him impostor. Dmitry was hacked to death (*below*), exhibited in the Red Square along with Basmanov, and cremated. Legend says his ashes were shot out of a cannon toward Poland. Basil Shuisky then had himself elected Tsar Basil IV. But by now Moscow was thoroughly demoralized. Basil IV was to last only four years.

COSSACKS

On top (and because) of the oscillating condition of Muscovy's throne during these "Troubled Times," Moscow had recurrent trouble with those Cossacks who, secure on island fastnesses in the Dnieper rapids, to which no women were admitted, were called the Zaporogs. To the Zaporog Cossack band were attracted reckless malcontents from Poland as well as Russia, in such numbers that their councils sneered at all who sought to curb or subjugate them (*above*). In one celebrated letter to Turkey's Sultan (it might easily have been written to a Tsar), they said:

"Thou, Sultan, art the devil's son, The grandson of Haspid himself. And thou a horned chort! . . . Thou art but a wretched innkeeper in Constantinople, A Macedonian brewer, A Greek and Moldavian swine and a Babylonian blacksmith; Thou oppressor of Serbia and Podolia, Crimean parrot, Egyptian swineherd, Owl of Jerusalem! No help of Christians art thou, but a fool; No protector of our God, Thou art not worthy to kiss anywhere—Nor worthy to hold our Zaporozhe. We shall fight thee By land and sea! Thou son of a dog—Such is our answer!"

AND TARTARS. A bloodthirsty remnant of the Tartar Hordes still lived in Crimea during the "Troubled Times"; still raided the steppe and carried off heads, herds and women (*left*). With a redoubtable capital at Bakchi Sarai (*below*), the Crimean Khan was a vassal of the Turkish Sultan and very useful, too, as a thorn in large, confused Russia's soft underside. Though he pacified and extended Russia's eastern marches, Tsar Boris Godunov (and other Russian rulers down to the late 18th Century) paid respect if not bribes to the potent Crimean Tartars.

AND MORE PRETENDERS

While Tsar Basil Shuisky strove manfully to lay the Dmitry ghosts at Moscow, another pretender arose. His pretense: that a posthumous child of Tsar Fedor had been, not a girl, but a boy named Peter. This "Peter" received backing from a rabble-rousing ex-serf called Ivan Bolotnikov (*left*) who so stirred up the east and southeast borders as far down as Astrakhan at the Volga's mouth that, when he entrenched himself with his mob in Tula, it took 100,000 of Basil's men to root him out.

Meantime, many a disgruntled retainer, and even nobles like **PRINCE TRUBETSKOI** (*right*) sought a new and better pretender. Poland supplied another "Dmitry" (whom Marina Mniszek and Ivan IV's widowed Martha embraced) and the Poles returned to the conquest of Moscow. They burned the city, occupied the Kremlin, besieged the Trinity Monastery for more than a year (*below, right* and *left*).

HERMOGEN, a humble abbot past eighty who had been made Patriarch by Basil Shuisky, for his own ends, now became Russia's rock of resistance. When King Sigismund of Poland openly bid for Russia's throne himself by besieging Smolensk, Hermogen refused to cooperate (*right*). Instead he sent messengers rallying all Russian factions to drive out the Poles. The Poles seized Hermogen, but his call was answered (*see next page*).

Hermogen's fortitude was truly remarkable. Taken by the Poles to the Red Square to tell the Muscovites to stop resisting, he said instead: "Blessed be those who come to save the Moscow sovereignty; and you, traitors, be accursed." The Poles threw him back into prison, starved him to death — one of Russia's real martyrs.

PRINCE AND BUTCHER

One of Patriarch Hermogen's messengers reached Nizhny-Novgorod and the ear of Cosmo Minin, chief elder, a butcher by trade. Minin also thought he had a visitation from the shade of St. Sergius telling him what to do (*left*). He offered all his goods, and urged his fellow citizens to do likewise, in a sort of Liberty Loan drive to raise an army (*below, left*).

Minin and friends chose for their leader Prince Dmitry Pozharsky (*below*), who had already fought the Poles manfully at Moscow. Butcher Minin remained in charge of fund-raising but also took the field.

A GOOD PICTURE of how deep-rooted was the feeling between Poles and Russians is the one above, of Minin watching his executioners prepare to decapitate Polish prisoners with a scythe.

For their part, the Poles were ruthless in their treatment of Moscow's populace, which they disarmed. On one occasion, to quell a carter's strike, they slaughtered 7,000 citizens. Entrenched in the Kremlin, they burned the rest of the city.

Pictures like this help to explain the deep rift between Russians and Poles.

MOSCOW LIBERATED

Long and bitter was the attack on the Poles in the Kremlin, by the troops of the Prince and the Butcher (*top*). Opposed to them was many a skilled Polish commander such as Hetman (General) John Carl Kotkevich of Lithuania (*above*), who arrived with a relief column but was driven off.

CANNIBALISM by the beleaguered Poles in the Kremlin was added to the horrors of the "Troubled Times" before Pozharsky and Minin, aided by the Cossacks, won out. Their victory restored independence to Russia at last (and forever since), earned them a joint statue in Moscow's Red Square (*above*).

ENTER, THE ROMANOVS

Ever since Ivan IV chose one of its daughters, Anastasia, for his bride in 1547, the easy-going, unpretentious family of Romanov had been on the rise. Fedor, son of Ivan's friend Nikita Romanov, whom Boris Godunov had driven to cloisters as the Monk Philaret, was one of the handsomest and ablest Romanovs (*above*). After years of being bumped around by warring factions, he emerged after Moscow's liberation as a great church patriot. The aged Patriarch Hermogen gave his blessing to Philaret's young son Michael as candidate for Tsar (*above, center*), with Philaret as regent. The Zemsky Sobor (popular assembly) hailed Michael's name before it was presented. His mother, Martha (*above, left*), hesitated but the notification committee assured her that this time all Russia would be loyal to its ruler. So a new dynasty was founded, linked to the old Rurik line through Great Uncle Ivan the Terrible.

BRIGHT IN ROMANOV ANNALS is the name of Ivan Susanin (*center*), a peasant who, though he knew where young Michael was hidden, refused under mortal torture to tell the Poles.

The Romanov house on the outskirts of Moscow (*left*) was destroyed by fire, rebuilt and preserved for posterity as a typical example of boyar architecture and furnishing, but no Romanovs lived there after Fedor and Martha, who had spent most of their adult lives sheltering in monasteries.

THE CORONATION of Russia's first Romanov tsar took place July 11, 1613 — five months after his election — in the Kremlin. Old paintings (*above* and *below*) record the ceremonial procession to all the Kremlin shrines and churches, followed by a state banquet at which the new young monarch sat alone at a high table while priests and boyars drank his health in honeyed wine. A new, splendidly encrusted hat (*left*) was provided for the occasion, far outshining the old hat handed down from the time of Vladimir Monomach. The new young tsar had little character. Court favorites really ruled.

THE TSARDOM

The church having played so big a part in its revival, and Divine Right having weighed so heavily with the people, Russia's tsardom now became an office more than ever sacrosanct. Michael Romanov might take his young son Alexis out hawking (*below*) but he was primarily a servant of God and the Russian people, who must wash his hands after receiving a foreign emissary (*right*).

THE SECOND ROMANOV TSAR, Alexis, came to the throne aged 16 and, being more addicted to hawking, drawing (*above*) and writing verse than to cares of office, relied heavily upon advisers to run his state. After the Patriarch Nikon (*see next page*), his ablest adviser was Athanasy Orduin-Nashchokin (*right*), native of Pskov, son of a poor official, whose able settlements of Alexis' difficulties with the Poles and Swedes earned him the position of chancellor, the reputation of being Russia's first modern-minded diplomatist and statesman. Orduin-Nashchokin's vision of Russia's role on the Baltic and in foreign trade helped to inspire the great career of Alexis' son Peter. He built the first Russian merchant vessels and advised Alexis to adopt the best practices of Europe. "There is," said he, "no shame in borrowing what is good, even from your enemies. . . . It is better to sell half your army and buy a military organizer." He encouraged trade with Persia, and state trade control.

ALEXIS AND THE CHURCH

Like his grandfather and father, Alexis Mikhailovich (*left*), who reigned from 1645 to 1676 and sired Peter the Great, was profoundly pious and strongly under Church influence. His "intimate friend of soul and body" was Nikon, an irascible peasant-priest whom he made Patriarch. Rewriting of the Greek-Orthodox liturgy and prayerbooks, to purge them of Russian corruptions, had been agitated ever since the introduction of printing under Ivan IV, to strengthen Orthodoxy against Roman competition. Nikon took up this reform with zeal and vengeance. After bitter debates against opposition led by the priest Avvakum (*below*), he got the new order made official, unfrocked the rebellious Avvakum.

RUSSIA'S "OLD BELIEVERS" hated Nikon's reforms, and a lasting schism resulted. For the masses, the controversy focussed on how to signal benediction and cross oneself: with two fingers, old style (*left, below*) or with three, new style (*right, below*). Also whether to spell Jesus "Isus" or "Iisus," a question raised simply by a slip made by an early translator from the Greek. Of such things, many Russian quarrels were composed.

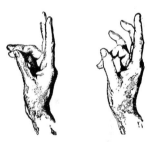

NIKON carried the fight to such extremes that Alexis cooled toward him. Nikon withdrew to a monastery (*left*) and a Church assembly (*below, left*) deposed him. But not before many a leading citizen, such as the Boyarina Morozova (*below, right*), had been sent into bitter exile for dissenting.

67

SERFDOM

In the reign of Alexis (1645-1676) the condition of Russia's peasants became intolerable. They were bound to the land by laws increasingly severe, because only by them could the land be worked and the state exact tithes and taxes (*above*) to support the tsar's armies. In 1649 Alexis signed a decree which virtually made serfs chattels and heavily punished runaways or persons who harbored them. Land could be sold only with the serfs that lived on it. In 1664 huge serf-hunts were begun by the state, for the miserable peasants were fleeing regardless to Siberia or to join the Cossack bands.

WORKERS in the cities — especially Pskov and Moscow (*below*) — rioted fiercely against corrupt taxation (especially on salt), scarcity of food and debasement of the currency, which inflated consumer goods. (*Right*): a shoe store in the time of Alexis, a contemporary print clearly suggesting the poverty of the time.

GOVERNMENT

Theoretically, Tsar Alexis ruled his land in consultation
with a council of boyars (*above*). Actually all administration was through a corrupt bureaucracy. One of the few
state functions of this period that improved was the postal
service (*right*), promoted by far-sighted Orduin-Nashchokin to keep roadless Russia in touch with the outer world.
But even postal costs were inflated by corruption. Every
state office was a clamorous nest of petty thieves with quill
pens (*below*). Meantime, justice for the poor was in the
hands of the landlords, whose officers could heavily fine or
knout the offending or even the complaining (*below, right*).

STEPAN ("STENKA") RAZIN became a name to conjure with under Tsar Alexis. A haughty Don Cossack (*above*), he organized the swarms of fugitive slaves and serfs that flocked to his camp into a proletarian army and navy. He preached class warfare far and wide, raided government forts and even large cities of the middle Volga, even plundered the Persian coast of the Caspian Sea. He was finally overcome in a raid on Simbirsk, turned in by the chief of the Don Cossacks, sent to Moscow and executed. But class warfare in Russia had acquired another precedent for the explosions to come.

THE UKRAINE became Russian under Alexis by a combination of opposition to Turkey and defense of Orthodoxy against Polish Catholicism. Alexis agreed to let the Cossacks there number as high as 60,000 (the Poles had tried to keep them down to a few hundreds). But when Sweden invaded Poland and again fought Russia, the Cossacks switched to Sweden and Alexis wound up his reign with few territorial gains on the west and southwest. (*Below*): Ceremony of annexing Ukraine.

V. TSAR PETER AND THE EMPIRE

Everything about Peter was unusual: his upbringing, his accession to the throne, his behavior as tsar; in short, his entire reign was a revolution. Peter was the son of Alexis by a second marriage. When Alexis died the throne was occupied by his older son Fedor (1676-1682), a weak and sickly youth. When he died the throne was to pass either to the feeble-minded Ivan, who was older, or to Peter, the youngest. A revolt of the guards, the so-called Streltsy, who had not been paid for months, was utilized by a girl in the family, Sophia. The two boys, Ivan and Peter, were proclaimed a sort of joint tsar, and Sophia became the regent. Sophia's prime minister was the highly educated Prince Basil Golitsyn. Peter and his mother lived in virtual semi-exile on an estate near Moscow.

The young tsar got very little formal education. He was taught to read and write by the deacon Zotov, who was not an abstainer. The young Peter made a number of friends among the foreigners in the foreign settlement near Moscow. With other lads of his age he liked to play war. The boys were divided into two companies, which soon became battalions, then regiments. The war games were highly realistic, with actual casualties. The two regiments were named Preobrazhensky and Semenovsky, after the two villages near the tsar's estate. Thus the Imperial Guard was born. In a barn young Peter located an old boat. The boat was tried out on a lake, with some of the foreigners instructing Peter and company how to set up sails. In virtual retirement the boy tsar already knew what he wanted: Russia was to have a modern army, was going to reach the sea and build a navy, everything was to be modernized and made to look like western Europe.

In August, 1689 Peter was informed that Sophia intended to exile him. Out of bed he jumped, seized a horse and rode to a nearby monastery. Soon his two beautiful regiments arrived, and then other troops joined. Sophia tried to negotiate and assemble troops, but in one month's time she was incarcerated in a convent. For the first few years Peter left the actual government to his mother. He took a trip to Archangel on the White Sea, just in order to ascertain how the real sea looked. He continued his war games and studied arithmetic, geometry, artillery. An old Scotsman, Patrick Gordon, was instructing Peter in military science. A gay Swiss, Franz Lefort, introduced him to western amusements. Timmerman from Holland was the mathematics instructor. In 1695 Peter went south to attack the Turks on the Sea of Azov. Playing at war was ended; the real thing was to begin. The city of Azov was besieged, but Peter had no navy. All winter ships were built with Peter acting both as engineer and carpenter. In the spring of 1696, to the amazement of the Turks, a Russian navy sailed down the Don, and Azov fell to the Russians.

The apprenticeship was finished, but Peter felt that he needed some graduate training. In 1697 a big Russian mission went abroad, including Peter Mikhailovich, the tsar himself in disguise. Peter visited Germany, then Holland, where he worked as a carpenter in shipbuilding, then France. From France he went to London and attended a session of Parliament, then to Vienna to persuade the emperor to enter into an alliance against the Turks. While abroad Peter received news that the Streltsy were planning to depose him and bring back Sophia from the convent. In the summer of 1698 the revolt actually broke out, but the Scotsman Gordon suppressed it without much difficulty. Peter returned to the capital unannounced and unexpected. The boyars who came to greet him were not allowed to kneel before the tsar. During the reception the tsar himself started cutting the beards of the visitors with a pair of big scissors. Russia was going to be modernized at once. On the squares of Moscow the rebellious Streltsy were hanged, and on the Red Square Peter himself chopped heads off. Sophia was left in exile and forced to become a nun.

To get to the sea one had to beat the Swedes. In order to keep the Turks quiet Peter gave them back the fortress of Azov. An alliance was entered into with Denmark and Poland. In 1700 Peter besieged Narva. Charles XII of Sweden hastened to deliver Narva. The Russian army suffered a crushing defeat. The Swedes thought that Russia was out of the war. Peter regarded the defeat as the first serious lesson inflicted on him by the best army in Europe at that time. The great northern war was only beginning. A year later Peter began to advance. In May, 1703 the foundation was laid for the fortress of St. Peter & St. Paul on the river Neva. This was to become St. Petersburg, the new capital of Russia. In the same year the first Russian warship was launched in the Baltic. Russia had broken through to the sea at last.

In the war against Poland the Swedes were successful. In 1707 Charles XII was marching through Poland to Russia. It looked as if the Swedes might march on Moscow, but Charles went into the Ukraine, hoping that under the leadership of Ivan Mazepa, hetman of the Ukraine, the country would rise against Russia. The hetman betrayed Peter, but the Ukrainians remained loyal. Charles approached Poltava and besieged the city. On June 27, 1709, the Russians and the Swedes met near Poltava. The young Russian regular army annihilated the Swedish force, capturing nearly all of Charles's generals. Overnight a new military power appeared on the European horizon. The up-to-then unconquerable Charles escaped to Turkey. After the battle Peter entertained the Swedish generals, his prisoners, at dinner, and the first toast was drunk by the tsar to the health of his "teachers," the captured Swedish staff.

Peter marched on into Turkey, but was surrounded by a superior Turkish force and had to bribe the Turkish commander-in-chief to get out. The war with Sweden went on. In 1714 the young Russian navy won its first victory in the Baltic. In 1721 peace was signed with Sweden. Russia obtained Viborg, Narva, Reval (now Tallinn) and Riga. The balance of power in Europe changed. To accentuate the significance of the changed role of Russia, Peter proclaimed himself emperor.

There was hardly an aspect of Russia's life that escaped Peter's attention. The army was reorganized from top to bottom. It was now to consist of regular regiments, the soldiers recruited from the peasantry, the officers from the nobility. Russia had a navy and was intent on ruling the Baltic. From Germany, Peter borrowed the regulations concerning ranks. The entire nobility, whether in the armed forces or in the civil service, was broken up into ranks. Boyars and petty noblemen all had to serve and be promoted in accordance with merit. Education and service to the state were made compulsory for the nobility. Those noble youngsters who were disinclined to study were beaten up by the tsar himself.

Trade and manufactures were encouraged. The first blast furnaces were introduced in the Urals. The country was divided into provinces, with governors responsible to the tsar. A sort of advisory council to the tsar, the Senate, was formed. Minutes of discussion had to be kept, the tsar participated in the deliberations, and occasionally cracked a Senator on the head with his long stick when somebody in the discussion disregarded the agenda. The administration was organized into collegia, precursors of departments in a modern government.

When the patriarch died, Peter decided not to have a new one elected. The church was to be ruled by a synod of bishops with a lay secretary appointed by the tsar. Thus the church became but a cog in the imperial bureaucracy, staying in that position up to the revolution of February, 1917.

The old Slavic alphabet was replaced by the modern Russian script. New Year's Day was moved from September to January. The first newspaper was published. A museum containing "mon-

strosities" from animal life, preserved in alcohol, was erected, and people were made to go there, whether they liked it or not. Evening parties, or so-called assemblies, were held by Peter in his new capital, St. Petersburg. Attendance was compulsory, and the tsar saw to it that everybody showed up in proper European dress, with wigs, and enjoyed himself. Peter smoked a pipe and drank coffee, and the same had to be done by all those who wanted to be active in public affairs. Peter the emperor began to bestow western European titles, like count and baron. This new nobility was very often of the most lowly origin. Peter's prime minister, Prince Menshikov, began as a pie salesman, and Shafirov, a Jew, became a baron. Old Muscovy was being reformed with a vengeance along all lines and in all directions.

The merchants, the artisans, and the soldiers were all for Peter. For a debt-laden serf to become a tsar's dragoon was certainly an advancement. Some of the old boyars grumbled in Moscow, but what could they do? The Old Believers, many of the regular Greek Orthodox clergy, and all types of other religious fundamentalists regarded the tsar as Anti-Christ. They constantly attempted revolts, but were mercilessly crushed. Peter was as harsh and as ruthless in his taxation policy as in everything else. The burden of taxation fell of course on the peasants. There was grumbling and there were revolts, but all this was crushed.

Peter's son, Alexis, also could not stand the uprooting of everything that was holy in old Muscovy. He fled abroad, was brought back, tried, and died during the questioning. Peter, confining his first noble wife to a nunnery, married a non-Russian girl who started as a washerwoman. The ex-washerwoman later became Empress Catherine I. Having deprived himself of an heir, Peter promulgated a law according to which the succession to the throne was to be determined by the tsar. Just after Peter had changed everything around and uprooted most of the old traditions, he caught a cold while saving sailors in a shipwreck. Losing consciousness, he died without assigning the throne to anybody. Thus in 1725 the great revolutionary tsar, who had made over Russia from top to bottom, passed away right in the midst of his great work.

"FATHER OF THE FATHERLAND, PETER THE GREAT, EMPEROR OF ALL RUSSIA." (1672-1725)

So proclaimed by the Russian Senate in 1721 after two decades of bitter war with Turkey on the south and Sweden on the north, this tempestuous giant did more to "modernize" Russia and make it a world power than anyone for two centuries before or after him. His performance on the throne was exactly like his character — full of extremes both good and bad. (*Left*): Life-size wax effigy of Tsar Peter on view among many other Petrine relics in Leningrad, the city that Peter built.

YOUTH AMIDST VIOLENCE

The mother of Peter was gentle Natalia Naruishkina (*right*), second wife of Tsar Alexis Mikhailovich. By his first wife Tsar Alexis had two weak-minded sons, Fedor and Ivan, and three strong-minded daughters, of whom the strongest was Sophia (*lower right*). After Alexis' death, Fedor ruled quietly for six years. Then he died and Natalia became regent for her son Peter whom the boyars and the church deemed better fitted to rule, even at 10, than his 16-year-old half-brother Ivan. This aroused the dominant Sophia, who had a strong following among the palace guards (Streltsy). An uprising amongst them against Natalia ended in the slaughter, before young Peter's very eyes, of the Streltsy's commander, Prince Dolgoruky, and of Artamon Matveyev, his mother's guardian, closest adviser, and their best friend. The convulsions from which Peter later suffered are ascribed partially to these shocking experiences of his childhood.

The contest thus begun between Sophia and her half-brother Peter was inevitably long, bitter and bloody. Also it was characteristically Russian, and tragic, for Sophia was an able woman with ideas for Russia almost as ambitious as her great brother was to generate.

Peter's mother, Natalia.

The Streltsy marching on the palace.

Sophia serving drinks to her Streltsy friends.

Sister Sophia (in later life, a prisoner).

ON THE RED STAIRCASE of the Kremlin, Natalia bravely met the drunken, angry Streltsy. Their pretext was concern for the welfare of her sickly stepson Ivan. She showed them Ivan and Peter, both safe and sound. The Streltsy's chief, Prince Dolgoruky, made a conciliatory speech. But another officer, Hovansky, who sought Sophia's favor, inflamed them again and they stormed the palace, butchering right and left. They insisted that Sophia become regent and that Ivan be crowned with Peter as joint Tsar, to assure Sophia (and themselves) the real authority.

(In Russian, the word for "red" and "beautiful" may be used interchangeably. Hence Moscow's "Red" Square and the Kremlin's "Red" Staircase, long before the "Red" Revolution of 1917.)

So the two boys were crowned together (*left*) and Sophia had a **TWIN THRONE** of silver made (*above*) through a rear panel of which she is said to have dictated their pronouncements. To her credit should be placed legislation improving the status of Russian women. She even contemplated emancipation of the serfs.

SOPHIA, REGENT

In her seven years as Regent, Sophia was well advised (and loved) by Prince Basil Golitsyn, brother of Prince Boris who was later to counsel Peter. They recovered Kiev permanently from Poland in return for Russia's crusading against Turkey. Renewed agitation among the Old Believers occupied much of Sophia's time but when the disputants became disorderly, she acted firmly (*right*). She executed Hovansky and disciplined other Streltsy who had stirred up the trouble.

PETER'S EDUCATION

Until he was eight, Peter's only tutor was Nikita Zotov, an old clerk who later became a leading court mummer (*center*). Peter learned Latin from the prayerbook, but wrote badly. During Sophia's regency, he lived with his mother in Preobrazhenskoe, a suburb of Moscow near the German quarter. There he met General Patrick Gordon, a Scottish soldier of fortune (*above*) who became his military tutor. Peter "played soldiers" with a regiment of young aristocrats (*right*) so realistically that both he and Gordon were wounded at times. The Preobrazhensky Regiment grew up to be Russia's proudest, its banner (*above*) bestowed by Peter himself.

PETER THE MARINER

Peter obtained from Europe an astrolabe (*above*). Franz Timmerman, a Dutch merchant of Moscow, showed him how to use it. Thereafter Peter was sea-struck, had Timmerman teach him arithmetic for navigation. They discovered in the Romanov flax-yard an old British boat that would "sail into the wind" (*above*). A Dutch shipwright was found to repair it and Peter, impetuous in all things, could not rest until he learned not only to sail but to build boats himself. He launched his first boyish "fleet" on Lake Plestcheyev near Pereyaslavl (*center, right*)

Among his many enthusiasms, Peter's love for ships remained dominant all his life. Ships represented to him the means of reaching the great world beyond Russia. His first boat, which he sailed on the muddy Moscow River (*right*) was perhaps given to Nikita Romanov by Queen Elizabeth.

PETER GROWS UP

When he was 17, Peter scotched a plot by Sophia and the Streltsy to depose him. He incarcerated Sophia in a nunnery but left state affairs to his mother. He was too busy sailing, playing soldiers and sowing wild oats. In the latter his teacher was Franz Lefort (*below*), a sardonic young Swiss sophisticate for whom Peter built a mansion where he could take hundreds of guests for long days and nights of high revelry. Some historians say that Peter drank brandy and whisky only *between* meals and that at his parties there was more horseplay than debauchery. Others point at his huge travelling liquor chest (*right*) and to a six-week hangover he suffered in 1692 (when he was 20), which left lasting marks on his health and character. In any event, Lefort permanently inflamed Peter's enthusiasm and curiosity about the wonders of western Europe.

To calm him down, Peter's mother married off her high-stepping "Petrushka" at 17 to Eudoxia ("Dunka") Lopukhin, beautiful but dumb, whose kinswomen swarmed around to share her good fortune (*below, center*). But this measure had small effect. Peter went right on blowing off steam. But he worked as hard as he played, learned a great deal at great speed.

Franz Lefort

PETER'S MOTHER ran the realm for the two boys while Sophia fumed in her nunnery and young Peter continued his sailing experiments in the north. He went to Archangel in 1693 and took instruction from European skippers frequenting that port.

The mother died in 1694, the half-brother two years later, and at last Peter felt the weight of being Tsar. Sophia's unfinished war with Turkey appealed to him as a means of winning for Russia a southern sea outlet. Lefort encouraged him in renewing the attack on the Sublime Porte, as Turkey was then called after the main gate of Constantinople (*right*). Peter's plan was to seize Azov at the mouth of the Don River (*see next page*).

TAKING OF AZOV

In 1695, Peter took an army down the Volga and the Don but found that the Turks were immovable in Azov unless he could blockade their oversea supply lines. He sent all over Europe for shipwrights and carpenters, had his forests felled and in one winter built at Voronezh (far upstream on the Don) a flotilla including two men-o'-war and 23 galleys (*left* and *left below*).

During this period Peter conceived and began a characteristic project: a canal to link the Volga and the Don (not completed in his time).

THE FIRST RUSSIAN FLEET, commanded by "Captain Peter Alexeivich," defeated the Turk ships in the river (*above*) and blockaded Azov until it fell under amphibious assault (*left*). Peter promptly built Taganrog and other fortresses to clinch his hold on the Don estuary and Sea of Azov. He ordered (and his word was now sole law, with his brother Ivan dead) that ships be built for his wars by all kinds and conditions of Russians. Then, advised again by Lefort, he headed for Europe to seek allies and education. The motto of his mission was: "I am among the pupils and seek those who can teach me." The start of this expedition, which was to mean so much to Russia's national development, was delayed by one more Streltsy plot, led by a colonel who had sided with Peter before but later grown jealous. Tortures and executions ended this affair, and Peter was off.

Richard Edes Harrison

WHAT PETER SAW

Whatever his selfish motives may have been, Peter's inseparable Lefort aroused in the young Tsar a deep respect for Europe (c. 1700). Looking westward into it from his own crude Russia, Peter's mind's eye could see not only all the states and principalities with whom he, as Russia's head, might war or ally himself. He also saw skills, techniques, sciences which he passionately coveted for his Russia. When he went abroad, after ruthlessly

exterminating another minor Streltsy plot against himself in Moscow, he went as plain Peter Mikhailovich, volunteer seaman. He made enemies in Sweden by being too curious about Riga's fortifications; but in Courland, Prussia, Hanover, he made friends. He learned and pondered the fact that Poland and Denmark were planning to fight potent Sweden. In Holland he haunted the factories, picture galleries, printshops, medical schools, everywhere engaging technicians to serve in Russia. But his deepest passion remained shipbuilding (*see next page*), of which he became, in person, Russia's foremost exponent.

PETER IN EUROPE

In Holland, the young Tsar slipped away from his official party, donned the blouse and pantaloons of a laborer, lived in a humble room near the Zaandam shipyards, took up smoking Dutch clay pipes. His landlady adored him, upbraided him for the litter he left on her floor (*below*). His incognito did not last long and he moved into Amsterdam where he consulted the master mariners about charts, navigation, ship construction (*right*). Here he also visited factories, picture galleries, surgeries, everywhere signing up experts to go to Russia and introduce their skills. About 1000 technicians were thus acquired to westernize Russia.

Ship construction was the thing which Peter was most anxious to improve upon. The Dutch ships were cumbersome and slow. He learned from Witsen, a master builder, that every ship builder made his own proportions. Immediately he sent an order to Voronezh that all Dutch ship carpenters should be put under the supervision of Danes or English. Peter liked the long lines of the new British ships, and sent Major Adam Weyde to obtain the King's consent to a visit of the Tsar. Immediately King William sent his fleetest and best vessels to bring Peter and the great embassy to the British Isles (Jan. 17, 1698).

HERE WORKED
AS A SHIP CARPENTER
PETER,
CZAR OF ALL THE RUSSIAS
AFTERWARDS
PETER THE GREAT.
·1698·

IN ENGLAND, Peter arrived with ceremony, passing up the Thames amid royal salutes. But when King William III called on him, the carefree young Tsar remained en deshabille (*right*). He inspected Parliament, the law courts, museums, libraries, but his chief goals were the shipyards of Deptford, Woolwich, Chatham where he hewed and sawed, studied ordnance and gunnery. William provided a mansion, Sayes Court, at Deptford which Peter and his merry crew of dwarfs, jesters and drinking companions left in such a mess that Sir Christopher Wren estimated £350 as the cost of repairs for the owner. (*Above*): Peter working at Deptford, and (*insert*) a memorial plaque.

KING WILLIAM presented Peter with his finest yacht, the *Royal Standard,* mounting 20 cannon. Peter manned her with a crack British crew, loaded her with various British technicians, consigned her to Archangel and set off himself for Venice to complete his navigation studies. (*Left* and *right, below*): the stern and bow of a man-o'-war designed by Peter.

PETER'S PURGE

Peter never reached Venice from London. At Vienna he learned that the Streltsy were up again, this time seriously threatening to murder him and reinstate Sophia. He rushed to Moscow, to find that his lieutenants, led by Shein, already had the situation in hand (*right*). Peter determined upon fierce retribution, to bring the country completely to heel for the sweeping plans he had evolved. With his own hand he slew five plotters and made several of his officers do likewise. He then tortured and executed scores, hundreds, thousands of others. He sent Sophia to a more remote nunnery, incidentally ridding himself of Eudoxia the same way. Lucky indeed was Sophia to escape the long Moscow gallows that creaked and groaned for months that summer of 1698 (*below*). Another of Peter's half-sisters, Martha, was also made to take the veil. Peter wanted his decks entirely clear.

FOR SAVAGERY and public shock there have been few purges equal to Peter's. He had the plotting Streltsy whirled through the streets in tumbrils to the Red Square before the Kremlin, where their women could watch (*above*). He gave them the knout (leather and wire whip) to extract their guilty secrets, had them slowly broken on wheels and beheaded. From some 50,000 he reduced the Streltsy to a harmless handful. Peter taught later Russian rulers about discipline.

OFF BEARDS AND KAFTANS

Symbolic to Peter of the reactionary spirit which opposed him and held Russia back from European modernity, were the bushy beards and oriental *kaftans* (robes) worn by the old-line boyars. At his headquarters in Preobrazhenskoe, Peter one day personally sheared the beards of his chief boyars (*below*) and ordered all other boyars to shave their chins forthwith. Merchants and lesser folk might go bearded by paying a tax. Beards were tax-free only to peasants. Peter put his soldiers into European-style jackets and gaiters, with tricorn hats. He outlawed the old civilian costume, personally chopping off some sleeves himself.

Old-Style Boyar and Wife (Palm Sunday).

Peter Trimming Beards.

Peter Chopping Kaftans.

A NEW CALENDAR to synchronize Russia with Europe was proclaimed (*above*) and enforced by Peter, moving the Russian New Year from Sept. 1 (Old Testament style) to Jan. 1 (Julian calendar). (But the religious calendar remained the same.) He also Europeanized Russia's architecture, speech, manners.

Peter's Soldiers at Work.

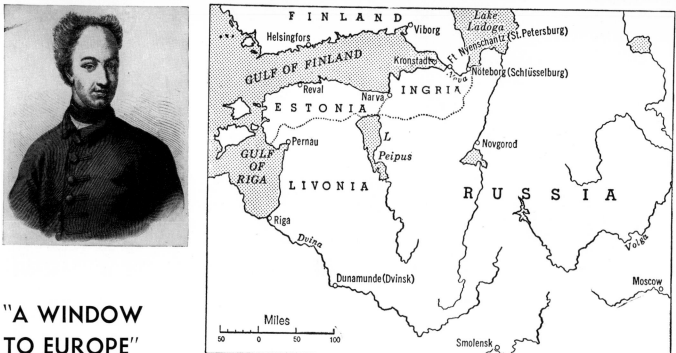

"A WINDOW
TO EUROPE"

Peter's dream was nothing less than to carve for Russia "a window to Europe" on the Baltic. The man to beat for this was 17-year-old Charles XII of Sweden, whose ancestors had nailed shut Ingria, Estonia and Livonia (*see map*). Poland and Denmark were tired of Sweden's sway. They welcomed Peter into alliance and started to fight. Peter waited until he could strike a truce with Turkey (1700). Then he charged precipitately north to challenge rugged young Charles (*above*).

PLAYING AND FIGHTING were the only two things Charles XII really understood. A picture of him, armed only with a forked stick, approaching an enraged bear (*left, below*), expresses his contempt for the raw Russian troops of Peter, who were now minus their tough backbone, the Streltsy. Any Swedish horseman (*below*, with barber-pole lance) considered two Russians an easy match. Practical jokes were Charles's delight, like smashing shop windows. And he preferred runaway horses.

THE BATTLE OF NARVA (*above*), first round of what was to be a 21-year war, taught Peter a lesson. After spanking Denmark, Charles sent his army after Peter, who was invading Livonia. In a blizzard, the Swedes sliced into Peter's hosts and swept them into the river where they drowned when a bridge collapsed.

AFTER NARVA, Charles turned on Poland, leaving garrisons at Sweden's strong points along the coast between Lake Ladoga and the Gulf of Riga, to keep Peter penned inland. Experimentally, using small task forces under General Sheremetev (*above, left*) Peter chipped at these garrisons — Narva, Reval, Pernau, Riga, Dunamunde (Dvinsk) — until his men learned how to fight the Swedes. Meantime he sent in hordes of Kalmycks and Bashkirs to "scorch the earth" of Livonia and Estonia so that they could not supply the coastal fortresses — a strategem he had learned from the steppe Tartars. For his own troops he personally planned supply with infinite care.

TWO YEARS AFTER NARVA Peter felt strong and smart enough to storm Nöteborg, the Swede fort where the Neva flows out of Lake Ladoga. After a thorough mortaring (*left* and *below*) he took it (October, 1702), renamed it (Schlüsselberg), strengthened it vastly.

PETER'S BIG CITY

Moving down river the spring after his capture of Schlüsselberg, Peter seized a small fort called Nyenschantz near the Neva's mouth. He also seized an island there and at once converted it into a capacious naval base which he named Kronstadt. For little Fort Nyenschantz was his idea of just where to build his new capital: St. Petersburg.

Not many conquerors have built a new capital in enemy territory. But that is precisely what Peter did. It was seven long years before he could reduce all the Swedish forts along the Gulf of Finland and around into the Baltic, but Petersburg and Kronstadt were begun in 1703, with flourishing naval salutes (*above*). They were rushed to completion by 1718, using thousands of peasants to drive piles in the marshy ground (*below*), to haul millions of tons of red granite from far inland.

SWEDEN'S SHIPS attacked the new capital before much of its mortar was dry. Serving under Admiral Apraxin (*left*) in his own battle fleet, Peter helped repel the blow. Several of the Swede vessels were captured. Twenty years after its founding, St. Petersburg was mapped by a German with deep respect (*below*).

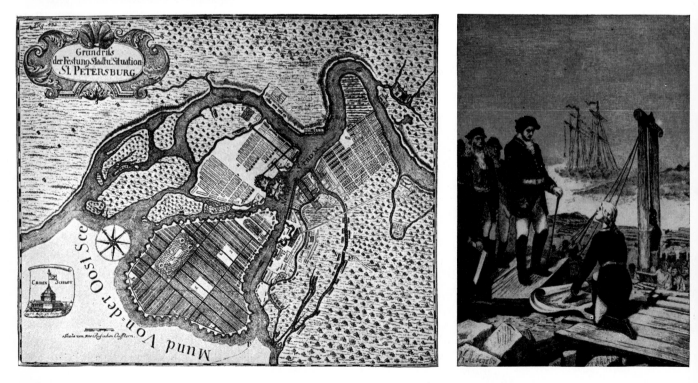

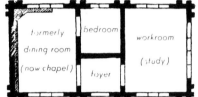

formerly dining room (now chapel) | bedroom | workroom (study) | foyer

PETER'S LITTLE HOUSE

The scale on which Peter, the Tsar, did things can be seen in his architect's drawings for his Big City (see p. 98). The scale on which Peter, the man, liked to live can be seen in the pictures on this page, of his "Little House" in St. Petersburg. The house was 55 x 20, of logs, and shingled. There were three small, low-ceilinged rooms, and many small, leaded windows, through which he could see the water. He later had another building (*below*) erected outside of this cabin to preserve it from the damp climate, and many of his relics are stored there now.

The bedroom was made into a chapel, where prayers were said before a miraculous image which accompanied Peter in his campaigns and was present at the Battle of Poltava (p. 88).

For his wife and friends, he demanded luxury, entertainment, fine raiment, fine palaces and courtly manners, but Peter loved simply furnished quarters without servants, or ceremony, where he could wear old clothes, eat simply and recoup his energy. He wore an old surtout, with many state papers and engineering plans in its pockets, and rolled it up into a pillow at night.

COSSACK TROUBLE

In Peter's time, the Cossack bands resumed their old custom of raiding outpost settlements, carrying off women and livestock (*above*) and putting villages to the torch. In the order of their troublesomeness in Peter's time were: the Bashkirs of the Middle Volga, the Kirghiz of Astrakhan, the Cossacks of the Don and, fiercest, the Zaporog Cossacks of the Dnieper. Just when Charles XII completed his subjugation of Poland and turned his full strength against the rising Russian challenge, Peter was confronted by all four of the above-named steppe peoples going on the warpath simultaneously.

Peter sent able Prince Y. Dolgoruky (*left*) to stamp out the steppe fires. The Cossacks surprised him by night, slaughtered him and his expedition.

Prince Dolgoruky was sternly revenged, but now the Cossacks fought Peter everywhere on principle, for their freedom. Sensing this, Charles XII of Sweden, who had penetrated eastward nearly to Smolensk in a threat to Moscow, turned south down the Dnieper to enlist the Zaporog Cossacks.

The Zaporog chief was a crafty oldster named **MAZEPA** (*above*) whom Peter had known as a friend for years. But Mazepa joined Charles. His promised aid proved picayune, but Charles pushed rashly on, besieged **POLTAVA.** At that he nearly smashed Peter's army when it fell upon him at 4 o'clock one morning, but the dependable Menshikov enveloped him (*left*), and a chance cannon shot smashed Charles' carriage.

SWEDES AND TURKS

Though badly wounded, young Charles had henchmen carry him on a litter of pikes, continued in command until his rout was certain. Then he escaped just before Peter rode up (*above*). With Mazepa he fled southward into Turkey. Said Peter, vastly relieved, to the captured Swedish generals: "I drink to my teachers in the art of war."

While Peter returned north with the invaluable Menshikov (*left*) to mop up Estonia and Livonia, Charles persuaded Ahmed III, Sultan of Turkey (*right*) to declare war on Peter. Result was a campaign on the Prut River which might have been a shambles for Peter had not the Turk stayed his hand when promised all that Peter had won at Azov.

HAVING RETRIEVED his own chestnuts, Ahmed kicked Charles out of Turkey. His return to Sweden failed to stem the Russian tide. Menshikov swept the Swedes out of Poland, Germany, Finland. He even threatened Stockholm after the Russian fleet whipped the Swedish in its biggest victory yet, off Gangut, (Hango) in 1714. Peace was signed at Nystadt (1721).

AFFAIRS OF STATE

When he was away at war (which was most of the time), Peter entrusted domestic affairs largely to Prince Boris Golitsyn (*left*), who had helped him against Sophia. Foreign affairs, Peter left to his sister's husband, Prince Boris Kurakin (*right*). The Astrakhan Cossack uprising of 1706 destroyed Peter's faith in Golitsyn, who drank heavily, and he was replaced by Andrei Matveyev. Kurakin performed with consistent brilliance, especially in keeping England from saving Sweden toward the end. He is called "Father of Russian Diplomacy." He lived until 1727. His autobiography ends with 1709 but remains a classic.

PETER'S CONTEMPT for Russian institutions (compared to Europe's) and his imperious manner of changing them, were exemplified by his transfer of the Patriarch's authority to a Holy Synod of the church, and his substitution of a yesman Senate for the Council of Boyars. To the Senate, as a judicial and legislative body (*left*), he added executive ministries on the Swedish model. These innovations angered the pious people and the proud boyars, so that only Peter's alertness and towering will kept revolt suppressed.

THE POLL TAX which Peter levied to support his armies was crushing (*left*), but it did result in a great increase in cultivation by peasants who had to work to pay it. Peter was lenient toward the Jews, whom he considered clever and commercial. (*Above*): Peter cordially receiving a Jewish deputation.

PETER'S COURT

From France, Peter imported the function called "assembly" (*right*), a pleasure-mixed-with-business gathering where news, affairs of state and military plans were mingled with affairs of the heart, gossip and champagne. Peter was insatiably gregarious and kept around him, besides kindred and faithful spirits who could share his work, a horde of jesters, entertainers and dwarfs. The marriage of two of his drawfs he made into one of the great galas of his time (*below*). His black friend Hannibal, whom he bought as a slave boy in Paris (*left, below*), was so favored that one of his descendants became Russia's great 19th Century poet, Pushkin. After the marriage of one of his fools, Jacob Turgenev, which was made the occasion for a three-day party in a special pavilion in the fields, Peter and his comrades masqueraded through Moscow in sledges drawn by pigs, dogs, oxen, even bears (*see below*) with the bridal couple on a camel. This party was too much for poor Turgenev, who died in a few days. Peter's love for masquerade seems to have derived from his German friends' custom of Christmas Eve mummery.

PETRINE INDUSTRY

One of his biographers observes that Peter moved so indomitably into the teeth of popular winds that he increased their velocity against him. Repin's picture of Peter striding off to supervise the work at some of his factories, followed by a retinue staggering under his impedimenta (*left*), expresses this accurate metaphor. Constantly on the move, Peter's personal industry was almost too much for the unleavened lump that was then Russia, but they did say of him admiringly: "He works as hard as any muzhik." He whizzed around to all corners of his empire, commanding, planning, stimulating, exploring, usually accompanied by his second wife, Catherine, who alone had power to soothe him and make him rest from his work.

PETER SENT hundreds of students to Europe to learn arts and skills, examined them rigorously himself when they returned (*above*). He was constantly on the lookout for talent, foreign or domestic, which might add to the greatness of his expanding state.

WINTER AS WELL AS SUMMER the headlong cavalcade that was Tsar Peter's might turn up at any moment anywhere (*above*). For stays on his ships, Peter built a wire factory, with artisans imported from Germany (*below, left and right*). His system was to form a company, endow it, exempt the managers from taxation, draft labor from the peasantry.

NIKITA DEMIDOV (*left*) was the designer of, **WILHELM GENNINS** (*right*) the engineer-manager of, a series of metallurgy plants built by Peter in the Urals. One of the most important was a copper smelter, for making bronze cannon (*below, right:* exterior, *left:* interior). Peter well understood the strategic value of the Urals to Russia in peace as well as war.

UNHAPPY LABOR. In its cinema account of Tsar Peter, the present Soviet regime does not omit the scene (*below*) of workers, outraged by autocratic conscription of their labor, striking against Peter's tyranny and being shot down by his soldiers.

PETER AND CATHERINE

In 1711, Peter divorced Eudoxia so that he might marry Catherine Skovronsky, a husky, healthy Lithuanian wench who, captured by General Sheremetev, had been sold to General Menshikov, in whose house Peter found and enjoyed her. Among other things Peter wanted from her a son, because Alexis, by Eudoxia, was a weak reed. Catherine bore him two legitimate daughters Elizabeth and Anne. Peter rushed off to France in 1717 to see if he might not pledge Elizabeth to the boy Louis XV, whom he picked up bodily in his hands to inspect thoroughly at their first meeting (*below*).

THE WEDDING FEAST of Peter and Catherine (*below*) was a sumptuous state affair, but thereafter she was content to act as safety valve for his "intolerable" energy and emotions, sharing the ordeals he put himself through. He had her crowned Tsarina in 1713. She often interceded for courtiers who fell into disfavor.

REGALIA

Peter loved to slide into his naval coat and overcoats (*below*), tattered by work and campaigning. This over-grown-boy habit endeared him to peasant-motherly Catherine, who personally sewed and patched for him.

Sailing on the Neva with Catherine (*above*), Peter would dress like a simple sailor (except for his star of St. Andrew) and take the tiller.

(*Left*): Catherine's coronation gown, a creation of massive scarlet and gold brocade. (*Above*): Coats worn by Peter at court ceremonies, modeled after the French style — but hated by him for frequent use. Too fancy. Everything huge Peter wore had to be out-size, especially his shoes.

THE SUCCESSION

Peter's son Alexis wanted nothing so much as to get out of being Tsar. But ambitious people around him intrigued to keep him in line. Peter angrily announced a new rule: the Tsar might name his own successor.

Not knowing just which he would do — marry according to his father's dictate or renounce the throne — Alexis ran off to Austria. Haled home (*above, right*) he admitted he might have

connived at Peter's overthrow. Peter forced him to renounce the succession publicly (*left*), and Alexis soon died (1722) under torture.

Peter's basic dislike and distrust for Alexis was doubtless partly rooted in the boy's inability to "take it" physically as his father could. In his 53rd year, Peter carried his rigors too far. Sailing in the White Sea he was shipwrecked, heroically rescued several people (*below*) but caught a chill which sapped his resistance and undermined even his phenomenal ruggedness.

PETER'S END

Peter's serious reason for going to the White Sea in 1725 was to inspect and inspire work on his projected canal from Lake Ladoga to tidewater. He had thousands of peasants toiling (*above, left*), drove himself (in spite of his shipwreck chill) as hard as them. He returned in time for the New Year's "Blessing of the Waters," a frigid ceremony performed on the river ice (*left*). Seizures followed, and Peter died while trying to dictate his will about the succession to his womenfolk (*bottom*). His death mask on the pillow (*above*) was that of a burned-out volcano of fifty-three.

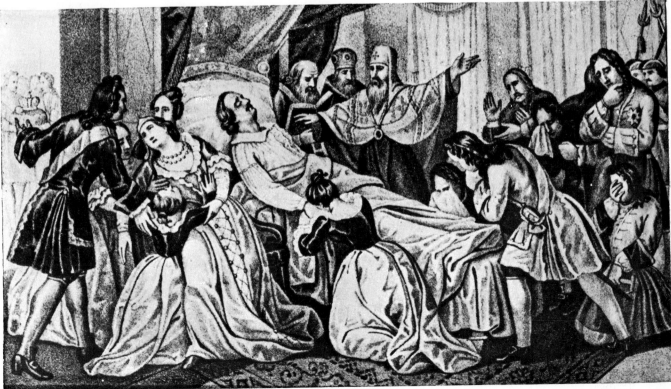

MARK OF PETER

St. Petersburg, Petrograd, now Leningrad was the conception and monument of one man — Peter the Great. No other great city in the world can refer its origin so explicitly to a single driving force. It stands today as Peter's mark. On this page may be seen what amount to architects' drawings of some of the buildings ordained by Peter. They were mostly dull yellow.

(*Right*): **MONASTERY OF ALEXANDER NEVSKY.** A road to it was cut straight through the woods, and was called Nevsky Prospect.

EKATERINHOF was a beautiful palace set in a park which Peter built for Catherine.

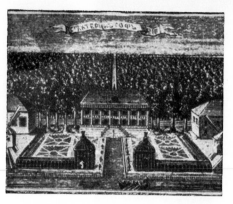

The house of the most serene **COUNT MENSHIKOV,** where Peter liked to entertain — later a cadet school.

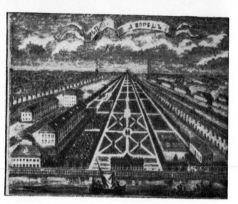

THE SUMMER PALACE, an example of Peter's preference, was really three separate, small buildings.

GOSTINNY DVOR on Troitsky Square, a group of shops where merchandise from all parts of the world was sold, reflecting Peter's interest in foreign trade.

THE WINTER PALACE was of brick, 250 feet wide, its portal decorated with a naval crown and two wings — Peter's idea of swanky decoration.

THE ADMIRALTY was surrounded by a deep moat, and Peter had its spire gilded. He had shipways put on its river frontage, and made canal approaches to it.

ORANIENBAUM was a beautiful menagerie and formal park, lavishly planted with carnations Peter's favorite flower.

KOTLIN ISLAND, or Retu-Saari, was designed in Dutch manner with canals, but in Spring and Fall was badly inundated.

KRONSTADT was the fortress on Kotlin Island built (with great effort) to defend Peter's capital.

VI. GROWTH AND DE-CLINE OF THE EMPIRE

Tsar Peter the Great was dead, but his product, the Russian empire, remained. His successors were limited and petty people. During thirty-seven years (1725-1762) Russia experienced five palace revolutions. The Imperial Guard, a powerful tool in the strong hand of Peter, now became master of the situation, overthrowing and even murdering sovereigns.

In 1762 Tsar Peter III was murdered by the officer friends of his wife. The young lady, a petty German princess, became empress and is known as Catherine the Great. In the beginning of her reign Catherine was a liberal. She corresponded with Voltaire and Diderot, and even drew up a plan for a constitution. She also wrote a few plays, fostered the theatre and encouraged Novikov, the first publisher of popular-priced books.

Under Catherine the empire continued to expand. This expansion slowed down in the interval between Peter and Catherine, but never quite stopped. In 1760, for instance, the Russian troops were in Berlin, and Frederick the Great of Prussia was in flight. Only the accession to the throne of Peter III, an admirer of all things Prussian, saved the great Frederick. The Russians had reached Kamchatka and were on the Pacific long before Catherine. Bering discovered Alaska after the death of Peter, but his expedition was encouraged by Peter. In the reign of Catherine the Great, Russia fought repeatedly with Turkey. In 1783 the Crimea was conquered. As a result of these wars, Russia now stood firmly on the Black Sea.

In 1773 there took place the first partition of Poland, followed by the second partition in 1793. Finally in 1795 a third partition wiped unfortunate Poland off the map of Europe for over a hundred years. Russia now bordered directly on Prussia and Austria. She could now participate in European politics directly; the buffer state was gone, and Catherine, a skillful diplomat, made ample use of her newly acquired position. Russian arms were successful not only on land, but also on sea. In 1770 the Russian fleet inflicted a crushing defeat on the Turkish navy in the Mediterranean.

While the empire was expanding, Catherine was also instrumental in strengthening serfdom. In the course of her reign she donated to various noblemen over 800,000 serfs. Serf girls were sold for ten rubles, and one noble lady managed in the course of ten years to torture to death 140 serfs, mostly women and girls. Various nationalities subjugated by the Russians, like the Kalmyks on the Volga, staged revolts. In 1773 a Cossack named Pugachev began to spread the tale that he was Tsar Peter III, who miraculously escaped the murder plot of his wife Catherine. Pugachev had no resemblance whatsoever to the dead tsar, but the Cossacks in the Urals flocked to him, the peasants on the Volga rose, and again began burning noblemen's estates. The suppressed minorities also joined in the movement. As in the days of Stepan ("Stenka") Razin a hundred years earlier, a vast territory was in revolt. At one time there was even a threat to Moscow, but the well disciplined troops of the empire finally managed to crush the peasant war.

The liberal Catherine now became a conservative. The French revolution that soon followed turned her into a reactionary. But the era of Catherine gave permanent root to new values in the field of culture. The first great modern Russian scientist, Lomonosov, appeared even before Catherine. He was a most remarkable man, a peasant's son who became a philosopher, physicist and poet. In Catherine's days there lived the poet Derzhavin, and the first great Russian historian, Karamzin, began his work. Among the high nobility there arose two intellectual movements. Freemasonry was imported from Scotland, and several Russian lodges were formed. Another group

among the nobility, more cynically inclined, became followers of Voltaire. The seeds that Catherine had sown in her liberal period, when a woman was made president of the Russian Academy of Sciences, began to sprout in the second, reactionary part of her reign.

The days of Catherine also brought forth the greatest Russian general of all time: **Alexander Suvorov.** He believed that an army is a team, that every soldier should have a chance to become a field marshal, that the best form of defense is the attack. Under Catherine's eccentric son, Paul I, Suvorov accomplished the seemingly impossible: In a war against France he crossed the Alps with his army from Italy into Switzerland.

The reign of Catherine's son Paul was short (1796-1801). A man of many extraordinary ideas, but of a most unruly temper, he was murdered by the nobility. His son, Alexander I, disliked by the father but the favorite of the grandmother, began his rule with many liberal ideas. He even dreamed of liberating the serfs, and again like his grandmother, worked on a project of a constitution. All this, however, went on in high court circles. The peasants continued to suffer under serfdom.

Alexander annexed Finland to Russia and granted Finland a constitution fairly liberal for that day. He continued fighting the Turks, attempting like his grandmother Catherine to capture Constantinople and to re-establish the Byzantine empire. These plans, however, had to be abandoned. A new danger began to threaten Russia: Napoleon.

After the Russians had suffered several defeats from Napoleon, Alexander and Napoleon met in 1807 in Tilsit and decided to divide Europe between them. But Napoleon, like most would-be world conquerors, could not tolerate a powerful neighbor. In the end of June, 1812, he crossed the Russian border with an enormous army of allies and recruits from all over Europe. The continent of Europe was now marching on Russia. The Russians retreated, drawing the conqueror deeper and deeper into the vast space of Russia. For a few days Napoleon wavered in Smolensk, unable to decide whether to go on or not. But the die was cast, and the emperor of the French followed the retreating Russian armies. On the field of Borodino near Moscow the Russians finally gave battle. Napoleon was unable to dislodge the Russian army, but half of the Russian force perished. Kutuzov, a pupil of Suvorov, led the Russian troops through and around Moscow and abandoned the old capital. Moscow was empty, the people had fled. Fires broke out in several parts of the city. Surrounded by flames, Napoleon wrote to Alexander from the Kremlin, but received no reply. Alexander was in St. Petersburg, stubbornly silent.

In the meantime all around and in the rear of Napoleon's army, the Russian peasants rose. The regular Russian army was still intact; it was gathering strength beyond Moscow. All around the invading forces of Napoleon there emerged the flames of a much more dangerous fire than the fire of Moscow. The invaders were engulfed in the flames of a people's war. Napoleon decided to retreat over the devastated road through Smolensk and Vilna. Kutuzov followed with the regular Russian army. The peasants and the Russian winter did the rest. Having crossed the Berezina river going into Russia with over half a million men, Napoleon recrossed the same river on the way out with approximately 60,000.

Alexander continued the war into Europe. The powerful coalition against Napoleon was formed and in 1814 the Russians entered Paris. Alexander played the leading role in the peace congress assembled at Vienna. Having liberated Europe from Napoleon, he became a mystic. A period of reaction followed in Russia. One of Alexander's aides even tried to militarize the serfs, thus further aggravating the condition of the peasantry. Russia seemed all-powerful, and Alexander was the leading monarch of Europe. The Russian people, still in the bonds of serfdom, had passed the test for nationhood. The serfs who liberated Europe did not become free, but the consciousness of what the Russian nation was capable of could not be erased.

PETER'S SUCCESSORS

AND THEIR MINISTERS

The Imperial Guards saw to it that Catherine (*above, left*), who had campaigned with them, succeeded Peter the Great in place of young Peter II, son of the foresworn Alexis. She lived only two more years (1727), spending money so wildly that even old Prince Menshikov, her chief adviser, protested strongly. Succeeding at twelve, Peter II (*above, center*) exiled Menshikov and broke his betrothal to the Menshikov daughter. He returned Russia's capital to Moscow and let Russia's affairs be handled by the Dolgoruky family. Then he died of a chill at fifteen (in 1730).

The Supreme Secret Council invited Peter the Great's niece Ann, widow of the Duke of Courland, to be Tsarina under strict controls. She agreed. Peter's old regiment, the Preobrazhenskoe Guards, stepped in and kicked out the Council and let Ann, who was coarse and provincial, run an extravagant show with her German lover, Count Ernst Johann Biron (*below, right*). This performance lasted ten years (1730-1740), during which Russia suffered internally from fires, storms, epidemics, taxation, persecution, famine. (*Above, right*): Ann, with Biron at her right elbow, shooting animals in the Peterhof Zoo. The "sport" was to have game chased past her majesty by hounds.

Except for the Dolgoruky and Golitsyn families, Russia was now run by foreigners, for Peter the Great had broken the boyars and relied on imported talent. Two of his importations were superior characters: Ostermann, (*below, left*), who stayed until young Peter II became completely insupportable; and Münnich (*below, center*), a military man of the first order who kept Russia in the running with Poland and Turkey. After Ann's death, Münnich sent Biron off to Siberia, but both he and Ostermann lost their liberty when Peter the Great's youngest daughter, Elizabeth, was brought in by the Preobrazhenskoe Guards to oust Ann's depraved niece and her infant Ivan VI whom Ann had named as her successor.

Count Biron (*below, right*), lover of Ann, was a polished sycophant incapable of any thought save for his own income and pleasure. He was as much loathed in his native Courland, where he was grudgingly elected to the dukedom, as he was in Russia. At Ann's coronation he was made grand chamberlain, and a count of the Empire, whereupon he adopted the arms of the French ducal house of Biron. The Russian guardsmen detailed to bundle him out of their country did not handle him gently. He was sent to Siberia for twenty-two years (1740-1762).

ELIZABETH (*above*), who died with a glass of cherry brandy at her lips, was a drunkard and nymphomaniac but at least she was a Russian. She ruled twenty years (1741-1761). Her advisers were the Shuvalov brothers who, though not the calibre of Menshikov or the Golitsyns were, again, at least Russian. Count Peter Shuvalov, Elizabeth's treasurer, was hard put to pay her bills, which became so large that her Paris dressmaker stopped her imperial credit. Shuvalov debased the coinage, and Elizabeth built the Winter Palace for ten million rubles, while the peasants starved and groaned. Yet her loyal armies won the respect of Frederick the Great, whom they whipped in the Seven Years' War.

An able man who might have served Russia well had Peter II lived, was **PRINCE DMITRY GOLITSYN** (*above, right*), whom Peter the Great trained abroad. He was a constitutionalist who understood Peter the Great's mistakes of haste, as well as his great objectives. He was for restricting the autocracy of Russia's ruler, enhancing the power of the Supreme Secret Council of which he was president. Ann sent him to prison where he died. **A SORRY FIGURE** in Siberian exile when Peterless Russia needed him most was the aged Prince Menshikov (*below*), shorn of his estates, nearly blind, comforted only by his daughters. He endured only two years and died in 1729.

CATHERINE THE GREAT

The accident by which an obscure German princess, Sophia Augusta of Anhalt-Zerbst (*above, right*), daughter of a Prussian field marshal and of one of Frederick the Great's female spies, became tsarina was this: Peter the Great's daughter Ann, married to the Duke of Holstein, had at the time the only available male descendant of the Romanov line, a hare-brained zany also named Peter (*right*). The Tsarina Elizabeth paired this youth off with Sophia Augusta. Not everyone would have married him. Rechristened Catherine in honor of his grandmother, Sophia devoted her talents, which had been sharpened by adversity and a worldly upbringing, to becoming the autocrat she knew her husband could never be.

There was more than poise in Catherine's expression as she attended the funeral of Tsarina Elizabeth (*above, left*). There were also premonition, premeditation, gloating. It seemed she knew her idiot spouse would behave so much like a Prussian that the Imperial Guards would remove him and install her — which they promptly did. He left for confinement with only his violin, his dog, his Negro slave and his mistress. Prince Gregory Orlov, one of Catherine's first lovers, was in charge at a drunken dinner from which Peter III emerged dead. Catherine lost no time in getting crowned Autocrat (*below*) and in all things being one.

CATHERINE RODE ASTRIDE (*above*) at the head of 20,000 Guardsmen the day they deposed her husband. She had the "news" of his death brought to her at a public function so that she could burst into tears and flee the room. Then, having spent patient years of preparation amid what she considered Russia's barbarism, she squared off to rule for thirty-four years. In a general way, she began where Peter the Great had left off. Not least of her accomplishments was to give Russia what it had never had: Style. She said Autocracy "requires certain qualities."

Serenity and good cheer were the keynotes of Catherine's court. She cultivated imperturbability in the face of crisis. Vigorous in body and mind, she rose at 5 A.M., lit her own fire, kept four secretaries busy during a fifteen-hour work day. Her basic technique was exerting her charm on people to gain ends for herself and Russia. Her whims and moods, which she at all times indulged fully, ranged from reading the French encyclopedists or quietly walking her dog (*below, left*), to promiscuous lovemaking, intensive letter-writing, hawking with her paladins (*below*). As a ruler, she was contemptuous of system, preferring to rely on "circumstances, conjectures and conjunctions."

CATHERINE'S MEN

Of Catherine's many lovers, four were important: (1) and (2) the brothers Orlov, Gregory (who poisoned her husband) and Alexis, under whose command the Russian fleet whipped the Turks at Chesme (*below*); (3) General Sergius Saltykov who led her victorious armies in Poland; (4) Prince Gregory Alexandrovich Potemkin (*above*) who won for her the Crimea. She had the faculty of retaining her cast-off lovers as friends, also of inspiring sincere friendship and service without necessarily giving her love. Count Peter Panin, one of her best generals (*right*) was in this last category. Potemkin, after her passion for him was spent, retained his influence by finding for her able younger lovers, while he fought her battles.

CATHERINE'S MIND

Buffon, Diderot, Locke, Blackstone, Voltaire, Montesquieu were Catherine's favorite authors. She herself undertook a history of Russia; she sculpted, made cameos, painted. She was one of the leading humanists of her time — but purely doctrinaire. The intellectual style which she (*above*), as a benevolent despot, set, was destined to backfire when other Russian minds took seriously the thinking that led to the French Revolution.

At her court besides Lomonosov, who painted one of her many portraits (*above, right*) and filled the air with ponderous odes and brilliant physics, Catherine encouraged the poet Derzhavin and the encyclopedist Grimm (her favorite correspondent). But the satirists Radishchev (*bottom, left*) and Novikov lost favor by outdoing their mistress in their "liberalism."

Catherine built the **HERMITAGE** (*below*), now one of Russia's chief art museums, as a retreat where she could house visiting literary lions like Grimm and Voltaire (*left, center*) who wrote intimately and often but never came. Catherine also built foundling homes, a public library, the Smolny Institute for young ladies, a medical college (where she led the way in taking smallpox inoculation). Sievers, the governor of Novgorod persuaded her to found the Free Economic Society, to investigate agricultural conditions. In a word, Catherine was "modern."

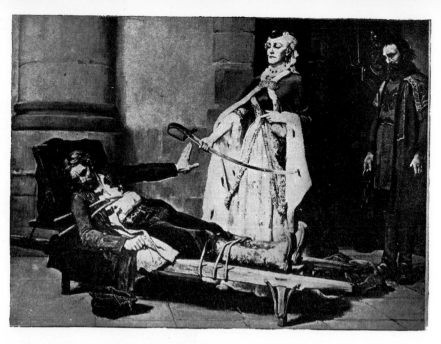

CATHERINE
AND EUROPE

Peter III's downfall was precipitated by his slavish adulation for everything Prussian right after his Aunt Elizabeth had whipped Prussia's Frederick the Great (*above, left*). The Tsarina Catherine did not endorse Frederick but, since he could be useful, she was cordial to him and let him in on the carving up of Poland. Their correspondence was cheerfully cynical. Said she: "Where is there a happy anarchy which we can work at will?"

Having fought in the American revolution and visited Paris after the French one, Thaddeus Kosciusko felt his Polish blood boil when Russia and Prussia carved all but the heart out of his homeland in 1793. As dictator he roused and freed the serfs,

flung his volunteers at the Russian juggernaut. He was wounded and captured. When, for gallantry, Catherine offered him his sword back if he would fight for her, he bitterly refused (*above, right*). The extinction of Poland then proceeded as caricatured in an old print (*below, right*), with Catherine presiding.

Nicholas Esterhazy, French diplomat in Russia's service (*below, left*) tried without success to get Catherine to intervene in the French Revolution.

Count Simeon Vorontzov (*bottom, left*) was one handsome Russian who declined to succumb to Catherine's charms. She philosophically utilized his talents as her ambassador to England, where he lived until his death. His son became British.

PUGACHEV

Catherine called a Great Commission of 564 members from all corners and classes of Russia (except the gentry's serfs). It sat for eighteen months (1766-1768) to reform civic and social conditions (*above, left*). Accomplishments: zero. Serfs were still auctioned, peasants fastened tighter than ever to the land, though their gentry owners were now freed from state service. Crying class war, up rose a shrewd Don Cossack: Emelian Pugachev (*above*).

Starting in the Urals and along the Volga, posing as Peter III with a complete bogus court, Pugachev quickly had an immense following. Factory serfs brought him guns from the imperial cannon works (*left*).

After raiding the provinces, where he despoiled and executed the gentry wholesale (*below, left*) Pugachev threatened Moscow, promising to send Catherine to a nunnery.

It took repeated efforts by Golitsyn, Panin and other generals to put down Pugachev's monster class war, take him in a cage to Moscow for execution (*bottom, right*). It was characteristic of Catherine that she affected to treat the whole affair as a minor incident, and would not let Pugachev be tortured before he was quartered on the scaffold.

"POOR" TSAR PAUL

Lacking any legitimate title of her own, Catherine blandly, completely usurped her son Paul's tenure from his eleventh to his forty-fifth year. Even then she nearly passed Paul over for his son Alexander. For this reason and because he was ugly (*left*) and eccentric almost to the point of Peter III's lunacy, Tsar Paul, who reigned only five years (1796-1801), is often called "poor" Paul. From the exploits of his mother's fleet at Chesme he inherited a vantage in the Mediterranean which, quaintly, resulted in his Orthodox Catholic Majesty becoming the proud Grand Master of the Knights of Malta (Roman Catholic), with their twin-pointed cross (*below, left*).

PAUL'S IDEAS were not all crazy. He restored primogeniture as the basis for the Tsar's succession. He clipped the gentry's wings. He limited the labor of serfs. But he was tyrannical, in Prussian style. He made ladies kneel in the slush at his passing. He chivvied his generals. He drove his guards nearly crazy with the goose-step (*above*). Beside his dead mother on her bed he laid the exhumed remains of his murdered father, which he ceremoniously crowned, and forced his mother's aging lovers to stand guard over the pair. It was summer. Catherine II was fat. There was no embalming. The scene and scent were grisly. When he refused to abdicate, Paul was strangled by a group of officers (*below*).

SUVOROV

Born of gentlefolk at Novgorod, wiry little Alexander Suvorov (*above*) rose from the ranks and never forgot that an army's blood-drops are its common soldiers. He usually scouted ahead of his lines and entered battle carrying a cane. He was sixty-eight and full of honors when Tsar Paul, who had pettishly dismissed him, had to recall him to fight the French Republic. Suvorov quickly disposed of Italy, and was headed for Paris when told to relieve the Austrian commander at Zurich. Suvorov went up through St. Gothard Pass, which he brilliantly negotiated (*left*) only to enter a trap near Zurich whence the French had ousted the disorganized Austrians.

THE DEVIL'S BRIDGE (*above*) was only one tight spot through which Suvorov had to push in the Alps. There were other, tighter spots coming out and down (*left*), but Suvorov extricated two-thirds of his army. Tsar Paul made him Generalissimo and planned a homecoming triumph, which was then capriciously cancelled. Suvorov died in obscurity but, against Paul's orders, all Russia mourned him. The Soviets have revived his memory with the Order of Suvorov, for offensive action annihilating Russia's enemies, bestowed on very few.

NORTHERN SPHINX

Catherine's favorite grandson, Alexander, played with military cadets from small-boyhood (*above,* seated under cannon) and wanted to be a great general when he grew up. From his tutor, a French Republican named La Harpe, he also acquired strong liberal tendencies. From his mother, a princess of Wurtemburg, he inherited big blue eyes and a magnificent physique; from his grandmother, great charm. At sixteen he married Elizabeth, a princess of Baden (*right*), and longed to rusticate with her. He might well have remodelled Russia internally if he had not had to fight Napoleon, who called him "Sphinx of the North" because he, like Napoleon, could dissemble so well. In periods of peace or truce he put his mind on reforming the government and emancipating the serfs. His closest friends were ardent liberals. (*Left*): Alexander standing beside a bust of his grandmother Catherine.

LITTLE CORPORAL

To Alexander's father, Napoleon (*above, left*) had been a welcome force restoring order in the "dangerous" French Republic. After Napoleon conquered Italy and Egypt, he and Paul planned together a conquest of India, which worried England. Alexander vetoed this wild project but Napoleon cherished it. After he became emperor and meddled in Holland and Switzerland, Alexander became fearful of his tyranny and sent Novosil-tsev to London with a vague project of world peace. Pitt was skeptical and Frederick Wilhelm III (Prussia), Francis II (Austria) and Gustav IV (Sweden) hoped for Russia's help against the tyrant who would swallow up the world.

In a surprise move, Alexander and Elizabeth paid a dramatic visit to Berlin, where, at the tomb of Frederick the Great (*above*), he pledged aid to Prussia. This pledge financially curtailed his reform policies, but fired his enthusiasm for stopping Napoleon in the field. He became an ardent amateur soldier.

NAPOLEON quickly knocked out Austria (1805), reducing Alexander to tears of despair. "We are babies in the hands of a giant," he said. Then Napoleon took Berlin and Warsaw. Alexander levied all the troops he could and had Napoleon anathematized in his churches as an Anti-Christ.

The Russians met Napoleon in Prussia, first at **AUSTERLITZ** (*right*), then at **EYLAU** (*below*) and then at Friedland. The Eylau battle, in a snowstorm, cost both sides dearly and was a draw. It made Napoleon realize how far from home he was, how tenuous were his lines of communication and supply. He was as ready as Alexander to mark time a while (*see next page*).

TRUCE AT TILSIT

A floating pavilion was anchored midstream in the Niemen river at Tilsit. The two rulers went out to it in their barges (*above*) and struck a bargain (*upper left*). They would rule Europe jointly, from its two ends. Alexander would abandon his allies, even help enforce Napoleon's blockade of England. Prussia was whittled down and Poland became a French protégé. Russia took Finland and the Danubian provinces. Turkey was to be expelled from Europe, but was to retain Constantinople. This was the occasion of Napoleon's remark: "Constantinople — that is the empire of the world!"

Napoleon dined Alexander, and Alexander proudly introduced to Napoleon his Cossacks and Kalmyks (*left*). But each knew that the Peace of Tilsit was only a truce, the whole meeting a charade, like a later agreement between Hitler and Stalin. Alexander privately reassured the bereft Frederick Wilhelm: "Wait, we will get it all back. He will break his neck. I am your friend."

With England hammering him in Spain, Napoleon anxiously sought to clinch his new friendship with Alexander by a meeting at Ehrfurt in 1808. In the picture (*lower left*), Napoleon is receiving the Austrian ambassador while Alexander (*far right*) looks on. There was plenty of double-crossing at this meeting. Russia secretly agreed to help France if the latter were attacked by Austria. And Napoleon's foreign minister Talleyrand (*center,* beyond table) turned against his master, began corresponding secretly with Alexander.

Meantime, Napoleon proceeded to build up his Grand Army, ostensibly an army of occupation in Germany, actually as a mighty force to invade Russia when the time should seem propitious. The time came in 1812.

NAPOLEON'S MARSHALS

Above are four of Napoleon's marshals: (1) Marquis Laurent de Gouvion Saint-Cyr, who had served France as a general in Germany, Italy, Spain and Poland, received his marshal's baton for breaking the Russian stand at Polotsk, before Moscow in 1812. His apathy toward Napoleon, and sometimes towards war, had cost him more rapid promotion. France's famed military college was named, not for him, but for the village near Paris where it stands. (2) Marshal Louis Nicholas Davout, Duke of Auerstadt and Prince of Eckmuhl, was in Egypt and Austria with Napoleon, later became his War Minister during the "100 Days" of 1815. (3) Marshal Joachim Murat, son of an innkeeper, brother-in-law of Napoleon with whom he served in Italy and Egypt and who made him King of Naples, was the Grand Army's cavalry specialist. (4) Prince Joseph Anton Poniatowski commanded Napoleon's large Polish contingent, was made a Marshal of France in 1813.

THE LINE-UP — 1812. For the war when it was resumed in 1812, Napoleon assembled 600,000 troops from France and captive countries into the Grand Army. He was his own generalissimo with brave Marshal Ney (*right*) his No. 2 man. Alexander had 200,000 men ready, first under de Tolly and Bagration (*bottom*) then under Kutuzov (*below, left*), pupil of Suvorov. Napoleon called him "Old Fox of the North."

ALEXANDER'S GENERALS

Below are four of Alexander's leaders: (1) Prince Michael Andreas Barclay de Tolly was a Livonian of Scottish descent who, wounded at Eylau, was War Minister when Napoleon returned in 1812. He took command of the larger of two armies into which Alexander's forces were divided. (2) Prince Peter Bagration, a Georgian who had commanded Suvorov's advance guard, led the second Russian army. At Borodino, he was killed. (3) General Denis Davydov was Murat's dashing counterpart. An adventurous cavalry hero well beloved by comrades and peasants, he was chief of the militarized guerillas. But most interesting was (4) a young Prussian named Karl Von Clausewitz, who had lately assisted in the reorganization of the Prussian Army under Scharnhorst. Like many other Prussian officers he took service with his country's nominal enemy. Serving as a staff officer, he evolved in the wide spaces of Russia that fluid strategy which was to become basic for the German Army. His famed war philosophy: Don't just take cities. Destroy the enemy and his will-to-fight. Clausewitz died in 1831 of cholera.

THE GIANT DUEL

Resumption of Napoleon's war on Russia was inevitable. It came in 1812 because Napoleon was ready. He still thought he could make Alexander his ally by beating him. Together they would then seize India. But Alexander was angry as well as determined to free Europe. Napoleon had absorbed Elizabeth's homeland and criticized Alexander's love-life, which was expansive, and he had asked for the hand of Alexander's sister Ann, then married Marie Louise of Austria. Moreover, Russia wanted British goods, which she was not supposed to accept under Napoleon's "continental system" for destroying England by closing Europe to her exports. Napoleon seized the initiative by crossing the Niemen with his Grand Army on June 23, 1812 (*below*) using highly efficient pontoon bridges.

Alexander was dancing at a ball in Vilna when news came of Napoleon's move. Accepting deep curtseys from his favorite ladies (*above*) he departed to declare war.

BORODINO. Alexander went to Moscow to rally the home front, leaving the fighting to his generals. Bagration was for attacking Napoleon, de Tolly for retreating, to fight the invader with space, time and hostile population, whom Alexander persuaded to scorch the earth. Battle was evaded, except for delaying actions at Mogilev, Polotsk and Smolensk, until Borodino was reached on the big main road to Moscow. There Kutuzov, who had been given command after popular outcry against the retreat, felt he must stand. The Borodino battle (*below*) wound up as a fierce, confused melee in which both sides lost 40,000 men and several generals.

KUTUZOV (*above,* seated at left of table) paused at Fili west of Moscow for a council of war. He decided not to risk his army before Moscow but to keep it in being by retreating through and around the city. The governor of Moscow, Rostopchin, roused the citizens, freed criminals and even serfs, evacuated the city taking with him all the fire engines, then had the city carefully ignited at several points.

NAPOLEON paused on one of the low Sparrow Hills west of Moscow for his first look at his prize (*left*). After leagues of lonely, inhospitable wilderness, he and his army looked forward to the comforts of home, and a quick surrender of the Russian arms.

After Borodino (*below*) both sides were exhausted. A 7-hour armistice was declared so the Russians could evacuate Moscow, since the French knew that street fighting in the wooden city would mean fires, and what they wanted was rest, food and ammunition. Napoleon slept well that night just west of the city, and next morning rode to the Kremlin.

MOSCOW AFIRE

The fires organized by Governor Rostopchin swept into Moscow from every quarter, to the dismay of the triumphantly entering French. Their ammunition, stored in the Kremlin, was threatened. Napoleon had to leave there (*left*) for the Petrovsky Castle in the suburbs until the conflagration subsided. When he and his men returned two days later (*below*) they beheld a gutted city where home comforts were few indeed.

When he heard in St. Petersburg about the Moscow conflagration, Tsar Alexander said: "After this wound, all others are trifling." Napoleon debated marching on St. Petersburg.

RETREAT FROM MOSCOW

Napoleon wrote to Alexander, offering peace. Alexander would not even reply. Realizing his predicament with the onset of winter, Napoleon sent an emissary to obtain "peace at any price." Alexander would not retreat. To his entourage he said: "I and the people at whose head I have the honor to be, are determined to stand firm." Lonely in the cold Kremlin (*right*), Napoleon received bad news from home; he was losing in Spain.

The stores Napoleon had hoped to capture with Moscow were largely incinerated. Roofs were so scarce that, through necessity and not impiety, horses had to be stabled in the Ouspenskaya Cathedral (*left*). Meantime, General Kutuzov rallied his army and moved around Moscow to the southwest, threatening Napoleon's communications with an offensive action. This increased Napoleon's sense of being miles away from anywhere, without supplies, in a dead city. For long hours he brooded.

THE FIRST SNOWSTORM decided Napoleon: he must get out of Russia. He feinted at Kutuzov to the south and then, his army decimated by desertions, gloomily struck out of the smoldering city on the road by which he had come. Alexander (*above*), stricken by the burning of Moscow, vowed piously to form a Holy Alliance to free Europe.

NO MIRACLES

Many famed paintings depict this turning point in the career of Napoleon and the history of Europe. One is the Russian Vereschagin's picture of Napoleon, urged by his generals to withdraw, studying maps to try and evoke a miracle (*above*). Another is the Frenchman Meissonier's picture of a grim-faced Napoleon on his white charger during the long trek homeward through snow and mud (*below*). Until he reached Smolensk he rode along in a black pit of despair and misery.

THE ROAD BACK

Another great painting by Vereschagin (*above*) shows Napoleon after the snows really came being driven in a sleigh while clouds of scavenging birds arise from corpses left along the way since the advance a month before. The same theme, of human folly and war's futility, informs Vereschagin's "On the Great Road" (*below*) which Alexander's grandmother, Catherine, built.

GUERILLAS

As the tattered, freezing Grand Army retreated, Russian guerillas sprang out of the snowy forests to snap at their heels (*left*). "Revenge! Hurrah!" was their cry. By their fortitude in scorching the earth at his approach, and now by savage acts of vengeance, the Russian People are credited with beating Napoleon. But the climate, distances, forests, bad roads and epidemics had a lot to do with it.

To typify the spirit of the guerillas, Vereschagin painted the picture (*above*) of a proud old patriot and his neighbors defending their village.

Many soldiers who escaped from the French led these patriots. Yermolai Chetvertakov, of the Dragoons, escaped and organized a group of 300 near Smolensk which mushroomed into 4,000 guerillas, many of them Cossacks.

THE TECHNIQUE of guerilla warfare, thus improvised in Alexander's struggle, was not lost on later Russian commanders, who carefully studied and organized it during a later, greater moment of peril for Russia (see Chapter XII).

VASILISA KOZHINA of Sitchev is a peasant immortal of Napoleon's retreat. An old Russian cartoon (*right*) shows her mounted on a farm horse, armed with a scythe, chaffing a captured Frenchman, Prussian and Pole. One of her followers derisively holds up a frog, while a Russian rooster pecks at the fallen Napoleonic eagle. Cries Vasilisa:

"You didn't get fat in Moscow. If you'd gone to Petersburg you'd have collapsed!" The other crone: "Good people, we honor. Brigands and thieves, we knock out!"

THE REAR GUARD

As the ill-clad, starving French plodded toward the Polish border, Kutuzov followed them with the Russian army at a distance. Only at Maloyaroslavets did he engage them, briefly. The army of St. Petersburg and an army from the Danube threatened to intercept Napoleon but through a ruse, and valiant rear-guard action by Marshal Ney, Napoleon escaped. Guerillas and swift bands of Cossacks who cut down stragglers (*right* and *below*) remained the chief threats besides General Winter. Cornered at Losmina, Ney made his classic statement, "A Marshal of France never surrenders," and wriggled out. He emerged fighting almost alone, with a musket, but he survived.

The French artist Philippotaux painted the sorry scene above: a wounded French veteran, unable to go farther, sitting in the snow with drawn pistol awaiting the end, meantime comforting a perishing young recruit. (*Below, right*): Some of the 875 cannon captured by the Russians from the Grand Army and racked up in the Kremlin.

COUNT MATVEY IVANOVICH PLATOV (*below*) was one of the Cossack commanders who pursued Napoleon's army not only across the Russian border but all the way to the Rhine.

TRIUMPH IN PARIS

Napoleon left his Grand Army in Poland, rushed home to get a new one of a million men, reappeared in Central Europe ready for battle early in 1813. Meantime Alexander, taking full credit for Napoleon's defeat, pressed on into Europe. Beaten Prussia and Austria arose to join him. Napoleon won two battles and obtained a truce in June, but thereafter the Allies beat his lieutenants one by one and in October smashed his new army at Leipzig in the "Battle of the Nations." Following the Allied invasion of France, Alexander called on Paris to surrender, which it did. Alexander, received warmly by the sly Talleyrand, entered Paris in triumph in March, 1814 (*above*).

PEACE IN VIENNA

Austria's entry into Alexander's new Alliance made it something less than Holy. Instead of the welfare of Europe's peoples, Austria's cynical Count Metternich sought gains for Austria at the peace conference of 1814 in Vienna (*below*). Italy was partitioned. Germany and Poland were re-carved instead of re-united. Alexander was furious and wanted to fight a duel with Metternich (standing, sixth from left). Biggest gainer was Talleyrand (seated at right, arm on table). He even managed secretly to align England and Austria with France against Russia. When Napoleon returned in 1815 from Elba, he sent this agreement to Alexander, who tore it up under Metternich's nose.

MARK OF ALEXANDER I

Napoleon's "Hundred Days" in 1815 were ended by the battle of Waterloo, from which the Russian Army was absent. But Alexander promulgated his Holy Alliance that autumn: an agreement among Europe's monarchs to keep the peace. To keep the Alliance in line for liberty and peace, Alexander threatened to "release the Beast" (Napoleon) from St. Helena. In St. Petersburg the arch celebrating the Peace of 1815 represents the tremendous (though impermanent) mark that Alexander, or at least the Russian people under him, made upon history.

WINNING OF THE EAST

Even as the United States had to win its Western wilderness by exploration and the suppression of native tribes, so did Russia have to win its East. This process, begun under Ivan IV, was continued under Peter I, Catherine II and Alexander I. Explorer Vitus Bering, a Dane in Peter's navy, in 1725-1728 investigated the strait and sea named for him but failed to reach Alaska until 1741. He died in the Aleutians during his return voyage (*below*). The harbor of Petropavlovsk (Sts. Peter & Paul) was his base in Kamchatka (*above*), which Cossacks had

occupied in 1697. One of Bering's captains, Chirikov, got home with some furs which stimulated the settlement of Alaska. Gregory Shelekov ("The Russian Columbus") settled Kodiak Island in 1784. Novy-Archangel (Sitka) followed in 1805, when the Russians penetrated to Bodega Bay in northern California, seeking furs and red-wood timber.

Peter's ambition for eastern expansion extended to India and even China but he got no further than the Irtysh River, the Altai Mountains, the Yaik River and the Caspian Sea. Under Tsarina Ann, Ivan Kirilov commenced extending the border to the Aral Sea, but the Bashkir, Kalmyk and Kirghiz tribes prevented this until 1847 under Nicholas I (*see next chapter*).

VII. RUMBLINGS OF THE STORM TO COME

For over a hundred years before the 1917 Revolution, the history of Russia presents a picture of strife. The sudden death of Tsar Alexander I served as a signal for the first organized effort to overthrow tsarism. This was the so-called Decembrist Revolt, which took place on December 14, 1825. The Decembrists were officers and aristocrats who had seen a good deal of Western Europe, had formed secret groups of a revolutionary nature, and thought they could bring about a more liberal regime in Russia by utilizing the death of the tsar. Some of them were constitutional monarchists, others favored a republic. The revolt was crushed before the Winter Palace in St. Petersburg, and the main leaders executed. This, however, was only the beginning.

Up to the last century writing and vocal political thought were confined nearly exclusively to the nobility. Now certain middle-class elements began to percolate into literature. The influence of the German philosopher Hegel began to be felt, largely replacing the influence of the ideas of the Frenchman Voltaire. Among Russian intellectuals two groups began to develop. One called themselves the Slavophils. They believed that Peter the Great had gone too far and that there was a good deal in the old Muscovite culture and tradition which Peter discarded too hastily. The Slavophils wanted to revive some of the things the great reformer threw overboard. The other group were the Westerners. These believed that the path indicated by Peter was the correct one, but that the main trouble lay in not having followed it well enough. The Westerners realized more and more the economic backwardness of Russia as compared to Western Europe and stood for further westernization.

In the 1860's there appeared the Nihilists, revolutionaries who had practically no contact with the people and who took a completely negative position toward everything. A decade or so later a new movement arose. The so-called Narodniki, or Populists. These people wanted socialism, but opposed modern industrial development. Their teachings somewhat resembled the later doctrines of Mahatma Gandhi in India, who also opposed industrialization and praised the virtues of primitive peasants. In 1883 there was formed the first Russian Marxist circle under the leadership of George Plekhanov. In 1898 there took place in Minsk the first congress of the Russian Social-Democratic Labor Party. Thus throughout the century there grew in Russia a conscious vocal opposition to tsardom.

But autocracy was still very firmly in the saddle and had no intention of giving up easily. Tsar Nicholas I (1825-1855) became known as the "gendarme of Europe." In 1830 he crushed a rebellion of the Poles, after which Poland lost most of the privileges granted to it by Alexander I. In 1849 Russian troops invaded Hungary, helping the Austrian emperor to crush the Hungarian movement for independence. The Hungarian national leader, Kossuth, was picked up by a United States warship and received tremendous ovations in the United States. Throughout Europe Nicholas was active almost everywhere in defense of autocracy. But the Russian autocratic giant had clay feet. The crucial test came in the Crimean War of 1854-1855. A joint English and French army landed in the Crimea and besieged Sevastopol. The Russian soldiers and marines fought heroically, but Russia lost the war. Russia had scarcely any railroads. Russian arms were the same as were used against Napoleon in 1812. Heroism alone could not defeat the industrial backbone that the western nations now had. Nicholas died before the war was over, and his successor, Alexander II, understood that reform had become imperative.

On February 17, 1861 (old calendar) Tsar Alexander II affixed his signature to a decree liberating over 20,000,000 serfs. The tsar said, "It is better to do this from above than have it happen from below." In this step the tsar went somewhat beyond the proclamation of Abraham Lincoln liberating the slaves. Alexander gave the peasants land. It is true that he did not give them enough land, and that he made them pay for the land they got from the noblemen, but land they did get, which the American ex-slave was not granted.

Alexander also revised court proceedings in Russia, establishing the Russian bar, introducing trial by jury, and carefully selecting the judges. The old Russian professional army, where soldiers served for twenty years or more, was abolished, and universal conscription introduced. Alexander also initiated a system of local self-government in which the merchants and the middle-class groups had a voice. All this, however, did not seem to catch up with the rate at which dissatisfaction was growing. Revolutionary terrorists haunted Alexander wherever he went. In 1881 they finally blew him up with a bomb on the very day he expected to sign a draft of a limited constitution.

While the internal struggle proceeded, the empire continued to push its borders outward. Under Nicholas I and Alexander II the Russians finally conquered the Caucasus. In the reign of Alexander II, Russia penetrated deeply into Central Asia and extended the empire to the borders of India. In 1877-1878 Russia again fought the Turks, but was deprived of the fruits of her victory by the western powers, for whom Russia was no match industrially.

Alexander III, the father of the last tsar, attempted to do two irreconcilable things. He wanted to industrialize Russia and thus strengthen her. In his reign foreign capital began to flow into the country, railroads were built, and factories erected. But Alexander also wanted to turn the clock of history backward. He was determined to crush the liberals and radicals. He tried to "Russify" the various national minorities by force. The penetration of industrialism into Russia, begun under Alexander III and continued under his luckless son, Nicholas II, brought about extensive changes. An industrial working class began to emerge. The old patriarchal ways of life and work in the villages began to give way to modern conditions. The peasantry, rather uniform before that, started to divide into layers of rich, middle and poor peasants. From the last group came most of the recruits which made up the industrial working class.

It must be noted that this period was also most significant in the development of Russian culture. Present day Russian literature emerged with the great Russian writer Alexander Pushkin, who was followed by Lermontov and Gogol. In the middle of the century there developed the Russian novel. Tolstoy, Dostoevsky, Turgenev and many others established Russian literature not only inside Russia's culture, but internationally. A similar development took place in music, with Glinka, Rimsky-Korsakov, Tschaikovsky and many others. In the field of science the Russians were by now also able to compete with the best that Western Europe had to offer. Mendeleyev, the great Russian chemist, devised the periodic table of elements. Pirogov, an outstanding surgeon of the Crimean War, laid the foundations of modern war medicine. Pavlov became the great psychologist. The more Russian culture and learning expanded, the more glaring became the contrast between the educated and cultured layers in the city and the predominantly illiterate peasantry in the country. Economically Russia was unable to keep pace with the times. In spite of the tremendous inpouring of foreign capital, Russia's industry was in a less advantageous position relative to western Europe in 1913 than was the case in 1900.

Nicholas II, crowned in 1896, was the last of the Romanovs. His reign began with a gruesome occurrence. Following the coronation ceremony, the people at a large festival stampeded, and hundreds of persons were trampled to death, earning for Nicholas the ominous tag of "Bloody" from the very start. In 1904-1905 occurred a preview of things to come. The great empire got involved in a war with little Japan.

This war proved disastrous, and a revolution followed. For the first time in Russian history, country and city revolts coincided. For the first time there was an approach to unified leadership. For the first time the phenomenon was nation-wide. Century old rumblings produced the first real storm. The tsar signed peace with Japan, obtained a loan in western Europe. He still had some of his best troops intact, and all these factors combined allowed the monarchy to weather the storm. It did, however, emerge from the experience with its wings clipped. The tsar was forced to grant a limited constitution and to establish a consultative-legislative body, the Duma. The tsar was still strong and another period of reaction ensued. But the revolutionary forces had tested their strength. The rehearsal of 1905 was followed by a brief interlude, before the real thing in 1917. Most significant aspect of the 1905 revolution was the formation of the first soviets (councils) of striking workers and the first collaborations of revolutionary workers with revolutionary peasants.

CONSTANTINE, ALEXANDER I's BROTHER. Alexander I died of gastric fever in 1825 while visiting Empress Elizabeth, who was also ill, in remote Taganrog on the Sea of Azov. Having no heir, he had carefully arranged for his youngest brother, Nicholas, to succeed him — but had told few people about it. Younger brother Nicholas did not know that a middle brother, Constantine (*above*), who looked very much like Alexander, had in 1822 expressed his wish to continue as viceroy of Poland and had signed away his claims to the Russian throne. When news of Alexander's death reached the north, Constantine in Warsaw had his people swear fealty to Nicholas, while Nicholas in St. Petersburg acclaimed Constantine. This mixup gave plotters a chance to attempt a *coup d'état* (*see next page*).

NICHOLAS I

Nineteen years younger than Alexander, Nicholas (*above*) was a very much overshadowed younger brother. He never knew his brilliant grandmother, and he came to the throne saddled with Alexander's unfinished projects at home and abroad. Social and governmental reforms were now sought by leagues of the gentry and officer classes who had lived in Europe and seen how constitutions and parliaments worked. A group led by Colonel Paul Pestel was working to overthrow autocracy entirely, substitute a strong central government, free

the serfs, divide up the land. This was the group which, on December 14, 1825, assembled in the Senate Square to prevent the accession of Nicholas. Their cry was "Constantine and Constitution!" Many soldier followers of Pestel actually thought Constitution was Constantine's wife.

GOVERNOR-GENERAL MICHAEL MILORADOVICH

of St. Petersburg (*above, right*) was killed by the Decembrists (as Pestel's rebels were ever afterward called) when he tried to parley with them. Nicholas had to put down the commotion with his soldiers (*below*), thus martyring the Decembrists.

"REFORM"

Col. Pestel (*left*) and four other Decembrist leaders were executed but the serf problem was at once handed by Nicholas to the first of six study commissions, under Count Kisilev (*right*). Alexander's aide Arakcheyev (*left, below*) had made a botch of trying to militarize the serfs, teaching them the goose-step in what amounted to military barracks instead of crown villages. Kisilev started with the crown peasants, relaxed their instructions, gave them schools. By Alexander's law of 1803, industrious serfs were supposed to be able to obtain freedom with land. Under Nicholas and Kisilev between 1827 and 1842 the serfs were supposed, instead of being bartered for dogs as in Shevchenko's famed painting (*above*), to be assured enough land for sustenance, protected against family split-ups, and given new, moderated ceilings on their unpaid labor. These measures however, bogged down badly under bureaucratic administration.

Two reform efforts under Nicholas did go well. The able Michael Speransky (*right, below*), home from long exile under Alexander, codified (but did not rewrite) all Russia's laws in forty-five volumes. This at least enabled serfs to learn what rights they did have. And the able Count Kankrin overhauled the imperial treasury, tightened up on spending and graft.

Nicholas also took over the political police, but always pretended he didn't.

THE KNOUT

Under the silken glove of reform, the iron fist of an autocrat kept Russia in line. The knout (leather and wire whip), lustily and publicly applied across the bare back, male or female, continued as a common punishment for all manner of offenses under Nicholas. Queen Victoria was urged by a leading London magazine to protest to the Tsar when Madame Kalergi, kinswoman of the distinguished Nesselrode family, was knouted in Warsaw in 1846 (*above*) for aiding a pro-French friend to escape the police.

EXILE remained standard Russian practice, especially for political offenses. One famed exile under Nicholas I was the Slavophil Yury Samarin (*left, below*) who returned and lived to see his Town Statute adopted under Alexander II. Another was Fedor Dostoevsky (*below*) who, chained and exiled at twenty-seven for discussing socialism, returned under Alexander II to write socially powerful memoirs and novels (*Crime & Punishment, The Brothers Karamazov*). Some 40,000 people attended his funeral in 1881. His political importance equalled his literary stature.

RUSSIAN CULTURE COMES OF AGE

Despite (or because of) the grim repressions of Nicholas, seeds sown by the French Revolution and spread over Europe by Napoleon's wars sprouted in Russia during the time of Nicholas. Now came the break from 18th Century neo-classicism. The Russian nature, rich in natural feeling and aspiration, found expressions of its own which for the first time commanded world attention.

First and greatest to be heard was Alexander Sergeivich Pushkin, born in 1799, a descendant (on his mother's side) of Peter I's Negro friend, Ibrahim Hannibal. Before his early death he became to Russians what Shakespeare is to the English. An old nurse filled him with Russian folklore like *The Lay of Oleg,* while French tutors supervised his dandified upbringing. He wrote verse at eight, published at fifteen, and astounded his elders by reciting a brilliant original ode at his precocious graduation (*above*).

His "Ode to Liberty" (1820) went too far and he was sequestered in the south, where he wrote *Boris Godunov.* This so voiced the Decembrists' sentiments that Pushkin became involved in their indictment. Nicholas pardoned him, personally censored *Boris,* put him under surveillance in the Foreign Ministry.

Pushkin in 1831 married a celebrated young beauty of Moscow, Natalia Goncharova (*right,* with Pushkin before mirror). Six years later, by an anonymous letter calling him cuckold, his enemies involved him in a duel with his wife's brother-in-law, the Baron d'Anthès, society rake and crack pistol shot. Pushkin fell in the snow (*below*) with a wound from which he died two days later.

TWO POETS AND A CRITIC

LERMONTOV. The foul play done Pushkin was bitterly and brilliantly assailed in 1837 by a new voice. A poem was circulated in manuscript entitled *A Call to Revolution*. A copy soon reached Tsar Nicholas. The author, Michael Urievich Lermontov (*right*), twenty-three, was immediately sequestered in the Caucasus. His rich grandmother interceded but the irrepressible Lermontov's ensuing military career was spent largely under a cloud. In 1840 he published a volume of verse and *A Hero of Our Times* (novel). His promise was great; by eighteen he had written fifteen narrative poems, three dramas, three hundred lyrics. But in 1841 he, too, fought a fatal duel. By his own terms it was conducted on the brink of a precipice and he, when hit, toppled off.

Interesting about Lermontov, who rates next to Pushkin as Russia's foremost poet: he stemmed from the Learmont who fought with Malcolm against Macbeth.

BELINSKY. A navy doctor's son, born in Finland, frail and consumptive, Vissarion Belinsky (*above*) was expelled from Moscow University for writing a narrative drama excoriating serfdom. In 1834 his "Literary Reveries" established him as Russia's first critic. Publications for which he wrote were usually suppressed. Fearlessly honest, he quarreled with Gogol and frightened Tsar Nicholas, but encouraged a whole school of realist and individualist writers. He died in 1848 aged thirty-seven, too early to get into as much trouble as he promised to cause. His importance lay in the intellectual plowing he gave Russian minds, which helped prepare them for, among other things, Marxism. When he died of tuberculosis in Germany, the chief of Tsar Nicholas' secret police, who had had him under constant surveillance, said: "Too bad . . . for we'd have made him rot in prison."

TARAS SHEVCHENKO (*below*) was a serf, born in 1815 in the Kiev province. His freedom was purchased thanks to Poet Zhukovsky (later the tutor of Alexander II). A poet, his material was the old days of the Ukraine. He was so outspoken as to suffer ten years of hard-labor exile (1847-1857), the physical effects of which he survived for only four years after his return. He could paint as powerfully as he could write — witness his canvass of serfs being traded for hounds (p. 128).

PUBLIC EDUCATION

Alexander I believed that public education must precede a constitution and liberation of the serfs. He founded what became the University of St. Petersburg, six other colleges and forty-two gymnasia (secondary schools). Repin's humorous painting of a student "cramming" for examination by blowing kisses to a belle across the court (*right*), clearly depicts the petty bourgeois type of youth who now became exposed to intellectual exercise and whose callow self-expressions made Nicholas feel the need of stern censorship. Yet these youths were the material for revolutionary groups when they grew up and took with Russian literalness and seriousness all the theory, especially social theory, they had read. And they had read everything — poets, novelists, philosophers. The foremost European thinkers of the time began to have great influence in Russia, including Germany's greatest conservative and greatest radical (*below*).

GERMANS v. FRENCH

The French rationalist influence of Catherine's day was replaced, under Nicholas, by German introspection — Schelling, Fichte, Hegel (*left*), and later, Kant. Hegel especially, mystical exponent of the World-Spirit, succeeded Voltaire as lode-star of the Russian intelligentsia. But a more profound German influence was developing. Seven years before Nicholas was crowned, a man named Karl Marx (*right*) was born in 1818 at Trier, Prussia. His writings on social and political philosophy kept him shuttling by expulsion through the 1840's between Cologne, Paris, Brussels, until he landed and was allowed to stay in London. He published *Das Kapital* in 1867 and its first translation was into Russian. (*Below*): Cologne, where in 1848 Marx was tried for treason for fomenting revolution. He was acquitted but sent away.

THREE GREAT ONES

"Every one got his — but I most of all!" said Nicholas I after seeing **NICHOLAI GOGOL'S** play *The Inspector General.* Like most great social diatribes, the piece plays as a comedy. It caricatures, like Dickens, the brutal and corrupt hypocrisy of its time. Gogol (*left*) quit Russia in 1836 (he was twenty-seven) and lived mostly in Rome. *Evenings On a Farm, Taras Bulba* and *The Overcoat* are his best known works besides *Dead Souls,* which was so strong that, after being converted to religion, he burned all but the first volume of it.

As a means of examining and satirizing all of Russia, Gogol gives Chichikov, the hero of *Dead Souls,* the idea of scouring the country to buy up serfs who, though they have died, continue legally alive as names in the census. As such, until the next census, they cost their owners poll-taxes and remain mortgageable and saleable property. Chichikov's scheme is to float a bank loan on these "dead souls" and make a fortune in live serfs.

IVAN TURGENEV'S kinsman Nicolai was one of the principal Decembrists. His family's estate contained 5,000 serfs, and he suffered the knout as well as they, from his mother. His *Hunting Sketches* (1852) helped precipitate emancipation. Turgenev (*right*) lived in Italy and Germany, died near Paris (1883). His *Fathers & Sons* introduced to Russia the term "Nihilism" to describe the new pessimism of his mystical friend Bakunin and others. Critic Belinsky was his chief idol.

In 1828, three years after Nicholas took the throne, Russia's greatest literary giant was born: **COUNT LEO NICHOLAIE-VICH TOLSTOY,** son of a rich boyar family of Tula. Orphaned at nine, he lived with a gay aunt through whom he learned all about worldliness, including gambling, to which he was prone until his middle years. He studied law and oriental languages but never finished college. He served in artillery in the Caucasus and the Crimean War. He lived for a while in St. Petersburg and in 1857 made the grand tour: Germany, France, Italy, England.

By 1859 his growing interest in social welfare took him to Europe again. Not till 1860 did his great writing begin, with *War and Peace.* He then married an eighteen-year-old girl, who was to bear him thirteen children, and retired to his ancestral acres which thereafter, with brief interludes, became his world. He, working in it, became a titan looming above and apart from the Russian literary sphere. (*Left*): A photo study of Count Tolstoy. For more about his life, self and works, see next page.

TOLSTOY'S RUSSIA

"Radiant Meadow" was the name of Tolstoy's pastoral paradise (*below*), and of a periodical he published to express his views on serf uplift and education. He joyfully obeyed Alexander II's edict of 1861 and liberated all of "Radiant Meadow's" serfs. He gave them land and built progressive schools for them, until the Government felt he was going too far. Upset, he went off among the steppe nomads to drink *koumiss* (mare's milk) and rusticate.

He wrote *Anna Karenina, The Death of Ivan Ilyich, How Much Land Does a Man Need?* (His answer: "Six feet, from head to heels"), *Three Deaths,* and *The Cossacks,* but became increasingly mystical, more interested in evolving a way of life and religion for the peasants than in writing. He gave up alcohol, tobacco and meat, learned bootmaking. He made over all his property to his wife and children. Repin's painting of him at the plow (*above*) is not symbolic but factual. He fed his people in famine.

For his open sympathy (in *Resurrection*) with the communistic Doukhobor sect of the Caucasus, he was excommunicated. It is ironic that the Soviets should have found him dangerous for other reasons and removed Repin's life-size portrait of him (*left*) from public view. He died at a railroad way station in 1910, aged eighty-two, after quitting "Radiant Meadow" to retire into obscurity. Non-Russians consider him supreme.

TOLSTOY AS TOLSTOY In the cinema *Resurrection* (United Artists), Count Ilya Tolstoy, the eldest son, gave an astonishing portrayal (*above*) of his world-famed father.

135

MUSICIANS

Music belonged to the stomach and soul of Russia always. That it did not come out as a formal product until the 19th Century is puzzling, except as proof that Russia was really cut off from "civilized" forms until then. Reading clockwise on this page from upper left:

MICHAEL GLINKA (1803-1857) of Smolensk studied in Italy and Berlin to become Russia's first operatic composer with *Life for the Tsar, Russlan and Lyudmila* (on Pushkin's poem).

ANTON RUBENSTEIN (1829-1864) was a baptized Podolian Jew, a piano prodigy who toured Europe and settled in St. Petersburg to produce opera (1845-1853). With Carl Schuberth he founded the St. Petersburg Conservatory (1862).

ALEXANDER BORODIN, illegitimate son of a prince, born in 1834, studied medicine and did not write memorable music until 1867 — *Prince Igor,* finished by Rimsky-Korsakov — and *In the Steppes* (1880).

PETER ILYICH TSCHAIKOVSKY (1840-1893), son of a mining engineer, was one of Rubenstein's protégés. *Winter Day Dream* (1867) was his first success but many failures and emotional upsets intervened before his triumphal tours of Europe and America in the 1880's and 90's. His famed Sixth Symphony was first performed in St. Petersburg in 1893.

MODESTE PETROVICH MOUSSORGSKY (1835-1885) of Pskov joined the army early, but at twenty-two his musical inheritance asserted itself and he devoted the balance of his years to composing some of the most vigorous, barbaric and compelling Russian music yet heard. His famed *Boris Godunov* (based on Pushkin's drama) was produced in 1874, in St. Petersburg.

NICHOLAI RIMSKY-KORSAKOV (1844-1908) was one of the musical aristocrats who, with Borodin and Moussorgsky, gathered around Mili Balakirev at the Free School of Music (St. Petersburg). He wrote Russia's first native symphony (E Minor), eleven operas, many song and piano pieces, succeeded Balakirev as Russia's top conductor. Balakirev & disciples were called "The Mighty Band."

136

PAINTERS

Vereschagin, Repin, Vasnetsov — these are the three names to remember in Russian painting of the Alexander II-Nicholas II period. They painted historical pictures of all periods, especially **VERESCHAGIN** (*below*) who left the navy and became a military chronicler. His work frequents this book. Born in 1842, he was at his peak in 1904 when he painted Roosevelt I. He died aboard the Russian flagship *Peter & Paul* in the Russo-Jap war.

ILYA REPIN (*right*) (1844-1930) studied in France and Italy and, in his later work, parallels the French impressionists, especially Monet. Best known is his "Reply of the Cossacks to Sultan Mahmoud IV" (*see* p. 60) but his historical work was prolific and all of a high order. For several years after 1894 he taught historical painting at the St. Petersburg Academy of Fine Arts, where he had studied for six years as a humble and impoverished youth.

VICTOR VASNETSOV (*right*) was the time's foremost religious painter. He decorated the dome of St. Vladimir at Kiev. He liked blazing gold, barbaric splendor, the "mighty chord" effect.

SCIENCE

The Academy of Science, projected by Peter, was opened under Catherine I in 1726. It supported the Great Siberian Expedition of 1733-1743. Its first native celebrity was Catherine II's physicist friend Lomonosov.

As a nucleus for Russian scientific thought and development, the Academy's influence was pervasive. Russia early became the West's peer in science. **IVAN POLZUNOV** (1730-1766) perfected an industrial steam engine independently of Scotland's contemporary James Watt. **LOBACHEVSKY** evolved his post-Euclidean geometry in 1855. **LADYGIN** demonstrated an electric lamp in 1874, two years before Edison. **POPOV** sent radio signals five kilometers in 1897, when Marconi's ideas were still on paper.

The name and fame of **DMITRY IVANOVICH MENDELEYEV** (*right*) went farthest. Educated in the gymnasium at Tobolsk, Siberia and later at St. Petersburg and Heidelberg, he announced in 1871 his Periodic Law for the elements, postulating from it the existence of certain elements later discovered, and correcting mathematically the atomic weights of other elements. He thus laid under modern chemistry its first solid floor.

Medicine came forward under Tsar Nicholas, especially military medicine. **NICOLAI IVANOVICH PIROGOV** (1810-1881), a surgeon at the front in the Crimean War (*above*), developed new techniques in antiseptic surgery in the field. He established first aid stations back of the line of fire, where the use of ether and plaster (or gypsum) casts made medical history. His praise and encouragement of the Sisters of Charity gave women a permanent place in military nursing.

(On the other side of the Crimean lines, in the British base hospitals at Scutari, famed **FLORENCE NIGHTINGALE** (*right*) was performing enlightened nursing work which reduced mortality 40%.)

Other great names in Russian medical history are **PAVLOV** (*right*), **VORONOV** and **METCHNIKOV** (*far right*) who made studies of longevity. The first two were world-known for their experiments at resurrection. Ilya Metchnikov (1845-1916) was rewarded with the Nobel Prize for Medicine in 1916 for his studies of bacteriology. He worked with Pasteur, succeeded him as head of the Pasteur Institute in Paris, first postulated that the white corpuscles and leucocytes devour bacteria in the blood, and that inflammation in infected parts is caused by the struggle between white corpuscles and germs.

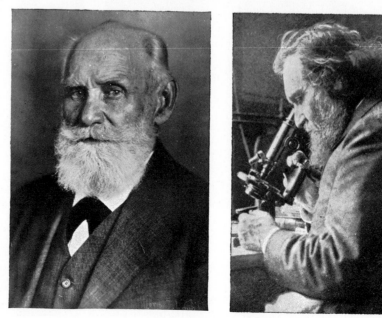

NICHOLAS AND EUROPE

After Napoleon's wars, all of Europe's thrones kept trembling except Queen Victoria's and Nicholas I's. She (*left*) became the moral preceptress, he the military policeman of the Continent. Whenever revolution raised its head, Nicholas took the reactionary side, except in Greece (1828-1829), when Britain (especially Poet Lord Byron) preferred the revolutionists to Turkey, and Russia did too. Nicholas helped the Bourbon cause in France, the Hapsburgs in Austria. After crushing the Poles' revolution of 1830 he took away the constitution his brother Alexander had given them.

Unifying the Balkan Slavs (dream of all great Russian rulers since Svyatoslav) and obtaining a southern sea outlet through the Bosporus, were projects of high priority with Nicholas. So Russia's chronic state of war with Turkey erupted twice under him, the second time leading to the Crimean War with England and France.

Nicholas helped young Emperor Franz Josef of Austria in 1848 by sending General Paskevich (*right, center*) and 100,000 men to suppress the insurgent Hungarian patriot dictatorship of Louis Kossuth (*left, center*), whose eloquence had made him Europe's No. 1 revolutionist.

SINOPE. In return for defending Constantinople against a revolt by the Egyptian Army in 1833-1834, Nicholas won free transit of the Bosporus and Dardanelles, but signed this away at London in 1841. In a new row with Turkey, over Orthodox rights in the Holy Land (1853), Nicholas invaded Moldavia and Wallachia (Rumania). Sultan Abdul Medjid declared war and the two armies met on the Danube. When the Russian Black Sea Fleet wiped out a Turkish squadron in the harbor of Sinope (*below*), England and France moved in to curb Russia (*see next page*).

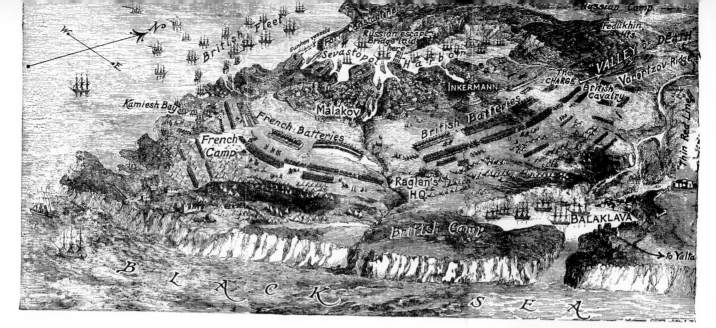

THE CRIMEAN WAR

SEVASTOPOL, Russia's Black Sea naval base, is a virtual fjord near the southwest tip of Crimea. The Allies resolved to reduce it. Russia's General Count Todleben (*right*) hastened to increase the fortifications, and the Russian warships were sunk to block the harbor. The *Illustrated London News's* contemporary sketch (*above*, with legends added) shows almost all sites of action in this war. The Allies under Lord Raglan (*right, below*) and Marshal St. Arnaud, landed some 51,000 infantrymen, 1,000 British cavalry and 123 guns on beaches about forty-five miles north of Sevastopol. Marching south to battle they fought past the Alma River bluffs and headed for Balaclava Harbor on the south coast to stay in touch with their fleet.

THE ALLIED SIEGE ARMY, including natty British Guards (*left, above*), dug in on an arc before Sevastopol's landward forts. To protect the besiegers against Russian flank attacks (*left*), the Allied right wing, including the British cavalry, took up positions along the low hills north of Balaclava. Weakest spot was the valley between Vorontsov Ridge and Fedukhin Heights (*see plan above*). This was to be, for the British, the "Valley of Death" immortalized by Poet Tennyson:

> *"Someone had blundered!"*
> *Theirs not to make reply;*
> *Theirs not to reason why;*
> *Theirs but to do and die . . .*

THE ALMA crossing was won after stout uphill fighting by the Highlanders (*below*). Sir Colin Campbell, their leader, cried: "We'll hae nane but Hieland bonnets here!" Thereafter the Allies proceeded to Balaclava unmolested. The Russian commander, Prince Alexander Menshikov (great-grandson of Peter I's stand-by), actually crossed their trail while withdrawing a force northward from Sevastopol to protect his communications to the mainland. Menshikov's inland base was Bakchisarai, ancient capital of the Crimean Tartars (*see* p. 60). The Alma battle cost the Allies (already weakened by cholera) 3,000 casualties to 5,700 for the Russians.

BALACLAVA. When Menshikov did pierce the Allied right flank and take Vorontsov Ridge, the British "Heavy Brigade" under General Scarlett counter-attacked with some success (*below*). Then the "Light Brigade" under Lord Cardigan (*above*), perhaps due to a misunderstanding charged suicidally into the "Valley of Death" to recover some captured British guns. Two-thirds were annihilated.

"THE THIN RED LINE" (*bottom*), the 93rd Highland Regiment, to cover the Light Brigade's repulse staved off repeated Russian cavalry thrusts north of Balaclava.

FIVE "FIRSTS"

The Crimean War is memorable for five "firsts." In it appeared the first modern army medicine and first good military nursing. Also, the first telegraph between home front and battlefield, first iron-clad warships and first news camera (*see next page*). The iron-clads, British, dared anchor close under the Russians' shore batteries and blast away. (*Left*): British warships shelling Odessa, exploding its mole.

THE MALAKOV

Principal Sevastopol forts were the Redan and the Malakov, which Allied artillery would daily blast and Russian work parties nightly rebuild. This went on for nearly two years. Todleben was wounded. Lord Raglan died, worn out. When in September, 1855 the French at last took the Malakov (*left*), Sevastopol fell.

THE END

The Russians streamed out of blazing Sevastopol across a causeway to the harbor's north shore. Tsar Nicholas, who had figured that "Generals January and February" would win for him, died suddenly in March of "nervous exhaustion." After another summer of fighting, with Russia getting nowhere because of the length of her supply lines to Crimea from the North, Nicholas' son, Alexander II, accepted peace at Paris. The war had cost Russia 256,-000 men (128,700 in the Crimea), $710,000,000 and much blood.

British men-o'-war in Balaclava Harbor.

Unloading ammunition, Balaclava.

British siege-gun crew.

Cannon balls within the Russian lines after the siege.

FENTON'S PHOTOGRAPHS

ROGER FENTON (1808-1869) was the first secretary of the Photographic Society of London (later the Royal Photographic Society). He went out to the Crimea in 1855 with a dark room mounted on a wagon, to make the world's first war photographs, of which six are reproduced on this page. Because his slow wet plates could not record action, there was no use his dragging his bulky box camera to the front lines under fire. But his still-life studies before and after battle rank close to Brady's record of the American Civil War, made in the next decade.

Where two British Army photographers had failed before him, Fenton, despite heat and other Crimean inconveniences, made a portfolio of which 159 pictures were published (now in the Victoria and Albert Museum). Besides developing his work on the spot, Fenton had to make his own plates, usually with white of egg as the fixative for his salts.

Captain Walker (38th English Infantry) reading an order.

French canteen worker.

ALEXANDER II FREES THE SERFS

Gentle son of a martinet father, Alexander II (*right*) was a mature thirty-seven when he faced Russia's moral collapse after the Crimean War. Historians seem to agree that the Poet Zhukovsky, his tutor (*right, below*), produced in this tsar a humanitarian ruler who did not entirely deserve his fate. Six years after his accession, on March 3, 1861, he signed a proclamation that went even further than Abraham Lincoln's forthcoming emancipation of the American slave. Tsar Alexander II said:

Some 20,000,000 Russian serfs are not only free, but they may have land, in proportion to their deserts. The state will recompense the landowners. The serfs will pay the state in installments.

Alexander also saw that Russia's natural resources must be developed, to keep pace with the European industrialism which had whipped primitive Russia in Crimea. Exploitation companies were chartered. Railroads were mapped. The Army and Navy were overhauled. So were the courts and local police. Though he had been abroad little, because his father distrusted European influence in Holy Russia, Alexander II was enlightened to the point of acting, often, without consulting his court advisers — especially on the basic serf issue, where he took his lead from the Polish petitioners and on his own authority called up rural emancipation committees from all over Russia.

UNCLE TOM of cabin fame could not have been more grateful to his "Massa" than was the Russian serf when his lord called all hands into the courtyard (*left, above*) and obeyed the Tsar's edict of 1861 by making a short speech and, in old Russian fashion, sealing the bargain with a drop of vodka. The serfs kissed the ground, which their kind had worked for centuries and of which some was now to be theirs.

Few serfs could read, except young ones, who spelled out the Tsar's unbelievable proclamation to their bearded elders in the fields and haymows (*left*). (It would be 75 years before most Russians could read.)

"BETTER FROM ABOVE"

"It is better," explained Alexander to the Russian upper-crust in the scene above, "to have this reform come from above, rather than from below."

His critics quote this remark, made apropos the basic issue of serfage, to show that he begrudged reform. Actually, he was as sore beset by the thin top layer of Russia's social structure as he was by the inarticulate lower masses and their violent spokesmen. He tried to steer a middle course. Freeing the serfs was not much more unpopular among the rich than was, for example, his granting certain tax powers to local assemblies.

Alexander II, though constitutionally suspicious, seems really to have taken a long view of his country and tried to reorganize it thoroughly by lights which, in his day, were pretty bright. The personnel of his thirty-six-man Reform Commission bears out this view: **GENERAL ROSTOVTSEV** (*lower left*), chairman, was the son of a merchant, grandson of a workman; **NICHOLAI MILYUTIN** (*below center, top*), the chairman's chief assistant, an honest bureaucrat, expert on famines, whom Alexander feared but respected, and on whose say-so he included as commissioners liberal **PRINCE CHERKASSKY** (*below center, bottom*) and Yury Samarin (the same one his father exiled). **COUNT MICHAEL TARIELOVICH LORIS-MELIKOV** (*lower right*), with whirring whiskers like Lord Raglan's, was a bluff admiral with no personal sense of riches or power.

Alexander, on the eve of his death, had signed the preface for Loris-Melikov's constitution. In effect, the constitution was assassinated along with Alexander.

CONQUEST EASTWARD

I. THE CAUCASUS

The coat-of-arms of Georgia — mountainous Caucasian homeland of romantic Queen Tamara and also of latter-day Joseph Stalin — displays a sling and a harp (*upper left corner*). This is because Georgia's King David II (1089) traced his descent to David the shepherd-harpist of Judea, slayer of the Philistine champion, Goliath. Through the centuries Georgia and her Caucasian neighbors were beset by "Philistines" of all sorts — and were not conquered finally until 1859, when General Baryatinsky of Russia brought to surrender the Circassian chieftain, Shamil.

So respectful of Caucasian valor were the Russians that they returned to Shamil his sword, (*bottom*), and bound the mountain peoples to Russia's cause, which at that point was expansion east and southeast.

The Russians at once got busy blasting a military road through the Georgian mountain's rocky hips (*left*), which later became a motor highway (*above*).

II. CENTRAL ASIA

Bismarck said: "Russia has nothing to do in the West. She only contracts Nihilism and other diseases. Her mission is in Asia. There she stands for civilization."

The map on Page 149 demonstrates what areas Alexander II, his generals and his engineers, found it necessary to subjugate so that Russia might expand eastward and exploit the continent which Russia obviously dominated.

The Khivans, who stuck their enemies' heads on poles after battle (*right*), were Problem No. 1. In 1847 Aralsk was built by Russia on the Aral Sea to control the Khivans. Then the southeast border was inched forward to Lake Balkash, Bukhara and nearly to Samarkand. In 1865 the province of Turkestan was gained and General Chernyaev took Tashkent.

Alexander's **GENERAL SKOBELEV** (*far right*) now shared effort and glory with the German-blooded **GENERAL KAUFMAN** (*right*) as the Russian conquest, paced by Cossacks, pressed expansion. Samarkand fell in 1868 after desert fighting in which plenty of Russians had opportunity to exhibit their toughness. (*Below*): A Russian patrol ambushed by nomads somewhere in Central Asia.

III. THE FAR EAST

The Cossacks who penetrated to and settled Kamchatka in the 18th Century were followed by fur traders, much as Canada's explorers were followed up by posts of the Hudson's Bay Co. By 1872, Vladivostok on the eastern coast of the Asian land mass was a thriving Russian naval station and seaport (*above*). Earlier there was a mystery: was Sakhalin part of the mainland or an island? In 1849, Captain Nevelskoi sailed the brig *Baikal* around into the Sea of Okhotsk to prove it was an island — and Russia traded the Kurile Islands to Japan for the lower end of Sakhalin Island.

Admiral Count Muravyev (*right*) was allowed to add "Amursky" to his style after he boldly took over the entire left bank of the Amur River in 1858, and enough of the right bank to consolidate Vladivostok. Seals for fur and fish for food were the immediate gains of this expansion, which Japan was not then strong enough to challenge.

148

OCCUPATION OF RUSSIA BY THE RUSSIANS, III.

Philip

Legend:

Russia	under	Ivan IV		Russia after Nicholas I
Russia	after	Peter the Great		Russia after Alexander II
Russia	after	Empress Catherine		Later acquisitions

Poland 1772

Line of the Congress of Vienna 1815

Place names and features:

BERING SEA, East Cape, Wrangel I., ATLANTIC OCEAN, GREAT BRITAIN, NORTH SEA, Spitsbergen, Fridtjov Nansen Land, ARCTIC OCEAN, Severnaya Zemlya, C. Chelyuskin, New Siberian Is., Novaya Zemlya, SEA OF OKHOTSK, Okhotsk, Kamchatka, SAKHALIN, Amur, Khabarovsk, Vladivostok, SEA OF JAPAN, Tokyo, KOREA, Port Arthur, Mukden, Harbin, MANCHURIA, S. MANCHURIA RY. 1903, CHINESE EASTERN RY. 1903, MONGOLIA, Irkutsk, Baikal, Chita, Krasnoyarsk, TRANS SIBERIAN RY., Novo Simbirsk, Semipalatinsk, L. Balkhash, Omsk, Syr Darya, Samarkand, Bukhara, Aral Sea, Amu Darya, Pamirs, AFGHANISTAN, PERSIA, TURKEY, CASPIAN SEA, Baku, CAUCASUS, Batum, Astrakhan, Saratov, Volga, Don, Rostov, BLACK SEA, CRIMEA, Odessa, Kharkov, Kiev, UKRAINE, Moscow, Smolensk, POLAND, Berlin, GERMANY, Warsaw, Riga, Dvina, Petersburg, BALTIC SEA, Stockholm, SWEDEN, NORWAY, FINLAND, White Sea, Archangel, N. Dvina, Kazan, Tobolsk, Ob, Irtysh, Yenisei, Lena, Yakutsk, Kolyma

Miles
0 100 200 300 400

MORE RUMBLINGS

To hear both sides tell it, Russia's internal trouble now (after 1861) was that too much liberalism had been shown, and too little. Agitation by gentlemen in December, 1825, had been replaced with agitation by "intelligentsia." Imperial sternness drove underground all manner of serious students who disguised themselves to appear among the Russian masses as propagandists (*left*).

Novelist Turgenev in 1862 first used the word "Nihilism" to describe the black defeatists, the have-nots with nothing but destructive ideas, of whom **BAKUNIN** (*far left*) was the leader. He advocated armed uprisings, village by village.

"Anarchists" were another cult of rebels among whom, after study outside Russia, the most "scientific" was whiskery **PRINCE PETER KRO-POTKIN** (*left*). Like the Nihilists, the Anarchists favored complete overthrow.

Tsar Nicholas reacted to subversive movements as would most other executives of comparable responsibility: he got tough. Anarchists, Nihilists, suspect intelligentsia of all sorts were arrested and imprisoned. "Nihilist" became a world-word like Ku Klux Klan. Arrests at dead of night (*below*) underscored Bismarck's supercilious but accurate wisecrack about Russia's diseases.

AND
REPRISALS

Now the road to exile, to Siberia, became crowded (*above*), as Alexander II, reformer, cracked down to give his reforms a chance. The two extremes of Russian character were now in full play: gentle idealism and cruel insistence. Offenders believed really bad (and this was far past the middle of the 19th Century) were branded on the brow and cheeks (*above*).

In the early spring of 1880, an explosion shook up the Winter Palace, wrecking the guard room (*left*), but nobody important was hurt. A Nihilist bomb! The Siberian prisons filled to capacity (*below*).

RUSSIA AND THE U.S.A.

I. VISIT OF THE FLEETS — 1863

In 1863, the government of Abraham Lincoln, who believed slaves should be free, was fighting not only the South but also British pro-Southern sentiment — which wanted cheap cotton. Russia, which had just freed its serfs, still smarted from Britain's beating in Crimea. Also, Russia feared British intervention in the current civil war in Poland. Presently a Russian fleet paid a courtesy call in New York Harbor (*above*), while another dropped anchor in San Francisco Bay. The local notables turned out to do the potent visitors honor.

There was a grand Ball at the Academy of Music, and hoop-skirted ladies of the North were whirled by gallant Russian and Union officers (*below*). This was a new chapter in Russia's foreign relations.

II. PURCHASE OF ALASKA — 1869

In 1869, President Andrew Johnson, the martyred Lincoln's not-too-popular successor (*below*), concluded a treaty with Russia whereby the U. S. paid $7,200,000 for Russia's holdings in North America. Herds of seal and walrus (*left*) — and then-unforeseen stores of gold — did not appeal to editorial opinion. Said influential *Harper's Weekly:* "Their value [our new possessions] is another question. . . . Its entire population . . . is not more than 60 or 75 thousand (five-sixth Esquimaux), or about the same as that of the District of Columbia . . . the agricultural productions, trade, etc., of the country, like its population, are ridiculously disproportionate to its area, the former comprising principally icebergs and snowdrifts, and the latter amounting to considerably less than the 'Goshen butter' or 'Queens County milk' trade."

Harper's printed a bleak sketch (*bottom*) of Novy Archangel (which became Sitka) and a Boston photographer carefully photographed the Greek-Orthodox church (*left, center*), perhaps as a warning to good New England Protestants and Roman Catholics.

III. VISIT OF THE GRAND DUKE

The Grand Duke Alexis, Alexander II's third son, visited the United States in 1871-1872 when Ulysses Simpson Grant was president. Mrs. Grant from Illinois shook his imperial hand in the White House "Red Room" (*left*) and he was then embarked on a round of American entertainment which he never forgot. For the Grand Duke's American tour, see below. Every step that the Grand Duke Alexis took was covered by press artists (not yet news cameramen) and Mr. Frank Leslie's *Illustrated Newspaper* did not miss a trick — see next page. Interesting in this series of pictures are the frankness and humor of the American journalists, who befriended, but did not bow and scrape to, Russian nobility.

THE DUKE'S TOUR (*l. to r.*)

1. Reception, Philadelphia Navy Yard.
2. Brooklyn Ball (ditto New York, Boston, San Francisco).
3. Niagara Falls (with icicle).
4. Chicago, right after the fire.
5. St. Louis, snowballed by small-fry.
6. With General Custer . . .
7. . . . to shoot buffaloes.

THE GRAND DUKE ALEXIS ON THE PLAINS—THE BUFFALO HUNT AS IT REALLY WAS.—FROM A SKETCH BY OUR SPECIAL ARTIST, FROM A TELEGRAPH POLE.

FROM LESLIE'S. To make Grand Duke Alexis feel completely at home, Publisher Leslie published a jovial full-page cartoonograph of the buffalo hunt with General Custer. If a magnifying glass is needed to read the script, get one.

ASSASSINATION!

Besides the Winter Palace bomb attempt of 1880, there had been a pistol attempt on the life of Tsar Alexander II in 1867 when a woman missed him in Paris (*top*). Mines and death traps lay in wait for him constantly, for his would-be assassins were organized. They called themselves "The Will of the People." On March 13, 1881, as he was returning in a carriage to the Winter Palace from dining with his Aunt Helen, the Tsar was rudely shaken by a bomb which killed horses and equerries (*left, center*), but did not touch Alexander. He got out on the pavement whereupon another bombster approached and, hands over head, let fly an explosive which left the embalmers little of Alexander II to work on below the chest (*above*).

"It is too early to thank God!" cried Assassin Grinevetsky, as he hurled the second and fatal bomb (*left*), which killed him, too. Perhaps it was too early, but Alexander had prepared to sign, that very day, the program of Loris-Melikov to push to a conclusion the constitutional plans which had been worked on ever since the beginning of Alexander's reign. The Tsar, his legs and stomach blown away, gasped: "To the Palace, to die there." With him died constitutional reform — but not the necessity thereof.

ALEXANDER III

Huge of frame, powerful and slow, Alexander III (born 1845) had prepared to be tsar since his twenty-first year when his elder brother Nicholas died. At the latter's express wish he married beautiful Princess Dagmar of Denmark, Nicholas' fiancée, who was renamed Marie Fedorovna. They were most happy. Alex-

ander III at thirty-six liked to think of himself as simple and rugged, like his subjects. Being Russian, and making Russia Russian, were his dominant motives. His father's assassination ended for him all enthusiasm for liberalism. The revolutionaries openly threatened to kill him, too, and when he and his bride drove handsomely in public (*below*), it is small wonder that they felt they were taking their imperial lives in their hands.

INDUSTRIAL EXPANSION

It is jumping ahead to look, in the beginning of Alexander III's brief reign (thirteen years), at Sergius Witte, the financial wizard who did not take over until 1892, only two years before Alexander's death. Yet it is necessary, for Witte was the logical result of this Alexander's Russia-for-the-Russians program, a program of resource development and industrial expansion which bounded forward impelled by two things:

(1) the new, free labor market, and (2) Alexander's desire for Russian self-reliance.

Sergius Witte, astute and placid in middle age, so smoothly integrated that he could be caricatured in few simple lines (*left*), started as a station-master and worked up to Minister of Communications, then of Finance. From him, Russia got railroads and a gold standard. What called him into office was the bursting growth of Russian industry and enterprise which Alexander fostered.

CHANCELLOR BISMARCK (*center, below*) personified for Alexander III all that was bad about Germany. Russia had helped Germany win empire in 1870, but Bismarck blocked Russia's pan-Slavic plans in the Balkans, where Alexander personally helped establish Bulgaria and a victorious Russian Army at last reached Constantinople. Bismarck favored German-Russian friendship, but he wanted Russia clearly and at all times to be the junior partner.

PROFESSOR CONSTANTINE POBEDONOSTSEV (*far left*), tutor of Alexander III, taught him three things: nationalism, autocracy and orthodoxy. He was the ascetic embodiment of reaction and, as Procurator of the Holy Synod, the suppressor of everything un-Orthodox — Doukhobors, Stundists (Baptists) and Jews. Because of him, under Alexander III came Russia's first pogroms in Odessa and Kiev.

One of the most memorable and far-reaching developments of Alexander III's era was gold mining on the River Lena in eastern Siberia (*below*). Here thousands of exiles, political and otherwise, were set to work extracting the metal which Witte needed to bring huge, backward Russia up into the line of modern nations. Labor troubles naturally ensued from time to time, but here was laid a foundation for Russia's still-unassessed fiscal power. Precious metal abounded in Siberia to an extent that dwarfed Russia's sold-out holdings in Alaska.

THE TRANS-SIBERIAN

The Ural Mountains never constituted the barrier to human expansion eastward in the Eurasian land mass that the Appalachians and Rockies did for westward expansion in America. The "Continental Divide" of the Urals (*above*) is tame. But building a railroad across 5,793 miles of steppe and tundra (as far as from New York to Patagonia) is still a big job. Russia did it beginning March, 1891, and the conquest of Siberia, begun by Yermak in 1582, continued by Muravyev in 1847-1861, was finally tied across with steel by Witte to Vladivostok ("Lord of the East") and southward to Port Arthur (by treaty with China) in 1903 (*see map* p. 149).

The track was single. The locomotives were crown-stacked chuffers. There were broad rivers to leap where painfully constructed bridges often washed out. And there was a gap at Lake Baikal where a ferry functioned. But Siberia was spanned.

By 1905, 20,000 mi. of this.

Trestle.

Baikal ferry.

Crown-stacked chuffer.

FAMINE, 1891-1892

While Alexander III and his ministers laid a basis for future Russian prosperity, the people starved. In 1891-1892 food was particularly short and suffering acute. One cause was plain: so many free people leaving the land to seek city life, where their factory labor brought hard money. Simultaneously, many people left Russia — more than 4,000,000 of them emigrating to North and South America. Famine was perhaps an inevitable growing-pain of a large, sprawling social organism which was trying to develop sinew without any experience in social diet. Things got so bad that peasants had to feed their roof thatch to the stock (*right*).

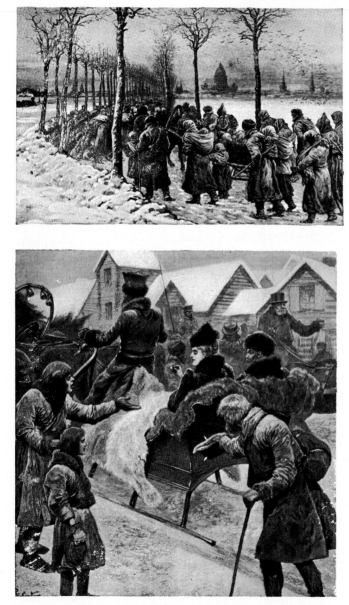

People trudged hungrily off the land into the big cities (in the picture, *left*, St. Petersburg). Fine, curious ladies doled out silver as they sleighed through the famine areas (*left, below*). Cossacks were sent to bar with their lances the surge toward the cities (*below*), a sorry ending for the reign of pro-Russian Alexander III.

(All pictures on this page from *The Illustrated London News*.)

"BLOODY NICHOLAS"

Nicholas II was a timid shadow of his father, Alexander III. He had charm, and a fatalistic personal courage, but in the face of Liberal stirrings ("senseless dreams") he took refuge in "unswerving adherence to the principles of autocracy." The bad omen which affixed the epithet "bloody" to his reign occurred during his coronation festivities in 1894 (*right*). At the customary distribution of presents (kerchiefs, cups, money) to the populace at Hodynka, suburb of Moscow, the crowd of 300,000 went out of hand due to poor policing arrangements. In the riot, several hundreds were trampled to death or crushed against the barriers (*above*). Nevertheless, the Kremlin continued to blaze festively (*below*) and Nicholas held the evening's reception as scheduled.

WAR WITH JAPAN

Nicholas' Minister of the Interior Plehve once opined that a "small, victorious war" would divert attention from Russia's internal troubles. But neither Plehve nor anyone was prepared for what came in 1904. Angered because Russia and other powers had obliged her to get out of Port Arthur after taking it from China in 1895, and because Russia had not removed her troops from Manchuria after the Boxer Rebellion (1900), Japan struck without declaring war.

Admiral Uriu at Chemulpo with heavy units and Admiral Togo at Port Arthur with torpedo boats, quickly crippled Russia's Asiatic fleet when it steamed out (*below*). They then clamped on an effective blockade, using mines freely. This opened the way for Japan's trained army of 270,000 to strike across from Korea at the 80,000 railway guards and garrison troops under Russia's General Kuropatkin (*right*). The latter was for tactfully withdrawing north for a better strategic position.

RUSSIA'S VICEROY of the Far East and commander-in-chief was Admiral E. I. Alexeyev (*left*), a passive, hesitant person with little military experience. Even so, Russia's fatal loss of superiority at sea was nearly averted by the bold counsels of Admiral Makarov, who lost his life on the battleship *Petropavlovsk* and remains enshrined as one of Russia's great naval heroes.

JAPAN'S NAVAL HERO was the sly old sea fox Heihachiro Togo (*right*), the speed and efficiency of whose ships were to startle the world before the war was finished (*see next page*).

Togo studied naval science and navigation in England (1871-1878), first came to fame in 1894 when, commanding the cruiser *Naniwa,* he precipitated war with China by sinking a Chinese troopship.

What the Russian Navy would do.

What the Japanese Army would do.

WAR WITH JAPAN

THE YALU. Both sides fought a lively cartoon war (*above*) but after the initial Jap naval successes, the contest settled down to an army affair with a sharp edge for Japan from the outset. Two pictures (*left* and *below*) tell the story. The Japanese, superbly accoutred, trained to the tick, landed near the River Yalu (*left*) and proceeded to win one of history's memorable battles: first victory of modern yellow men over white men.

The Russian Army was handicapped for reinforcements and supply by Siberia's vast distances over which the Trans-Siberian railroad and the Chinese Eastern down to Port Arthur could deliver only 40,000 men per month in summertime. Bottleneck was the gap at Lake Baikal where ferries in summer, sledges in winter (*below*) had to carry every man and every pound of supplies forty miles.

PORT ARTHUR

After their columns cut across the Liao-Tung peninsula, the reduction of Port Arthur by the Japanese was simply a matter of time. Commander-in-chief Nogi Kiten (*above*) implanted 11-inch siege mortars (*right*) and knocked out the inferior Russian defense guns (*above*) at leisure. Moreover, the Japanese battle fleet could steam by and add its weight of fire to the assault (*below*). But the Russian garrison was stubborn and cost Japan 57,780 men (to 28,200 Russians) before the final storming and surrender (January 1, 1905), which freed 100,000 Japs to join their main armies in Manchuria, to the north. The Russian squadron in Port Arthur made at least one effective sortie during the siege, momentarily paralyzing the Japanese land offensive; but then it returned to port.

MUKDEN

By mid-winter 1905 when Nogi struck for Mukden, the Japanese were whittled below 200,000 men and the Russians had amassed 250,000. Nevertheless, Kuropatkin left the initiative to Nogi, and after both sides had lost 70,000 men in a series of actions around besieged Mukden, relinquished his command. Russia's soldiers were far less keen for this war, which few of them understood, than were the fanatical Japs, who gave the world something to think about when they stormed and took the seemingly impregnable height of Takushan (*right*).

American opinion of the war was expressed by *Harper's* in a cartoon of March, 1905 (*below*). Extraordinary to democratic eyes today is the picture of Uncle Sam standing next to chesty Japan, England, France and the splendiferous Kaiser.

SIGN!

TSUSHIMA

The fight went out of Russia when her Baltic Fleet, which had steamed clear around Africa to redress the Eastern naval balance, was set upon by Admiral Togo as it entered the strait of Tsushima one night in May. The Japs so outsped, outmaneuvered, outgunned Admiral Rodzhestvensky that by the next nightfall only two cruisers, two destroyers could escape to Vladivostok. (*Below, left*): Explosion of the Russian warship *Korejez*. (*Right*): Russian battleships *Suvorov, Imperator Alexander III* and *Borodino*, all sunk at Tsushima.

The Tsushima disaster decided the Tsar to accept tenders which had been received from President Theodore Roosevelt to use the good offices of the United States to arrange a peace.

PORTSMOUTH

President Theodore Roosevelt persuaded Tsar Nicholas to send Count Witte to Portsmouth, N. H. and accept peace terms. These were arrived at late in August when Japan's Marquis Komura waived indemnities but obtained: undisputed sway over Korea; Russian withdrawal from Port Arthur and southern Manchuria; the southern half of Sakhalin Island. Far more important, what Japan had won abroad and Nicholas lost at home was Face. (*Right*): At Portsmouth — Witte, Rosen (for Russia); Roosevelt; Komura, Takahira (for Japan).

Roosevelt I umpired this settlement between two nations whose attitude *vis-à-vis* the United States were to alter so diametrically. On close inspection, perhaps the Portsmouth treaty can be found to contain the very seeds that wrought the change. Chesty Japan became imperialistic. The beaten Russian Empire turned toward democracy.

REVOLUTION!

During the unpopular war with Japan, bombs began flying in Russia. Interior Minister Plehve was killed; also the Tsar's uncle, Grand Duke Sergius, Governor General of Moscow, publicly, right in the Kremlin. Strikes became chronic. The loss of the war and the Portsmouth peace terms inflamed a situation already tensed by quarrels over how the new Duma should function (*see next chapter*). **REPIN'S PAINTING** (*below*) of the 1905 Revolution singles out the 17th of October demonstration, on which day Tsar Nicholas made a new promise: to give Russia representative government, freedom of speech, individual liberty. Some liberals were satisfied with these promised concessions and came to be called "Octobrists" (as the more violent agitators of 1825 had been called the "Decembrists"). So marched history toward an even greater Revolution.

IN ODESSA, in the summer of 1905, the crew of the cruiser *Potemkin* mutinied (*left*) and went on a Black Sea rampage until obliged to seek supplies, and internment, in Rumania.

IN SEVASTOPOL, revolutionary crowds were fired upon by the Tsar's soldiers (*upper right*).

IN MOSCOW in December, following a St. Petersburg strike by railway workers which so tied up things that it caused general paralysis, another general strike was attempted, with barricades in the streets (*left*). Again troops had to fire.

IN ST. PETERSBURG a priest named Gapon working with and for the Tsar's police, organized the radical factory workers into unions which could be watched and controlled. Railway workers formed a Soviet (council) and then a Union of Unions, of which the vice-president was one Leon Trotsky. (*Below*): Gapon and his followers, with police official eyeing watchfully.

"BLOODY SUNDAY"

The moment which Russia's workers never forgot or forgave was Sunday, January 22, 1905, when a great body of St. Petersburg labor unionists was led by double-dealing Priest Gapon to the Winter Palace to petition Tsar Nicholas in person for reform. The crowd carried icons, not arms, but the Tsar's Cossacks rode and shot them down in the square before the Palace. There was to be an encore of this "Bloody Sunday" performance, with quite opposite results, twelve years later on precisely the same bloody ground.

VIII. WAR AND REVOLUTION

The new parliament or Duma which resulted from the Revolution of 1905 was too Leftist to suit Tsar Nicholas II. Count Witte, the Finance Minister to the Tsar's father and signer of peace with Japan, was succeeded by Stolypin as prime minister. Arbitrarily he changed the electoral law so as to obtain a more conservative Duma. Stolypin also attempted an agrarian reform, wanting to create a broad layer of independent and prosperous farmers on whom the Tsar's government could rely. The nobility was losing its land holdings, and Stolypin realized that the dynasty needed a new, firmer base.

The strong hand of Stolypin subdued for a time the revolutionary movement. But in 1911 he was assassinated. In 1912 a peaceful demonstration of workers in the Lena gold fields of Siberia was fired on by the authorities. The country was aroused. Unrest increased. In June, 1914 over half a million workers in Russia were on strike. It looked as if 1905 were returning. But in August, 1914 the first world war broke out, diverting attention for a while to other things.

The start of the war was favorable for Russia. The Austrians suffered defeats, and the Russian armies marched into Galicia, returning to an area which had been Russian a long, long time ago, in the days of the Kiev state. The Germans were threatening Paris. In response to the pleas of France and England, the Tsar sent two Russian armies into East Prussia to march toward Berlin. At Tannenberg, Hindenburg and Ludendorff smashed the Russian advance, not far from the place where in 1410 a united army of Slavs inflicted a crushing defeat on the German Teutonic Knights. Two Russian armies were lost, but the diversion they had created saved Paris. Soon it became obvious that industrially backward Russia was no match for more advanced Germany. Galicia had to be abandoned, the Germans took Warsaw, and all the industries of Russian Poland, which were essential for the Russian war effort. Russian soldiers were dying heroically, with the artillery lacking shells and rifles lacking cartridges.

Mistrusting everybody around him, the Tsar was opposed to mobilizing many forces in the country that could have been of help in the war effort. In 1916 a large section of Central Asia revolted against Russian domination, and the natives were brutally suppressed by Russian troops. England and France were sending supplies and munitions to Russia, but the Russian transportation system broke down. Brusilov, one of the Tsar's ablest generals had developed a well prepared offensive on the southern front. In spite of all the help of the Allies and the fact that Russia had by now practically mortgaged herself and her resources to her western allies, the rest of the army was unable to support Brusilov's efforts. The prestige of the Tsar had practically vanished. Since 1905 the emperor was no longer "little father" to the workers whom he had shot down in St. Petersburg on "Bloody Sunday." Now millions of peasants were dying like flies in the enormous armies. They were dying for something they could not understand, because neither victory nor defeat held out any promise to them of a better lot. The disgraceful scandals that emanated from the court in connection with the self-styled "monk" Gregory Rasputin were discussed in the most faraway nooks of the empire.

In February, 1917 disturbances began in the capital. Crowds of people waiting in long queues at food stores lost their patience. Troops sent to suppress the demonstrations joined them instead. Drastic messages were sent to the Tsar, who was at the front, by the president of the Duma, Rodzyanko. The Tsar abdicated and a provisional government was set up. The thousand-year-old Russian monarchy suddenly collapsed.

The Provisional Government, presided over by Prince Lvov, set to work as an extremely mild affair. Its members believed in civil liberties, wanted to win the war, and to establish either a constitutional monarchy, as in England, or a conservative republic, as in France. The only Leftist member of the cabinet was the minister of justice, the young lawyer Alexander Kerensky. Independently, but simultaneously with the establishment of the Provisional Government, the soldiers and workers created their councils, or soviets, after a pattern already tested in the 1905 Revolution. The soviets wanted to go further than the Provisional Government: they wanted drastic reforms now, immediately, and not "later."

In April, 1917 the most conservative members of the Provisional Government resigned, as a result of popular demonstrations in Petrograd. That month there arrived from Switzerland V. I. Lenin, leader of the Bolsheviks (as the radical section of the Social Democrats were called after 1903) with a program that seemed then too drastic even to the Soviets. Not long after, Leon Trotsky arrived from New York. Before the end of the summer he switched his allegiance from Marxist middlemen to the Bolshevik Party and for a time was regarded as even more drastic a Revolutionist than Lenin. The only man who seemed to enjoy the confusion and conflict and had a speech for every occasion was Kerensky, the Leftist member of the Provisional Government. Soon, he became prime minister, secretary of war and navy, and commander-in-chief. In fact the Provisional Government in effect became the Alexander Kerensky government. But Kerensky did very little. He just talked and talked and talked.

In July a new crisis arose. A revolt against the Provisional Government broke out in Petrograd following the bloody failure of an offensive that Kerensky had tried to engineer on the Austrian front. Lenin, who had assumed leadership of the Bolshevik party, considered the revolt premature, but the people were rising, and Lenin and the Bolsheviks decided that they had to lead them. The revolt failed with a good deal of bloodshed. The Bolsheviks had to go into hiding, at least for the time being.

Kerensky and the commander of the troops at the front, General Kornilov, both now sought to stem the revolutionary tide. They could not, however, agree on which one of them was to be the Russian Napoleon. They started fighting each other. Now the workers of Petrograd had to rally to Kerensky, the man who had just suppressed their revolt, in order to crush Kornilov. The general was easily overcome, but Kerensky lost face with the reactionary army elements on the one hand and with the entire Left, with whose aid he had won so easily. Meanwhile the Bolsheviks were getting stronger and stronger in the soviets.

At the front the enormous army was disintegrating. Soldiers were going home by the hundreds of thousands. Lenin and the Bolsheviks were telling the men not to leave their rifles behind, but to carry them home. The men were going home in the vast majority of cases to get the noblemen's land. To the peasant soldier the overthrow of the Tsar meant one thing: at last he could get all the land and not bits of it as in 1861 when the serfs were liberated. To the Russian masses the war was the Tsar's war. A defeat simply meant at the worst a new master. The people wanted "Peace, Land and Bread," and the Bolsheviks made this their slogan. Parliamentary procedure was being discussed by the liberal intellectuals in Petrograd and Moscow, but this had very little meaning to 100 million Russians. They knew what they wanted, and they were going home to get it with rifles in their hands.

By October, 1917 Kerensky's power had nearly melted away. In Petrograd the Bolsheviks were getting ready to take power through an armed insurrection. Kerensky's government continued deliberating on a high intellectual plane in the halls of the Winter Palace of the tsars. The last card in the hands of the Provisional Government was to call elections for a

Constituent Assembly, which they had been putting off for the last eight months. This body was to have given the peasants land. But the peasants were already taking the land themselves. The elections proceeded throughout the country, but the Assembly did not convene before the overthrow of the Provisional Government. On October 25 (November 7 by the Western calendar) the soldiers and workers of Petrograd, led by a committee of Bolshevik leaders, finally struck against the Provisional Government. Only the military schools and some women's battalions came to the defense of Kerensky. The Winter Palace was stormed. The cruiser *Aurora* steamed into the river Neva and began shelling the palace. Kerensky fled abroad, first to Prague, then to Paris, then to Westchester County, N. Y.

to finish his days as an embittered and disillusioned man.

The Bolsheviks under the Red flag were now in control and delivered power to the Second Congress of Soviets of Workers' and Soldiers' Deputies, which convened on October 26. Lenin took the floor, proposing first, as he had promised, a decree to obtain peace immediately. The second measure was the nationalization of land, without compensation to the owners and for all time. The third measure — it was far past midnight now — was the establishment of a Council of Peoples' Commissars with Lenin as premier, Trotsky as foreign affairs commissar and Bolsheviks in most other posts. All three proposals received overwhelming support, and thus the first Communist government in history came into being.

THE LAST ROMANOVS

Nicholas' marriage was happy for him but most unhappy for Russia. The Tsarina, half German and half English (Queen Victoria was her grandmother) was psychopathic, mystical and strong-willed. Her influence completed the undermining of the

throne. Like Lady Macbeth, she grew in power and purpose as her husband declined. Almost a symbol of this family's tragedy was the fact that the son and heir, whom the mother bore after four daughters, was a hemophilic (addicted to abnormal bleeding). Clockwise around Alexandra Fedorovna and Nicholas II: Anastasia, Tatiana, Olga, Marie and the Tsarevich Alexis.

IMPERIAL LIFE at Tsarskoe-Selo between the troubles of 1905 and World War I was outwardly very splendid, with a strong martial note. The Tsar reviewed his immense bodyguard every few days, while the ladies watched from a balcony (*above* and *left*).

THERE WERE RELAXATIONS, such as wing-shooting in the South with relatives or on the imperial Black Sea estates of Orianda and Livadia. And there was motoring, especially in the Crimea where the roads were improved, in high-backed old chariots which, though imperial, were not immune to punctures (*below*).

171

PARTIES

In St. Petersburg there were grand parties and processions, like the one above in front of St. Isaac's Cathedral on the quay, where the Tsar is seen approaching the Tsarina (*center,* in white) with countless court ladies and gentlemen looking on. But another type of party also went on in the court. The Tsarina fell under the psychic domination of a shrewd, shaggy monk called Rasputin (means "debauchery"), whose powers of clairvoyance and hypnotism were believed capable of controlling the Tsarevich's hemophilia. A confirmed lecher and worse, Rasputin taught that salvation was to be found in his embrace: "Sin, to obtain forgiveness." He enjoyed himself with various high-born ladies, inspiring them to wear rough clothes like his own "holy" ones and go on loose picnics (*right* and *below*). The situation was as though Oom the Omnipotent were a revered intimate of the White House.

172

AND PARTIES

But Russia's people were not enjoying any parties except the kind where flocks of them, coming in hungry from the countryside, camped outside the Kremlin (*right*). The Kremlin clock shows 10:20 A.M. on this bright morning in 1911, but the hour was much nearer midnight for Imperial Russia.

STILL OTHER PARTIES were starting in Russia: political parties, who meant business. Nicholas II's attention was drawn so forcibly to them in 1905 that he invited all parties to submit programs for a national assembly. In August, an Imperial Duma (parliament) was announced, to be elected on a narrow, class franchise. This suited few people, and the strikes and riots that continued scared Prime Minister Witte into widening the franchise to include almost all taxpayers. The Constitutional Democrats ("Cadets") won control, with Labor in the minority, and Nicholas II received the First Duma on May 10, 1906, in the Winter Palace (*below*), with an Address from the Throne.

This speech was just so many high-flown words. It advanced no social or political program (as in the British models after which it was fashioned), leaving to the Duma the initiative in its answering Address to the Throne, issued from the Tauride Palace where the Duma went to sit. Russia now had representative government, in form, if not in substance, and the shadow of the feared thing became more dangerous than the reality might have been.

DUMA IN FINLAND

The First Duma at once submitted to the Government, which was now headed by Prime Minister Goremykin, a comprehensive program to reform Russia's administration from top to bottom. Goremykin replied that this program was almost all unsuitable. The Duma voted censure of the Government, but lacked power to force its resignation, or power to appeal to the electorate. The Government declared the Duma dissolved. Whereupon 200 members, Cadets and Labor, repaired to Viborg in Finland where, meeting in a forest (*above*), they called upon Russia for passive resistance to the Government until the Duma was restored. But Russia was not yet organized to resist, even passively. The call fell flat. But this was not the end of the Duma.

ZEMSTVO CONGRESS (1906)

The Zemstva (county and provincial councils) were the second of Alexander II's great reforms. Founded in 1864 (on a pattern devised by Speransky way back in 1811), they dealt locally with public education, roads, food, health — all subjects ignored by the central Government. Elective, they attracted some of Russia's best men who shrank from bureaucratic drudgery. Zemstva came into being in 33 provinces of European Russia and their chairmen formed a Congress which aided the Government often in overcoming popular discontents. Meantime, the Zemstvo Congress members worked constantly to extend representative government like theirs from country and provinces to the nation as a whole. These efforts were thoughtful, peaceful, constitutional, yet those who exerted them were accounted brave men in their day because active Reform was at all times suspect as Revolution. With the formation of the Duma and national political parties, the Zemstvo Congress' importance became secondary. In the picture above, of one of the last Congresses, some of Russia's best old families are represented. *Left to right, standing:* Lvov, Rodichev, Lvov, Golovin, Kovalevsky, Dolgorukov, Troubetskoi, Novosiltsev, Shakhovskoi. *Seated:* Korff, Heyden, Petrunkevitch, Fedorov, Nikitin.

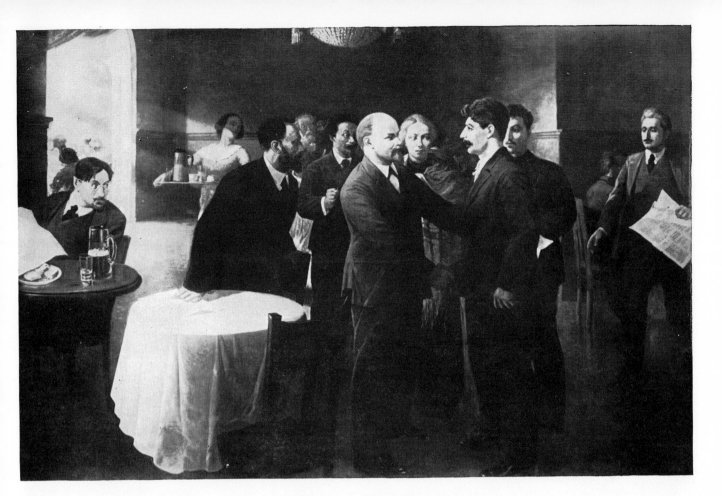

LENIN MEETS STALIN (1905)

Easily the world's foremost political figure of the 20th Century is Vladimir Ilyich Ulyanov, styled LENIN (from the Lena River). Clearly high in the same category is Joseph Vissarionovich Djugashvilli, styled STALIN ("steel"), who became Lenin's understudy and successor. It is interesting to know that these two met for the first time (*above*) at a revolutionary party meeting in Tammerfors, Finland, in December, 1905, just when the Zemstvo Congress was completing its work in Russia and the Duma was in gestation. Though these two men had no direct part in overthrowing the tsardom, but came to power through gaining control of the revolution, it is important to examine at this point a box-score of their origins and mental equipment, which contrasted strongly at almost every point (*see below*).

LENIN

Born: 1870, in Simbirsk (now Ulyanovsk), son of a schoolmaster and a doctor's daughter. His elder brother participated in a plot against Alexander III and was executed.

Educated: at Simbirsk Gymnasium (class of 1887) where he won the gold medal; then Kazan University, whence he was suspended two years for agitating. He studied law and, intensively, Karl Marx. In 1891 he passed the St. Petersburg bar examinations.

Worked: as a lawyer in Samara until 1893 when he settled in St. Petersburg as a Marxian propagandist, travelling abroad to meet other Marxists. He was imprisoned through 1896 for organizing and propagandizing workers.

Exiled: for three years (1897-1900) to Yenisei province, during which time he wrote *The Development of Capitalism in Russia,* and married Nadezhda Krupskaya, his collaborator (shown between Lenin and Stalin in picture above).

Subsequently (up to 1905): went to Switzerland (1900), founded *The Spark* to be the Marxian organ of Russia's Social Democratic Revolutionary Party. Central thought: let the proletariat organize and stick together within — then control — the democratic movement in Russia.

Characteristics: short, stocky, round-headed, sparse-haired, essentially intellectual; powerful but not violent speaker; tireless reader and writer; implacable toward class (but not personal) enemies.

STALIN

Born: December 21, 1879, in the hamlet of Gori, Georgia; son of a peasant shoemaker.

Educated: briefly, at a religious seminary in Tiflis, whence he was expelled.

Worked: briefly, in the Batum oilfields, where at 17 he joined a Social Democrat group and agitated among his fellow workers. He was first arrested in 1902 (aged 23) for organizing demonstrations.

Exiled: to Eastern Siberia in 1903, for three years. He escaped and returned in 1904 — the first of a series of shuttle trips to and from exile. He was thus only just fledged as a revolutionist when he met Lenin, who recognized him at once as promising material and in later years advanced him in what became the Communist Party. To him, Lenin was "the mountain eagle."

Characteristics: short, stocky, longheaded, with a shock of black hair; shrewd but essentially physical; a blunt, laborious, far from eloquent speaker; a man of action but also of diligent bookishness; largely silent and calculating, he doggedly espoused and ruthlessly advanced the cause of Communism.

ULYANOV

Lenin's early career was spent mostly underground, and after he came to power there was little time for party artists to recreate his early days. Remaining are his police pictures of 1896 (*left*) and a painting of his wife, Krupskaya, visiting him in his cell with guards standing by (*below*). She was to remain for 26 years his standby and co-worker; dispatcher of underground messengers; coder and decoder; secretary, wife and friend.

Born in 1869 of penniless nobility, Nadezhda Krupskaya attended private school, taught evening classes for workers. Her early approach to Revolution was the dreamy approach of the intelligentsia. She took fire when, arrested during the strikes of 1896, she was exiled to Minusinsk in Siberia where she married Lenin. Childless, she was always deeply concerned about children, became assistant commissar for Education in 1932. She died in 1939, aged 70.

DJUGASHVILLI

Through the long years of his ascendancy (after 1923), there was ample time for Soviet artists to record all the high points of Stalin's life, going far back of his best 1910 police portraits (*right*). The scene below shows the young Djugashvilli on the carpet before a stern preceptor of the Tiflis seminary, over whose ominous head hangs the portrait of Tsar Nicholas II. The charge against adolescent, wary-eyed Joseph: "unreliability," for which he was expelled.

Despite this early diversion from the priesthood, Stalin's speech and writing were to be strongly colored throughout later life by his beginnings in theology. Echoes of scripture (and of the classics) are to be found in profusion; for example, in the 1936 Soviet Constitution wherein he had a large hand, occurs the paraphrase, "He who does not work, does not eat." In Stalin's speeches are quotations from or allusions to Gogol, Pushkin, Saltykov-Schedrin, *et al.*

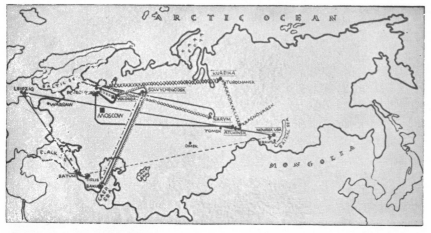

DJUGASHVILLI (cont.)

The Caucasus oil fields (the same ones which Germany was to covet and be denied by Stalin's armies in World War II) form the backdrop of all of Stalin's early political activity. The oil workers, constantly exposed to grime and danger, were ill-paid, ill-fed, ill-housed. Stalin repeatedly encouraged them to strike.

A chart of Stalin's exiles and escapes (*left*) looks like a piece of knitting. *Key:* arrested in 1902 in Batum, he was exiled to Novaya Uda in Irkutsk Province; escaped 1904 to Leipsig, returned to the oilfields, not rearrested until 1908 at Baku; exiled to Solvychegodsk in Vologda Province; escaped 1909 and returned to Baku; rearrested 1910, again exiled to Solvychegodsk; escaped 1911, went to St. Petersburg; rearrested after two months, exiled to Vologda; escaped after five months, returned to St. Petersburg; rearrested after two months, exiled to Narym; escaped after three months, returned to St. Petersburg; rearrested after six months, exiled to Kureika, transferred from there to Krasnoyarsk after three and one-half years, then to Aktubinsk (February, 1917); returned to Petrograd on the eve of the Tsar's overthrow. In all these comings and goings, he managed to keep himself supplied with political reading matter.

A moment to which Stalin's admirers still point with pride is his first imprisonment (1902-1903) when, behind bars, he continued agitating among his fellow prisoners and even his guards. The latter's consternation is shown (*left*) when he harangues a group of convicts who, like himself later, are off to Siberia.

CRACOW CONFERENCE

During Stalin's fourth term of exile (1911-1912), Lenin had him elected *in absentia* to the Central Committee of the Social Democratic party, at a meeting in Cracow, Poland. After his fourth escape, Stalin visited Cracow, attended a party meeting (*above,* Stalin with elbow on table in center) which Lenin addressed. This was about the moment when the Bolshevik wing of the party finally split with the Mensheviks, whom the Bolsheviks considered faint-hearted for believing that revolution must wait until Russia was more highly industrialized.

"DISPERSING A STRIKE" is the title of a painting by Artist I. Vladimirov (*below*) dear to the Bolsheviks, for it faithfully portrays the scene, enacted over and over again, of tsarist police charging with drawn sabres into the ranks of striking workers to drive them back to their jobs at the edge of the sabre.

STOLYPIN

One man dominates the period 1906-1911. His name was Peter Arcadievich Stolypin (*left*). He had proven himself as the firm-handed governor of Saratov Province during 1905's storm. Tsar Nicholas put him in as Minister of the Interior, under Prime Minister Goremykin, in 1906. The latter's job then fell to Stolypin when the government wanted to dissolve the First Duma. He got around this problem by calling another Duma within the prescribed time limit and struck for the heart of discontent:

(1) By wholesale courts-martial in which 600 people were executed; (2) by offering vast new tracts of land to the peasants at low prices, to put a broader agrarian base behind the government. Peasants could now get their land in blocks, instead of isolated strips, and could own it permanently.

The peasants never wholly believed or trusted Stolypin, but they took advantage of his reforms. He alienated not only Liberals but reactionaries. The Second and Third Dumas were almost as unsatisfactory as was the First, with the Cadets and their friends outstripping the Octobrists, and with the Social Revolutionaries (peasant party) and Social Democrats (workers) gaining strength. The Third Duma lasted its full five years, though Stolypin did not live to see this. A bomb attempt on his life in 1906 at his country home (*below*) had maimed his daughter but missed him. In September, 1911, while he was attending a gala at Kiev with the Tsar and the Court, he was shot fatally with a pistol by one Mordecai Bogrov.

GOOD FRIENDS

Right up to August 1, 1914, the Tsar and Kaiser Wilhelm II (Hohenzollern) of Germany were cordial friends. The Kaiser would attend Russian Army reviews wearing the uniform of a Russian fieldmarshal (honorary). The Tsar inspected the German Fleet aboard the German cruiser *Berlin* dressed as a German admiral (honorary), while Wilhelm dressed up in Russian regalia to be doubly polite and gay (*above*). They talked shop like old cronies. In 1897 for example, during a friendly drive, Wilhelm asked Nicholas not to mind if Germany took over Kiao-Chow on China's Shantung peninsula as a naval base, and Nicholas consented. Fact is, Wilhelm understood Nicholas and his weaknesses, and courted him to offset Russia's *entente cordiale* with France. He even got him to sign a protocol of alliance in direct breach of the French pact, out of which Nicholas' ministers had to extricate Russia, with embarrassment.

SARAJEVO

Russia's immemorial interest in the Balkans — protection of all the Southern Slavs there — was rudely threatened when, after the Balkan War of 1912, Austria got tough toward victorious Serbia. In June, 1914, Crown Prince Francis Ferdinand of Austria and his wife were assassinated at Sarajevo, Bosnia. Suspecting a Serbian state plot, Austria issued an ultimatum which compromised Serbia's independence. Serbia asked Russia's advice and help. Germany announced that if any power intervened she would back up Austria. The latter refused to accept Serbia's reply to the ultimatum, declared war on July 28.

The man whose death was to plunge the whole world into war was old Emperor Franz Josef's nephew, aged 51, a second choice reluctantly picked after the romantic death in 1889 of Crown Prince Rudolph. Because his wife was not royal, he had to sign away all rights of succession for their children.

The men whose fusillade at Sarajevo rang around the world were of Serbian birth but Bosnian citizenship. The leader was Gabrilov Prinkip (marked "x," *below*). There was evidence of official Serbian connivance at the murders. Prinkip and colleagues were, however, sincere hot-blooded patriots resolved not to let their small country be dominated by its large, imperialistic neighbor, and willing to shed imperial blood to make their point.

MOBILIZATION

Russia prepared to mobilize when Austria declared war. Foreign Minister Sazonov (*above, left*) explained to everyone that it would be *partial* mobilization only, aimed at Austria alone, if the latter should march on Belgrade. In London, Foreign Minister Grey (*above, center*) strove prayerfully to intercede, but German Ambassador Pourtales (*above, right*) told St. Petersburg that *any* mobilization would mean war with Germany. So Russia's mobilization was made general. The Kaiser wired the Tsar he would do everything to prevent war between them. But Germany mobilized, too. The Tsar wired the Kaiser that Russia's mobilization did not necessarily mean war, so long as Austria did not invade Serbia. The German Government demanded that Russia's mobilization cease, and in the next breath declared war on Russia. So much "mobilization" talk had been so much fluff. All Europe had been priming for war for years, and everyone knew it.

(*Below*): The Tsar inspecting troop movements just before mobilization, with thousands of enthusiastic Russians looking on.

WAR!

War against Germany and for the Southern Slavs aroused in the Russian people an access of patriotism. The country was electrically united as it had not been for years. Against his will, Tsar Nicholas appointed as commander-in-chief his second cousin, the towering (6 feet, 6 inches), silver-streaked Grand Duke Nicolai Nicolaievich, 58, whom he disliked but whose popularity with civilians as well as soldiers was immense. As commander-in-chief of the military district of St. Petersburg (now swiftly changed to its Slavic form, Petrograd), the Grand Duke had drilled home lessons of the Japanese war; had promoted humble but able field generals to high command. But for six years he had had no part in planning Russia's grand strategy. When the bands blared (*below*) and the vast Russian armies (15,000,000 men) started into motion, the Grand Duke had to execute plans made by others, had to rely on generals not picked by him. (*Left*): Tsar and Grand Duke.

POLAND was, as usual, in the nutcracker when Germany and Russia joined battle. Grand Duke Nicolai and the Tsar promptly promised that if the Poles would fight on the side of the Slavs, they would be granted their independence after victory. The Germans made similar promises, and the Poles split their allegiance. Many fought on the German side, including Pilsudski who organized a Polish Legion. Russian regiments were rushed to hold Warsaw. The net effect of this development was to interfere with Germany's swift application of pressure on the Western Front, but it imposed a heavy strain on Russia's inadequate supply system. The Russians were willing but bemused.

SUCCESS IN AUSTRIA

Russia's war plans called for a smashing offensive with four armies against Austria into Galicia. This operation proceeded splendidly under General Alexeyev, whose troops were soon tacking up posters (*right*) in Przemysl ("This town no longer belongs to the Austrians"), entering its massive fortress (*below*) and rounding up 200,000 prisoners.

For thus bringing Galicia back into the Russian fold for the first time since the Tartar invasion (13th Century), the Tsar gave Grand Duke Nicolai a diamond-studded sword, the honor and significance of which were to stand for less than a year, when Russia's Austrian drive went into disastrous reverse.

DISASTER AT TANNENBERG

Russia's war plans also called, under the *entente* with France, for an offensive into East Prussia within 16 days after war's outbreak. This undertaking was carried out on the dot. Popular outcry caused the German High Command, which had planned to let Russia have East Prussia until France was smashed, to withdraw several divisions hastily from the West, sparing Paris.

One night Russian General Rennenkampf (*left,* at far left) dined sumptuously in his staff car. The next night his I army and the II army under General Samsonov were shattered wrecks, after the battle of Tannenberg. More than 100,000 Russian prisoners were herded into Augustovo (*above*). Their arms were piled high in churches (*below, left*). Thousands of them were captured before having fired more than a few shots (*below, right*).

186

LACK OF SUPPLY

The German general who delivered the blow of Tannenberg was Paul von Hindenburg, aided by Chief of Staff Eric von Ludendorff and a team of crack generals, headquartered at Posen (*above*). Chief sufferer was the Russian II Army under Russian General Samsonov, five of whose divisions Ludendorff surrounded and slaughtered. General Samsonov committed suicide. But a greater shame lay upon others. Russia's supplies, and her system of supply, were woefully inadequate for her great spaces and her huge army, about 30% of which remained unarmed even after thousands of sacrosanct Russian church bells (*below*) were taken down to be melted and recast into cannon.

SUCCESS IN POLAND

The Russian campaign plan in Poland was a two-army drive on the Polish plain. Though Ludendorff moved 52 divisions toward Warsaw, the Russians prevailed here in October. The Western Allies demanded yet more of Russia: a further Polish drive, into Silesia. Fourteen more German divisions were thus drawn away from the Western Front. This time the tired Russians were stopped.

(*Above*): A Russian charge in Poland. (*Left*): A Russian trench. (*Below*): Russian gun.

AND MORE REVERSES

Germany now decided to whip Russia before smashing France. More and more power was sent east — and implacable General Mackensen of the Death's Head Hussars (*right*). From 63 divisions in 1914, Germany's strength in the East was raised to 161 divisions by September, 1915. Germany bolstered Austria in Galicia until the Russian triumph there was converted into a Russian rout (*above*). Against the fierce, systematic onslaught of Mackensen on the Polish plain, Russia's supply system simply could not stand up and the whole summer of 1915 was a long, bitter-retreat, yielding everything thus far gained and also the Russian parts of Poland, the Baltic states and White Russia. Short of food, guns, ammunition and transport, the Russians, though they had proved themselves brave and steadfast fighting men, had to surrender by tens of thousands (*below*). But the Russian Army stayed in being despite Germany's best efforts to destroy it.

THE TSAR TAKES OVER

The most potent war-making agencies in Russia — as the Allies began to understand — were the Duma and the Zemstva, which set themselves to lick Russia's supply problem and, by the autumn of 1915, were beginning to do so. To save his own and his Government's face — and because the rascally Monk Rasputin (who hated Grand Duke Nicolai) advised it — Tsar Nicholas suddenly announced that he would take over personally as commander-in-chief. With the Tsarevich at his side he took communion in the field with his officers and men (*above*), visited and reviewed detachments close to the front (*below*). Grand Duke Nicolai was sent to the Caucasus front, to fight Turkey. The Cabinet was shuffled and reshuffled. Net result: zero, except for a further decline of the Tsar's prestige with his country and his Allies.

COMPLICATIONS

Actual commander-in-chief for Nicholas was able General Alexeyev (*above*) but his work was embarrassed by this chain of circumstances: whatever he told the Tsar, the Tsar would tell the Tsarina, who would tell the Monk Rasputin, who would tell — heaven knew whom! Some people even thought Rasputin might have been planted amidst the Imperial Family by Germany (which he was not). Certainly he was a weird complication for any nation fighting a major war. He controlled nominations, dictated decisions, chiseled in on munitions contracts, yet persons who opposed him at once lost standing.

Rasputin was so close to the seat of power that he was photographed (*right*) sitting between two high court officials (one of them the Tsar's adjutant) who remained respectfully standing. The position of the "mad monk" was becoming intolerable to too many people.

END OF RASPUTIN

Late in 1916 a group of top-flight nobles determined that Gregory Efimovich Rasputin must go. The Grand Duke Dmitry and Prince Felix Yousoupov put potassium cyanide in his wine at a soirée in the Yousoupov Palace. When that did not overcome his tremendous strength, they shot him. When he lurched to his feet and went at them, they shot him some more, bashed and kicked his head, finally dumped his still-twitching hulk into an icy river.

(*Right*): **PRINCE YOUSOUPOV** (right) with Prince Nikita Romanov, leaving court in London in the 1920's during Yousoupov's wife's suit against a movie company which, she said, portrayed her libelously in a Rasputin picture. (She won the litigation.)

191

DUMA v. TSAR

Two million refugees from Russia's lost regions, plus the families of millions of soldiers, plus reduced crops due to diversion of manpower to munitions-making, plus the breakdown of Russia's railways, resulted in grave food shortages, especially in Petrograd. (*Right:* A food line, with policeman.) Fierce food riots ensued. The Duma asked the Tsar for a Cabinet in which people could have confidence. He replied by sending one battalion to Petrograd to restore order, and commanded the Duma to dissolve.

The one battalion was ineffectual. Petrograd's unrest continued. And the Duma refused to obey the Tsar's dissolution ukase. It continued meeting in the Tauride Palace, where crowds of soldiers as well as civilians assembled to see what would happen. On March 12 the mob arrested the Cabinet. The Duma's president, Michael Rodzyanko (*below*), was chosen head of a Temporary Committee to take control of what was now Revolution, and to notify the Tsar that. he must abdicate.

A deputation sought the Tsar, who was returning from the front to Tsarkoe-Selo. Railway employees stopped his train and the deputation confronted him at Pskov. Beaten, he abdicated; not in favor of the ailing young Tsarevich, whom he wished to spare, but in favor of his brother, the Grand Duke Michael (*upper left, next page*). The latter promptly declined unless the people — that is, the forthcoming Constituent Assembly — should ratify his accession whenever it should meet. This proposal was tabled and — when the Assembly met later — forgotten.

THE OVERTHROW OF RUSSIA'S 300-YEAR DYNASTY was thus quite "legal" and peaceful. The Revolution was purely political — so far. The Duma set up a Provisional Government with Prince George Lvov (*below, right*) as its chief.

MICHAEL RODZYANKO (1859-1923), scion of rich landowners, was typical in 1917 of the best in old Russia which was to be erased to make way for the new. As a Zemstvo leader he had worked long and hard for representative government. His efforts had rallied Russian industry to support the war. After the Revolution he put his energies into the Red Cross, died in Yugoslavia as a refugee from the Reds.

PRINCE GEORGE LVOV (1861-1925) was another such as Rodzyanko: gentle, honest, Tolstoyan but incapable of Revolution. As past president of the Zemstvo Congress he was the Provisional Government's logical head, but both its Cabinets headed by him were miserable though earnest failures.

THE FIRST SOVIET

When the Duma's Temporary Committee was formed, Socialist Alexander Kerensky accepted a place on it, and went on to be Minister of Justice in the Provisional Government. Socialist Nicholai Chkeidze (*above, right*), president of the Petrograd Soviet of Worker's & Soldier's Deputies (of which Kerensky was vice-president) held aloof from the Committee. Under him, the Soviet met in rump session in the Tauride Palace (*below*) while the Duma deliberated. The Soviet asserted its power and its control of the masses, but did not attempt to take over the government. Their policy was to dictate to the government. After an all-night wrangle between the rival bodies, the Provisional Government passed its first decrees, dictated almost

in toto by the Soviet, which at first agreed to support it.

These decrees declared a general amnesty for all imperial prisoners; provided freedom of speech, press and assembly, and labor's right to strike; proclaimed universal suffrage and called for a Constituent Assembly, through elections to be held in the autumn.

Having thus shaped the future, the Soviet did not disperse. It went right on sitting, and without consulting the Provisional Government issued to the Army on March 14 its own **"ORDER NO. I."** This told the soldiers to organize committees and obey the Soviet in political decisions; to obey no orders of the Duma which conflicted with the Soviet's; to regard their weapons as their own, not to be surrendered to their officers. These orders suited the tired, restless soldiers, whose discipline was thus basically undermined.

ENTER, LENIN

From Galicia, where the war's opening found him, Lenin had returned to Switzerland whence he preached, to Russia and the world, revolt of the masses to end the capitalists' war. When Russia revolted, he was anxious to get home. Germany, which had counted on revolution to take Russia out of the war, was glad to pass Lenin and his henchmen — Zinoviev, Kamenev, Radek, Lunacharsky, *et al.* — in a sealed car through to Denmark, whence via Sweden and Finland they triumphantly reached Petrograd on April 16 (*above*). Lenin took over a private house for headquarters, took charge of the Bolshevik wing of the Soviet (*below*), made "All power to the Soviets!" the Bolshevik slogan and set out to capture the Revolution from the Provisional Government by skilfull, tireless activities.

KERENSKY

From Minister of Justice in Prince Lvov's first cabinet, Alexander Kerensky, the voluble, electric little barrister (*right*), progressed to War and Marine Minister, then Premier. As commander-in-chief, he prepared an offensive to re-win Russia's lost territories. He harangued the troops to get them to fight some more and the offensive, on the Austrian front, was hugely successful at first — until the men got tired. The Bolsheviks encouraged them to fraternize with the enemy, call the whole thing off, take their rifles and go home to grab land for themselves or join in grabbing the factories. So many men did so that the war's tide soon turned back again.

As a matter of fact, Kerensky contributed to the Russian Army's disruption by appointing **COMMISSARS** to represent the Provisional Government politically at the front. The military commanders thus found themselves under pressure from above as well as from below, and this was the more confusing since the common soldiers' committees (under Bolshevik influence) were working at cross purposes with Kerensky's commissars.

Thus, this young lawyer who, by the vicissitudes of war, found himself at the trigger of a centuries-old fighting nation, was presently without an army. (*Right*): The young Kerensky reading a French socialist sheet.

"BABOUSHKA" (Little Grandmother) was the nickname of Katherine Breshko-Breshkovskaya, an oldtime Social Revolutionary brought back from long exile to be the Revolution's brooding matriarch.

GENERAL BRUSILOV, one of the Tsar's best, was made commander-in-chief by Kerensky for the summer offensive. When whole regiments of Red soldiers quit fighting, able Brusilov failed.

"PERSUADER-IN-CHIEF" was the nickname earned by Kerensky on his trips to the front to exhort the troops to keep on fighting. But even his oratory was no match for Red propaganda.

THE BOLSHEVIKS RISE

The Bolsheviks made more than one premature bid for power. The Soviet at Petrograd called for the formation of Soviets all over Russia, and a congress of these was held in June. The Bolsheviks had only 105 delegates to 285 Social Revolutionaries and 248 Mensheviks (of whom Leon Trotsky, fresh from New York, was one). Nevertheless the Bolsheviks most vigorously organized cells throughout the land and in Petrograd demonstrated so violently that Kerensky set police to fire upon them, producing the scene shown above.

LENIN HIDES

Biding his time, but writing and organizing incessantly, Lenin went into hiding from Kerensky for the summer, in a farm hut at Razliv on the Finnish border (*left*).

IMPERIAL PRISONERS

After his arrest and close-guarded confinement at Tsarskoe-Selo, Nicholas II behaved with utmost fortitude and resignation. It hurt to have the soldier-guards lounge about with their belts off, showing no consideration, talking roughly, shooting deer in the park. But Nicholas took refuge in hard physical work, which he loved. He chopped firewood, shovelled snow, and when spring came worked with his guards in a kitchen garden which yielded them vegetables (*above*). Evenings he read to his family. He organized them into a school and became the history teacher. The fallen Empress, who was ill, bore herself less nobly. She moped and brooded in her wheel-chair. When the train (with blinds drawn and flying the Japanese flag!) came in the summer to take them to Siberia for safekeeping, the once-dominant Empress had to be carried aboard, a pathetic shadow of her old self.

"WHY FIGHT ANY MORE?"

Within two months of the Provisional Government's accession, there were 2,000,000 desertions from the Army. One cause for this was "Order No. I," dictated by the Soviets, instructing the soldiers to form committees of their own which they would obey instead of their officers, especially as concerned control and disposition of weapons. Another cause was Soviet propaganda the theme of which was, "Why fight any more? Take your gun and go home and seize *your* piece of land." For a time, trains carried more men away from the front than to it (*below, left*). In rear area villages, the scene (*above*) was of returned soldiers laying down their rifles to pick up pitchforks. The Soviets also counselled fraternizing across the lines with German and Austrian troops (*below, right*) to end the war as soon as possible.

KORNILOV
v. KERENSKY

Now a strong voice made itself heard in the Army. General Kornilov, on the collapsing Austrian front, called for a restoration of discipline; for deserters, death. The country responded so heartily that Kerensky made Kornilov commander-in-chief (*right*, in light coat). Kornilov decided to suppress not only the defeatist Socialists but also the talkative Kerensky. He sent General Krymov to take over Petrograd and establish what would have been a military dictatorship. Instead of discipline and order, a military clash between the commander-in-chief and the Prime Minister ensued, Russia was more divided than ever.

KERENSKY'S WOMEN

To meet the Kornilov-Krymov threat, Kerensky had to call on the Bolshevik-led guards with whose backing he ordered Kornilov's arrest, and made it stick. Krymov committed suicide. Kerensky's call for help made it clear that, as prime minister, he was woefully weak. The only military support he could command personally in the showdown that was coming were cadets and some women's battalions. The latter, sworn to battle until death, were especially loyal to the charming "Persuader-in-Chief." (*Above*): A women's battalion on review. (*Left*): Wounded woman soldier receiving first aid from male corpsmen, a reversal of procedure somehow typically Russian.

THE BRIEF EXPERIMENT in diluted Revolution thus rapidly neared its end. The Provisional Government was powerless. The Army was disintegrating. The country was in turmoil.

199

OCTOBER 25

The Bolsheviks (whom Trotsky had now joined) dominated the Socialist Soviet through its Military Committee created by Trotsky. The turning point came in October, when Trotsky was elected vice-president of the Soviet. By now the Petrograd garrisons were thoroughly Bolshevized. With the Constituent Assembly only a few days off, the Reds struck, on October 25 (November 7, Western). Their troops and civilians, indiscrimi- nately armed, stormed the Winter Palace (*above*) where the Kerensky Government now sat. They brought the cruiser *Aurora* up the river from Kronstadt and gunned the palace from the water side (*see* p. 201). Before dawn of October 26, Petrograd was in the hands of Lenin and Trotsky. They made haste to clinch their hold, posted Red guards at their doors (*below, right*), hoisted the Red flag over the Imperial Palace (*see* p. 201), while joyous workers and soldiers paraded in the streets en masse (*below*). The Revolution was now theirs.

THE AURORA (*above*) was joined by the fortress of Peter & Paul (straight across the river from the palace) in shelling the palace and also the Admiralty, until resistance ceased. Kerensky escaped but most members of his Cabinet were captured and imprisoned. In memory of her part in this historic affray, the *Aurora* was kept at anchor off Kronstadt for years afterward with her little red firing pennant flying permanently at her masthead.

THE RED FLAG

The crimson standard of Revolution which was finally raised over the palace of the Tsars on October 26 (November 8), 1917, was never formally adopted by the Soviets as their official emblem. It so became simply by natural evolution. A blood-red flag, or kerchief or armband or shirt, had been the symbol of armed revolt at least as early as 1792 in Paris (some even say a red flag was raised in Massachusetts in 1776). Again over the Paris barricades of 1848 flew red flags, and during the Commune, and during Russia's social stirrings of the 1880's and 1905 when so much else of Revolution was imported from Western Europe including *The Internationale*. The Hammer & Sickle, signifying the Union of factory workers and peasants, came in during the early days of the local Soviets.

"PEACE, LAND, BREAD"

The victorious Bolsheviks turned over their power to the Second Congress of Soviets, which the Bolsheviks dominated. Lenin went at once to work, formed the Council of People's Commissars with himself as president, Trotsky for Foreign Affairs, Rykov for Internal Affairs, Stalin for Nationalities, Lunacharsky for Education. In his speech to the Congress, Lenin explained how he proposed to translate "Peace, Land, Bread" into concrete political action. Cried he: "Peace to the huts and war to the palaces!"

About the land, Lenin said: "The outbreak of armed insurrection, the second or October Revolution, clearly proves that the land must be handed over to the peasants." And he handed out the central committee's decree on the subject: "Landed proprietorship is abolished forthwith without compensation.... The land of peasants and Cossacks shall not be confiscated."

IX. CIVIL WAR AND RECONSTRUCTION

After the establishment of the Soviet government a series of new measures followed in rapid succession. All titles and ranks of the old regime were declared null and void. The church was separated from the state and the school from the church. Women were equalized with men in the enjoyment of civil rights, and civil marriage was introduced. A new, more simplified system of spelling was adopted, and the Gregorian calendar of the Western world was substituted for the old Julian calendar previously used in Russia. All banks were nationalized, and a government Supreme Council of National Economy was set up. There was issued a declaration granting full equality, including the right to secede, to all peoples of the former empire.

To combat the enemies of Communism a dread secret police, **the Cheka,** was created. This was a terrorist organization that dealt ruthlessly with anti-Communists. The authority of the Soviet government was rapidly extending to all parts of the former empire. It looked as if Lenin and his collaborators might achieve a gradual and peaceful transition to a socialist regime. This, however, did not take place, because very soon the government was confronted with innumerable difficulties and obstacles.

Russia was still at war with Germany. The Soviet government began peace negotiations, which were carried on in the city of Brest-Litovsk, with Trotsky representing the Soviet Republic. Early in 1918 the negotiations were broken off and the German high command began an advance with thirty divisions. Lenin wanted to obtain peace at all costs, but found himself in a slight minority in the cabinet. In February, 1918 there occurred the first clash between the newly formed Red Guards and the Germans who were moving toward Petrograd. This event is now regarded as the official birthday of the Red Army. In March, 1918, negotiations with the Germans were resumed, which led to the **Peace of Brest-Litovsk.**

According to the terms of this treaty the Germans occupied a vast area of Russia, including most of the Ukraine and parts of the Caucasus. Poland, Finland and the Baltic States remained under German control. But this treaty did not bring peace in Russia. It brought further breaches with other political parties and severe internal dissension, which grew into a bitter, bloody civil war and later also to nationalist wars with Poland, Finland and the Baltic countries. It brought also the opposition of the Allies who regarded the treaty as a betrayal.

The internal dissension broke out into civil war when Boris Savinkov, Kerensky's war minister, as leader of the Social Revolutionary party, led a revolt in July, 1918. It failed but Savinkov embarked on a program of terrorism which culminated in an attempt on Lenin's life, and the assassination of a Cheka official. The Cheka's vengeance against plotters and conspirators now became so swift and terrible that it became known as the "Red Terror." News of this terror, which spilled rivers of blood, aroused the rest of the world, and this together with the previous unpopularity of the Revolution, served to make the name Bolshevik anathema in most places. During 1918, the Bolshevik party became the Russian Communist party and thenceforth Russians, whether members of the party or not, were known as Communists.

General Kornilov again appeared on the scene and began forming a White Army to oppose the Red. Soon the entire country was engulfed in the fire of civil war. The Soviet government took over all of industry, and instead of a gradual transition to socialism there had to be introduced a regime which became known as War Communism. In the areas occupied by the Germans, guerilla warfare against the invaders began to spread rapidly. The Allied powers, which were still at war with Germany, lent their support to the Czechoslovak war prisoners in Russia, who had in the meantime organized themselves into an army. Soon all of Siberia was in the hands of the Czechoslovaks and the Whites.

At about this time in Ekaterinburg the Tsar and his family met death by execution, ordered by the local Bolshevik authorities.

Basing themselves on the Urals the Whites developed a wide offensive on the Volga. The leader of the White forces in Siberia after November, 1918, was Admiral Kolchak, who had the support of the Allies. On the western front Germany was defeated by the Allies and sued for an armistice. German and Austrian occupation of the south of Russia collapsed, but the Allies continued their undeclared war against the Soviets. In the south of Russia the leader of the White forces was General Denikin. In the Baltic area a White army was formed under General Yudenich. In the north, in Archangel, there also functioned a White government supported by the Allies. The Soviets were virtually surrounded in the center of Russia, with armies moving toward Moscow from all sides.

The White movement was most heterogeneous. It consisted of tsarists, dispossessed landlords and manufacturers, tens of thousands of officers of the old Russian Army, Constitutional Democrats, Socialist Revolutionaries, and Social Democrats of the Menshevik variety. It had one thing in common: a negative attitude to the Soviets. It had the military, financial and moral support of practically the entire outside world, but not a single positive point on which its various component groups could agree.

The first large offensive of the Whites took place in the spring of 1919. **Admiral Kolchak** was to proceed from the Volga toward Moscow, while the Denikin forces in the South and Yudenich and Miller from the North, with British and American aid, acted as auxiliary pincers. Kolchak was defeated by the Red Army and driven back into Siberia.

In the autumn of 1919 the second White offensive developed, with Denikin aiming from the South at Moscow and Yudenich and Baron Mannerheim at Petrograd. This time Denikin was defeated, and the plan collapsed.

The third onslaught took place in the spring of 1920, with the Polish Army occupying Kiev. The Poles were soon driven back. The Red Army nearly captured Warsaw, but was in turn defeated by the Poles and had to retreat. An armistice was signed with Poland in October, on terms most unfavorable to Russia, transferring land inhabited by 4,000,000 Ukrainians and Byelorussians to Polish sovereignty. Lenin wanted peace at any cost.

Thereafter the last embers of civil war flickered out. The defeated Denikin had been replaced by Wrangel who now operated from the Crimea. The Red Army drove his forces into the Black Sea by the end of the year. For a while fighting continued on a number of minor fronts, and only in 1922 did the Red Army enter Vladivostok after the departure of a formidable Japanese force which had occupied most of Russia's Far East.

In the course of the civil war, **the Red Army** grew to over five million men. While the fighting progressed the currency depreciated to zero. All monetary values were thus wiped out. In October, 1917, the Soviet government had seized power. Now, with the end of the civil war, this same government had consolidated its power. The country was cleared of numerous White armies and their friends and allies from abroad. This victory was achieved at a tremendous price. Millions of people were killed, and the country thoroughly devastated. Industrial production had declined to about one-ninth of the 1913 level. The railroad system barely functioned. There was a shortage of grain, and owing to the disorganization of transport, it was nearly impossible to transfer foodstuffs from those areas which still had a small surplus to those that were starving.

In March, 1921, Lenin announced the New Economic Policy,

or NEP. All land and heavy industry remained nationalized. Private trade was allowed to resume operations, and small-scale manufacturing of consumers' goods by private enterprise was also resumed. However, all important positions in the state continued to be held by members of the Communist Party. Lenin described the NEP as a "tactical retreat." He believed that the country needed to recuperate and gather strength for a further advance. Outside of Russia the NEP was nearly universally interpreted as a collapse of the idea of socialism. It was thought that the Bolsheviks would never be able to make good their promise to resume the advance toward socialism after the period of reconstruction and recuperation had been completed. Events, however, proved the expert opinion of the world wrong and the Bolsheviks right. In a few years the advance was resumed, but more of this later.

During the NEP period the Soviets tried to interest foreign capital in Russian reconstruction. Foreign capital, however, was either timid or holding out for better terms, one of which was the redemption of tsarist loans. Russia had to rebuild largely with her own resources, which were then very meager. Though trade agreements were signed with England and several other countries in 1921, Russia's first real recognition came in 1922 when Russia and Germany signed a full-scale mutual-friendship pact. This annoyed the other powers greatly. Apparently the two defeated powers of World War I wanted to collaborate in rebuilding their economies while the rest of the world was subjecting them to ostracism. The other powers feared the combination as a threat to the Versailles Treaty. The year 1924 was the first year of major Soviet diplomatic success. Great Britain, France and Italy followed the example of Germany and resumed full relations with the Soviets.

In 1923 the Russian Soviet republic forced the other three republics on the territory of the former empire to form the Union of Soviet Socialist Republics. These three republics were the Ukrainian, Byelorussian and the Transcaucasian Federation. Meanwhile reconstruction was progressing and by 1928 industrial production and the national income once more reached the level of 1913. Now the Bolsheviks could make good their promise to take the next step toward socialism. The NEP period was coming to a close, and the country was soon to move into a new era, that of planned industrialization.

Lenin, the man who was most active in the Revolution, in the establishment of the Soviet regime, and in the victorious conclusion of the civil war, was not destined to witness this step, which he had envisaged and planned. In January, 1924, after a prolonged illness, the founder of the first socialist state died near Moscow. Even before Lenin's death, his Politburo began quarreling as to who should succeed him. Chief contenders were Stalin and Trotsky. When Lenin died, at first the Politburo declared itself a "collective leadership"—the same slogan used twenty-nine years later by Kremlin stalwarts after Stalin's death. Oddly enough, the loudest supporter of "collective leadership" in 1924 was Stalin, who eventually killed most of the other collective leaders. Lenin died in the midst of this struggle which was to continue bitterly for some fifteen years among his successors.

In a message to the Party Lenin had warned against Stalin as his successor.

THE IMPERIAL INSIGNIA of Tsarist Russia started coming down in Kerensky days, but Lenin's people and Stalin's did not finish the job until 1935, when the big double-headed eagle was hoisted off the Kremlin to make way for the Red Star.

"NEITHER PEACE NOR WAR"

Peace was the first thing Lenin had promised Russia. Within 48 hours of the Bolsheviks' seizure of power, Foreign Minister Trotsky wirelessed all belligerents for an armistice. The anxious Allies appealed to General Dukhonin, still commander-in-chief of the Russian armies (*above, right,* on steps with hands clasped). He was deposed (and soon executed by Red soldiers). New commander-in-chief was an officer of the lowest commissioned rank, Army Ensign Nicolai Vassilevich Krylenko (*above, left*). Germany agreed to an Armistice and peace negotiations began in December at Brest-Litovsk. Delegate Trotsky's phrase, "neither peace nor war," described the upshot of this conference: Russia stopped fighting without accepting Germany's terms, which presently were made more severe after the German army moved on Petrograd. (*Below*): Prince Leopold of Bavaria, German east front commander, signing the Brest-Litovsk treaty while Russia's helpless delegates sit glumly opposite.

THE UKRAINE

Besides its Polish and Baltic territories, Russia lost the vast, rich Ukraine at Brest-Litovsk. Ostensibly the Ukraine had become autonomous in March, 1917. Actually its "Rada" (parliament) strove for complete independence. When Ukrainian grain was not delivered as scheduled in 1918, German and Austrian troops were sent in to collect, and General Skoropadsky was installed as Hetman (chief). This enraged the Ukrainians and in November when Germany collapsed, they threw out Skoropadsky, reasserted their independence under Simon Petlura (*above*). (*Left*): Hetman Skoropadsky and the Kaiser. (*Below*): German soldiers hanging Bolsheviks in the Ukraine (1918).

REFUGEES

The chaos that ensued throughout Russia after the beginning of the intervention and civil war had to be seen to be imagined. With peasants rioting for land and townspeople for bread, with "Whites" fleeing from "Reds" and vice versa, the roads and railroads were jammed with large segments of the population moving hither and thither to better their lot or save their skins. (*Above*): The "Hot Water Line" at a stop on the Trans-Siberian Railroad. (The kettles were for tea water, not bathing.)

Refugees sleeping like sardines in a church at Ekaterinburg.

Refugee life in a box car at Omsk, Siberia.

People lived for months in railway stations, like this crowd at Chelyabinsk.

Some made a break for the nearest border, and camped beside the tracks like these people who were trying to reach Lithuania.

VIOLENCE

Violence became commonplace. Where the Bolshevized peasants or workers gained control, landowners or employers were robbed, tortured, murdered. Where the Whites kept the upper hand, police or soldiers ruthlessly stamped out Bolshevism wherever found or suspected. (*Above*): A White execution squad shoots two suspects — then hangs two more, for the effect (*right*) — then lets the villagers take a look (*below*).

The Revolution which had begun as a bloodless overthrow of tsarism, now took a toll of millions. There was scarcely a nook in the vast expanse of Russia where the populace was not divided into Reds and Whites.

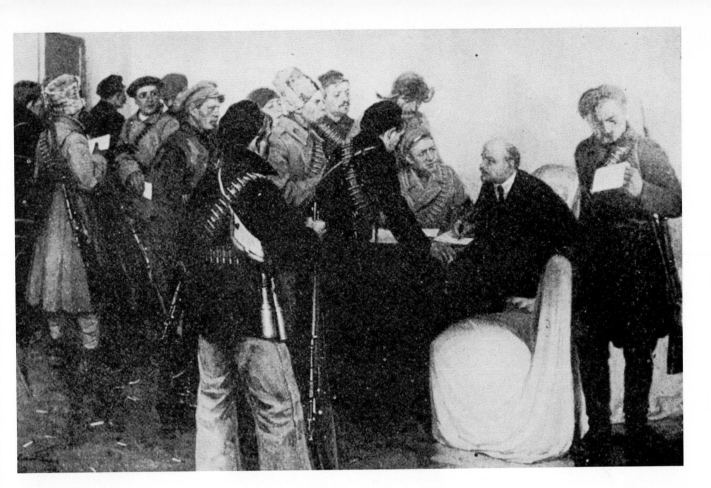

RED TERROR

Lenin, tireless at his desk in the Smolny Institute (*above*) whence the Government was moved to Moscow when the Germans threatened Petrograd, did not hesitate to use cruelty and violence systematically. He said it was ridiculous to expect a proletarian revolution to succeed without terror. His chief assistant in reorganizing Russia's industrial functions was Yakov Sverdlov (*left*), for whom Ekaterinburg in the Ural mining region was renamed. "Cheka," the Red Terror organization (Extraordinary Commission for the Suppression of Counter-Revolution, Sabotage and Speculation) was entrusted to Felix Dzerzhinsky (*right*), a brilliant Pole, who coined a slogan: "Better to arrest ten innocent people than let one guilty person go free."

CZECH LEGION

In March, 1918, the Soviet Government agreed to grant passage through Siberia to 45,000 Czech and Slovak soldiers who, encouraged by Professor Thomas Masaryk, had deserted Austria-Hungary and wanted to get around the world to fight on the Allies' western front. Strung out across Siberia in their trains (*above*), these Czech Legionnaires heard (erroneously) that the Bolsheviks were arming German and Austrian prisoners in Siberia for an ambush. The Czechs electrified the Allies by seizing the Trans-Siberian, easily overcoming local Bolshevik forces, including the guards of Russia's gold reserve, which they took with them from Kazan. They took Vladivostok, a White government was set up and, with Allied approval, the Czechs started back westward to fight the Bolsheviks. (*Left*): Czech General Gaida and staff at Ekaterinburg in the Urals, where they arrived too late to avert the massacre of the Romanov family, who thus died as hostages to the political clock.

END OF THE ROMANOVS

From Tsarskoe-Selo, Nicholas II and his family were moved to Tobolsk in Siberia by the Kerensky government. The Bolsheviks brought them back to Ekaterinburg in the Urals, where they were closely quartered in the home of a merchant named Ipatiev (*below*). This version of what happened there is generally accepted as true: When word came that the Czechs were headed for Ekaterinburg, the local Bolsheviks charged by Moscow with the deposed emperor's custody, became panicky. They voted a mass execution. The local Commissar, Yurovsky, roused Nicholas and family in the night (July 16, 1918) and took them to the cellar with a firing squad. He read the sentence. When Nicholas started to say something, Yurovsky whipped out his pistol and shot for the head. The firing squad did the rest. From jewelry and dental work found among certain ashes, it has been deduced that all seven bodies were later soaked in oil and burned at a remote spot in the forest. (*Above, left*): A photograph of Nicholas made by his wife at Tobolsk, where he suffered a chill. (*Above, right*): Nicholas and children sunning themselves over a greenhouse in Tobolsk (last photograph).

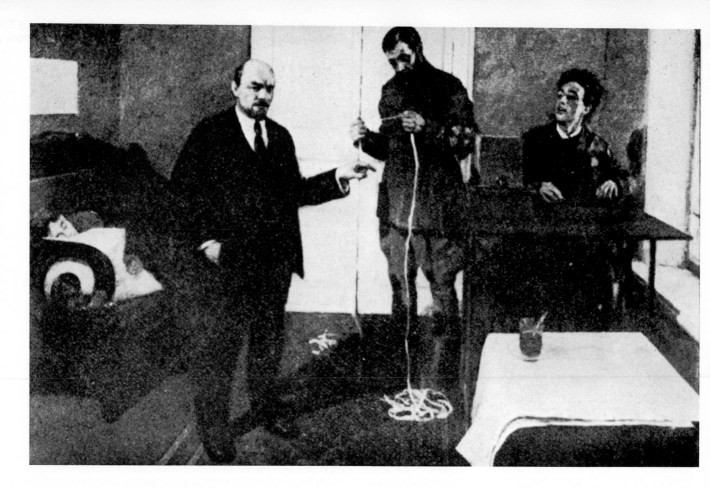

WAR ON SIX FRONTS

The Bolsheviks' belief that their revolution would be the precursor and inspiration for a rising of the world proletariat, aroused world-wide alarm. There was also a strong school of Allied thought which believed Lenin & Co. were tools of Germany, from whom Russia's withdrawal from the war removed great pressure, and the Allies viewed darkly the supplies promised at Brest-Litovsk. The Allies jumped in wherever they could to help Russia's Whites stamp out the Reds. Besides their internal problems, the Bolsheviks had to cope during 1918-1921 with the armed forces of fourteen foreign powers, on six fronts. Lenin spent a great deal of his time reading his generals' despatches at the direct wire from these war zones (*above*).

THE BALTIC. White Russians, Germans and Finns pressed the Bolsheviks on a Baltic front, with the British Navy joining in an ill-advised attack on the Kronstadt fortress. (*See below.*)

German General von der Golz, after Germany capitulated to the Allies, kept a large segment of the German Army intact, especially officers, by enlisting it in the anti-Bolshevik campaign along the Baltic. The Allies welcomed his aid, though it contravened Versailles.

White General Yudenich, with more than 150,000 men (including von der Golz's), was stopped at Pulkovo just outside Petrograd in October, 1919, by a last-ditch defense of the 7th Red Army, aided by the people of Petrograd, who dug trenches and filled sandbags.

Baron Mannerheim, with assistance from Germany, put down a rising of Finland's Reds and helped the Yudenich push for Petrograd. This was the first conspicuous appearance of a man who was to become anathema to all Soviet citizens.

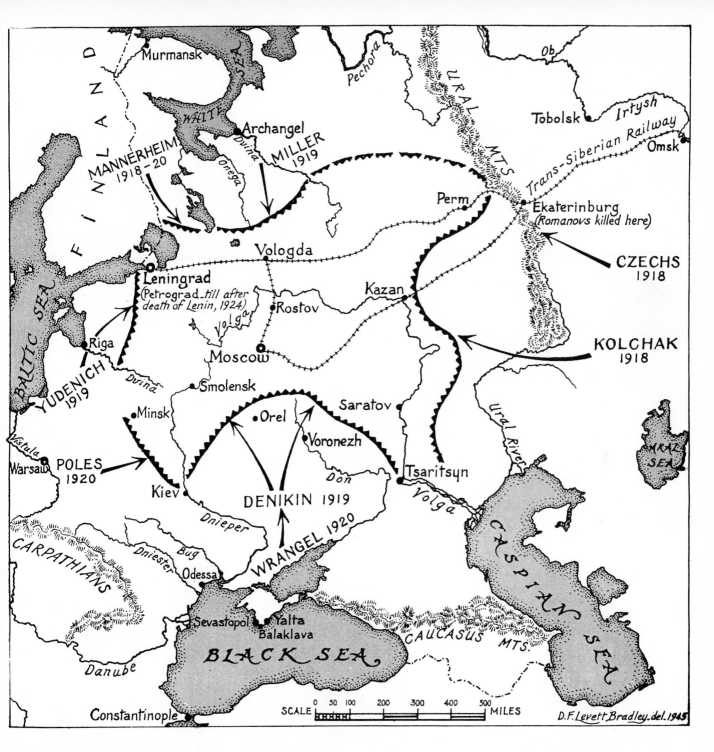

RUSSIA'S CIVIL WAR FRONTS

The above map is a synthesis in time. It shows how the Red Revolution was compressed and constricted by combined forces from the outer world, not all at one moment, but over a period of three years (1918-1921). It indicates how close Russian Communism came to early defeat in the civil war, which Soviet historians still have trouble explaining how Communism won.

The map also reflects the fact that, unlike the Civil War in the United States — which was strictly geographical in its economic aspect — the civil war in Russia was universal. On every front the Reds had local Whites to fight — the smallest village was often divided within itself in a confused, desperate turmoil that set kin against kin.

The Six Fronts were:

1. North — from Lake Ladoga to the Dvina River, and then vaguely east to the Urals.

2. East — down the Urals and the Volga basin to the Caspian.

3. Southeast — where the British struck for the oilfields.

4. South — where Denikin and later Wrangel struck out of the Crimean base.

5. Southwest — on the line Minsk-Kiev where the Poles struck in 1920.

6. Northwest — where von der Golz and Yudenich struck for Petrograd.

WAR ON SIX FRONTS

THE URALS

Following the success of the Czechs in Siberia, the Allies got behind Tsarist-Admiral Kolchak for an eastern front beyond the Urals. Kolchak set up as "Supreme Ruler of Russia" at Omsk. In the spring of 1919 he started an offensive which was soon halted on its northern wing but required all the Bolsheviks' efforts to stop short of Simbirsk and Samara. Guerrilla warfare at his rear then weakened Kolchak who withdrew his "government" that autumn to Irkutsk, where he was caught and shot by the Reds in February, 1920. (*Above*): White troops on their way to the Ural front. (*Left*): Admiral Kolchak's troops retreating after their defeat by the Reds near Ufa (northeast of Tsaritsyn).

Rear-Admiral Alexander Kolchak, brave and impetuous, was only 45 when he died. He entered the Russian navy at 13, served in the Russo-Jap war, explored polar regions, commanded a destroyer squadron in the Baltic in 1914, the Black Sea Fleet in 1918, land troops later.

Nicholai Sokolov was a White who, in this disguise, passed through the Red lines and joined Kolchak, for whom he investigated the mass-murder of the Imperial family at Ekaterinburg. He got the names of those responsible and first pieced the story together for historians.

Professor Masaryk gained most, as Kolchak lost most, in the Siberian interlude touched off by the doughty Czech Legion. On November 14, 1918, Masaryk was elected first president of Czecho-Slovakia, whose recognition by the Allies the Legion's performance had helped to win.

THE SOUTH

In the south of Russia, White resistance to the Bolsheviks was continued in 1918 by Generals Kornilov and Alexeyev. When the former was killed in action and the latter died, the Southern command passed to General Denikin (*left*) who, in June, 1919, succeeded where others had failed: he captured Tsaritsyn (now Stalingrad). He also took the Ukraine, the Don and Donets basins and was approaching Moscow when a slashing Red offensive that reached Rostov, cut Denikin's armies in two. Denikin's remnants were taken over by Baron Wrangel (*right*), but he had not gotten far from his base in Crimea when the Reds, in the autumn of 1920, pushed him into the Black Sea. Many of his men (perhaps 130,000), reached safety in Turkey, whence they made their way to Europe and the United States, becoming the familiar "White Russians." Stalin served as an army political commissar in these campaigns (*above*).

WAR ON SIX FRONTS

THE FAR NORTH

To keep Allied munitions out of Germany's hands, Britain swiftly landed troops at Murmansk soon after the peace of Brest-Litovsk. An expeditionary force to Archangel followed, commanded by Brigadier-General Ironside and including a U. S. contingent. Its history makes strange reading when laid beside the heroic efforts of the same nationals to supply the Red Army via the north a generation later. The British and American troops did little fighting, but supplied munitions to the local White Russians in an effort curiously akin to a later more heroic effort when the West would supply the Reds against Hitler's surprise attack and full-scale war (*see* p. 328).

(*Above*): Convoy landing the first U. S. troops in North Russia (September, 1918).

(*Left*): British replacements embarking for Archangel, wearing what they called their "Bolshie caps."

RUSSIAN GENERAL MILLER was the White chief on the Far North front.

BRITISH GENERAL KNOX represented the Tories behind Intervention.

BRITISH BRIG.-GEN. IRONSIDE was called "Baron of Archangel."

STEVENS COMMISSION

In the winter of 1918-1919, a commission of U. S. railroad engineers under John F. Stevens of the Erie R.R., one of the Panama Canal engineers landed in Vladivostok to recondition and run the Trans-Siberian and its feeder line, the Chinese Eastern. Supporting and guarding the railroaders' work was the chief mission of General Graves and his troops after the Bolsheviks came to power. (*Right*): The Stevens Commission in Vladivostok. The old gentleman with flaring whiskers is White Russian General Horvat, who for a time headed up anti-Bolshevik forces rallying in Manchuria. (*Below, right*): The railroad bridge over the Amur river at Khabarovsk, a prime link guarded by the Allied forces. (*Below*): General Graves who reported that 90% of eastern Siberia's populace were pro-Bolshevik; that it would be best to let the Reds run their own show. He and his U. S. troops left Vladivostok before midsummer, 1920 (*bottom*).

THE RED ARMY

One of the major considerations behind General Graves's judgment that Russia had best be let alone, was the Red Army. By the winter of 1919-1920, the Red Army had grown from a rabble to a trained force of 5,000,000 men. Its 1st Mounted Army, in which Stalin was commissar (*above*), split Denikin's armies and captured Rostov. When the Reds celebrated the Revolution's third anniversary, an impressive, disciplined force of Red Guardsmen were on hand in Siberia (*left*). But not until 1922 did the Red Army finally take over Vladivostok from the lingering Japanese.

OFFICIAL BIRTHDAY of the Red Army is February 24, 1918, when volunteer detachments of Bolsheviks clashed with the oncoming Germans on the approaches to Petrograd. These volunteers were factory workers who, with or without uniforms, after a few days of training, simply went to the front and started shooting off their guns in response to commands by Red officers whom they chose to obey.

UP FROM SCRATCH

Lenin said that the Russian Army "decided the question of peace or war with its feet." That is, it just walked home. About 2,000,000 men were marked down as "deserters." These men also decided the question of the Revolution's survival. They took their rifles home with them. When the moment came to go to the barricades, or fight as guerillas in field and forest, the Communists had a nucleus of arms which the ex-soldiers either used themselves or shared with civilians. From what desperate rock-bottom the Red Army was evolved is suggested by photos (*above* and *right*) of the kind of "soldier" the Bolsheviks started with in Polish territory.

"Communist Detachment" is the title of the painting below, which accurately reflects the mixture of "deserter" soldiers and sailors and stalwart civilians who, in the cities, formed the first units of "The Peasants' and Workers' Red Army."

TROTSKY'S JOB

"The Peasants' and Workers' Red Army is to be created of the most class-conscious and organized elements of the working classes," wrote Lenin, on the same day the Brest-Litovsk Peace was signed. In other words: no conscription — at first. The creating job was taken over by Leon Trotsky, whose chief problem was finding officers. Quite naturally he availed himself of Tsarist officers, but Communist Commissars were appointed to make and keep the new army Red. Trotsky's chief accomplishments were in whipping up martial patriotism (*left*), converting armed rabble into a disciplined army and in organizing officer schools which graduated 1,700 cadets in 1918, 12,000 in 1919, 26,000 in 1920. (*Above*): Cadets on parade before Trotsky. (*Below*): A review of some Red Army reservists in 1920.

Commissar Trotsky carried the use of posters to a new high. Mass meetings replaced recruiting booths. And to Trotsky may be credited the invention of the propaganda train — itinerant ensembles of speakers, agitators, leaflet writers equipped with printing presses, banners, even motion pictures. Trotsky himself, with his impassioned diction and gestures, was the greatest spell-binder of them all. "Father of the Red Army" he was called — until Stalinist propaganda later vilified him.

THE POLES — PLUS WEYGAND

In 1919, the Reds proposed peace and the end of intervention to the Versailles Peace Conference. The Big Four (Lloyd George, Orlando, Clemenceau, Wilson — *right*) approved, and President Wilson proposed a parley on the Isle of Prinkipo in the Sea of Marmora. But the Whites believed just then that they had the Red Army licked. They killed the Prinkipo plan. Intervention continued another two years.

The Soviets reaffirmed Kerensky's grant of Poland's independence but refused to grant Polish claims for the frontiers of 1772. Allying themselves with the Ukrainian turncoat Petlura, the Poles struck east and took Kiev in May, 1920. Red cavalry force-marched 600 miles from the Caucasus, retook Kiev. In August, 1920, Red armies stood before Warsaw and Lvov. Britain and France rushed support to Marshal Pilsudski (*below,* dining with his staff). France sent Ambassador Jusserand and foxy little General Weygand (*left*). The latter outgeneraled the impetuous, poorly supplied Reds and peace was signed at Riga in October with Poland's new frontiers including millions of Byelorussians and Ukrainians.

TROTSKY'S GENERALS

Dissensions among the Whites and the Allies; short interior lines of communication as against long exterior lines; the adherence of many whole units of the Imperial armies; stockpiles furnished to old Russia by the Allies but seized by the Reds — these are some of the explanations advanced for the miraculous feat of the Reds who, after being compressed into a tight corner by the coalition armies, broke out and recaptured their country. Basic explanation was Lenin's application of "war communism" — total war — to which the Russian proletariat responded. Some other explanations are to be seen on this page — some of the Red Army's founders and first leaders.

KLEMENTY ("KLIM") VOROSHILOV (*above*), son of a railway worker, had a revolutionist record going back to 1896 when, at 15, he began organizing and agitating in the mines and factories of his native Don district. At Lugansk in early 1917 he formed one of the first local Red regiments to fight the Germans. Out of such detachments, locally raised and led, were later welded the Red armies which ultimately whipped the Whites and in which Voroshilov, trusted by Stalin, rose steadily to become War Commissar (1925–1940) and the Red Army's second "father."

NICHOLAI SCHORS (hand raised) was another original organizer of Red detachments in 1917, recruiting and fighting primarily in his native Ukraine, where he was one of the few pro-Bolshevik leaders.

VASILI IVANOVICH CHAPAYEV, a village carpenter near the Caspian, typifies the local insurgents who, having fought as guerillas to win their homes and villages from the Whites, did not at first welcome it when the Reds sent officers and political commissars to incorporate them into the growing Red Army.

SEMYON BUDENNY, a herdsman of Voronezh, served the Tsar in the Dragoons, later became a Red guerilla. "To horse, proletarians!" was his recruiting cry. With Voroshilov, he created the 1st Mounted Army, later trained reserves. His men used to say that he could win battles by his superb profanity alone.

MICHAEL FRUNZE was a Kirghiz peasant, schooled in Socialism at St. Petersburg and in exile. During 1917-1918 he emerged as a leader in soldier Soviets, rising to command the Eastern Front. He succeeded Trotsky in 1924 as War Commissar. He authored the military strategy followed by Stalin's Russia.

ICONOCLASM

For its professed atheism, the Soviet Government was excommunicated by Patriarch Tikhon, who took office just as the Reds were seizing the Kremlin. The Reds clamped down on religion of all persuasions but especially, of course, upon the Orthodox Church. Whatever their sympathies were before, this move lined up the prelates and the church almost solidly against the Reds. Red soldiers were the government's agents of suppression, and smuggled pictures of them stripping churches (*above*) supposedly to convert church icons and other treasure to war uses or famine relief, helped arouse world opinion against Communism. (*Right*): Effigy of Patriarch Tikhon mocked by a crowd. Not for two decades was peace to be established between the Russian Orthodox Church and the Soviet Government.

FAMINE

Famine threatened Russia from 1916 on, but did not grip the country until 1921-1922. Then it was aggravated by a bad drought, and the condition of large masses of the populace was indescribably miserable. The Near East Relief authenticated reports of Russian children running wild in homeless, starving bands. (*Above*): Small beggars "indulging in cigarets as a nerve-soother." N.E.R. Worker Davidson with some children he rounded up in Transcaucasia.

Soldiers, war workers and children had priority on food during these dark, empty days. (*Left*): Even "poor" peasants — backbone of the Red Army — had to queue up for the few "industry products" (consumer goods, like clothes) available during the civil war. Fuel and transport were even more scarce than food in the cities.

(*Below*): A common sight in new Red Russia, dumping fuel logs in a public square where the people could "come and get it."

THE U.S.S.R.

Blazoned proudly by their publicists were the original members of the group who put over the October Revolution in 1917 and still had the country functioning when their first anniversary came around. Reading to the right from Lenin they are Pokrovsky (historian), Kamenev, Sverdlov, Lunacharsky (education), Kollontai, Krylenko, Zinoviev, Bukharin, Trotsky, Rykov and Radek. Conspicuous is the absence from this inner circle of Joseph Stalin who became Commissar for Nationalities and drew up the constitution whereby, in 1923, Russia became the Union of Soviet Socialist Republics. Below is the historic first meeting of delegates from the constituent republics to elect their first president (Michael Kalinin) in the imperially ornate coronation room of the Kremlin, August 4, 1923.

LENIN'S FUNERAL

In 1918, Lenin was wounded in an attempt at assassination by Fanya Kaplan, agent of Savinkov. It is undetermined whether this wound, or overwork, was responsible for a stroke he suffered in 1922. He retired, recovered, relapsed, and died January 21, 1924. Through the snow from his suburban retreat, thousands of mourners followed his body to its state resting place in Moscow, where nearly a million more filed by, standing in line for hours at 30° below zero, many of them for their first look at the man who had given them his life. The widow Krupskaya (*left*) lived for 15 years, a sort of mother-superior of the Communist Party. Finally, Lenin's embalmed body, under glass and still visible, was laid in a monster tomb of black granite in Moscow's historic Red Square (*see next chapter*).

X. PEOPLE, GOVERNMENT AND LEADERS

By the eve of World War II, the Soviet Union was a highly centralized federation consisting of 16 Union Republics. Inside many of these republics there existed further subdivisions. The Russian Republic, largest of the 16 both in territory and population, contained 15 subsidiary autonomous republics, six autonomous regions, ten national districts. When the Soviet Union was formed in 1923 there were only four Union Republics. By 1937 there were already 11, to which five were added before Hitler attacked on June 22, 1941.

Linguistic Autonomy was enjoyed by the Union Republics. Since a dictatorship can never be a true federation, the Stalin Constitution gave the U.S.S.R. central government full power over foreign affairs, defense, foreign trade, police, economic planning, taxes and budgets, banking, insurance, land, natural resources, education, public health, labor, and the judicial system. In addition, the U.S.S.R. central government owned and operated most industry, transportation and stores, as well as all state farms and machine-tractor stations. Thus the governments of Union Republics and other political subdivisions had little authority, and mainly served as local agents to carry out U.S.S.R. orders. The question is often raised: why do these Union Republics, autonomous republics, autonomous regions and national districts exist? The answer is found in the Soviet nationality policy.

Since the days of Ivan the Terrible (1533-1584) Russia was, as we have seen, a multi-national state. As Russia slowly expanded from a small Muscovite principality into a Eurasian empire, Ukrainians, Poles, Armenians, Turks, Mongols, Laplanders and more than fifty other nationalities came under the Tsarist yoke. Their languages ranged from Indo-European to Finnish, Semitic and Chinese; their religions from Roman Catholic and Lutheran to Buddhist and Moslem. Their native cultures varied just as widely. Often the upper class of these minority races became Russified and cooperated with the ruling Russians. But the native masses remained stubbornly nationalistic and anti-Russian. To control these minority races, which by the late 19th Century constituted half the population of the Russian empire, Moscow pursued a policy of "divide and rule." Each racial minority was turned against the other, and all were against the Jews.

To the increased anger of the minor nationalities, Tsardom attempted a policy of extreme Russification. The official slogan was "one Tsar, one language (Russian), and one religion (Russian Orthodox)." In discussing the nationalities problem before the Bolshevik Revolution, Lenin referred to Russia as the "prison of peoples." People who then had never heard of Lenin would probably have agreed with this description.

When Lenin's Bolsheviks seized power in 1917, Finland, the Baltic states, Poland, the Ukraine, the Caucasus and Turkestan all revolted from Russia in an attempt at racial independence. To the Finns, Ukrainians, *et al.,* Russians were anathema, no matter whether Tsarist or Red. By 1920, most of the racial rebels had been reconquered by the Red Army. But Lenin and Stalin, the Commissar of Nationalities, had to devise a nationality program which would ensure Moscow control, yet be at least partially palatable to the reconquered minorities.

The Nationality Policy of the Soviet government is a subtle change from that of the empire. All races are legally equal in the U.S.S.R. Most of them have the right to use their own language, have their own national press and theaters, send their children to their own schools. Native customs, culture and art are encouraged, as long as they do not become unduly nationalistic. The areas of the more important minority races are honored with the title of Union Republic, which ensures that the language of the racial minority is the official language of that region.

Lesser minorities receive the title of autonomous republic, autonomous region or national district for their living space, also retaining linguistic autonomy. Minorities who misbehave politically sometimes lose this language privilege. Some fairly large nationalities, such as Russia's 190,000 Koreans, never received linguistic autonomy.

Moreover, Soviet Russia continued the Russification program of the Tsars, though far more cleverly and quietly. Russian is a compulsory language in all non-Russian schools. In most non-Russian republics and regions, Russians held the real positions of power. The Soviet press constantly portrayed the Russians as the leading race, which all minorities should try to emulate. As in Tsarist times, many intellectuals of the racial minorities were wooed into the Russian camp. In many respects, the old Tsarist slogan remained true, with one Tsar (Stalin), one supreme language (Russian), one religion (Communism).

Besides political dictatorship and subtle Russification, **Economic Uniformity** tied the many races of the U.S.S.R. together. Most of the working population in the cities were state employees, living in state-owned housing. The majority of adults in rural regions were collective farmers, or members of fishing, hunting or shepherd cooperatives operated under tight state control. All people paid heavy taxes, which amounted to 60% of their income, to finance the armament and industrialization burdens of the Five-Year Plans. Both urban and rural workers, state or cooperative, were paid on a piece-work basis wherever possible, with sharp gradations in income according to the amount and quality of the work performed. Though little publicized, some private enterprise still existed in the form of self-employed artisans, non-collectivized peasants, peasant food markets in the cities, and the large private gardens of almost every rural resident. In general, because of the government's sacrifice of everything else to build a huge heavy industry, the economy was one of scarcity of consumer goods.

In Communist terminology, this economic phase was described as "Socialism." Official promises were made that in the future would come "Communism" with equal pay for all work, no private enterprise, and an abundance of consumer goods. Hope for this distant, better future somewhat encouraged younger Soviet citizens to endure the privations of the early Five-Year Plans.

Another unifying factor in the multi-national U.S.S.R. was the **Communist Party.** By the late 1930's, all pretense was dropped that this was a party of proletarians. Instead, it was openly proclaimed a "party of leaders." Most high officials in government, industry, army, education, and labor unions were party members. The Party had strict discipline, the members had to follow the Stalinist line, and in this way unified action and control were assured. Never very large, the Party had only 2,477,000 members and candidate members in 1939. But members were recruited for their leadership ability, rather than belief in Marxism alone. Stalin was the Secretary-General of the Central Committee of the Party, hence chief Party executive and actual ruler of the U.S.S.R., beginning soon after Lenin's death. So powerful was the Party secretaryship that the Georgian dictator did not bother to take any high governmental post until he assumed the U.S.S.R. premiership in 1941.

After Lenin's death, a bitter struggle for the succession ensued in the Party Politburo (policy-making body). The Soviet future was hotly debated. Trotsky insisted on fast world revolution, or in his words "permanent revolution." Kamenev and Zinoviev wanted the U.S.S.R. to export foodstuffs and minerals, but depend on imports from capitalist countries for its manufactured goods. Bukharin opposed collectivization of agriculture, offering heavy taxation of private farms as an alternative. In contrast, Stalin stood for collective farming, fast industrialization, and strengthening the U.S.S.R. before continuing world revolution. Cleverly maneuvering his rivals against each other, in a few years Stalin removed all of them from positions of power. Trotsky was exiled to Turkestan, and in 1929 was deported from the Soviet Union.

Large-scale industrialization was launched in 1928, accompanied by forced agricultural collectivization. The process was difficult and painful, and Russian industrial and educational backwardness was a terrific handicap. Suffering was immense, but the program progressed.

In December 1934, a young Politburo member, handsome **Sergei Kirov,** was assassinated by a Leningrad Communist. The murderer, whom Stalin immediately questioned in private, had been influenced by the writings of the dictator's old rivals. Stalin, apparently frightened, used the murder as an excuse to accuse these rivals of conspiracy and treason. The world was shocked by the spectacle of dozens of prominent men with extensive revolutionary records being publicly tried and executed. Each of these had hundreds of friends and followers who were also purged, then "friends of friends" fell victim, until finally almost no Soviet citizen was safe. Millions were arrested, imprisoned or demoted. In 1938 Stalin stopped this slaughter by purging the police. By then, most provincial and central high officials, half of the army field officers, and half the entire party membership were purge victims. Stalin had created a legacy of hatred, which 15 years later his successors tried to disavow.

The story of Russia's internal political development would not be complete without mentioning some of its external repercussions. In March 1919, the Comintern or Third (Communist) International was founded by Lenin to unite the Communist parties of the world under his leadership. In this organization, the U.S.S.R. Communist Party was always dominant. The Comintern openly strove for world revolution, and also constantly aided U.S.S.R. foreign policy.

Meanwhile, desire for Russian trade led to the gradual recognition of the Soviet regime by other powers. In 1922 Germany recognized the U.S.S.R. In 1924, England, France and Italy established diplomatic relations. The United States extended recognition in 1933.

"LENIN IS DEAD: LENINISM LIVES" — such has been Russia's watchword since 1924, such is the portent of Lenin's mausoleum in the Red Square where, embalmed under glass for all Russians to behold, Lenin's corpse lies in state after three decades. But all the world knows that within five years of Lenin's death, "Leninism" began to become "Stalinism."

THE COMMUNIST PARTY

The Communist Party (as the Bolsheviks renamed themselves after seizing power in Russia) was conceived by Lenin as merely the Russian mother-chapter of a worldwide workers' fraternity whose aim, as laid down by Marx and Engels, should be the overthrow of capitalism everywhere, the erection of a world fellowship owned and controlled for the benefit of all by the ultimate producers of wealth and power: the Workers.

To understand the pure Communist lexicon at all, two of its concepts are essential: (1) That the proletariat (persons without any capital or means of exploiting labor) must be society's dominant class; (2) That the proletarian state must own all means of producing wealth such as land, factories, mines, transportation, power.

The basic difficulty encountered by the Communists in Russia from the outset was that the people were 85% agricultural and the peasants, having at last obtained land during the Revolution, did not at all wish to regard it or its products as belonging to the State. Despite this obstacle, Lenin founded his Communist party so solidly as a series of political cells throughout the land, and as the only political party allowed (after July, 1918), that it managed to hold its position and carry out most of its program in Russia.

(*Above*): Central Committee Meeting in session. The higher a Communist official became, the more careful he had to be to dress roughly lest he appear bourgeois (*i.e.* propertied, and possessed of social graces).

(*Below*): The splendor of the throne-room in the Kremlin did not disqualify it as a meeting-place for Communists.

THE COMINTERN

The Third or Communist International (there had been two earlier Marxist Internationals, which petered out) was called together in Moscow by Lenin and Trotsky in 1919 while the capitalist world was still wrangling over the peace at Versailles. Amid terrific fanfare Lenin called for world revolution, which program met with no immediate success because: (1) most Western countries (unlike Russia) still had well-rooted social systems in which radicals weighed little; (2) countries like India, Persia, Turkey, where the masses might have listened to the Russian theme, were developing nationalist movements of their own (*Above*): Entrance to the Third International (1921).

The Comintern thus in time became an appendage of the party and government in Russia, though the latter was still regarded by the Communists only as a springboard for revolution throughout the world.

Two typical scenes in the early history of the Third International are shown below. (*Left*): The Oriental delegations at Moscow, flag-waving hopefully. (*Right*): Italy's socialist leaders looking like six of the seven Tailors of Tooley Street after "declaring their adherence to the Third International."

THE KOMSOMOL

Controlling all power, all privileges and the entire press, the Communist Party organized a political reserve for itself — the Young Communist League, or Komsomol. Youngsters who proved smart and disciplined in the Komsomol might aspire to Party membership and even to public office. Essence of the scheme is to be seen in the eager face of Dusya Vinogradova

(*right*), an able young weaver who "made" the Supreme Soviet of the U.S.S.R. She is addressing a Komsomol congress. (*Left*): Komsomol neophytes (railroad workers).

Junior auxiliary of the Comintern, was the Communist Youth International. When it met in Moscow's Grand Opera House for its convention (*below*), its top slogan banner read: "MILITANT GREETINGS TO YOUNG REVOLUTIONISTS LANGUISHING IN PRISONS OF CAPITAL."

BREAD BEFORE CIRCUSES

American housewives, who had a small taste of rationing in World War II, can understand faintly the plight of Russia's housewives (*left*) during the War Communism of 1918-1921. Not just a few food items, shoes and gasoline, but *all of life's necessities* were obtainable by government permit only. And only certain people could get permits. Private enterprise, buying and selling *anything*, were outlawed. Small wonder that Lenin had to "retreat" into a New Economic Policy, allowing some private manufacturing and return to private trade in consumer goods. Before he could win Russia's masses to Socialist ideas, he had to give them Bread. (*Above*): Queuing up under war Communism. (*Below*): A Moscow bazaar street after NEP lifted the bars and consumer goods became available.

TORGSIN

As the Soviet leaders planned for industrialization, they needed additional foreign exchange to pay for imported machinery and technical skill. For this purpose, "Torgsin" stores were opened to sell off, for marks, francs, dollars and sterling (from tourists or from any Russians who had it), art treasures and other wealth taken from churches, the nobility and rich bourgeoisie. In even greater volume, Torgsin also sold luxury goods. Foreigners could buy fancy cheeses, embroidered shirts, real cognac, champagne. This lasted until 1935. (*Right and lower left*): Two Torgsin stores and (*above*) some of their art wares. (*Lower right*): One of the first good state department stores opened for Russians, at Dnieprostroi, to raise the morale of dam-builders there.

"COMMUNISTS –
– BUT NOT COMMUNISM"

When a delegation from Russia went to Genoa in 1922 to discuss war debts and peace credits with the other nations, Soviet spokesman Radsutak (*right,* between Soviet Delegates Litvinov and Joffe) was able to say: "In Russia today you can find Communists — but not Communism." Lenin's retreat into NEP indeed was the end of pure Communism, and other nations breathed easier beholding it. But Russia's refusal to pay pre-revolutionary debts left the Russian issues dangling at the Genoa Conference (*below*).

Russia sought to obtain credits and attract foreign capital but the world remained distrustful, waiting to see if the Reds would swing even farther back toward capitalism.

RAPALLO AND REVENGE

For their "safety," Italy housed the Soviet delegates miles outside of Genoa, with guards at the gate (*left*). The Russians felt imprisoned — or quarantined. Before leaving, they slipped over to nearby Rapallo and signed a friendship treaty with the other European country then in disgrace — Germany. At once everyone began to fear these two might join hands in a war of revenge. This fear was ill-founded, for the democratic Weimar republic was toothless. All that it sought at this time was economic convalescence through trade with its equally needy neighbor. During the 1920's, hundreds of German experts went to Russia.

PARIS AND LONDON
– 1924

Chief wanglers for Red Russia's recognition by Europe were Foreign Minister George Chicherin (*above*), Leo Kamenev (who married Trotsky's sister) and the NEP's promoter, Leonid Krassin (*right, behind Kamenev*). In 1921 a trade arrangement was reached with Great Britain which *Punch* cartooned for what it was (*below, right*). Germany recognized Russia in 1922 and signed a mutual assistance pact, but recognition by Britain did not follow until 1924, in which year both Italy and France also unbent.

But all of these countries were afraid of the Comintern's propagandizing through native agitators like the lady (*below*) in London's Hyde Park who helped promote the general strike. Even the leftist government of French Premier Herriot told Krassin that Comintern monkey-business must stop — but it didn't.

ENVOYS EXTRAORDINARY.

PRIME MINISTER (*to Bolshevist Delegates*) "HAPPY TO SEE YOU, GENTLEMEN, BUT WOULD YOU MIND GOING ROUND BY THE TRADESMEN'S ENTRANCE, JUST FOR THE LOOK OF THE THING?"

TRIUMVIRATE TAKES OVER

When Lenin died, Trotsky was south resting. The triumvirate which took over, leaving him out, was Zinoviev, Kamenev and the laconic, calculating Secretary of the Party: Stalin. All three were longtime friends of Lenin, the basic difference being that Stalin had always worked for the Party and the Revolution inside Russia. Zinoviev and Kamenev were "internationalists" after long residence outside of Russia. A lot of old revolutionists who had constantly risked their necks at home disliked it when expatriates like these two (and Trotsky, who came all the way back from New York) returned to rule the roost in 1917. In 1924, Zinoviev (*above, left*) was head of the Comintern; Kam-

enev (*center*) was vice-chairman of the People's Commissars. They aided Stalin (*right*) in outmaneuvering the fiery Trotsky in party councils. Eventually Stalin was to execute them both, and exile Trotsky, who would meet an unpleasant and equivocal destiny far from home.

It was Ramsay MacDonald's first Labor Government which recognized the Russia run by this triumvirate. And it was a letter ascribed to Zinoviev, telling British Communists how to seize power, that overthrew MacDonald (*below, left*) within a year. Conservative Stanley Baldwin (*below, right*) pressed the Red issue and severed diplomatic relations with the Soviet Union in 1927, after Britain's paralyzing general strike in which the Comintern aided the strikers.

"E PLURIBUS ..."

The idea was to build up a strong Union by binding the parts into a whole under Moscow's strict control. The following pages show some of the 180-odd racial and national minorities now embraced within the U.S.S.R. Author of the basic constitution under which all these people were forcibly united was Joseph Stalin.

On this page are inhabitants of Outer Mongolia which, since a Red-fostered revolution of 1921, is nominally independent, but actually, for all economic and political purposes, an unincorporated 1,000,000 sq. mi. of the U.S.S.R., including the Gobi Desert. This part of the world, as much Chinese as it was Russian (if not more so), was to become an outlandish meeting-ground for Communism as developed in west and east Asia. (*Right*): Mongolian monk calling his people to prayer.

For chart and map of the U.S.S.R.'s components, see pp. 246-8.

FOREIGN MINISTER CHICHERIN dressed Mongol style to receive Mongol visitors, a courtesy extended to all racial groups. (*Below*): Mongols washing wool in a communal wool-washery.

TUVAN-NASTEE & FAMILY. He (in 1926) was assistant finance minister of Tannu-Tuva, in the northwest corner of Outer Mongolia, a statesman more astute than this pose suggests.

BALTIC PEOPLES

The U.S.S.R. forcibly annexed 3 Baltic countries in 1940, making them the Estonian, Latvian and Lithuanian S.S.R.'s, whose state emblems (typical of all — with Red Star, rising sun, hammer & sickle) are shown at right. The Karelian-Finnish S.S.R. (top emblem) was also added in 1940 along the Finnish border and the White Sea's west coast. Here the population is predominantly Finno-Ugrian except in the towns and on the coast, where the fisher-folk (*above*) are descendants of medieval emigrants from Novgorod.

THE PRIPET MARSHES (*left*) contain not only water lillies and wild fowl but, for centuries, have spelled security to Russia against attack from the west between Smolensk and Kiev. They lie in the Byelo (White)-russia S.S.R., which was one of the original four.

THE HAMMER & SICKLE, old time symbol of international socialism, representing the union of industry and agriculture, was criticized as archaic during debates on the new Constitution in 1936. Some critics wanted to substitute a drop-forge and a tractor, or other symbols of industrial and agricultural modernity. But Stalin said: "One could not change the Soviet seal every few years to keep pace with mechanical progress."

ARCTIC PEOPLES

From the White Sea eastward to Bering Strait along the Arctic Circle it is nearly 4,000 miles. In this zone the R.S.F.S.R. in 1918 incorporated all the tribes and nations corresponding to America's northern Indians and Esquimos. Richest and most advanced are the Yakuts, whose A.S.S.R. of 1,170,000 sq. mi. is biggest of any and contains the Lena River goldfields. The Yakuts (*left:* a rich bride; *above:* her horse) are of Turko-Tartar stock. Kindred people are the Tungus (*below*) and Lamuts. Of Mongoloid origin are the Chukchees (*below, left*) of whom a quarter-million inhabit the Chukhot National District in northeast Siberia. Before being Sovietized, they were polygamous, killed off their old folk.

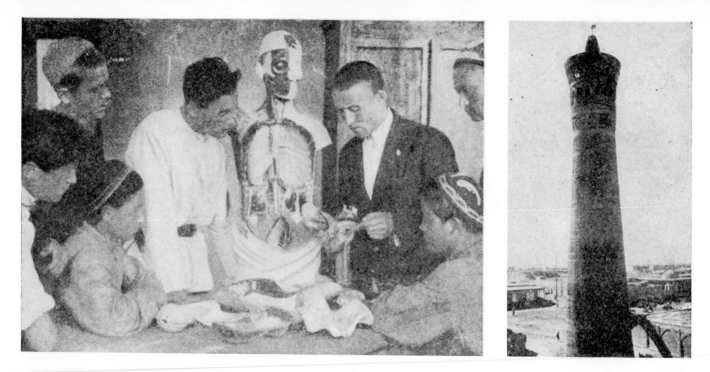

STEPPE PEOPLES

Second-largest S.S.R. is the Kazakh (1,060,000 sq. mi.) extending across the Khirghiz steppe from the Caspian Sea to the Tien Shan and Altai mountains. It was admitted to Union status in 1936. Four other, smaller S.S.R.'s were formed between the Kazakh and the borders of Persia, India and China. These are the Turkmen, Uzbek, Tadzhik and Kirghiz S.S.R.'s all containing various mixtures of steppe and mountain peoples left by the successive migrations of early times. The Uzbek S.S.R. contains Samarkand, which was Tamerlane's capital (*see* p. 41), and Bukhara.

(*Right*): **DEATH TOWER** in Bukhara, whence persons who displeased the Khan had to jump. (*Above*): **LIFE CLASS** in Bukhara, a Soviet physiologist expounding anatomy to pupils whose forebears depended on sorcerers for their medicine. (*Left*): Tadzhik oldster playing his *robob*. (*Below*): Kirghiz librarian reading the constitution to collective farmers.

MOSLEM PEOPLES

The many Mohammedans of old Russia received a special invitation from Lenin to restore their mosques and chapels, their beliefs and customs "trampled under foot by the tsars and oppressors. . . . Henceforth your beliefs and customs, your national and cultural institutions are free and inviolate. Build your national life freely and unhindered." And then the Soviets proceeded to educate and "Russify" such peoples, unveiling the Mohammedan women, discouraging their religion, encouraging them in sports, teaching them obedience to "Russian" Communism. The capital of the Tadzhik S.S.R. was named Stalinabad and from kindergarten days young Tadzhiks learned who was their Great White Father (*right*).

(*Above and below*): Tadzhik sportswomen.

THE SHIR-DAR MADRASSA, oldtime Mohammedan college in Samarkand, before which the warriors of Turkestan used to parade Russian heads impaled on spears, was carefully restored by the Soviets as a gesture to Turkomen nationalism and culture. Also restored was the tomb of Tamerlane (*right*), on which the ancient inscription reads: "And were I alive today, mankind would tremble!"

(*Below*): Uzbek dance in which the feet remain mostly in place.

(*Below, right*): Political propaganda being nailed to a wall in Tashkent urging downtrodden Islamites to rise.

The Soviets' policy of encouraging national, racial and religious self-expression (within confines of the Party line, and with emphasis on replacing religions by scientific ideology) gave thought to India.

242

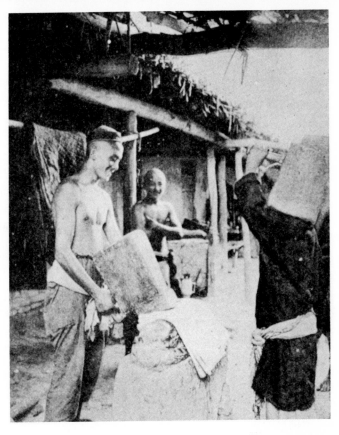

THE NOMADS' CHILDREN

The Moscow government has tried with indifferent success to make the descendants of Eurasia's nomad tribes wander no more but settle down to be solid U.S.S.R. residents. Mares are still milked in the steppe countries (*above*). Felt is still made — centuries-old textile of the herd-raising peoples — but no longer by hand as (*right*) in Tamerlane's capital. Now felt is made by machine.

A camel caravan of cotton (*below*), traveling Russia's wild and woolly Southeast (*Turkmenia*) is flagged Red to indicate government ownership and discourage bandits. But bandits and smugglers persist. As late as 1955 Red troops had to quell them.

MOUNTAIN PEOPLES

Russia's bulwarks against her ancient enemy Turkey were the Black Sea and the Caucasus Mountains. Small wonder that the mountain and valley peoples of Georgia, Azerbaidzhan, Daghestan and Armenia were reconquered to buffer this approach and the oil fields of the Caucasus. (*Left*): How the country looks, driving out of Baku toward the oil. (*Center*): Oil goes by pipe, wine still in bullock skins. (*Right*): An Azerbaidzhan belle. (*Bottom*): Village in Daghestan, of typical Near East mountain construction, clinging to its slopes like a honeycomb.

ARMENIA

The Soviets reconquered Armenia, which tried to secede during the Russian Civil War. The Armenians' S.S.R. is now among the most advanced. They make fine wine, raise fine herds, manufacture fine goods (besides rugs) and their population is now 1,500,000.

(*Above*): **MOUNT ARARAT**, seen from Erivan.

(*Right*): Armenian women workers on a collective farm being lectured by a local Communist propagandist.

(*Below, right*): Armenian Kurds, who no longer are savage desert robbers. (*Below, left*): Not a Biblical scene, but a shepherd on an Armenian collective ranch.

TABLE OF SOVIET STATES AND NATIONALITIES (as of 1968)

Republic, region or district	Date of formation	Population (1967)	Ethnic Strain	Major Nationality in per cent of total	Area in square miles (1968)
RUSSIAN SOVIET FEDERATED SOCIALIST REPUBLIC (R.S.F.S.R.)	1918	127,312,000	Slav	Russian, 83%	6,600,000
AUTONOMOUS SOVIET SOCIALIST REPUBLICS					
Bashkir A.S.S.R.	1919	3,757,000	Turco-Tatar	Russian, 42%	56,000
Buriat A.S.S.R.	1923	780,000	Mongol	Russian, 75%	135,500
Checheno-Ingush A.S.S.R.	1936	1,033,000	Japhetic	Russian, 49%	7,400
Chuvash A.S.S.R.	1925	1,192,000	Turco-Tatar	Chuvash, 70%	7,100
Dagestan A.S.S.R.	1921	1,361,000	Japhetic	Dagestani, 69%	19,400
Kabardino-Balkar A.S.S.R.	1936	530,000	Japhetic	Kabardin, 45%	4,800
Kalmyk A.S.S.R.	1935	248,000	Mongol	Russian, 56%	29,600
Karelian A.S.S.R.	1923	707,000	Finno-Ugrian	Russian, 63%	66,600
Komi A.S.S.R.	1936	974,000	Finno-Ugrian	Russian, 48%	158,900
Mari A.S.S.R.	1936	653,000	Finno-Ugrian	Russian, 48%	8,900
Mordva A.S.S.R.	1934	1,014,000	Finno-Ugrian	Russian, 59%	10,100
North Oset A.S.S.R.	1936	518,000	Iranian	Oset, 48%	3,100
Tatar A.S.S.R.	1920	3,127,000	Turco-Tatar	Tatar, 47%	26,200
Tuvan A.S.S.R.	1944	217,000	Turkic & Mongol	Tuvan, 57%	66,400
Udmurt A.S.S.R.	1934	1,379,000	Finno-Ugrian	Russian, 57%	16,400
Yakut A.S.S.R.	1922	646,000	Turco-Tatar	Yakut, 46%	1,188,300
AUTONOMOUS REGIONS					
Adygei A.R.	1922	366,000	Japhetic	Russian, 70%	2,900
Gorno-Altai A.R.	1922	169,000	Turco-Tatar	Russian, 70%	35,700
Jewish A.R.	1934	174,000	Jewish	Russian, 78%	13,900
Karachaevo-Cherkess A.R.	1926	330,000	Turco-Tartar & Japhetic	Russian, 51%	5,500
Khakass A.R.	1930	462,000	Turkic & Mongol	Russian, 76%	23,900
NATIONAL AREAS					
Agin-Buriat N.A.	1937	62,000	Mongol	Russian, 49%	7,900
Chukot N.A.	1930	89,000	Paleo-Asiatic	Russian, 61%	274,500
Evenki N.A.	1930	12,000	Mongol	Russian, 58%	287,600
Khanty-Mansi N.A.	1930	250,000	Finno-Ugrian	Russian, 72%	212,600
Komi-Perm N.A.	1925	216,000	Finno-Ugrian	Komi, 58%	12,700
Koriak N.A.	1930	37,000	Paleo-Asiatic	Russian, 61%	116,400
Nenets N.A.	1929	37,000	Nenets	Russian, 69%	70,100
Taimyr N.A.	1930	36,000	Mongol	Russian, 65%	332,100
Ust-Orda-Buriat N.A.	1937	154,000	Mongol	Russian, 56%	8,100
Yamalo-Nenets N.A.	1930	73,000	Mongol	Russian, 45%	289,600

Republic, region or district	Date of formation	Population (1967)	Ethnic Strain	Major Nationality in per cent of total	Area in square miles (1968)
UKRAINIAN SOVIET SOCIALIST REPUBLIC	1919	45,966,000	Slav	Ukrainian, 75%	240,000
BELORUSSIAN S.S.R.	1919	8,744,000	Slav	Belorussian, 81%	80,000
ESTONIAN S.S.R.	1940	1,294,000	Finno-Ugrian	Estonian, 73%	17,000
LATVIAN S.S.R.	1940	2,285,000	Baltic	Latvian, 62%	25,000
LITHUANIAN S.S.R.	1940	3,026,000	Baltic	Lithuanian, 79%	25,000
MOLDAVIAN S.S.R.	1940	3,425,000	Rumanian	Moldavian, 65%	13,000
GEORGIAN S.S.R.	1921	4,611,000	Japhetic	Georgian, 66%	30,000
Abkhaz A.S.S.R.	1921	471,000	Japhetic	Georgian, 39%	3,300
Adzhar A.S.S.R.	1921	301,000	Japhetic	Georgian, 73%	1,200
South Oset A.R.	1922	102,000	Iranian	Oset, 66%	1,500
ARMENIAN S.S.R.	1920	2,253,000	Japhetic	Armenian, 90%	12,000
AZERBAIDZHAN S.S.R.	1920	4,802,000	Turco-Tatar	Azerbaidzhani, 66%	33,000
Nakhichevan A.S.S.R.	1924	189,000	Turco-Tatar	Azerbaidzhani, 90%	2,100
Nagorno-Karabakh A.R.	1923	149,000	Japhetic	Armenian, 84%	1,700
KAZAKH S.S.R.	1936	12,413,000	Turco-Tatar	Russian, 43%	1,050,000
UZBEK S.S.R.	1924	10,896,000	Turco-Tatar	Uzbek, 63%	156,000
Kara-Kalpak A.S.S.R.	1932	638,000	Turco-Tatar	Karakalpak, 31%	64,300
TURKMEN S.S.R.	1924	1,966,000	Turco-Tatar	Turkmen, 60%	187,000
TADZHIK S.S.R.	1929	2,654,000	Iranian	Tadzhik, 53%	55,000
Gorno-Badakhshan A.R.	1927	93,000	Iranian	Tadzhik, 90%	24,600
KIRGIZ S.S.R.	1936	2,749,000	Turco-Tatar	Kirgiz, 40%	77,000
Total		234,000,000		Total	8,600,000

1. It is to be noted that all the chief peoples of the Soviet Union overflow to some extent the boundaries of the territorial divisions bearing their names. Thus each main division has within it a minority or minorities other than the predominant one.

2. The three Republics of Georgia, Armenia and Azerbaidzhan first united in 1922 in the Transcaucasian Soviet Federated Socialist Republic, which then became one of the four original Union Republics of the U.S.S.R. In 1936 this federation was dissolved and its three constituent members became Union Republics in their own right.

3. Totals of area and population are reached by adding figures for the 15 Union Republics, abbreviated as "S.S.R."

Prepared by Ellsworth Raymond

TOTALS OF NATIONALITIES IN ALL U.S.S.R. (1959 *census*)

Abkhaz	74,000	German	1,619,000	Latvian	1,400,000
Armenian	2,787,000	Greek	310,000	Lithuanian	2,326,000
Azerbaidzhan	2,929,000	Gypsy	132,000	Mari	504,000
Balkar	42,000	Hungarian	155,000	Moldavian	2,214,000
Bashkir	983,000	Ingush	106,000	Mordva	1,285,000
Belorussian	7,829,000	Iranian	21,000	Oirot	45,000
Bulgarian	324,000	Jewish	2,268,000	Ossetian	410,000
Buriat	253,000	Kabardin	204,000	Polish	1,380,000
Chechen	418,000	Kalmyk	106,000	Rumanian	106,000
Cherkess	30,000	Karachai	81,000	Russian	114,588,000
Chinese	26,000	Karakalpak	173,000	Tadzhik	1,397,000
Chuvash	1,470,000	Karelian	167,000	Tatar	4,969,000
Czechoslovak	40,000	Kazakh	3,581,000	Turkmen	1,004,000
Dagestan Peoples	945,000	Khakass	57,000	Tuvan	100,000
Estonian	969,000	Kirgiz	974,000	Udmurt	623,000
Finnish	93,000	Komi	431,000	Ukrainian	36,981,000
Gagauz	124,000	Korean	314,000	Uzbek	6,004,000
Georgian	2,650,000	Kurd	59,000	Yakut	236,000

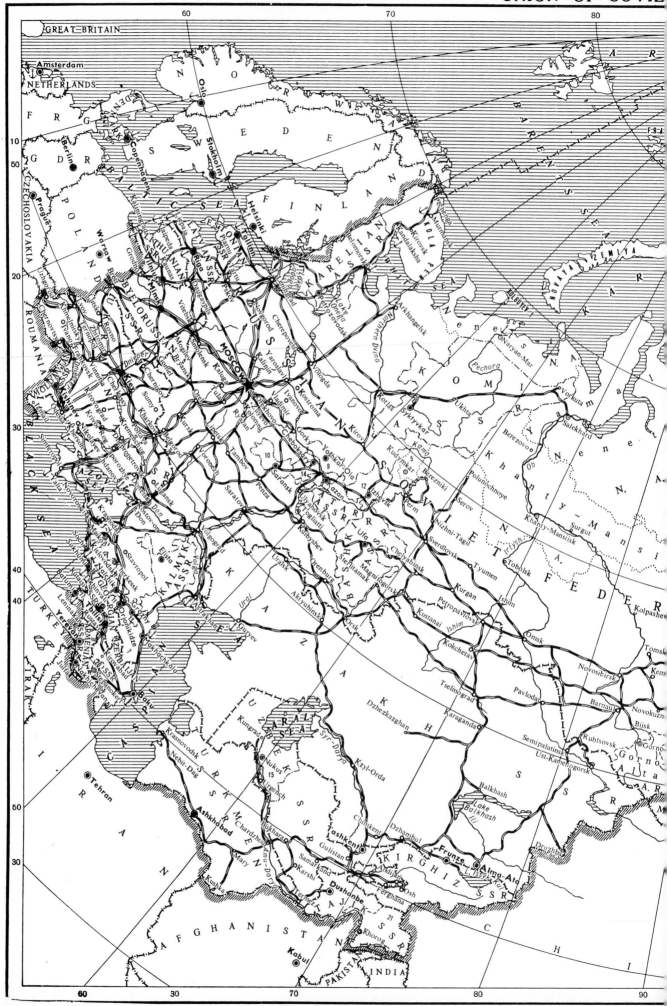

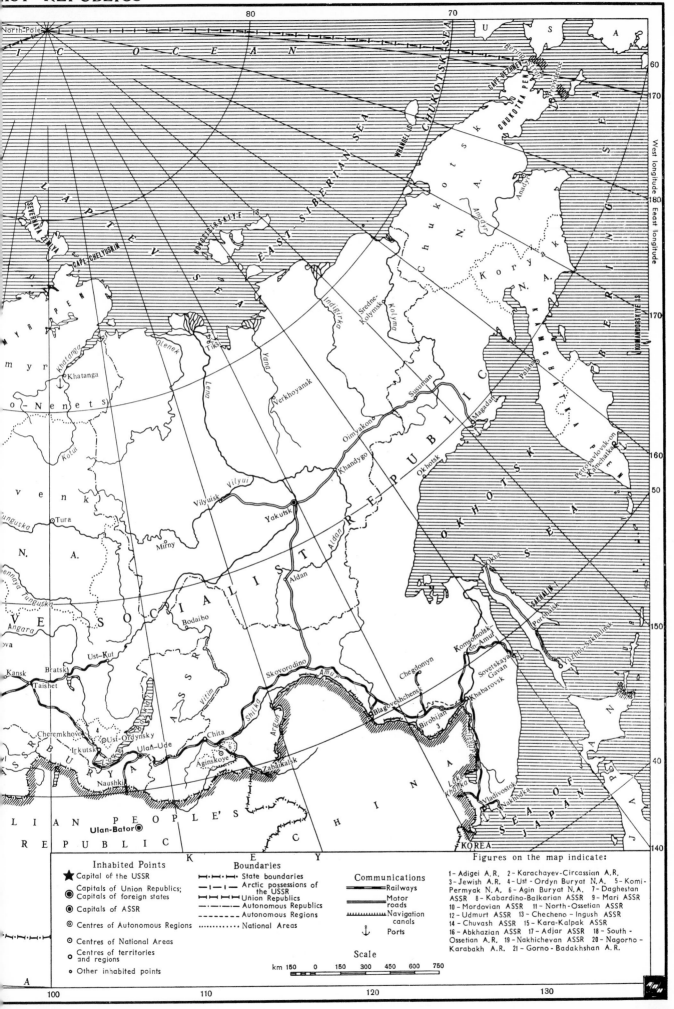

ACCENT ON YOUTH

"WELCOME, PIONEERS OF ALL LANDS" says the greeting under this windowful of crowing moppets in a Moscow nursery. They are an example, not at all staged or unusual, of the tremendous emphasis placed by the Soviets on their rising generations — seed-crops of new Communists, of manpower for the state. Below are two frank shots of Red soldiers rounding up for rehabilitation the "wild children" left homeless by the Civil War, foraging for themselves like little beasts. As fast as it could the state caught, scrubbed, fed and educated hundreds of thousands of such urchins thus "given to Lenin" by their uprooted parents. The children of parents busy helping build the new state were national wards from birth, organized as Pioneers to be raised and trained for citizenship. Education was to receive heavy emphasis in the new U.S.S.R.

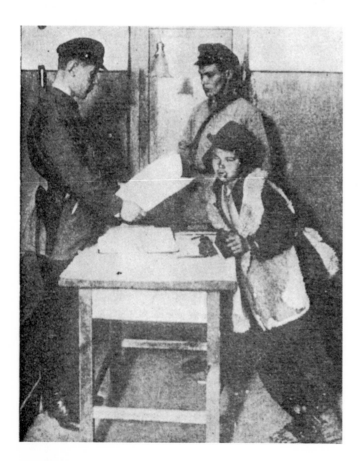

EXIT TROTSKY

To give Trotsky his due as the colleague of Lenin and Stalin in Communist annals, herewith is a box-score on him comparable to theirs.

Born: 1879, in Elizavetgrad, of middle-class Jewish parents. Real name: Lev Davidovich Bronstein.

Educated: at high school and University of Odessa.

Worked: from age 19, strictly as a professional revolutionary and journalist. Arrested in 1898 for Social Democrat activities.

Exiled: to eastern Siberia whence he escaped to England in 1902 using Trotsky as his passport name, which he thereafter kept. In London he met Lenin, collaborated with him on *The Spark* (newspaper) for a while. Went to St. Petersburg in 1905 and was chairman of its workers' soviet when all were arrested. Sent to Tobolsk but escaped at once to Vienna where he worked in a chemical plant. He went to the Balkan wars as a reporter (1912-1913) and enhanced his interest in military matters. France expelled him in 1914 for anti-war writings. He went to Spain and thence to New York where he worked as a columnist on Bukharin's *Novy Mir* (New World).

In the Revolution: Friends financed his return to Russia in 1917. The British detained him at Halifax but the Provisional Government obtained his release and he reached Petrograd soon after Lenin. whose Bolshevik wing of the Social Democrats he finally joined that July. As Commissar for Foreign Affairs, then for War, he contributed hugely to Red success.

(*Right*): Trotsky as Foreign Minister arriving at his office. (*Below*): Trotsky (center with star on sleeve) as War Minister reviewing troops. This is the high moment in Trotsky's entire career.

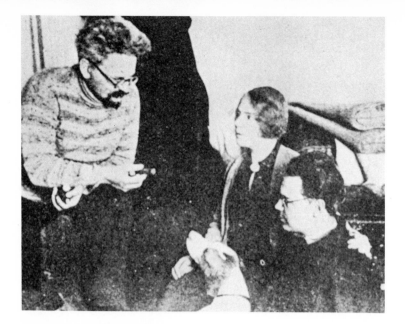

TROTSKY'S GOODBYE to Russia (*right*) was said in 1928 after Stalin had him expelled, then permanently banished, for opposing him. It seems Trotsky underestimated Stalin, whom he regarded as but a Lenin henchman. Trotsky, expatriate and internationalist, was for "permanent revolution," Stalin for "Socialism in one country." To Alma Ata in the Altai mountains went the Trotskys (*above*), then to Constantinople, then Norway (1936). In that year, Trotsky was accused with Zinoviev and Kamenev of plotting Stalin's death. They were tried and executed; Trotsky went to Mexico. The figure on the right is the Trotskys' son, Leon, who was murdered in Paris ten years later.

GREAT WAS THE FUROR in world Red circles over the Trotsky-Stalin schism. All Reds had to take sides, call names, make speeches. When the Trotskys (*above*) reached Tampico, they were welcomed by Artist Diego Rivera's picturesque wife, and Max Schachtman of the U. S. Trotskyites (*above, right*).

ASSASSINATION

On May 24, 1940, parties unknown fired 300 machine-gun slugs through Trotsky's bedroom in Mexico City. Trotsky and his wife escaped by rolling on the floor, playing possum.

On August 20, 1940, one "Jacques Mornard," a Spanish Communist, attacked Trotsky with a pickaxe in his study, inflicted a head wound which proved fatal. (*Right*): Trotsky dying, in Green Cross Emergency Hospital.

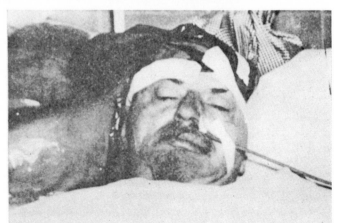

DEATH OF KIROV

Six years before Trotsky's assassination, in the year 1934, when Stalin finally ousted Zinoviev and Kamenev, he installed his favorite lieutenant, Sergei Kirov, at Leningrad to replace Zinoviev. Kirov was promptly assassinated by his secretary's husband, one Nikolaiev, whose testimony Stalin used in an attempt to show Zinoviev and Kamenev to have been in cahoots. They and scores of other anti-Stalinists were subsequently tried for treason, declared guilty and executed (*see* p. 293). A Red Army guard of honor accompanied Kirov's casket (*above*). Molotov, Voroshilov, Stalin himself and Kalinin publicly carried the cremated remains (*left, above*).

PURGE TRIALS

The Kirov murder and other "wrecking" and sabotage led to a long series of highly publicized trials. The world was mystified by the curious fact that most of the accused abjectly confessed the alleged sins and put up very little defense. (*Far left*): Andrei Vishinsky, attorney general, summing up. (*Left*): Vassily Ulrich, presiding judge, reading a verdict. (*Below*): A duly impressed court audience.

THROUGHOUT THE UNION during Stalin's purging of the Party, scenes like the above (on a Uzbekistan collective farm) were enacted. Every party member, even leaders like Rustan Khalbekov, who is the defendant here, was cross-examined by the local party committee to be sure he was (1) not slacking, (2) not actively sabotaging the party program.

COLLECTIVE SECURITY within the Union, against possible plots by Fascist Germany which he was sure would some day attack, was the alleged purpose of Stalin's party purges. Collective security outside the Union became the U.S.S.R.'s foreign policy keynote, and Foreign Minister Maxim Litvinov led a delegation into the League of Nations in 1934 (*below*).

XI. THE U.S.S.R. IN CONSTRUCTION

Large-scale building was started in the Soviet Union only toward the end of the 1920's. The new Soviet government was faced with a double task: to build a new type of society and also to overcome Russia's backwardness. These two tasks had to be tackled simultaneously. From the empire of the tsars the Soviets inherited a vast country predominantly agricultural. In the last decades of the empire considerable industrial progress did take place, but almost entirely with foreign funds. Before the Revolution, Russia was rapidly becoming an economic colony of the more advanced Western powers. In spite of all this progress and the billions of foreign capital that poured into Russia, industrial production of the empire remained below that of France.

A very formidable obstacle to the modernization of the country was the illiteracy of the people. The census of 1897 showed that only about 30% of the people of Russia could sign their first and last names.

In the course of World War I, Russia's foreign indebtedness doubled. After the Revolution the currency became inflated and the value of the ruble finally declined to zero. In the course of the civil war, industry and transport were of course subjected to heavy destruction. Thus in the early 1920's, having won the civil war, the Soviet government found itself firmly established in a country nearly altogether ruined and devastated. Industrial production had sunk to approximately one-ninth of the 1913 level. The new Soviet had to rebuild almost from scratch.

Only by 1928 did the level of industrial production and the annual national income exceed the corresponding amounts of 1913. The reconstruction period was coming to a close; now one could begin to build further. The years 1926-1928 were devoted to the working out of elaborate plans for an all-out construction drive. In 1928 this drive was finally launched, known as the First Five-Year Plan. Just as in the civil war, the country had to tighten its belt once more. Enormous sums of money were diverted to the building of heavy industry. In less than five years a powerful iron and steel industry was established. In the same period the Soviet Union began to develop large-scale production of agricultural machinery. A third achievement of the First Five-Year Plan consisted in the laying of the groundwork for mighty industrial centers in the East. Tremendous difficulties had to be overcome in this drive, but Russia entered the 1930's with a rapidly expanding heavy industry of her own and with industrial production beginning to extend deeply into the East.

The Second Five-Year Plan that followed in 1933 continued the expansion of iron and steel production, but also allowed for the manufacture of consumer goods. The population was now beginning to receive dividends from all the investment sacrifices that were incurred five years earlier. The Soviet Union also initiated its own automobile production and began to manufacture electrical appliances. The Third Five-Year Plan, begun just before World War II broke out in Europe, laid great stress on the development of the chemical industry. By 1940, industrial production in the Soviet Union was four times greater than that of tsarist Russia in 1913. Russia had become a great industrial power, with a productive capacity surpassed only by that of pre-1939 Germany and the United States.

In agriculture the changes introduced under the Soviet regime were as violent as those in industry. In the course of the First Five-Year Plan the centuries-old organization of Russian agriculture was for all intents and purposes scrapped, and

a new system introduced. Instead of 18,000,000 individual peasant households, there now appeared 250,000 collective farms. These collective farms are virtually state estates embracing as a rule from 150 to 300 peasant households. The land is tilled in common and the proceeds are divided among the members of the collective after payment of taxes. The collective does not own its land, since all land is common property, but enjoys the perpetual use of the land it tills. What an individual farmer never could afford, a collective farm can pay for. A collective leases tractors and other machinery from Machine & Tractor Stations. These stations are owned by the state, and before the outbreak of World War II there were already 6,000 such stations. By the time Hitler invaded Russia there were half a million tractors operating in Russian agriculture. Most collective farms still lacked electrification. In comparison, the United States had three tractors for every tractor in the Soviet Union.

This mechanization of agriculture somewhat stabilized agricultural production. What in the old days used to be a good crop year now became an average crop year. Periodic famines, which always used to threaten the Russian peasant, were now no longer a constant menace. The Soviet Union also began to develop very rapidly all types of other agricultural production, in addition to grain, like the growing of cotton and citrus fruit. Extensive use of machinery in the countryside enabled the release of labor power to industry. In 1913 only one-tenth of Russia's population lived in cities. By the end of the 1930's one-third of the population of the Soviet Union was urban. Agricultural production increased all along the line, but the very nature of agriculture does not permit as rapid an expansion as is feasible in industry. Great qualitative improvements were achieved by Soviet agriculture, but agricultural production was in 1940 only about 20% above that of 1913. During the same span of time, industrial production increased fourfold.

All this could not have been achieved without a considerable change in the cultural level of the population. Right in the midst of the intensive industrial drive of the First Five-Year Plan, millions of adults were being taught how to read and write. In the 1890's approximately eight-tenths of the population were illiterate; by the end of the 1930's only one-tenth of the people were, 90% of the people could read and write. The vastly expanded net of specialized schools was turning out engineers and other professional workers by the tens of thousands. Only the college population of the United States still exceeded that of the Soviet Union.

The present Soviet constitution is the third since 1918. The first constitution of Soviet Russia was adopted in 1918. This document stated the economic objectives of the Soviet regime. The second constitution was that of the U.S.S.R., adopted in 1923 after the formation of the Union. It also contained several paragraphs in the future tense. The Constitution of 1936, known as the Stalin Constitution, or the Constitution of Victorious Socialism, is all in the present tense. The claim was that socialism in one country had been achieved and was working, and the Constitution merely reflected the existing state of things.

While all this building was going on and while millions were poured in for the industrial development and the raising of the cultural level of the previously backward peoples, clouds of war were gathering beyond the frontiers. In 1931 Japan began her aggression in the Far East. In 1933 Hitler came to power in Germany. Russia took notice of the threat. Collective security became the slogan of Soviet foreign policy. In 1934 the Soviet Union joined the League of Nations, although previously Soviet statesmanship had been highly critical of it. In 1935 the Soviet Union entered into treaty relations with France for mutual protection. Russia tried to stop Mussolini's aggression against Ethiopia, but failed. Russia tried to mobilize the powers to prevent the domination of Spain by the fascists, but failed again. In 1937 large-scale Japanese aggression developed in China, and the Soviet Union proceeded to help China. The collective security idea collapsed completely in the fall of 1938, when at Munich the western powers sold Czechoslovakia down the river.

Now the Soviet Union seemed isolated, with hopes for collective security shattered. Moscow proceeded to secure peace the best way she could by adroit diplomatic maneuvering. The rest of the world was shocked when on August 24, 1939 Russia signed a non-aggression pact with Germany. One week later World War II started when Germany invaded Poland with her new brand of war called *blitzkrieg*.

The Red Army had already tested its strength in the Far East. In the summer of 1938 the Japanese were defeated in an undeclared war on the Korean border, and in the summer of 1939 an even more crushing defeat was inflicted on them in Mongolia. When the German armies started to sweep through Poland, Russia, although still neutral, marched into Poland and took over Western Byelorussia and Galicia, incorporating them in the U.S.S.R. The Germans did not resist this and not long afterwards agreed with the U.S.S.R. on a stabilized border of Poland, once more partitioned.

In the winter of 1939-1940 the Red Army fought a war against Finland, which aroused the sympathy of much of the rest of the world for Finland. The Russians seemed singu-

larly unsuccessful at first. The U.S.S.R. did not seem to show up as a great military power. But eventually the Red Army smashed through the famous Mannerheim Line of fortifications and a peace was made pushing the Finnish border away from Russia's second largest city, Leningrad.

In August, 1940 the three Baltic states, Estonia, Latvia and Lithuania, were forcibly annexed. In June of the same year, without war but after pressure, the Soviet Union re-acquired Bessarabia from Rumania which had taken it twenty years earlier. The U.S.S.R. was not only expanding and enriching itself, it was strengthening itself. With a tremendously powerful, dynamic nation across its borders, Russia was getting prepared for anything.

A good deal of peaceful construction had to be discontinued. The military budget was increased. Tractor production was converted into tank production, and projects for large urban housing developments were postponed to better days. Just as in the Revolution and in the First Five-Year Plan, Russia for the third time began tightening her belt. Everything that was built and achieved was now in danger. To meet this threat a strong war economy was being developed. On the surface, things still looked peaceful. On the night of June 21, 1941 Shakespeare's *Midsummer Night's Dream* was being played in Moscow. After that midnight came Hitler's invasion of Russia.

THE RAW MATERIAL

Said Lenin: "Put the muzhik on a tractor and you will have Socialism." The story of Soviet Russia from 1928 to 1939 is basically just that: how Stalin put the muzhik (peasant) on a tractor. Russia had plenty of muzhiks — some 100,000,000 of

them. But she had few tractors. Getting the muzhik on the tractor after it was built and making him happy there, was no small feat. The Five-Year Plans and the Collective Farms, by which the feat was accomplished, are the chief substance of the ensuing chapter. (*Above*): Some typical muzhiks, their women and children along a muddy village main street.

THE PLANNERS

The 15th convention of the All-Union Communist Party, which met in December, 1927, made decisions quite as revolutionary for Russia as the violent acts of 1917. It backed Stalin in his fight to eliminate Trotsky and other oppositionists. It embarked the nation on a vast industrialization program worked out over many months by a State Planning Commission. And it renewed the effort to sovietize agriculture, which would make administrative supervision and tax-collecting more effective: 250,000 collectives were easier to observe and manage than 25,000,000 small private farms.

(*Right*): Stalin with Author Maxim Gorky, whose popularity with Russia's peasants, and sympathy for them, helped propagandize collectivization. (*Below, left*): President Krzyzanovsky of the State Planning Commission and Alexander Vasilievich Winter, U. S. engineer who designed the Dnieprostroi power plants (U. S. engineer Hugh Cooper designed and built the dam). (*Below, right*): Chairman Kuibyshev of the State Planning Commission and (*bottom*) Grigory Ordjonikidze, Peoples' Commissar for Heavy Industry.

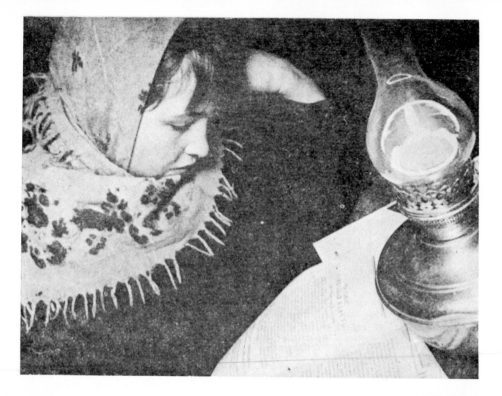

LITERACY

To make Socialism work, the proletariat must be able at least to read and write. The census of 1897 showed 72% illiteracy in European Russia, 85% in Siberia. The Duma's education program, begun in 1908, had reduced illiteracy to 55% by 1914, but the Soviet Planners of the 1920's had far to go. By 1925 they had opened 50,000 schools for adult illiterates, and in 1926 the U.S.S.R. was 51% literate. By 1934 the Planners achieved universal primary education. By 1940 illiteracy was down to 10% in the Union, non-existent among people under 30 years old. (*Left*): A Siberian girl studying.

In 1935, not less than 263 new schools were built in 39 cities of the Union. (*Below*): One of 72 new schools in Moscow alone: Middle School No. 23 in the Kirov District with 1,500 pupils, a fair example of size and architecture.

SHOCK TACTICS were adopted by Young Communists and Pioneers to stamp out illiteracy among their elders. (*Above*): A truckload of Pioneers out to canvass a section of Moscow. (*Below*): Typical scene in a workers' library. (*Upper right*): Tadzhiks learning arithmetic. (*Right*): Reading room at a textile plant. (*Lower right*): Schoolroom in Buriat-Mongolia.

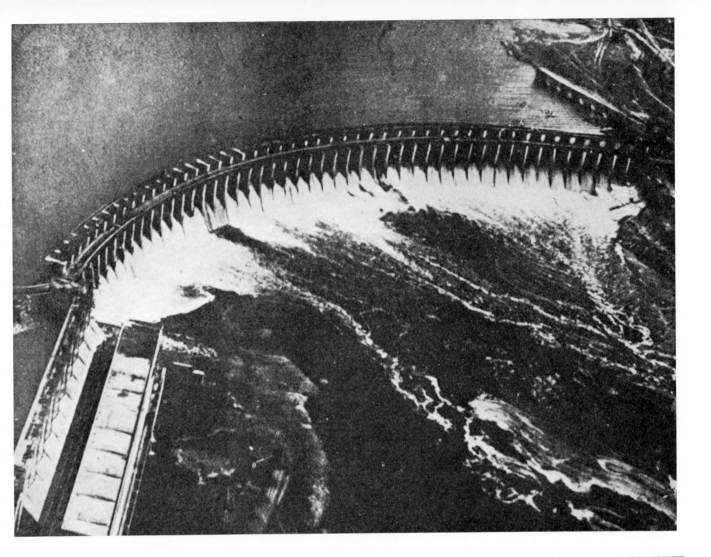

WATER POWER

A BASIC BLUEPRINT for the Soviet planners was provided by Engineer V. I. Grinevetsky in a book called *Postwar Prospects of Russian Industry* (1919). He proposed developing Russia's vast natural resources regionally — combining the fuels and power of the Urals, for example, with the metals and chemicals to be found there — instead of transporting the ingredients of industry from one region to another across Russia's great distances. Harnessing Russia's mighty rivers to produce electricity thus constituted a prime item of the first 5-Year Plan. (*On page opposite*): Power dam in the Ural River at Magnitogorsk. (*Above*): Dnieprostroi dam on the Dnieper River, completed in 1932, with a capacity of 625,000 kilowatt hours. (*Right*): Kuibyshev hydroelectric station in the course of construction. It was planned to be the world's largest, with 3,400,000 kw.h. (Grand Coulee: 1,900,000 kw.h.) The Planners estimated Siberian rivers' potential at 140,000,000 kw.h.

RUSSIA'S ELECTRIC POWER	1913	1,945,000,000 *kilowatt hours*
	1928	5,007,000,000 *kilowatt hours*
	1937	36,400,000,000 *kilowatt hours*
U. S. ELECTRIC POWER	1937	121,836,813,000 *kilowatt hours*

IRON & STEEL

PETER THE GREAT KNEW that the Ural Mountains contained iron ore. But not even in Nicholas II's day was it known what a colossal storehouse of metals and minerals lay there. And not yet is it fully known what other storehouses lie in remote parts of Siberia, such as the Soviets found in the Kuznetz region between headwaters of the Irtysh and Ob rivers. (*Above*): A view of Kuznetz in 1928 when the Soviet builders first moved in. (*Top of page opposite*): Kuznetz in 1932, a huge steel town. U. S. engineers and tools, like the shovel at the right, were called in. But not lacking were Soviet brawn, like that which dug the pit for a Magnitogorsk blast furnace (*below*), and Soviet brains, like that of Master Steelworker Matushenko (*left*).

THE "MAGNET MOUNTAIN" at Magnitogorsk (*right*) is estimated to contain 250,000,000 tons of ore averaging about 50% iron (compare: 1,123,000,000 tons left in Minnesota's Mesabi Range, 50-55% iron). Since the day of Peter the Great, smelting was conducted here by crude hand methods. Plants like the Magnitogorsk blast furnaces shown below in construction (1931) soon outstripped Russia's Ukrainian industry.

The Planners estimated the iron ore content of the whole Ural system at 2.5 billion tons. They planned a vast complex of plants like Magnitogorsk as an arsenal for their Union. Second giant was located at Nizhni-Tajil.

RUSSIA'S IRON AND STEEL	1913	8,447,000 *tons*
	1928	7,534,000 *tons*
	1937	32,170,000 *tons*
U. S. IRON AND STEEL	1937	87,696,000 *tons*

IRON AND STEEL: Coke-plant, Kuznetz. (*Below*): Coke-chemical plant No. 4, Magnitogorsk; channel-bars, Magnitogorsk.

IRON AND STEEL: Hot steel pig, Zaporozhstal (Ukraine); shears in slabbing mill, Zaporozhstal (*right*); rolled sheets, Zaporozhstal (*below*); rails, Dnieprodkerzhinsk (*right, bottom*). Such industry made the Ukraine alone a great industrial power, although its major importance remained agricultural.

MOTORS

NAMED FOR THE ELITE of the U.S.S.R. were scores of the new industrial towns — and plants — which sprouted under the Five-Year Plans. Nizhny-Novgorod was renamed for Author Gorky, and the big motor plant there was called Molotov, after Stalin's closest economic adviser. (*Left*): Architect's-eye view of the Molotov motor works at Gorky. (*Below*): Photo of the plant's actual facade, with gas-generator trucks in foreground. For some other Soviet models, see lower half of page. But heavy transport sooner than passenger cars was the obvious pre-war aim of the Soviet motor industry.

"ZIS-BUS" — a 27-seater (Stalin plant, Moscow). (*Below*): Polishing an "M-1" (Molotov plant).

The "ZIS-102" (Stalin plant), a seven-seater, eight cylinder, 110 h.p. (*Below*): "ZIS-SPORT" (100 m.p.h.).

TRACTORS, SOONER THAN AUTOS, were the U.S.S.R.'s crying need. The muzhiks were rounded up and settled on collective farms long before there were tractors for them to drive. The biggest tractor plants were located at Stalingrad and Chelyabinsk (Urals). (*Above* and *right*): Some of the first 75-h.p. gas-generator jobs turned out by the Stalin plant at Chelyabinsk. (*Below*): Grand opening of the Chelyabinsk plant (1935).

RUSSIA'S MACHINE PRODUCTION			
	Trucks	Tractors	Combines
1913	0	0	0
1928	670	1,272	0
1936	132,900	115,595	42,500
U. S. MACHINE PRODUCTION			
1936	784,589	221,246	16,900

RAILROADS

RUSSIA IS MOSTLY FLAT. But huge distances, extreme temperatures, boggy soils, dusty deserts had to be overcome to lace the land with railways. The Soviets double-tracked the Trans-Siberian, linked it around Lake Baikal (*above*). They built the Turk-Sib line from Tashkent to Alma Ata and Novosibirsk.

(*Above*): A Red streamliner. (*Below*): Roadbed crossing "Moscow Sea," a vast artificial water supply system.

RUSSIA'S RAILROADS	
1913	58,549 *kilometers*
1928	76,887 *kilometers*
1936	85,080 *kilometers*
U. S. RAILROADS	
1936 (Class I only)	360,074 *kilometers*
FREIGHT (Russia)	
1913	65,700,000,000 *ton - kilometers*
1928	93,400,000,000 *ton - kilometers*
1936	323,500,000,000 *ton - kilometers*
FREIGHT (U. S.)	
1936	544,700,000,000 *ton - kilometers*

TRACK-LAYING MACHINE (*above*) which puts down rail in sections complete with cross-ties. (*Below*): Locomotive works at Voroshilovgrad.

(*Above*): Fastening ties by hand. (*Below*): Electrification of U.S.S.R. railroads was slowly starting in 1939.

AIRWAYS

Russia seems made to be flown over and Russians are born flyers. A tight network of passenger and cargo airlines was projected by the Five-Year Plans, accelerated by military plans. (*Above*): Six-motored *L-760*. (*Below*): Tashkent passengers.

RUSSIA'S AIRLINES	1913	0 *kilometers*
	1928	9,300 *kilometers*
	1936	89,500 *kilometers*
U. S. AIRLINES	1936	46,000 *kilometers*

ROADS

Peter the Great and Catherine both realized how badly Russia needed roads, but not much was done about it until the Soviets, characteristically, started national "Road Day" to get roads built and maintained. In tsarist days, Russia had only 24,300 kilometers of highroads, of which 4,823 kilometers were paved. By 1938, Russia had 87,500 kilometers of paved highways, mostly asphalt. The camel caravan (*below*) keeps left on the old Silk Road to China, newly scraped for motor traffic.

(*Top of page*): Great Uzbek Highway. (*Below*): Krymsky Bridge, Moscow. (*Left*): Chuisk Highway to Mongolian border.

"METRO"

IN THE TEMPLE AT THE LEFT the gods worshipped are the pride and convenience of the Russian people. It is a station on "Metro," the Moscow subway system, to build which all of Moscow's trades and professions, and volunteers from all parts of the Union, pitched in. Above is the handsome interior of another station. No two are alike. Begun in 1932, "Metro" ran some 25 miles under Moscow by 1940, carrying 2,000,000 riders daily for 15 kopeks (3¢) the ride. (*Below, left*): Tickets are vended automatically. (*Below*): Wide, shiny cars; proud, comfortable passengers (no strap-hangers shown).

BUILDING

"OVERTAKE AND SURPASS AMERICA" was the Soviets' determined cry during the Five-Year Plans. Among other things, they built 90 new cities.

Old Russia and new were best seen, during the Plans, in Moscow where they flowered first and finest. (*Above*): A view down Gorky Street showing new stores and apartments, spruced up a bit by Soviet statues on top.

(*Right*): To house her urban industrial population, so enormously increased by the Plans, the U.S.S.R.'s living-space was shot quickly aloft, but was still very inadequate and would so remain for some time.

Functional architecture, using lots of glass and metal, was a Western development especially popular with the Soviets' rising generation of architects and builders. But air-conditioning, even adequate plumbing and heating had to wait. Behind the brand new facades, life remained fairly rugged. This was, perhaps, just as well, for thousands of the new structures were destined so soon to be knocked down by bombs and shells.

HOMES FOR ENGINEERS AND TECHNICIANS in the Molotov motor works at Gorky. (*Left*): Marx-Engels-Lenin Institute at Tbilisi (Tiflis). (*Right*): **PLANT OF PRAVDA** ("Truth"), organ of the Communist Central Committee, on Moscow's north outskirts. (*Bottom*): Bureaucrats' sanatorium at Kizlovodsk, where overtired elite rested at state expense.

WATERWAYS

"PORT OF 5 SEAS" is what inland Moscow called itself after the Planners projected canals linking the Moscow river to the Volga, the Volga to Lake Onega, Lake Onega to the White Sea and the Baltic, and the Volga to the Don (*see map*). All but the last of these was completed before the war. It was to store water for this system that the "Moscow Sea" was impounded. Streamlined excursion boats, as well as immense cargo barges, were put in service to show Soviet citizens the glories of their river system. Taking a vacation ride on it was like going on a Great Lakes cruise in America, only much, much more fashionable. (*Above*): Locking out of Lake Onega with the Communist Red Flag flying astern.

OIL

The Caspian oilfields (*below:* Baku) from which millions of tons of wealth for export were piped and tanked even in tsarist days, are one of Russia's best-known riches. Unpublicized, unpictured, are oil-bearing formations of untold volume stretching all the way up from the Caspian through and beyond the Urals. These fields the Planners exploited in time to have a comfortable second line of oil defense by 1940. But they had to import refineries to make aviation fuels and lubricants.

RUSSIA'S OIL, 1920	25,400,000 *barrels*
U. S. OIL, 1920	442,900,000 *barrels*
RUSSIA'S OIL, 1930	135,200,000 *barrels*
U. S. OIL, 1930	898,000,000 *barrels*
RUSSIA'S OIL, 1940	212,900,000 *barrels*
U. S. OIL, 1940	1,351,800,000 *barrels*

GOLD

"SECOND IN THE WORLD" (after South Africa) is about the U.S.S.R.'s only statement on its gold production, except for such figures as 26% for the increase in 1936 over 1935. But that one generality implies much in world fiscal adjustments. The wild, cold taigus (scrub forest) watershed of the Lena River is still the chief scene of operations by Lenzoloto, the state gold trust. (*Below*): Drilling. (*Right*): Placering. (*Bottom*): Dredging. (*Right, center*): A fair-sized nugget, and a Chinese golddigger made happy by Soviet amenities. The government grubstakes quite a number of "artels" (private groups) and individuals, even provides them with machinery and gives them wage and tax concessions, to encourage gold production. When a big strike is made, the state trust of course moves in.

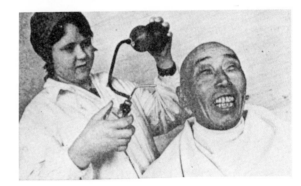

PHOSPHATES were found in the frigid Murmansk region and exhumed by the Planners on an impressive scale (*above*). Kirovsk is the name of this development, in honor of Stalin's martyred friend Sergei Kirov, boss of Leningrad after Zinoviev.

FISH, especially salmon, abound in Russia's rivers but none is so famed as the sturgeon, from which big green-gray caviar (roe) comes when the sturgeon is taken mature. The monster sturgeon below (9 feet, 298 pounds) was taken near Leningrad. Russia's southern rivers, especially the Don and Volga, are best for sturgeon. Azov and Astrakhan, the caviar centers, became state-run under the Plan.

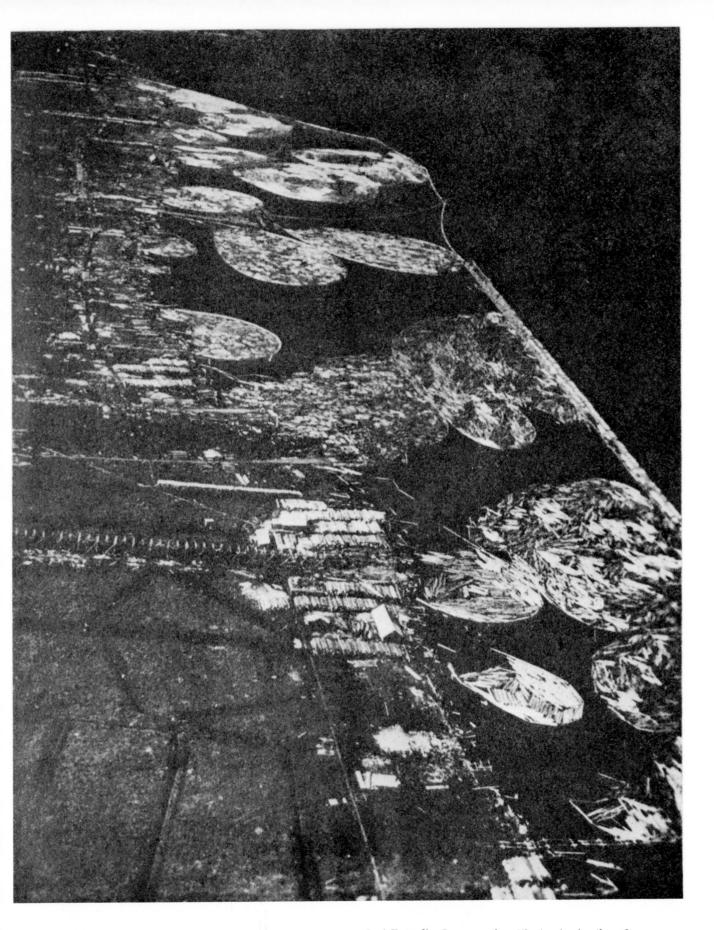

WOOD

Lumber rafts of the Planners looked like this to Explorer Lincoln Ellsworth when he flew over Archangel in 1931 in the *Graf Zeppelin*. Spruce, cedar, Siberian larch, silver fir are some of the chief trees cut for lumber and pulp upon which the Planners depended heavily for export trade balances. Cutting pulpwood in Siberia was found to be useful, healthy work for foes of the Stalin regime.

IRRIGATION

WATER FOR CROPS as well as for power and transport was figured into the Plans: vast irrigation projects to stabilize the balance of nature in drought areas. (*Above*): Completed section of the Malo-Kabardinskaya irrigation project on the Terek River (north Caucasus). (*Below*): Fergana River Canal in Uzbekistan receiving finishing touches before its opening.

COTTON

In Uzbekistan, water on the land meant bumper cotton crops, as two Uzbek farmers listening to a State engineer (*left*) could well understand. (*Above* and *below*): The whole performance: watered rows; crop picked by machine, and stacked neatly under one of Russia's towering mountain barriers. Most of Russia's best long-staple cotton now comes from Uzbekistan and Tadzhikistan.

RUSSIA'S COTTON	
1913	1,631,700 *bales*
1932	2,800,350 *bales*
1938	5,931,450 *bales*
U. S. COTTON	
1938	11,900,000 *bales*

"MUZHIK ON TRACTOR = SOCIALISM"

WITH PROPAGANDA, tax pressure and guns the Communists began collectivizing the stubborn Russian peasantry. During execution of the Plans, Joseph Stalin often tramped forth with the Planners (*above:* Ordjonikidze, Stalin, Kalinin, Kaganovich, Zhdanov) to see how things were going. More revealing than this state painting is the photo below, made in 1935, showing a group of young farmers, led by a girl, trying to persuade an oldster to join their *kolkhoz* (collective farm). The oldster, if he is not a kulak (rich peasant), is a middle-class peasant who hopes to become rich. If he is collectivized, away will go his independent farm and private gain. The Planners cracked down heavily on the kulaks, sent many of them to hard labor in Siberia, so maddened them that they struck at raising more crops than they needed for themselves. Frightful famines resulted in the early 1930's in some of Russia's richest black-soil regions. But eventually the Planners, aided by shock brigades of Young Communists, made most peasants join the collective farms by rather rough means.

THE KOLKHOZES

The Plan said that the *kolkhozes* (collective farms) should increase from 38,000 in 1928-1929 to 100,000 in 1930-1932 and their area from 4,000,000 hectares to 16,000,000. But until 1930 there were only 25,000 tractors in all Russia and not before 1933 were there 200,000, with 25,000 combines. To make machinery go as far as possible, Machine Tractor Stations serviced the collectivists, sending forth columns of tractors each day to a different area (*above*), training mechanics (*right*) to repair machines (*below*) which were worked overtime.

THE PLAN'S MACHINES did catch up with the Collectives in time and, after much bitterness and hardship, the U.S.S.R. began to be a country whose farmers were "industrialized" like the city workers. Huge cultivator seeders roamed the plains in the autumn (*above*). In the late summer, teams of monster reapers and binders scoured the ground as far as the eye could see (*left*). Wheat straw piled up like young mountain ranges in the collective threshing yards (*below*). But these results were not achieved without compromises and intensive persuasion. What angered the peasants most, was that the famines they suffered resulted from their wheat being shipped abroad.

RUSSIA'S WHEAT CROPS		
1913	560,000,000 *bushels*	78,700,000 *acres*
1928	590,173,000 *bushels*	68,420,000 *acres*
1937	1,080,700,000 *bushels*	101,550,000 *acres*
U. S. WHEAT CROPS		
1937	875,676,000 *bushels*	64,422,000 *acres*

BRIGADES OF AGITATORS, enlisted from the Young Communist ranks, were trained to deliver choral declamations (*right*) about the Five-Year Plans and the collective farm movement upon which the whole new Soviet structure must rest. Before farm machinery was available, and even afterwards, newspapers like *The Collective Farmer* were composed and printed on trucks right out in the fields (*below*) to drive home the new doctrine.

Besides these peaceful tactics, the government organized "shock brigades" of town workers to go out and drive the peasants into collective production, or to harvest the crops themselves. Little local pitched battles resulted. The death penalty was decreed for hoarding grain. By the spring of 1930, some 55% of the peasantry was collectivized, but the movement did not begin to catch up with the country's food requirements until after one more grave famine in 1932. The livestock situation was bad, too, because the angry peasants killed and ate their animals rather than let them be taken for the collective farms. Others killed their stock lest they be rated "rich."

MOLLIFICATION

Periodically during its peasant war, Moscow would relent a little. In 1930, Stalin ordered collectivizers no longer to use force. In 1933, a new Act was passed, which oldsters read with some satisfaction (*right*), guaranteeing to collective farmers not the ownership but at least the perpetual use of their land.

Restored also was the peasants' cherished right to keep up to three private cows, and any number of private pigs, sheep and poultry. Also, the farmers' taxes were alleviated and farmers' earnings were guaranteed by the government as their private property, which they could invest in interest-bearing bonds. Looser forms of group farming were permitted. (*Bottom*): View of the Karl Marx Collective farm, clearly showing private garden plots and poultry flocks.

PRIVATE EARNINGS were made possible once more by the 1933 Act, which levied a heavy percentage of farm output for the state but left a balance to be divided or sold for the benefit of the collective farm members, to each according to his work. (*Above*): Distributing shares of grain in kind. (*Right*): Bookkeeping department of a rich Uzbek collective, figuring accounts with the abacus (and one adding machine). (*Bottom*): Parade to a collective cotton harvest.

AMENITIES OF COLLECTIVE FARMING

To entertain the farm workers, theatrical troupes were occasionally sent into the fields, like the Uzbek performers above, with drums, robobs and the long-tubed karnai (bugle). (*Right*): Kolkhoz women received free maternity care. Profitable kolkhozes might build their own club, barn, silo or store. Such structures were invariably adorned with Stalin's picture. There was even barber service in the harvest field.

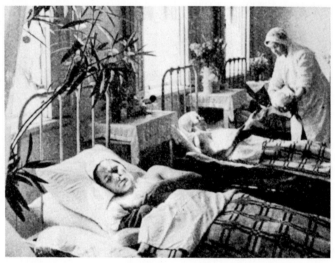

SOMETHING NEW WAS ADDED to the Plans, and to all Soviet effort, when Alexei Stakhanov (*above*), a Donbas coalminer, presented a pregnant idea to his superiors in 1935. He, Alexei, was a demon with a pneumatic drill, but only mediocre at putting in pit props. By teaming with two expert proppers, he proved that he could take out many times his quota of coal for a six-hour shift. "Stakhanovism" swept the country — a speed-up system based on division of labor, with rewards for record-breakers in all industries — and Alexei became a national hero in a fur coat (his wife got one, too).

EVEN FUR WAS
COLLECTIVIZED

From earliest times, Russia gave the world the fur of her forest animals. The Planners found this export product worth collectivizing for itself, or as a seasonal by-product of other occupations like lumbering and mining. In order of volume-value, Russia's furs are: squirrel, wolf, ermine, hare, fox, skunk, bear, marten, lynx, wild cat, sable, beaver, seal. Fur-laden trappers (*above*) carry their catch to airplanes for quick marketing. East of Lake Baikal, peoples like the Evenks of the Buriat Republic produce women hunters who can shoot squirrels from reindeer-back. Others take foxes (*lower left*). Persian lamb (*lower right*) was collectivized in Turkmenia and elsewhere in the Caspian-Altai area. The immemorial fur-seal harvest along Siberia's eastern coast was organized to enrich the state.

FUR PALACE

The State's take of fur, from its own farms and from collectives, was auctioned to world buyers at Leningrad beginning July, 1938, in a special Fur Palace (*above*). This auction replaced the oldtime Leipzig fur fair which declined after 1933. View of fox cages of a state fur farm and scenes of preparation for the Leningrad auction are shown here.

SOVIET CULTURE

Revolution and civil war severely disrupted Russia's cultural life, but not for long. Under the Red regime, along with the Plans for economic and industrial reconstruction, official stress was laid upon arts and letters, to encourage creative work propagandizing Communism.

The famed Ballet Russe was continued and reinvigorated, its greatest production, Tschaikovsky's *Swan Lake* (*above*), becoming semi-officially the state's prime entertainment.

Writers, artists, musicians became some of the most privileged and highly paid persons in the Union. A Big Three, repre-

sentative of the best the Soviets produced, is shown below. In the center is the late **KONSTANTIN STANISLAVSKY**, creator (with V. Nemirovich-Danchenko) of the Moscow Art Theater which gave the world Russian realist drama. **DMITRY SHOSTAKOVICH** (*right*) overthrew classicism, invented brave new sounds for the brave new era. His work was considered so important that he was flown out of besieged Leningrad, where he was a fire-control officer, to Kuibyshev so that he might finish his famed *Seventh Symphony*. **MICHAEL SHOLOKOV** (*left*), of Don Cossack descent, linked past and present with his epic novel *Quiet Flows the Don* and other works expressive of the transition from imperial to Communist life.

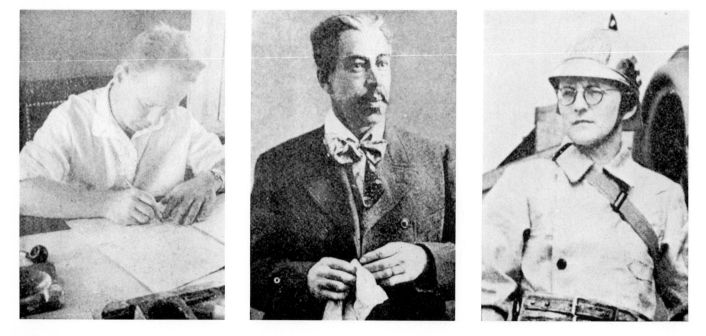

MAN WITH A PIPE

During all the prodigious Planning and executing of 1928-1936, hidden strife tore at the vitals of the Communist Party. The masses affected by the changes over which the contest raged were little aware of this trouble. The Man With a Pipe in the Kremlin carried on stolidly, eliminating more political enemies such as Bukharin, Radek, Rykov, (*above*), and Sokolnikov; finally even purging the Red Army command of several high generals and its No. 2 man, Marshal Tukachevsky, on false grounds that they were collaborating with Germany. Also purged was the top man of the dread OGPU, fox-eyed Genrikh Yagoda, on charges of conniving with the Trotskyites to bring about Stalin's death. (*Below*): Yagoda, Sokolnikov, Tukachevsky.

These trials and executions (1936-1938) were the internal culmination of the Trotsky-Stalin feud (*see* pp. 254-56) and served the multiple purpose of: (1) consolidating once and for all Stalin's control of the Communist Party; (2) eliminating most old Bolsheviks from positions of power; (3) packing the Soviet bureaucracy with young Communists who were careerists more than Marxists. Trotsky's demise in 1940 (p. 255), whether or not engineered by Moscow, removed the tough root of anti-Stalinism, ensured a future under the Stalinist hierarchy, which bordered on the ridiculous in that no one truly worshipped the All-Wise One, as pretended.

FOREIGN AFFAIRS I. ASIA

In 1929, young Marshal Chang Hsueh-liang, warlord of Manchuria, raided the Soviet consulate in Harbin. He sought evidence that Russia was abetting large, moon-faced General Feng (*left*) against the Nationalist regime that had squelched the Reds in China. Chang found enough evidence to expel the Reds from Manchuria, including the manager of the Chinese Eastern Railway. U. S. Secretary of State Henry Stimson sought to invoke the Kellogg Pact but the Reds moved into Manchuria from both ends of the Chinese Eastern, regained their 50% control in a new treaty.

This aroused Japan, which in 1931 started taking over Manchuria as "Manchukuo." Again Stimson sought to intervene, but got nowhere. Japan simply marched out of the League of Nations (*below*) when that body protested.

Russia stopped the Jap encroachment at the Amur River, but meekly surrendered her half of the Chinese Eastern for 10¢ on the dollar. The era of aggression was begun, and none knew it better than Russia, who set out to expand and improve the Red Army.

II. EUROPE

STRESA. Russia's foreign policy now focussed on Disarmament for all. Litvinov reiterated: "Peace is indivisible." But when the Powers met at Stresa to talk Peace, Russia was not invited. (*Above*): Flandin of France being playful at Stresa with Mussolini while Ramsay MacDonald and Pierre Laval look on.

GENEVA. Again in 1932, at Geneva, the U. S. was represented by Hugh Gibson (center with cane) and a big staff (*below*) — but Russia was not invited to join that Disarmament discussion either. These rebuffs arose from Europe's distrust of the Comintern. Meantime — (*see next page*).

ON JANUARY 30, 1933, ADOLF HITLER became Chancellor of Germany. On March 21 he addressed to the new Reichstag and to aged President Paul von Hindenburg (*above*) a speech which sounded the knell of parliamentary government in Germany and ushered in the Nazi dictatorship. Since Hitler had openly pointed, in *Mein Kampf,* to Russia as Germany's natural prey, Russia's attention and all her building and planning henceforth were focussed on defending the Motherland when Hitler should attack. In the light of later events, this explanation of everything Stalin did, and even of the Comintern's efforts to form a world-wide "United Front" against Fascism, is not implausible.

PREVIEW IN SPAIN

This gutted tenement in Madrid, blown horribly open by a Rebel air bomb if not by a German or Italian bomber flying for the Rebels, was one of the world's first foretastes of what airpower was to mean in World War II. Fascist Italy and Nazi Germany both sent men and equipment to help General Franco attack the Leftist government of Spain in a civil war that raged through 1936-1938. Russia sent Red troops and equipment to help Spain's Leftists. She was asked by the Powers to cease and desist from "intervening." The Fascists won, since Russian aid was too little to win.

297

RUSSIA AS WELL AS THE FASCISTS learned in Spain about bombing and siege techniques against masonry structures. In Madrid, the building of International Telephone & Telegraph. Co. withstood months of medium shelling and bombing. In Toledo, the Government army had to resort to huge dynamite mines to reduce the ancient Alcazar (*above*) in which a lot of Rebel cadets were holding out. Chief observer in Spain for the Red Army was a bulky little staff officer named Zhukov. (*Below*): Russian Army fliers captured in Spain. (*Right*): Banner proclaiming: "Madrid shall be the tomb of Fascism."

TOTAL PREPAREDNESS FOR TOTAL WAR

INSTEAD OF FOOTBALL OR BASEBALL, sports and studies directly preparatory for war were pressed upon the vigorous youth of the U.S.S.R. from one end of that broad land to the other all through the 1930's. "Voroshilov Horsemen" were enrolled and trained for war, instead of in polite hunt or polo clubs. (*Above*): Voroshilov troop of a collective farm in the Tadzhik S.S.R. (*Below*): Young boys were taught in school about planes and bombs; older ones learned bayonetry and competed for the national championship therein at Dynamo Stadium.

OSOAVIAKHIM

"Voluntary Society for Assistance to the Air Force and Chemical Defense," contracted from its Russian first syllables into Osoaviakhim, was the name of a body of 15,000,000 civilians, mostly athletes, who were coached by Red Army reservists for Russia's anticipated total war of defense. On this page, some shots of the lengths to which gas-mask practice was carried, even in remote regions like Azerbaidzhan (be.ow). More important than gas-masks were parachutes, which hundreds of thousands of Osoaviakhim members learned to use — and later did use as guerillas dropped behind the German lines. Most important of all, Osoaviakhim constituted a close link between the Red Army and the war-conscious civilian population.

ARMED WORKERS were the saviors of Leningrad against the Whites in 1918. By 1939, workers everywhere were not only armed but drilled and disciplined as civil defense auxiliaries, like the ranks above, marching and singing in Moscow.

HOUSEWIVES BRIGADES to fight air-raid damage were trained and sharpened by All-Union competitions. (*Below*): The All-Union champions of 1940, from the apartment house N-3 Gagarin Street, Leningrad, led by Housewife K. Kisseleva.

SWIMMING WITH HAND GRENADES, military skiing, diving, field nursing, markmanship were some other Osoaviak-him pursuits. By 1938, not less than 6,000,000 members had won marksmanship medals — a fine reservoir of guerilla fighters.

MUNICH

"PEACE IN OUR TIME" was the pious hope expressed by Britain's Prime Minister Chamberlain when he returned, in October of 1938, from throwing Czechoslovakia as one last sop to Adolf Hitler at Munich. Russia, though one of Czechoslovakia's sworn protectors, was not invited to this memorable Munich meeting (*above*) of Chamberlain, France's Daladier, Hitler, Mussolini and Count Ciano. (*Below*): Signing the Pact of Munich (Goering and Mussolini chuckle while Hitler signs).

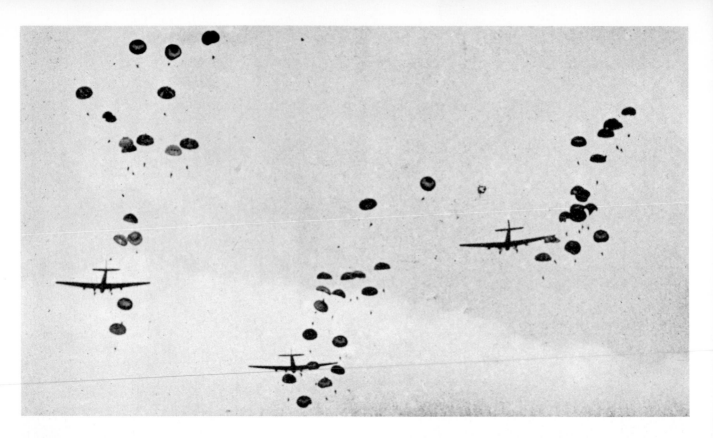

MORE PARADES

RUSSIA'S REPLY to Munich was silent but manifold. She abandoned Collective Security as a will-o'-the-wisp. She staged bigger and better parades, of the Red Air Force and Red Army, hoping to delay war by displaying her strength. Litvinov, high priest of Collective Security, was replaced as Commissar for Foreign Affairs by poker-faced Molotov.

TILSIT No. 2.

DEEPLY SHOCKING to the anti-Nazi world was the announcement, on August 24, 1939, of a non-aggression agreement between the U.S.S.R. and Germany. The picture of Stalin shaking hands with Foreign Minister Ribbentrop (*right*) seemed a new high in international cynicism. Followed as it was, one week later, by Germany's blitz of Poland, this Stalin-Hitler "deal" appeared to be the opening of an abyss from which Liberty might never rise again.

On September 17, the Red Army moved westward and occupied a large part of eastern Poland. As Red tanks rumbled into Brest-Litovsk (*below*), where the Reds had bowed to Germany twenty years prior, suspicion of a double double-cross arose, and recollections of Alexander I's temporizing "deal" with Napoleon at Tilsit. Perhaps the Stalin-Hitler deal was Tilsit No. 2 — a move to gain time and make ready.

A French news agency reported that in August, while telling the Politburo about the Soviets' plan to seize its share of Poland, Stalin said: "If . . . we accept the Reich's offer of collaboration, the latter will not hesitate to crush Poland. England and France will thereupon be drawn fatally into war. There will result a thorough destruction of Western Europe, and remaining outside the conflict we can advantageously await our hour. . . . If Germany wins, she will emerge from the war too exhausted to dream of an armed conflict against us. . . ." Stalin denounced this report as a lie, but said: "It was not Germany who attacked France and England, but France and England who attacked Germany, assuming responsibility for the present war."

COUNTER-OCCUPATION

The Russian counter-occupation of the Polish plains extended to the line Suwalki, Brest-Litovsk, Lvov, Przemysl — approximately the old Curzon Line. Soviet photographers had little difficulty finding inhabitants, rural and urban, who would welcome the Russians (*above*), for the population of western Byelorussia and the western Ukraine was predominantly non-Polish. Therein lay the crux of the age-old Russo-Polish "question." The Poles in the east did not welcome either German or Russian occupation. But they had little choice in the matter. As for Russia, at that moment the German "question" was infinitely more important than the Polish. When the two armies met, the Russians were polite but not fraternal toward their German "allies" (*left*). They simply settled down on the agreed demarcation line along the Rivers Bug and San.

The peasants divided up the lands of Polish nobles (*below*), while the U.S.S.R. divided them between the Byelorussian and Ukrainian S.S.R.'s (*see next page*).

WAR ON FINLAND

Next shock, to American sensibilities particularly, was Russia's war on Finland, begun November 30, 1939. This move was to enforce demands made for strategic sites deemed essential to defense against Germany (*see map below*). Small, brave, popular "because she paid her debt," Finland received much outside sympathy. At first tiny Finland defeated the Red Army, then, with great casualties, Soviet troops stormed the Mannerheim Line, named after the Finnish war minister.

When England and France threatened to intervene, Russia abruptly made peace, taking some naval bases such as Porkkala and buffer territory but not exacting any substantial reparations.

(*Right*): Nazi Air General Stumpff with Baron Mannerheim (wearing Iron Cross) in 1941. Baron Mannerheim was still Finland's strong man but now the Russians could for a time trust in their pact with Germany.

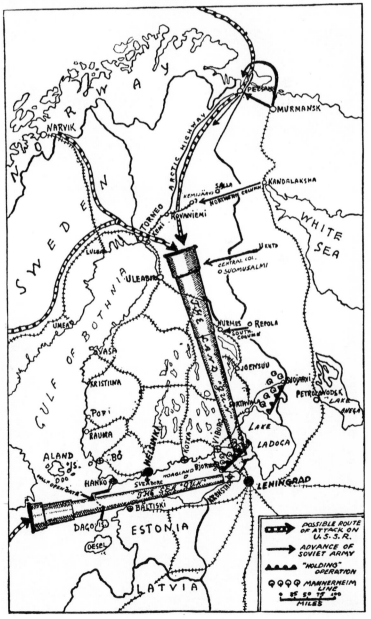

"GUNS AT LENINGRAD." The map (*right*) by former Cossack Captain Sergei N. Kournakoff in *Russia's Fighting Forces* presents the Russian view of the threat to its Baltic and Arctic "windows" latent in Finnish possession of Hango, Viborg, the Mannerheim Line across the Karelian Isthmus, and the port of Petsamo near Murmansk. It was to protect Leningrad that Russia fought Finland while Germany was still preoccupied in the west. Finland's gallantry, and pitiful pictures like the frozen horse (*above*) aroused sympathy from the entire non-Communist world. In its anger the United States nearly severed relations with the U.S.S.R. Italy sent volunteer pilots and planes; Britain and France, ski troops.

307

MORE BUFFERS

Somewhat to Germany's surprise and alarm, the Soviets next forcibly annexed the Baltic states of Lithuania, Estonia and Latvia; also Bessarabia and Rumanian Bukovina. These moves were consummated while the Nazis were overrunning the Lowlands and France. Russia gave the Baltic states S.S.R. status, like the Finno-Karelians, and also set up a Moldavian S.S.R. which included Bessarabia. These imperialist annexations were made the year before Stalin joined in the Atlantic Charter, at which juncture no request was made for Russia to dis-annex them. (*Above*): Red warships in the strategic Baltic harbor of Tallinn. (*Left*): Red troops occupying Kishinev, Bessarabia. (*Below*): Demonstration of welcome to the Soviet occupation forces in Bukovina.

XII. THE WAR FOR THE MOTHERLAND

In the early hours of Sunday, June 22, 1941 the Hitler armies struck across the Soviet borders without a declaration of war. The armed forces of Germany by then had behind them the industrial and human resources of nearly the entire continent of Europe. The invasion proceeded in three directions at once. One German group attacked through the Baltic republics in the direction of Leningrad. The second group proceeded directly east toward Moscow. A third group plunged through the Ukraine.

On July 3, Joseph Stalin appealed to the entire population over the radio, calling for a scorched earth policy and reminding the people how over a hundred years ago Russia had withstood a similar threat from Napoleon. Near Smolensk the German army was held for several weeks. The blitzkreig that succeeded so well elsewhere was slowing down against Russian resistance. The first two months were the decisive period for Hitler. He expected to reach Moscow, Leningrad and Rostov before the Red Army could be fully mobilized.

In the first days of October, Hitler announced that the Russian armies were destroyed and that only a mopping up operation was necessary. The Red Army had resisted heroically and though the Germans kept advancing it was not until November, when the Russian winter had begun, that they reached the vicinity of Moscow. They had reached Leningrad earlier, besieged it but could not capture it. As the battle of Moscow developed toward the end of November, divisions of armed civilian workers and employees were assembled in Moscow and thrown into battle. Seeing men without uniforms opposing them, the Germans thought that this was the end of Russian resistance. For Russia, however, this was only the beginning.

Large armies were being trained in the meantime by two old heroes of the civil war: Marshals Voroshilov and Budenny. These forces were assembled in the forests around Moscow, and on December 6, 1941, Russia struck back. For the first time the Nazis were really stopped. In the winter campaign of 1941-1942 the Red Army managed to push the Germans back from Moscow, but Leningrad was still besieged, and the Ukraine was in German hands.

In the summer of 1942 Hitler began his second campaign. This time the German military machine concentrated all its resources on one drive. The plan was to break through in the south, to reach the Volga, then go up the Volga and capture Moscow from the rear. The German hordes did break through in the south, poured toward the Caucasian mountains, and reached Stalingrad on the Volga in the fall. Everything the Germans could muster was thrown at Stalingrad, but the city held. The colossal, unrelenting bombardment destroyed every structure, the city was completely in ruins. But what metal and stone could not take, men could withstand. In the ruins of Stalingrad the resistance continued. While the soldiers of Stalingrad with their backs to the river Volga were resisting the might of the German assault, new armies for an offensive were being assembled and equipped. In November, 1942, the Red Army struck again, quickly surrounded the besieging forces of the German General von Paulus, and early in 1943 Stalingrad was liberated. An entire German army of 330,000 men was captured or destroyed.

The summer of 1943 was to witness, according to Hitler, the final German drive. Stalingrad was to be avenged and Russia crushed. In a salient near Kursk the Germans assembled even more mechanical equipment than they had at Stalingrad. They knew that they were going to face the flower of the Red Army, which was also preparing an offensive. This third German drive progressed only a few miles, and then the Red Army counter-offensive began. From this point on, the Red Army proceeded to liberate occupied territories and destroy the invaders.

Guerilla warfare, which the Russians employed so well against Napoleon in 1812, was organized in 1941 on a much larger scale, much more systematically, and from the very start of the war this time. Guerillas operated virtually everywhere behind the German lines; they often had professional military leadership, and were in radio communication with the Red Army, co-ordinating their activities with those of the regular troops. The Germans were faced not only with a defense in depth, but also with an attack in depth, because far behind their lines the Russians were also attacking. As the Red Army moved on, its numbers were augmented by the guerilla fighters.

As soon as Hitler attacked, the Soviet government started evacuating industry to the east. Men, tools and machines were loaded on trains and unloaded in the Urals or beyond. The new industrial centers constructed during the five-year plans now received evacuated equipment and skilled help from the older industrial centers overrun by the enemy. Although the Germans managed to capture the industries of the Ukraine and the Don Basin, and besiege the manufacturing city of Leningrad, they did not destroy the industrial potential of the Soviet Union. The armies that liberated Stalingrad and captured von Paulus were equipped from the Urals, where new production of the tools of war was being developed on an unprecedented scale, too far for the enemy to reach.

Considerable Lend-Lease aid began to arrive by 1943. By the same time the merger of local industry in the east with the evacuated factories had apparently been completed. The Hitler armies no longer had the tremendous superiority they enjoyed at the beginning, particularly in the number of tanks and trucks.

The war brought untold suffering to the Russian people in the occupied areas. Behind the fighting lines everything was mobilized for the war. The distinction between the front and the rear disappeared. Men, women and children engaged in production, in collecting the harvest, in providing fuel for the cities. The colossal production of tanks, airplanes and other instruments of war could be achieved only at the expense of curtailing all other production. Life again became difficult. As one area after another was liberated, cities had to be rebuilt, population provided with food and clothing. This process of reconstruction, which had to be started right in the midst of war, provided an additional drain on the hard-pressed resources of the Soviet Union. But the Soviet people had made up their minds to win this war, just as in the days of Napoleon. Russia had seen the Tartars, Swedes, Poles, French and Germans come and go. Through incredible hardships the people had survived in the past, and they were determined to survive and win this time also.

On the day of the invasion, Winston Churchill announced that England would stand with the U.S.S.R. in fighting the common enemy. After Pearl Harbor the United States officially joined this partnership, having begun to extend Lend-Lease to Russia even before that date. Churchill went to Moscow and Molotov went to Washington. Finally in November, 1943, Churchill, Roosevelt and Stalin met at Teheran to map a joint attack on Germany from the East, South and West, toward the destruction of Hitlerite Germany. In the fourth year of the Soviet-German war the fascist enemy, hemmed in from the South and West by the Anglo-American forces, and on the East by the Soviet forces, was being crushed.

During these four years of war the Union had achieved undoubted recognition as one of the great powers. Great Britain, the U. S. and the U.S.S.R. were the acknowledged Big Three of the world.

Victory neared, and the Big Three became more than ever appreciative of each other's power. This was good; the

alliance continued effective on the battle front; but with each military success the problems that came up for discussion and solution multiplied.

The great Allies began to discuss these postwar problems, with the result that as early as May, 1943, a Soviet delegation arrived in the United States to join the United Nations food conference at Hot Springs, Va. While the Anglo-American forces were battling from the beaches of Normandy inland, the Soviet Union's representatives were meeting with those of a score of other nations at Bretton Woods in New Hampshire but Russia soon showed that it attended these conferences to observe rather than to cooperate.

In the autumn of 1944, United Nations representatives met again at Dumbarton Oaks, in Washington, D.C., where they tried to build a permanent organization of nations to preserve the peace of the world.

In the meantime France was being cleared by Anglo-American forces in the West (to Russia's great relief), and the Red Army was driving the German army back toward German soil; liberating the Balkans; encircling and crushing, on the Stalingrad pattern, division after division of the German and satellite armies.

The war was coming to a close, and the Big Three met again, this time in liberated Crimea, near Yalta in January, 1945. Final victory plans were discussed and a date set for an international gathering at San Francisco to discuss the setting up of the machinery to preserve the peace after victory.

Franklin D. Roosevelt suddenly died on April 12. Fate prevented him from witnessing the final victory and from setting in motion the post-war plan for a community of nations pledged to peace. Roosevelt represented America to the citizens of the Soviet Union, whether they were Byelorussian or Bashkir, Ukrainian or Tartar. He personified the American ally, and now he was gone, just on the eve of victory. Never before had the passing of a foreign statesman evoked so general a sorrow throughout the U.S.S.R., or such expressions of public sympathy.

At San Francisco the delegations met to go on with the task begun at Dumbarton Oaks. Molotov came to represent the U.S.S.R., and there were also present Ukrainian and Byelorussian delegations. But events moved faster than diplomacy. A post-war charter was finished and signed after Germany's collapse, not before as anticipated. The chief delegates were hurried home to construct the peace.

On the River Oder, after taking Budapest, Vienna and Konigsberg, the Red Army fought its last big battle, the battle for Berlin. The battle of the Oder was won by the Red Army with the greatest concentration of tanks and the heaviest artillery barrages yet witnessed. The maps of Berlin used by the Red Army in this offensive had been prepared two and a half years before in cold, hungry and besieged Leningrad by cartographers who knew that the day would come. On May 1, 1945, the main citadel of Fascism collapsed: Marshal Zhukov took Berlin.

"Victory will be ours," Stalin had said when the invasion began. Now victory was achieved. A few days earlier the Red Army and the American expeditionary forces had joined hands on the river Elbe. Germany was cut in two. A week after the fall of Berlin, Hitlerite Germany surrendered unconditionally.

Germany was divided into zones and occupied by the allies. In Berlin a joint occupation was set up. The U. S. A., U.S.S.R., and Great Britain were faced with a new task. The Big Three — this time Churchill, Stalin and Truman — met again, now on conquered Nazi soil, in Potsdam, to plan the peace. A Labor landslide in Britain swept Churchill out of office and Clement R. Attlee in, much to the astonishment of Stalin, who could not understand this non-Communist democratic process.

In August the pace of events speeded to a terrific crescendo. The U. S. unleashed its atomic bomb. Russia declared war on Japan. Abruptly the war in the East ended — *pro forma* — bringing peace to the whole world for the first time in 14 years.

THE CRISIS

Some Russians are prone to deny that the Battle of Stalingrad was zero hour in modern world history. If the Russian armies had not turned back the Nazi armies at that time and place, they would (say Russians) have done so further east later on. Never would they have stopped fighting until the Germans were beaten. Never would they have permitted the Nazi system to conquer the Soviet system, and, in so doing, become supreme in the Old World. Thus January, 1943, the month of Stalingrad's liberation, was not a time of absolute crisis, not a last possible hour. It just happened (in this Russian view) to be the moment when the turn did come, when the Nazi machine did get smashed.

Nevertheless, the record stands clear. It was at Stalingrad that the crucial chapter of World War II was written, in stupendous suffering and courage and valor. It is to the stand at Stalingrad that historians must forever point to mark the peak, the supreme crisis, of the greatest threat free peoples have known in modern times. It was to Stalingrad that the King of England, whose nation had made a similar stand in the Battle of Britain, said: "To the steel-hearted citizens of Stalingrad, the gift of King George VI, in token of the homage of the British people." (*Below*): Lieut.-Col. Demchenko, commandant of the city, holding the Sword of Honor.

One of Stalingrad's defenders coined this slogan:

"The city is tired.
"The houses are tired.
"The bricks are tired.
"We are *not* tired!"

(*Above*): One of the classic photographs of the fighting at Stalingrad — Red riflemen pressing in to retake the siege-battered city.

BLITZ!

ON JUNE 22, 1941 Germany struck without warning, in the middle of the night, in the blitzkrieg pattern practised and perfected in Poland, Norway, the Lowlands and France. Some 165 divisions, including at least 20 panzer divisions, were increased to more than 200 in the first month. About 80% of the Luftwaffe, some 8,000 planes, were hurled in at the outset. The Soviets had ready 165 divisions and perhaps 10,000 first-line planes, to meet the onslaught on its three main lines — Koenigsberg-Leningrad, Warsaw-Moscow, Lublin-Kiev — with secondary drives on the Finnish and Bessarabian fronts. The German strategy called for quick and overwhelming assault, an early knockout. What Russia's frontier cities soon looked like (*see page opposite*), how the panzers plunged and thundered across the plains (*above*), how Russia's motorized columns suffered (*left*), were all too familiar after Germany's performance in the west. But the Russians stood up to their punishment, fought back hard while retreating, did not become demoralized or permit an early major breakthrough. Poor though their preparation had been, they proved, to themselves and to the world, their stamina.

The cost to Russia of her all-out defense was half a million casualties per month and loss of most of her front-line tanks and planes. But still the Russians did not crack, and the war pattern began to change.

BLITZ !

ELEVEN MILES A DAY. How well the Russians resisted is indicated by the speed of the German advance — an average of about eleven miles a day along the three main lines in the first three weeks — as against their average of 21.5 miles per day going from Aachen to Calais in two weeks of 1940. German shock-troopers like the ones pictured on these two pages (all from summer, 1941) early learned respect for the Red Army as it retreated from house to house, factory to factory, city to city, river to river — but always fighting back, not once routed.

WAR IN DEPTH

Nazi blitz campaigns, prior to Russia, had been won by bold thrusts into the enemy's rear areas, followed by destruction or demoralization of enemy forces flanked or by-passed. Russia's reply was to make war in such depth that there were, in effect, no rear areas; a war of "offensive defense" so planned that the invader had at all times to protect his own rear. For this strategy the Red Air Force was, of course, the prime arm. From the first day it attacked the legthening Nazi lines of supply and communication, with results like those shown below.

SCORCHED EARTH

Like Peter the Great in his war with the Swedes, the Soviet commanders from the first steeled their people to a "scorched earth" policy, to deny the invader any profit or comfort from the areas he occupied. This meant the removal of vehicles, animals and supplies; the demolition of utilities, roads and bridges. It meant also burning crops in the field and putting peasant homes to the torch, to destroy all shelter. If Russians protested this destruction, they were silenced by the Soviet police.

GUERILLAS

Red soldiers were trained not only to fight on when flanked or encircled but, under some circumstances, to remain in the enemy's rear, break up into small groups or disperse as individuals, to join and lead guerilla bands from towns and "inhabited places" (often, collective farms) left behind by the withdrawing armies. Russia's guerillas were mostly trained in the far-flung Osoaviakhim. On this page, some official photographs of Russian guerillas, systematically organized and supplied to harass the enemy's rear. (*Above, left*): A guerilla bivouac. (*Above*): Guerilla T. Balavenskaya (with Order of Red Star). (*Left*): Red officers at guerilla headquarters. (*Below*): Guerilla bread in the Byelorussian marshes. (*Below, left*): Red soldier demonstrating German gun to guerillas.

HOME FRONT

The extent to which the home front was mobilized as the People in Arms is at least intimated by this photo of trench-digging outside of Moscow — an operation for which the Red Army's fighting retreat gave plenty of time. Women and school-children did this work while Workers' Divisions went to the fighting fronts.

IN THE RED SQUARE, heart of the Soviet Union, with St. Basil's Cathedral and the Kremlin looming like History's sentinels, regular units of the Red Army passed in review as they braced for the coming showdown struggle to save Moscow. The picture below was taken about November 7, when in winter's first chill, Russia's leaders calmly celebrated their Revolution's 24th anniversary in this manner, with Hitler's armies only 40 miles away.

GRAND STRATEGY

Military men revere the writings of Prussian General Karl von Clausewitz (1780-1831) and cite the fact that the grand strategy adopted by Russia in 1941 was one of four schemes of defense laid down by Clausewitz in his classic *On War*. Fact is, Clausewitz (*left*) fought for Russia against Napoleon and saw with his own eyes the strategy of General Kutuzov in 1812, which was a fighting retreat, with earth-scorching that included even Moscow, to a depth inside Russia which overtaxed Napoleon's supply lines. As adapted by Marshal Stalin (who took supreme command in the fourth week of the invasion) and Marshal Semyon Timoshenko (*right*), in active command of the western front, Kutuzov's plan was modified to include a determined stand west of Moscow, whose capture the Nazis had scheduled for the war's first month. (*Below*): Powerful reserves of Red tanks and infantry were held ready for the stand before Moscow.

Powerful rings of anti-aircraft guns were thrown around Leningrad and Moscow, which the Nazis did not start bombing until the war's second month, when they began to realize they could not reach these cities with ground forces to take them intact.

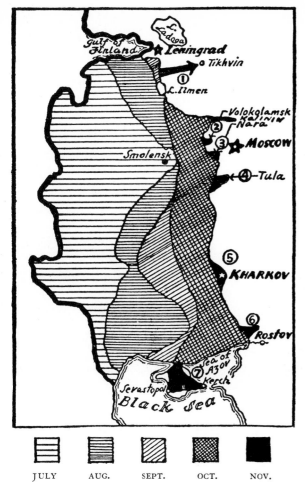

JULY   AUG.   SEPT.   OCT.   NOV.

STAND AT SMOLENSK

Smolensk was the area chosen for the Red Army's first big holding point. Map at left (from Captain Sergei N. Kournakoff's *Russia's Fighting Forces*) shows where the blitz was blunted and held up for two months, thus knocking out the whole Nazi timetable. Thereafter the Nazi advance proceeded more slowly, along the whole long line from Leningrad to Rostov, until the Nazis' reserves had been whittled down and winter came and the Soviets' counter-offensive was mounted, ready to go. (*Below*): Red infantry digging in to defend Smolensk.

MOVE TO THE URALS

A carefully planned part of the Soviet war-in-depth was the wholesale transfer of key industries from sites vulnerable to German bombs to new sites hundreds of miles east, in and beyond the Urals. While the Red Army held the battle line, completed its mobilization and prepared to counter-attack, other armies of the People in Arms hustled night and day to dismantle and pack up machinery for making shells, tanks and tires, guns and planes. Thousands of trains carried these machines, and the people to operate them, to the east, where not only new factory sites but homes for the workers had to be built. Much of the machinery was damaged in evacuation, but at least it did not fall into Nazi hands. On this page: some of the very few pictures released showing the move to the Urals. Workers in the lower right hand picture are converting sheds and warehouses into temporary homes, somewhere in the Urals. Not pictured: the machinery — and the people — left behind.

GENERAL MUD When the autumn rains came, Germany's motorized war machine bogged down. Mud hampered the Soviets, too, but they were better prepared for it, with their cavalry and with wider tank treads.

GENERAL WINTER

After General Mud came Russia's old ally General Winter, with temperatures well below Zero before December. Just when the Nazis launched their final pushes to encircle Leningrad and Moscow — with 15 Panzer, 4 motorized and 33 infantry divisions in the latter sector alone — they discovered their men were not dressed warmly enough. A few officers got special togs (*above, left*) but most of the Nazis looked and felt like the others on this page.

ON DEC. 7, 1941

Height of the German effort to win by an early knockout came in late November, 1941, when the Nazis hammered at the gates of Leningrad, Moscow, Rostov. Marshal Zhukov, who was put in to replace Timoshenko, hit back hard in the north and south but reserved his greatest counter-blow for the Moscow sector where, beginning December 7 — Pearl Harbor day — about 56 Nazi divisions, including four Panzers under General Guderian and 11 others under von Kluge, von Strauss and von Schmidt, were smashed backward in a fortnight by five Russian armies. Kalinin, Klin, Mozhaisk and Tula were the foci of this master-stroke, which relieved Moscow by blunting the German spearheads beyond repair for months to come. (*Above*): Nazi column after strafing by the new Stormovik fighter-bombers. (*Right*): Red mortar team going into action. (*Bottom*): Red infantry surging forward past a gun of their own (*left*) and a wrecked German one.

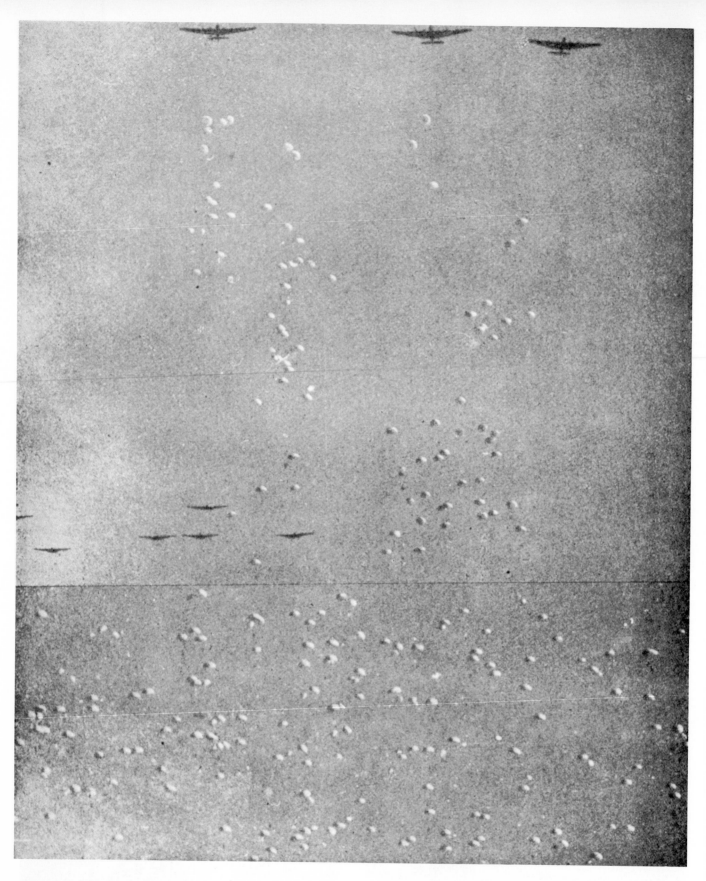

PARATROOPS

The first use of Red Army parachute troops was against Central Asian rebels in 1931. The winter of 1941-1942 saw this arm for war-in-depth put to great good use by the Red Army. With an enormous reservoir of civilian parachutists to draw on (more than 1,000,000 jumps were made by civilians in 1940 alone), the high command's strategy was not to try landing large masses of men in the enemy's rear. Instead it sent them continuously, in small groups seldom larger than a platoon, to land usually by night and accomplish innumerable small jobs of sabotage and harassment, then thread their way back, or join with the guerillas. In this picture 230 parachutists are seen, one small company with equipment. For technique, *see next page.*

Troops assemble in dispersal areas.

They board their planes.

They land in cover, well armed.

Even anti-tank guns are dropped.

A detail mines an enemy railroad . . .

. . . and neatly blows it up.

69th PARALLEL

American supplies and munitions started flowing to Russia via the icy northern sea route before 1941 was out. British and U. S. war vessels convoyed the long lines of plodding freighters around the North Cape under low-hanging, leaden overcast out of which Heinkel torpedo and dive-bombers would swoop to kill. In the fierce saga of those voyages, the Red Navy and Air

Force also had a part, for they would go out to meet their Allies and the vital cargoes they brought. The Soviets made a film called *69th Parallel* (latitude of Murmansk) to memorialize this traffic and the grim battles that were fought to protect it. Some shots from the film appear on this page.

(*Above*): Heinkels swing low into a convoy . . . and score a hit from which the smoke pillar towers into gloomy overcast. (*Below*): A Soviet escort sustains two near misses . . . and fires back furiously with ack-ack.

Long lines of ships lie at the Russian docks. (*Right*): A Churchill tank being swung overside to fight Germany where,

25 years before, Allied forces landed to prevent "lend-lease" munitions sent the Tsar's armies from falling into German hands.

SPECIAL WEAPONS

One of the finest new weapons evolved by the Russians was the low-flying, cannon-firing Stormovik fighter-bomber to "bust" tanks. In the rare photo above, a flight of Stormoviks is seen after it has strafed a Nazi tank column on a highway and busted three out of five. The Stormovik was heavily armored to protect it from ground fire. Relatively slow, it had great fire-power.

THE AERO-SLEDGE, propellor-driven on skis, whisked raiding parties cross-country at 60 m.p.h. — another weapon for war-in-depth.

In their fighting retreats, **LAND-MINING** (*below*) to impede tanks and shock troops was brought to a new peak by the Soviets. The Nazis copied this when their turn came to retreat.

The two-man **ANTI-TANK RIFLE,** of special large calibre with a long barrel to give terrific muzzle velocity, was another Russian invention, mass-produced within three weeks of the blue-prints being approved.

THE ROCKET GUN was first perfected and used by the Soviets. It played a major part in turning the tide at Stalingrad.

SPECIAL REASONS

THE PICTURES on this and the following pages are printed not just to be gruesome but because they constitute a very real and important aspect of World War II. They are some of the special reasons for fighting with bitter hatred which the Russians absorbed as the Nazis pushed into the U.S.S.R. and tried to pacify the captured areas by terror. There are sometimes two sides to stories of atrocities in war. In the case of the Nazis, the record is indelibly against them by proven brutalities inhuman beyond belief.

Only clue as to how one mass of men could do such things to other men — and to women and children — is that the Master Race was taught to regard and treat all other races, especially Jews and Poles and Russians, as sub-human. This teaching, this record, accounts for no small part of the Soviets' furious will-to-win.

(*Below*): Six Russian Citizens—a photo found on a dead German at Stalingrad.

SPECIAL REASONS (Cont'd.)

When the Germans shot captives, like those above (out of 200) at Pyatigorsk, they usually left them lying for relatives to come and bury. The scene below (in Warsaw) is merely the first act in a criminal tragedy that was repeated wherever the Nazis herded Jews into ghettos and then destroyed them. Mothers and children were included in Hitler's order for the extermination of non-combatants. In Kerch alone 7,000 were hanged. (*Bottom of page*): Pictures taken from Nazi soldiers.

THE GREAT SIEGES

LENINGRAD remained under siege for 29 months, ringed about by enemy cannon, without relief except by air and precarious lines across Lake Ladoga, by boat in summer, by rail when the ice was thick enough. Yet Leningrad not only lived but resumed making its own munitions, eventually cracked its blockade when troops from the Volkhov River front joined joyfully with the garrison of the Workers' Settlement (*right*).

SEVASTOPOL, main base of the Black Sea Fleet, fell to the Nazis July 3, 1943, after a siege of 250 days. Even then, thousands of guerillas went on living (as others did at Odessa) in the city's catacombs (*below, left*), darting out by night to make life miserable for the Nazi garrison. Sevastopol's stand delayed that summer's German drive to the Caucasus by at least a month. (*Bottom*): Smoke screen being laid across the besieged harbor to blind the attacking German artillery.

But **STALINGRAD** was the greatest stand of all. Hallowed as a bastion of the Revolution, when it was defended by Stalin (for whom its old name, Tsaritsyn, was changed), the great city on the Volga was triply important to the Soviets in 1942: (1) as the key to the Volga supply artery; (2) as a bulwark

before the Asian hinterland; and (3) a bulwark against the Nazi plan to take Moscow with a right hook. Its siege began August 22, 1942, when Marshal von Bock, who had some 100 divisions spearing east from Voronezh down to Mozdok at the peak of the Nazi's great summer push, sent General von Paulus and the VI Army Group (about 50 divisions) against it from north, west and south. When pincer tactics failed, the assault was made frontally and massively. (*Below*): House-to-house fighting in Stalingrad, and oil depots going up.

FOR 47 DAYS Stalingrad was hammered daily by 1,000 planes, and then by monster mortars (*below*). Von Paulus spent at least 250,000 men on the ground. But Stalingrad held, and Generals Rokossovsky and Yeremenko engineered one of history's greatest victories: a "super-Cannae" of encirclement and annihilation for about 330,000 Nazis. Two adjacent pictures at right show how Stalingrad's Square of the Fallen Heroes looked before and after the siege. The defenders' watchword was: "There is no land beyond the Volga." As the city was reduced to rubble, the Russians just dug deeper in with the river at their backs.

AFTER 140 DAYS, the 162-day siege began to turn when a wide Russian double pincers pressed around behind the besiegers Then the city's liberation proceeded as its defense had gone — house-to-house fighting of the fiercest kind, charges across footbridges (*bottom right*), heroic feats of mining and sniping. Finally, the pincers clamped shut.

Captain Kournakoff writes of Red tactics: ". . . Pincers were formed which not only bit off, but chewed up what they bit off."

VON PAULUS. The Nazi general von Paulus, who had stood in a fair way to become one of the Wehrmacht's all-time heroes (had he opened the back road to Moscow), was accorded the hollow honor of a Marshal's baton a few days before his VI Army Group was finally crushed. His capture came ignominiously, in the basement of a battered department store, by a business-like young Red 2nd lieutenant. With him were bagged 24 German and Rumanian generals. (*Left*): von Paulus (hands in pockets) with one of his staff.

THE TIDE TURNS

After Stalingrad, the westward march of the Red Army was irresistibly triumphant. Voronezh, Kharkov, Rostov, Kerch, Sevastopol, Odessa, Kiev — one after another all of Russia's big cities except a few Baltic ones were recaptured through 1943-1944. All of Russia's arms shared the glory, particularly the artillery which battered through the Nazis' "hedgehog" strongpoints like Kursk. But now was the greatest hour for Russia's traditionally valorous cavalry, of which the Reds had more than 60 divisions. New and ingenious was their coupling of horse and motor. Tanks and planes complemented the hard-riding horsemen (*above*), a development new to modern warfare. Red cavalry was often equipped with steel helmets and tommy-guns (*below*), but there was still work for sabres (*left*). One thing about cavalry pictures, like the bottom one: you can always tell a charge from a retreat. You don't retreat with your sabre raised aloft.

MARSHAL ZHUKOV

Marshal Timoshenko was wounded in May, 1942 and thereafter was not very active in the field. He became one of the co-ordinators of the Red Army High Command. But long before then the world had learned who was Russia's No. 1 soldier under Marshal Stalin. Grigory Konstántinovich Zhukov (*above*) was called in by Stalin to replace Timoshenko at Moscow's darkest hour (October, 1941). He organized the reserves brilliantly. He timed the counterblows precisely. He ordered: "Not a step back! Halt the Fascists! Every man must fight like ten!" He saved Moscow.

From then on Zhukov functioned like a MacArthur-Eisenhower-Montgomery rolled into one. As supreme field chief of every big operation in every theatre — Stalingrad, Leningrad, Crimea, the Ukraine, Poland, Hungary, finally Germany itself — he was his Motherland's busiest fighting son.

Maps and dates of the blows he struck from Stalingrad to the gates of Berlin appear at the right.

Like almost all the other rugged young Russians who whipped the proud Prussian school of war, Zhukov came from Russian peasant stock (born 1896). A furrier's apprentice, he was drafted into the Tsar's army, invalided out, then joined the Red cavalry and the Communist Party. He went through Frunze Academy (the Red war college) and went to Germany (prior to Hitler's advent) to hear lectures given by the German General Staff to Russians and Chinese. By 1936 he had so won the confidence of Stalin and Voroshilov that they sent him to Spain to preview World War II.

He commanded the Red Army on its proving ground against Japan in Mongolia (1939), then understudied Timoshenko in the Finnish campaign. He inveighed against oldsters and politics in the Red Army and was appointed to reorganize it, just in time to meet the German attack. Upon him, before Germany's last gasp, his country had lavished every decoration. Remained only to name a decoration after him, like the Order of Suvorov.

NOV. 1942 - FEB. 1943. Stalingrad freed, Mannstein and Bock smashed backward to the Donetz. (*Below*): **JULY 1943 - MAY 1944.** Ukraine, Crimea, Leningrad freed.

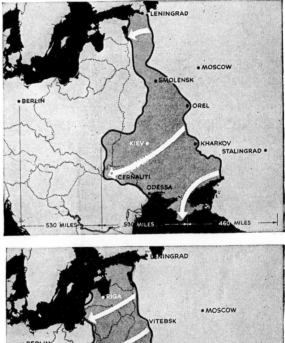

JUNE 1943 - JAN. 1945. Baltic states freed and Poland to Warsaw, Hungary to Budapest. (*Below*): **BY MID-FEBRUARY,** Warsaw and Budapest taken.

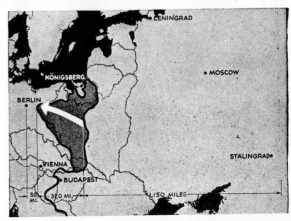

WESTBOUND JUGGERNAUT

After the fearsome German war machine was stopped and thrown into reverse, the Red Army juggernaut increased steadily in size, maneuverability and momentum westward. Seeing it coming, the Germans in panic recruited young boys and old men to dig anti-tank trenches (*upper left*) to protect their Reich's "holy soil." They erected dragon-tooth barriers (*above*) like those fringing the Siegfried Line and the Westwall, but without the latter's hill-country elevations for the bunkers and fortresses. The Eastwall was no pushover, however, and the Russians had to wait for wide rivers to freeze before they could smash through. While they waited for liberation, captive inhabitants painted ominous signs like the gibbeted swastika at left.

WARSAW AND BUDAPEST were two of the most stubborn obstacles in the Red march of retribution. Warsaw (*below* and *bottom left*) was reduced to rubble by the Nazis. The revolting Polish underground did not get the help it expected from the Red Army. (*Bottom, right*): Backyard fighting in Budapest.

700,000 SQUARE MILES

Fighting across rivers, fighting house-to-house through their ruined cities, crashing through forests with their big self-propelled guns, surging forward with shock units aboard troop-carrying tanks, the Reds cleared nearly 700,000 square miles of the Motherland in 156 weeks. They carved down the Wehrmacht (and themselves) as shown by the table below:

LOSSES TO MAY 8, 1945 *(in round figures)*		
	GERMANY	RUSSIA
Killed and missing	2,500,000	20,000,000
Guns	45,000	48,000
Tanks	35,000	49,000
Planes	30,000	30,000

BATTLE OF GERMANY

(*Above*): Red forces inside the historic Brandenburg Gate.

NOT SINCE BATU in the 12th Century had any force overrun eastern Europe so irresistibly as the Red Army in 1944-1945. Fearful of "Asiatic" revenge, the Germans now fought their hardest. After Warsaw and Budapest had been taken, and the Russian power under Tolbukhin and Malinovsky moving up the Danube toward Vienna threatened to outflank Germany from the south, Marshal Zhukov opened the Battle of Germany with a monster wedge-shaped operation: himself in the center with heaviest armor and artillery on the straight Warsaw-Posnan-Frankfort route to Berlin; Chernyakovsky, Rokossovsky and Bagramian to push his right flank to the Baltic; Konev and Petrov to push his left toward Dresden and along the Carpathians.

On the Red Army's 27th birthday (February 24), General Eisenhower began the Allies' drive into Germany from the West. While this drive was fighting its way across the Rhine to head for the Elbe, Zhukov consolidated his strength on the Oder, widening his wedge to a broad-axe, clearing up tough rear pockets like Koenigsburg, Danzig and Breslau. When Eisenhower's team of Montgomery and Bradley were rolling well across the north German plain, and Patton and Patch were spearing through to join Konev and Tolbukhin in cutting off escape to the "redoubt" of the Bavarian Alps, Zhukov closed in frontally and from north and south on the bristling Berlin area with overwhelming masses of artillery and armor.

One element of the Russian juggernaut that did savor of Asia was a transport corps of Siberian camels (*above*) that had plodded all the way from Stalingrad.

In Berlin, the frantic defenders holed up in the subways, whence they were routed out like rats by Red shock troops (*above*) employing grenades and tommy-guns.

WHAT WAS LEFT OF BERLIN after months of Allied bombing was systematically shelled and mortared (*above*) by the entering Russians, many of whom carried the names and street addresses of Nazis on whom they wanted to wreak personal vengeance for atrocities done their folks at home.

HITLER'S REICHS-CHANCELLORY, where he was reported to have stayed (deep underground) until a few hours before the end, when he either died or vanished, was a prime target for the Reds' siege guns. It was thoroughly gutted when Red soldiers arrived to comb the shattered ruins (*above*).

UNCONDITIONAL SURRENDER

By May 7, the shattered, disorganized, decimated Nazi forces were ready to surrender finally and unconditionally. They had been surrendering locally by hundreds of thousands before that day to the Americans and British, sooner than be driven into Russian hands. (*Right*): Some 160,000 Germans in one U. S. Army prisoner camp. In the middle of the night, General-Admiral von Friedeburg, c.-in-c. of the German Navy, Col.-Gen. Jodl, chief-of-staff of the German Army and Maj.-Gen. Oxenius, his aide (*below, right,* backs to camera) were received in supreme Allied headquarters at Reims by deputies of the Allied commanders, including the Russians. In this historic picture, Lt.-Gen. Susloparov (third from right on far side) is signing for Russia.

But Russia was not yet content to declare V-E Day, because resistance to the Red Army continued in several remaining pockets, especially in Czechoslovakia, where Nazi die-hards preferred death in battle to the "night of long knives" which they expected from Poles and Czechs as well as Russians if they surrendered. At length, Russia was satisfied and on May 8, in Berlin, the German commander-in-chief, Marshal Keitel, was allowed to ratify the Reims surrender. Air Chief Marshal Sir Arthur Tedder, deputy to General Eisenhower, signed for the American-British Supreme Command, Marshal Zhukov for his commander-in-chief, Marshal Stalin. (*Left*): Keitel signing. (*Below, left*): Zhukov, showing the strain of a 46-month war, checking over the documents before using his pen.

"IVAN" AND "JOE"

'We made contact at 1:32 Wednesday afternoon [April 25] on the banks of the Elbe River northwest of Dresden. There were no brass bands, no sign of the titanic strength of both these armies. The Americans who met the Red Army were a couple of dust-covered young lieutenants and a handful of enlisted men in their jeeps on reconnaissance. For days we had known that the Russians were near. More than a week before, General [Omar] Bradley had ordered our 1st Army to stop.

(This moment, described by Columbia Broadcasting Correspondent Richard C. Hottelet, had actually been anticipated for weeks. The Russian "Ivan" and the American "G.I. Joe" had looked forward with strong male curiosity and pleasure to meeting each other at the broken heart of Germany — as suggested by the photo above of a U. S. 406th Infantry demonstration in March.)

Hottelet continued: " . . . In the town of Riese, a 69th Division patrol spotted some Russians. And that was it.

"Some hours later another lieutenant got to Torgau on the Elbe and crawled out to the middle of a wrecked bridge. He brought back some Russian officers to division headquarters, which made it official.

"That's just the way it was — as simple and untheatrical as that. Just some men meeting, shaking hands, slapping each other on the back — glad to see each other. . . . These were the sort of men who for two and a half years have fought their way half way around the world to reach this moment — to meet and complete the destruction of Germany."

These were the war's real winners — the common soldiers of the grand alliance. For they not only had done the physical fighting. They and their kind were the populations involved. (*Below* and *top right*): "Ivan" and "Joe" fraternizing.

(*Right*): The formal joining of Russian and American colors was performed by Maj.-Gen. Reinhardt of the U. S. 69th Division (steel helmet) and Maj.-Gen. Rusakov of the 58th Guards, I Ukrainian Army.

Harry Hopkins visited Stalin, August, 1941.

Wendell Willkie in Moscow, November, 1942.

Joseph Davies revisited Stalin, May, 1943.

Eric Johnston, in March, 1944.

THE U.S.S.R. AND U.S.A.

The joining of "Ivan" and "Joe" (*see* p. 350) was the culmination of a long process. America's understanding of the Axis threat to all the western hemisphere was not sufficiently clear before Pearl Harbor for American politicians to do much more than start Lend-Lease, legislate conscription and get war-production rolling. Japan's attack at Pearl Harbor precipitated matters but it was to be long months thereafter before the hard-pressed Russian nation felt the weight of America at her side.

At the left are pictured a few high-lights of the rapprochement of America and Russia before and after Pearl Harbor. Above is the historic scene of U. S. Secretary of State Cordell Hull, in Moscow in October, 1943, signing with Russian Foreign Commissar Molotov, British Foreign Minister Eden and China's representatives the Pact of Moscow whereby these United Nations agreed to joint action in winning the war.

In addition to the visits recorded at the left, it should be remembered that Russia's worldly-wise Litvinov went to Washington for conferences, and so did Molotov, who astounded White House servants by toting a revolver and black bread in his suitcase.

TEHERAN. Britain and America were informed that Marshal Stalin, Russia's operational chief, could not go far outside his Union's borders to confer with Russia's allies. So the heads of those nations — Churchill and Roosevelt — traveled all the way to Teheran, capital of Iran, to talk with Stalin in December of 1943, and ratify what their foreign ministers had done at Moscow. This was historic indeed — the West going to Russia to consult — as well it might: for Russian man- and woman-power were soaking up the impact of three-quarters of the *Wehrmacht* and the *Luftwaffe*. At Teheran, the signatories agreed on joint action, and also upon Anglo-American invasion of France rather than the Balkans.

LEND-LEASE

Teheran was an inconvenient place for Churchill and Roosevelt to go to meet Stalin. But it was appropriate, as the capital of the country in which British and Russian interests clash most sharply, and the country through which an even bigger mass of Lend-Lease war-materials was by then flowing than went through the Arctic ports. The grand total of Lend-Lease to Russia was to reach $9,000,000,000 before V-E Day.

Some of the items:

638,000 tons of chemicals
294,000 tons of explosives
135,000 machine guns
12,200 planes
6,000 tanks
1,800 self-propelled guns
1,200 half-tracks
13,000 pistols
3,300 armored scout cars
8,200 guns
5,500 artillery prime movers
1,700 ordnance vehicles

331,000 motor vehicles, including —
45,000 jeeps
1,045 railroad locomotives
7,164 flat cars
1,000 dump cars
100 tank cars
60 power trains (to replace blasted hydroelectric stations)
1,300,000 tons of oil products
11,000,000 pairs of army boots
97,000,000 yards of cotton cloth
50,000,0000 yards of woolen cloth
58,000,000 yards of webbing.

Britain sent huge quantities of **ROLLING STOCK** (*above*) which U. S. Army trainmen operated up across Iran. U. S. Army engineers built a **NEW HIGHWAY** (*right*) over which fleets of U. S. trucks carried the goods from Persian Gulf ports to Russian control points.

SECOND FRONT

Russia's constant plea to her allies was that a Second Front be opened in the West, to draw at least 50 German divisions off the Red Army's front. Allied operations in Africa, and later Italy, comforted Russia, but not until the vast landings in Normandy beginning June, 1944, was Russia really happy. Then Marshal Stalin said: " . . . It may be stated without hesitation that the forcing of the Channel on a wide scale and the mass landing of Allied troops in the North of France have fully succeeded. This is undoubtedly a brilliant achievement of our Allies.

"It cannot but be admitted that the history of wars knows no other similar undertaking so broad in conception, so grand in scale, and so masterly in execution.

"As is known, in his time the 'invincible' Napoleon failed ignominiously in his plan to force the Channel and seize the British Isles. The hysterical Hitler, who for two years boasted that he would force the Channel, did not venture to make even an attempt to carry out his threat. It was only the British and American troops who succeeded in effecting with honour the grand plan of forcing the Channel and landing troops on a mass scale. History will mark this performance as an achievement of the highest order."

(*Left*): Supplies on Anzio beachhead, and equipment in France. (*Below*): D-Day, Normandy.

BRETTON WOODS

Russia's two great allies, Great Britain and America, had conferred closely on joint action, notably in Quebec and at Casablanca, with Russia not represented.

By July, 1944, with the Italian and French fronts powerful realities, Russia was ready to join in further discussions looking ahead to post-war organization of world order. She sent a delegation to a conference on monetary and financial stabilization, held in the Mount Washington Hotel at Bretton Woods, N.H. Even so, she mostly listened, held aloof.

Like all such meetings at this time, the Bretton Woods Conference could only blue-print a plan. Proposed were a short-term fund to help stabilize world currencies and an international bank to make long-term loans for post-war reconstruction. Russia seemed as cooperative at Bretton Woods as any nation, even agreeing to issue statements on her gold production when the proper time should come. The proper time never came. Russia refused to join the World Bank and International Monetary Fund resulting from this conference. (*Right*): The Bretton Woods money parley, of which U. S. Secretary of the Treasury Morgenthau was elected chairman, at its opening session.

DUMBARTON OAKS

Next, in August, 1944, came the full-dress, grand effort of the United Nations to plan a world security set-up. Again Russia joined, though only sending her young career diplomatist, Ambassador to Washington Andrei Gromyko, to sit in at the sessions instead of a big-wig from Moscow. The sessions were held in "Dumbarton Oaks," an old mansion on the outskirts of Washington (*left*). Here were proposed: (1) a Security Council dominated by the Big Five (Britain, the U. S., Russia and China, and later France); (2) a General Assembly in which all "peace-loving" states would participate on equal footing; (3) an International Court of Justice to settle disputes. The "sovereign equality" of all states was proclaimed. The Security Council would take "any measures necessary for the maintenance of international peace" should the Court fail or nations flout it.

Scores of reservations, amendments and objections to the Dumbarton Oaks plan were, of course, forthcoming from all 43 nations represented at this planning session. Especially disturbing was Russia's insistence on her right to an ironclad veto over all United Nations actions and procedures—an insistence which was to become a pattern as Russia, sensing her "foreignness" to the West, started to hold back and play international poker with her Allies.

YALTA

Early in February, 1945, President Roosevelt and Prime Minister Churchill met at Britain's war-torn island of Malta. Thence they flew to Yalta, in Crimea, where Marshal Stalin joined them at Livadia Palace (*inset above*), oldtime winter resort of the tsars. There for eight days, attended by their military and diplomatic chiefs (*below*), the Big Three attempted to chart the world's immediate future.

They first addressed themselves to the "final defeat" of Germany, resolved upon military co-operation "closer than ever," promised "new and even more powerful blows . . . by our armies and air forces into the heart of Germany from the east, west, north and south."

"Nazi Germany," they announced, "is doomed."

They asserted their "inflexible purpose" to destroy German militarism and Nazism . . . "to disarm and disband all German armed forces; break up for all time the German General Staff"; to eliminate or control German war industry, bring war criminals to justice, wipe out the Nazi party. They also said:

"It is not our purpose to destroy the people of Germany, but only when Nazism and militarism have been extirpated will there be hope for a decent life for Germans and a place for them in the comity of nations."

Russia agreed to enter the Pacific War three months after V-E Day. For this, it would receive the Kuriles, South Sakhalin, the Chinese Eastern and South Manchurian Railways and the two Manchurian ports: Port Arthur and Dairen. Nobody admitted it, but the idea was tacit: Russia would police and plunder Asia.

CRIMEAN CHARTER

Postwar problems sprouted like weeds at the heels of the retreating German armies in liberated territories. Feeding, housing, clothing the liberated peoples were only a fraction of the task. The self-determination of small countries was, as after World War I, basic among Allied intentions and promises. To reaffirm the so-called Atlantic Charter, which was necessarily vague and non-binding, the Big Three at Yalta issued a "Crimean Charter" which promised to concert their policies "during the temporary period of instability": to establish peace, supply relief, set up provisional governments "broadly representative of all democratic elements."

President Roosevelt was credited with evolving a formula, which Marshal Stalin accepted, for Poland. There was to be established a "Polish Provisional Government of National Unity" including "democratic" members of the new Lublin government fostered by Moscow, plus "other democratic leaders from within Poland and from abroad." The so-called Curzon Line of 1919 would be the Russo-Polish boundary, and Poland would be given German territory on the north and west. Britain, the U. S. and the U.S.S.R. would recognize this new Poland, at least until the Peace Conference. After President Roosevelt's death in April, disagreement arose as to just what this formula meant.

(*Above*): The Yalta conference table was round, and places measured exactly, so that each Great Man, or none, sat at the head.

(*Left*): Pipesmoker Stalin watching cigar-smoker Churchill. The Messrs. Roosevelt and Churchill in earnest colloquy before Marshal Stalin's arrival.

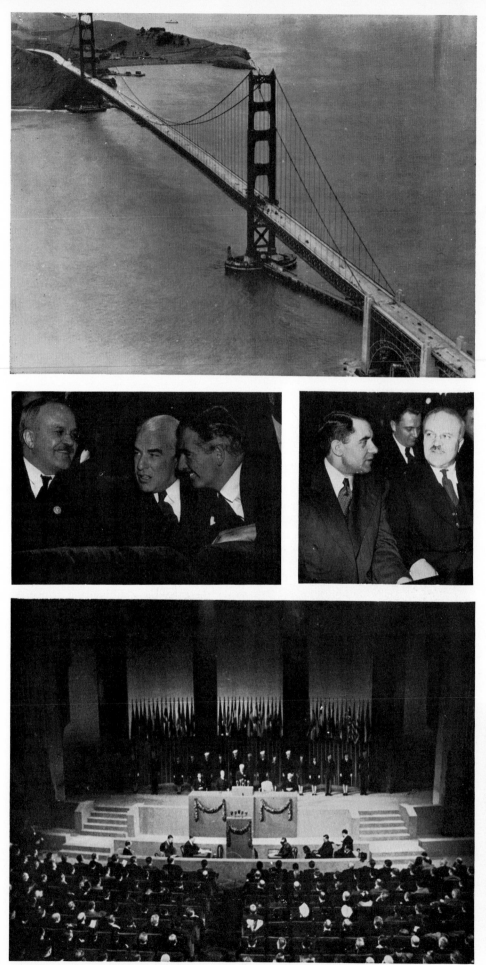

SAN FRANCISCO

At Yalta, the Big Three called for a United Nations conference on world security, to amend and elaborate the Dumbarton Oaks blueprint. The date chosen was April 25 — the date by which, unless she wished to renew it, Russia must denounce her friendship treaty with Japan. Before that date, Russia did denounce that treaty, and it was understood that Russia chose the place for this conference — San Francisco — which suggested that, with Germany beaten, Russia was ready to turn her attention if not her armed might to affairs in the Orient.

President Roosevelt died on the eve of this meeting, which he had designed to be the greatest one yet. Foreign Commissar Molotov traveled from Moscow to attend the affair in response to an appeal from the new U. S. President, Harry Truman. But neither Molotov nor Britain's Foreign Minister Eden stayed long. Victory in Europe and the pressing details of making peace overshadowed and delayed the nations' effort to draft finally, for ratification by their 50 governments, a world security system.

(*Top*): San Francisco's Golden Gate, where the new world order was designed. (*Center*): Commissar Molotov with Secretary Stettinius and Minister Eden. Ambassador Gromyko and his chief, Commissar Molotov. (*Bottom*): Opening of the conference in San Francisco's Opera House. (*Below*): President Truman addressing the Conference's closing session (June 26) after the delegates had signed the charter. Said he: "Oh, what a great day in history this can be! You have created a great instrument . . .

"Let us not fail to grasp this supreme chance. . . . !"

POTSDAM

Ten weeks after V-E Day, the Big Three leaders, with their foreign ministers, met in the former palace of Frederick the Great at Potsdam just outside Berlin, not to pursue peace as at San Francisco, but to palaver as politely as possible about the spoils of the war.

Franklin D. Roosevelt was dead, and before the meetings at Potsdam ended, Winston Churchill was voted from office by the war-weary British. Thus, seasoned Joseph Stalin had a pair of eager freshman-statesmen to deal with (one of whom thought "good old Uncle Joe" was "all right"). These were Harry Truman from Missouri and Clement Attlee from Putney. (*See left*, with Admiral Leahy, Truman's military adviser and No. 2 Statesmen Bevin, Byrnes, Molotov.)

PARTITIONING GERMANY

This was the main business of the Potsdam meeting. It was pretty cut-and-dried. It had been discussed at Yalta and predetermined by the strategy of the Grand Alliance whereby Britain entered Germany from the northwest, the U. S. from the southwest, the U.S.S.R. from the east to a line well past Berlin (*map, below*). By the axiom (*not* original with Lenin) that "who controls Germany controls Europe," the Soviets were thus entrenched for any and all future tussling on that continent. The little Saar corner allotted to France clearly reflected her reduced status in postwar Europe.

Reparations in coin or kind, peace treaties with the van-quished powers, the present feeding and future fates of captive peoples like Poland, Austria, Hungary — all such problems were left to the Big Three's foreign ministers, who were to meet many, many times, for years to come, trying to agree. As the fraternal wartime mood among the Big Three changed to moods of self-security, the partitioning of Germany was to provide one of history's all-time stumbling blocks.

If the two freshman-statesmen realized this, only one of them could afford to be smug, and that was Harry Truman. Up his sleeve he had a surprise that he thought would be the answer to everything, including peace not just for Europe but for the whole world (*see next page*).

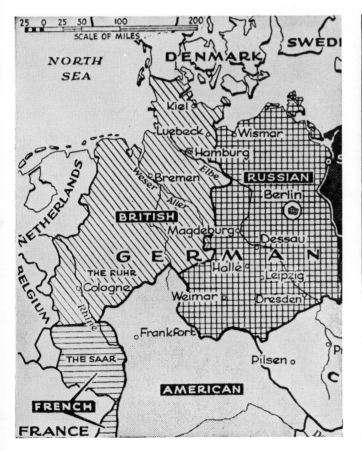

HISTORY MAY LOOK BACK at the acquaintance now formed by Eisenhower, generalissimo of the West, and Zhukov, his Soviet co-equal. Their armies having obliterated a hate-state, it was conceivable that these professionals would urge laymen never to permit further fighting among nations.

A **Potsdam Declaration** to Japan, probably worded by Winston Churchill before he left the scene, was signed by the U. S., Britain and China, but not by Russia, which was not yet at war with Japan. This ultimatum read: "Surrender or die!"

AN ERA OPENS

Up U. S. President Harry Truman's sleeve was a power — a horror — that dwarfed mankind. It was nothing less than the universe's prime force — nuclear energy — and Truman took the decision to unleash it on Hiroshima, then on Nagasaki, to bring the Japanese Empire finally to its knees. The use of this force in international affairs opened a new age in man's troubled history, at a cost of 97,159 dead and missing, 91,368 wounded in two explosions only.

What men would do further with atomic power, for worse or better, was a question posed to all humanity; and Russia, not yet having this force in its possession, stood somewhat aghast. The Soviets had been at war with Japan only one day before the second bomb fell, but they flew some officers over to be in on Japan's surrender (*see below*). (Ten years later, they had not relinquished their war status with what became virtually a U. S. protectorate.) The new force caused them to think fast and grimly. Atomic power was still in their laboratories. They would spar for time and consolidate their new space while their scientists caught up with the West. (*Above, left*): What an A-bomb explosion looks like seconds later! This photo was found in a Hiroshima news office. (*Above, right*): Corpses broiled stiff where they writhed (Nagasaki).

EMPIRE'S END

Japanese military and political functionaries went aboard U.S.S. *Missouri* ("Big Mo") in Tokyo Bay and, with General Douglas MacArthur (*right*) towering austerely above them, capitulated abjectly, retaining their Emperor only as a civilian symbol. Russia, while participating in this ceremony, kept its forces moving in Manchuria, scooping up prisoners for labor and indoctrination, amassing martial and industrial plunder.

XIII. COLD WAR

A change in the international political climate after San Francisco, Potsdam and the surrender of Japan was not unexpected, but it came with startling speed. It went from warm to cool to frigid. Immediately apparent when the smoke cleared and arms could be laid aside was the new world fact that the U.S.S.R. and the U. S. faced each other across the globe, no longer as titans allied in a common cause but now as the leaders of two rival systems which total war had conditioned for future action.

Capitalism, sobered in all its senses by havoc and sacrifice, was in a mood to repair the damage and restore general economic health as soon as possible. The United Nations sent relief through UNRRA, which was succeeded by the Marshall Plan, to pour U. S. billions into Europe's economy. When Russia took umbrage at the Marshall Plan and blockaded Berlin, the emphasis was shifted from economic to military security for western Europe, resulting in NATO.

Communism was shaken by its sacrifices but inspired by enormous potential gains made through it. It focused on consolidating these gains, this new dominance. Its victory was intoxicating to its leaders; and its masses' war spirit, instead of being allowed to subside, could be turned against the U.S. and Britain. World revolution, laid aside in 1943, was revived as the ultimate goal. Purges, terror, subterfuge, deceit — any means would be justified by these ends. And justification was made clearer (if Communist amorality needed clarification, which it did not) by two historical factors, one old, one new. These were: Western opposition to Russia's expansion southeastward; and the West's new super-weapon — Nuclear Power.

When at Yalta, Potsdam and after, the West firmly refused to give Russia, as part of her war prizes, warm-water egress at the Bosporus, dominance over Greece and Turkey and a free hand in oil-rich Iran, the first of these factors was underscored. When atomic secrets were withheld, seemingly (to Russia) as a fierce whip in unfriendly hands, the second factor was menacing. It was so interpreted by the Soviet leaders to discipline their war-torn peoples and keep them in line, unrelaxed.

The character of Joseph Stalin hastened and sharpened the world's new cleavage. How deeply he might differ from the original Roosevelt-Truman picture of a stern but good gray "father" to the Red masses was suggested not only by talkative high Reds like General Barmine and Colonel Kravchenko, who fled his power in fear and revulsion; but also by his postwar stratagems abroad as well as at home. Efforts by the Soviet spy apparatus to steal atomic and other secrets — exposed in Canada by Gouzenko, discovered by Washington in Eisler, Hiss and the Rosenbergs (who were executed) and by Britain in Klaus Fuchs, Allan Nunn May and several more (who escaped) — intensified Western distrust of the Red system and purposes to a pitch matched only by the Reds' suspicions toward the West.

Playing for time until their scientists could even the balance in nuclear power, the Soviets stalled the arrival of true peace by haggling at treaty parleys and by using the veto and even a boycott to jam the new United Nations machinery. They adopted a policy of keeping the West off-balance and of splitting it apart wherever possible. This was "cold war." They lowered an Iron Curtain for political privacy, kept more than 100 divisions ranked close behind it, ruthlessly rearranged the politics, populations and production of Eastern Europe to further their plans.

After accepting much UNRRA aid, Moscow turned and fought the Marshall Plan, forbade its friends to accept it. In one country after another which the Red Army had retaken from the Germans, the Russians set up one-party (Communist) governments, with dictators answerable to Moscow and a Cominform (the Comintern revived) to exert discipline. Poland, Rumania, Bulgaria, Albania, Hungary all heeled up. Czechoslovakia was more difficult, but a brusque coup in 1948 brought Prague, too, into line. Britain and the U. S. kept Greece and Austria out of Moscow's satellite ring, and Tito took Yugoslavia out when Moscow seemed to him too grasping. Otherwise, the extraction of reparations in cash, kind and labor proceeded unopposed and unimpeded in Eastern Europe, to resume building "Socialism in one country" at the expense of others.

The Soviets also exploited the fruits of their six-day war with Japan to establish a Red Axis clear across the world's largest, most populous land mass. When the U. S. failed to support Chiang Kai-shek's Nationalist Government in its civil war with Red Mao Tse-tung, Moscow swung in behind Mao and helped him win out. The new line-up, with Washington's MacArthur ruling in Tokyo, Mao in Peiping and Moscow itself in Manchuria, Sakhalin and the Kuriles, recalled a prescient forecast by Commodore Matthew Perry, who first entered Tokyo Bay in 1853 and later wrote:

"To me it seems that the people of America will extend their domain and power until they shall have brought within their mighty embrace multitudes of the islands of the great Pacific and placed the Saxon race upon the eastern shores of Asia. And I think, too, that eastward and southward will her great rival in future aggrandizement (Russia) stretch forth her power to the coasts of China and Siam; and thus the Saxon and the Cossack will meet once more, in strife or in friendship, on another field. Will it be friendship? I fear not!

"The antagonistic exponents of freedom and absolutism must thus meet at last and then will be fought that mighty battle on which the world will look with breathless interest; for on its issues will depend the freedom or the slavery of the world. Despotism or rational liberty must be the fate of civilized man."

Debatable is any interpretation of how the American people, properly advised, might have reacted had Washington stood more firmly than it did, in Truman's time, against extension of the Red Axis into the East and its testing of the West in Korea. Undebatable are: the temper of the European peoples at that time; the nature of the Soviet masses; the degree of control over the latter acquired and exercised by Stalin & Co.

The European countries, especially France, were sick and sore from war. Under the muzzles of the Red Army they had no stomach for rearming. Massive injections of Marshall Plan money were required to revive their will to survive, to join in at least a show of resistance against further Red conquest. They were slow to raise divisions for the common defense army and, in France's case, viewed with alarm the freeing and rearming of West Germany, until unifying Germany and using it as an East-West buffer proved truly impossible. They listened nervously when the Reds told them that America sought to use them as pawns and A-bomb fodder, after Red scientists came up with the atomic answers.

The Soviet peoples, on the other hand, reacted like well-trained troops. A whole generation of them had been conditioned, under the glass bell of Soviet ideology and isolation, to obey the Kremlin implicitly. Coerced by legions of secret police, the working hordes performed, albeit slowly and clumsily, prodigious tasks set by clever planners and engineers, whose demands rose ever higher as progress was made. Humanity, pleasure, humor had little place in their lives, which were imbued only with a blind will-to-build imposed from the top.

Stalin's control had been galvanized by the furious prewar purges. Now it was intensified by elevating him to the status of a superman, an all-wise heroic leader who had won the war practically single-handed. Stalinism as a cult was superimposed on Marxism without demur. The continuance of privation — putting heavy industry, heavy construction and armament ahead of consumer goods, housing and even food production — was suffered not in silence but with hosannahs from well-rehearsed choruses of workers and peasants chanting praise for Stalin's wisdom.

The rebuilding of the Soviet economy back to and, by 1955, well beyond its 1940 levels (*see table,* p. 369), was, indeed, little short of a miracle, even taking into account the slave labor and the leeching of the satellite states that made it possible. By 1952, when the Communist Party held its first Congress since 1939, results seemed to justify methods so well that the faithful received as gospel a promise from Stalin that Capitalism would crack and tear itself apart while Communism surged on to world dominion. By the time of Stalin's demise the following year (1953) no potentate since Tamerlane (unless it was Ivan the Terrible) had wielded such absolute one-man power over the Russians as the cold-eyed Georgian with the withered arm and ruthless power-complex. They laid him to rest beside Saint Lenin in the national shrine on Red Square and pilgrimaged in antlike millions to gaze on him in death.

THE PORTENT OF PEENEMÜNDE

Of all the war prizes taken by Russia in the Battle of Germany, perhaps none was so portentous as a small island at the mouth of the Peene River off the Baltic coast of Mecklenberg. Here, inaccessible except to the highest Nazi war chiefs, were the laboratories and production lines for the weapons with which Hitler hoped to — and very nearly did — win the Battle of Britain.

Hitler's "buzz bombs," as the British bravely nicknamed them, were something new in warfare. Unmanned, rocket-propelled packages of destruction, they could be launched into the stratosphere from well-hidden sites and guided to far-distant targets by built-in "brains" which earned them their other nickname: "robot bombs." Pushbutton warfare had arrived.

The R.A.F. spotted and heavily bombed Peenemünde as early as 1943, but the lethal research continued. The small V-1 buzz bombs of the early part of the war were succeeded by larger V-2s which could be fired from mobile launchers (*see above*), shifted from night to night along Germany's western coasts. Guidance problems were not sufficiently solved, however, in time to make the V-weapons decisive. In April, 1945, the Russians took Peenemünde before the scientists there had these problems finally licked.

The Russians destroyed Peenemünde in toto, but not before extracting all its secrets and "recruiting" the brains that made it tick. Some of the latter, including Dr. Wernher von Braun, escaped to the West, where their knowledge was eventually appreciated and put to work. (Dr. von Braun, "father of the ballistic missile," wound up leading the U. S. Army's missile-development team at Redstone Arsenal, Ala.)

Meantime, in the months and years following V-E Day, seafarers in the Baltic, especially the Swedes, who were too polite to say much about it, had frequent evidence that Red Russia was carrying on long-range, high-altitude rocket research from the point at which the Nazis had left off. Their capture of Peenemünde could be seen, a decade later, as giving the Soviets a formidable head-start in a fantastic race to develop "the ultimate weapon" — an unstoppable, 15,000-m.p.h. staged-rocket carrier for nuclear warheads which could cross oceans or poles in an intercontinental war.

V FOR VETO

When rules for the new United Nations were drawn, the Big Five agreed that each must have veto power lest its national sovereignty be infringed by the Security Council. Happiest adherent to this idea was Russia's Andrei Gromyko, who was to employ it time and again as a weapon in his country's "cold war" with the West.

First case to come before the Council, in January 1946, was Iran's demand that Russia get out of Azerbaidzhan. Going even beyond the veto, Gromyko led his delegation out of the Council in a boycott (above), reminiscent of Axis behavior in the old League of Nations (which was formally dissolved come that

April). Other delegates gasped at the young Red's stubborn disregard for the (supposed) new spirit of international conduct pledged by all U. N. members — but he had his orders from Moscow.

In May, Russia did bow to the world consensus and withdrew from Iran, but Russia's interpretation of collective security was clear: she would play ball only when it suited her long-range interests and her momentary moods. V had stood for Victory. Now it stood for Veto.

When the Anglo-American bloc decided to withhold its atomic secrets until the U. N. should establish controls over the awful new force, Gromyko was Russia's agent to prevent any such controls from interfering with the Soviet atomic program, which was now proceeding secretly at crash pressure and speed.

S FOR STUBBORN

Chief delegate for the U. S. in atomic-control planning was elder statesman Bernard M. Baruch. A curious pair they made — the tall, white-crested financier-philosopher, one of the most persuasive men of his time, and the pug-nosed little Stalinist career-man, one of the stubbornest. Moscow wanted no foreigners "inspecting" inside the U.S.S.R. Gromyko steadfastly resisted Baruch's intellect and charm (right) — even such blandishments as being taken by the former amateur heavyweight champion to the Louis-Conn world title fight; even such warnings as another huge, highly publicized blast touched off by the U.S. at Bikini atoll (above). When the Security Council voted otherwise unanimously for Baruch's plan, Gromyko abstained and had Poland do likewise. Tantamount to veto, this killed A-bomb control at its birth.

UNRRA

The Soviets applauded and signed up with the United Nations Relief and Rehabilitation Administration but contributed nothing to it, pleading prostration. The agency was headed by another U. S. financier-statesman, **Herbert H. Lehman.**

The Ukraine and Byelorussia alone got $163,000,000 worth of this assistance, which the Soviets could ill afford to acknowledge but worse afford to refuse, since fierce famines were but one of their postwar problems. Rebuilding a war-wrecked world was the universal task, but Russia had its own blueprints for a Red world and proceeded with these on its own as soon as possible, in its own grim way.

(*Left*): Lehman arriving with UNRRA aid in Greece, one of the sorriest sore spots.

FOR THE SECOND TIME THIS CENTURY delegates from the world's warring nations met at Paris, this time in the old Luxembourg Palace (*above*) instead of more grandiose Versailles, to attempt contriving just and durable settlements of World War II. If the peace they made this time did not end war, World War III probably would, and mankind with it. Movies of the Bikini blast were hurried to Paris to heighten the delegates' diligence. But they were in no hurry. In eight months they wrote treaties for Italy, Hungary, Bulgaria, Rumania, Finland; but Austria's was to take nine years, Germany's even longer.

THE MARSHALL PLAN

Perceiving how vast and vital was the task of rehabilitating Europe's peoples and economy and how popular UNRRA was among its recipients, the U. S. in April 1948 decided to go far beyond the U. N.'s meager resources and pour $5,300,000,000 into European recovery within a year. The name of (General) **George Marshall,** then Secretary of State, went on this plan and presently the great transfusion began. At the same time, $275,000,000 was voted for military aid to Turkey and to Greece (where Red guerillas were seeking to take over), thus implementing the doctrine proclaimed by President Truman that never would the U. S. let these two nations go Red. And $463,000,000 went to China (where more Reds were fighting for power) for economic and military aid.

To the Soviets these acts of enlightened self-interest naturally looked like, and could easily be called, "Capitalist Invasion and Encirclement." The Kremlin was quick to forbid countries under its control from accepting Marshall Plan aid (except through black-market purchasing channels), and to tighten its grip on such countries.

A few items of U. S. largesse, which by 1952 had totaled $13.6 billion, are pictured below. The Marshall Plan's name was later changed to "Strength for the Free World from the United States of America," emanating from the Mutual Security Agency.

Electric plant for Denmark.

New airports for Paris.

Haystacker for Holland.

Tractors for Turkey.

Hybrid corn for France.

351

To lick its wounds in private, to solve its internal problems as crudely and brutally as might be necessary without Western scrutiny — and to prevent millions of despairing captives from escaping its grip — the Kremlin erected what Winston Churchill, in a famed speech at Fulton, Mo., in 1946, named the Iron Curtain. Running along its new borders from the Baltic to the Black Sea, this structure, manned by the MVD and other special troops, consisted physically of leagues and leagues of electrified barbed wire, strung through a no-man's land studded with watch towers, searchlights, land mines, machine guns and guards with police dogs. Bare strips were grubbed out and kept weeded by slave labor, mostly women (*above*). This ground was examined daily for the footprints of escapees.

The Iron Curtain was also an ideological barrier against Western thought — a strict news censorship, a blackout of all information from or about the West which might embarrass the Red regime and its intensified plans. Behind the curtain the Soviets tried to condition their own and captive peoples the way physiologist Pavlov conditioned his laboratory animals until their reflexes responded as desired to chosen stimuli.

SEVERE PENALTIES, of which death was not the worst, were imposed on breakers of, or conspirators to break, the Iron Curtain's security. Radio, balloons carrying leaflets, and the age-old osmosis called the "grapevine" or "underground" by which desperate people everywhere manage to communicate through such police membranes, came into play all along the Iron Curtain. To shoot through the Curtain as far and as accurately as he could, one ingenious German mounted his tele-camera on a rifle stock (*left*).

ESPIONAGE

While preserving outwardly polite relations with its erstwhile allies, the Kremlin prudently energized its spying mechanisms to steal the atomic secrets otherwise denied. **Igor Gouzenko,** a code clerk in Moscow's Ottawa embassy, exposed the spy network operating in Canada. (*Right*): Gouzenko testifying in protective hood.

Washington's F.B.I. smoked out **Gerhart Eisler** as the No. 1 Red operative in the U. S. He stowed away on a Polish liner, was dragged ashore in England for questioning (*below, left*), later released to Moscow. Washington also pinned subversion on several U. S. Government employees including Alger Hiss, high in the State Department, who was jailed for perjury.

Ethel and Julius Rosenberg (*below, right*), he a Manhattan machinist with a brother-in-law (David Greenglass) working on A-bombs at Los Alamos, were electrocuted after trial, conviction, highest appeals.

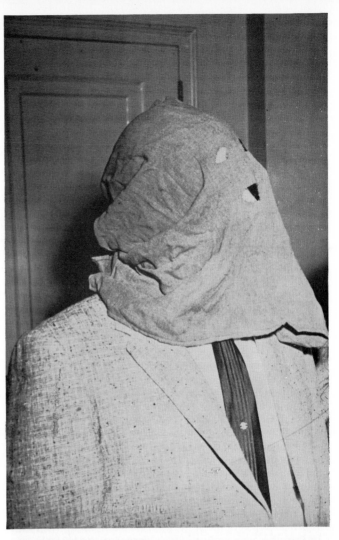

RUSSIA ACCUSED many persons of spying inside the Iron Curtain and jailed or did away with them summarily. Two celebrated cases of innocence (*above*) were **Cardinal Joseph Mindszenty** of Hungary and **William Oatis,** AP correspondent in Prague.

THE MOSCOW ART THEATRE, world-renowned for its esthetic conscience, was ordered to mend its ways, bend to the Party Line. (*Above*): Grandstand scene from *Anna Karenina*.

PURGATORY

Release from war's tensions is well-known as a force for dissolution. Joseph Stalin feared it in all members of the vast organism which he dominated. Ivan the soldier had tasted Western delights and hated going home. He must be redisciplined. Intellectuals had sniffed a heady atmosphere conducive to free creativeness. They must be regimented to work within the state's ideology. Food was short, farmers were discouraged: so the collectives had to be whipped up, forced to produce.

Exposure to the Germans — and to friendly foreigners — had vitiated the blind zeal of too many Party members. They must be purged.

As the new War Minister (succeeding Stalin), **Marshal Bulganin** took care of the Red Army, even putting **Marshal Zhukov** on ice for a while in the Odessa district. As the boss of the Party, Stalin himself took care of that apparatus, with iron purpose, first overhauling the secret police (now MVD) to make it tick sharply.

The coming and going of the Germans had truly aroused those hardy nationalists, the Ukrainians. They almost imagined they were free, white and independent. A burly, little-known Politburocrat named **Nikita Khrushchev** (*below*), former Donbas coal miner, was turned loose among them and he presently announced "mass replacement of the Party's leading personnel," 64% of regional Soviet heads, 67% of tractor station directors. (Nothing was said or admitted, meantime, about how UNRRA kept the Ukraine alive.)

Even the population's wartime savings were purged. In December 1947, all cash rubles had to be turned in at the state banks. For every ten old rubles surrendered, Ivan received one new ruble, while prices for everything stayed about the same.

If other postwar purges were sweeping, none was more so than the one assigned to Stalin's trusted lieutenant (of that moment): dapper, dynamic **Andrei Zhdanov** (*below*). Leningrad, whose defense he had commanded, was his adopted home. He plumed himself on his cultural superiority. Forcing art and literature to promote Stalinist dogma now became his chief task. He flew into it with happy passion.

He told Russia's movie-makers their products were too realistic, too politically primitive. He bade the Moscow Art Theatre produce more Soviet plays, fewer from the Tsarist era.

Forbidden further publication were top writers like poetess Anna Akhmatova and satirist Mikhail Zoschenko (rated Chekhov's peer), for their "decadence" and "rotten lack of ideology." The leading literary magazines were suspended for ignoring "the vital foundation of the Soviet system, its political policy."

All writers, said Zhdanov, must be "engineers of human souls." Even composer **Dmitry Shostakovich** (*above, right*), twice a Stalin Prize man, was denounced for backsliding in his cacophonous celebration of the Soviet ethos.

SINEWS FOR SOCIALISM

Russia in 1946 turned down a U. S. proposal that all Germany be disarmed for at least 25 years. Thereafter the West was of two minds as to dismantling or remantling German industry in its own control zones. In the end, remantling (except for munitions plants) won out, and in 1949 the West German republic was set up at Bonn.

The Soviets were ever single-minded about what to do not only with their portion of Germany but with all the other living space, wealth-producing plant and labor-producing peoples they had overrun. They would crate and ship not only all the machinery suitable for rebuilding their factories, but they would also crate (in box-cars) and ship home untold hordes of captive workers as the literal blood and sinews for rebuilding and expanding "Socialism in one country," if not eventually in all countries.

Pictures of the mass evacuations of Baltic, Polish, German, Austrian, Hungarian, Czechoslovakian, Rumanian and Bul-

garian "political offenders" and "enemies of the state" and of the atrocious slave-labor camps where they were sent to work, wear out and die are of course not available. Also unpictured are added millions who were debased, regimented and worked like slaves under the Red Army and the MVD on collective farms, in factories and in mines (especially uranium) right in what had been their homelands. "Legal" authority for this genocide was easy for the Stalin regime to find, and cynically pervert, in the Marx-Lenin social, criminal and political codes.

Originally, at Paris, Russia demanded $10 billions of reparations in cash and kind. In the end, it got much more — the slave labor count was estimated by the U. N. as high as 20,000,000.

Pictured above (*left*) are crated machinery from the Daimler-Benz motor works and (*right*) a steel press being removed from Dortmund. The picture below, of a heroic bronze statue of Peace being dismembered to feed Soviet smelters, suggests more perfectly just what victorious Russia did on its side of Europe.

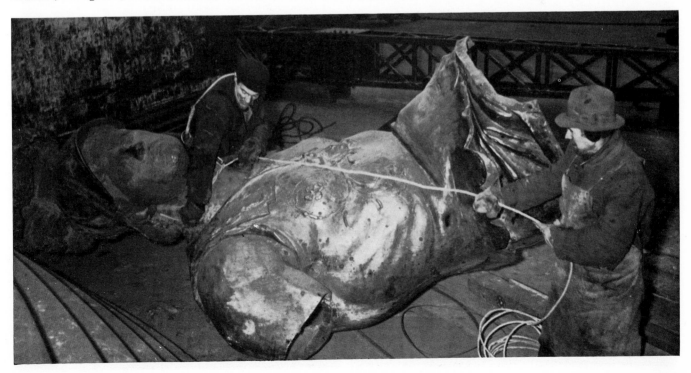

SQUEEZE PLAY

In June 1948 the Soviets tried to squeeze the Western powers out of their Berlin enclave by making life there physically miserable. Pretext was found for a blockade of Berlin, to which the Reds controlled all access by land and water. They closed the Autobahn (*above*), halted barge traffic, even ripped up rails (*right*). Food shortages threatened and, come autumn, fuel would soon run out.

But the Soviets did not control the air. Through that medium, Britain and the U. S. responded quickly, massively, in a way that gave them good practice for such an emergency elsewhere, in peace or war. The Berlin airlift, organized almost overnight and maintained for nearly a year, made air history.

"OPERATION VITTLES" was the name given the huge Berlin airlift. A thousand transport planes kept Berlin stocked with necessities from June 21, 1948 to May 12, 1949, when the Russians gave up. The planes shuttled mostly between Frankfurt and Tempelhof Field (*left*), lugging everything from coal to nylons. To the British went the honor of carrying the 1,000,-000th ton (*below*). Total tonnage airlifted by the U. S. alone: 2,231,600.

356

FORCE PLAY

The great airlift was but a small part of the West's reaction to the Berlin blockade. Having watched the Comintern's revival, disguised as the Cominform, and the Communization of one captive country after another by strong-arm methods, the U. S., Britain, France, Canada and the three little Benelux countries welded their various mutual defense agreements into a **North Atlantic Treaty Organization,** with teeth in it: a joint army, air force and navy designed at least to impede the 100-odd Red divisions poised at the Iron Curtain, should they ever march west.

Moscow uncorked Berlin almost immediately. Nevertheless, into NATO hastened all the other Western countries, from Iceland clear around to Turkey (omitting only Ireland, Sweden and Spain). President Truman recalled **General Eisenhower** from retirement at Columbia University to command NATO. Air bases, motor pools, port facilities, fuel pipelines, supply dumps, radar networks — all the costly paraphernalia that had been used to crush Hitler — were called back into being to check Stalin. By spring of 1952, when General Ike turned over his command to General Matt Ridgway (*see right*) and started his march to the White House, NATO's design called for 50 divisions, 4,000 planes, 300 naval vessels (including a call on more than 100 aircraft carriers).

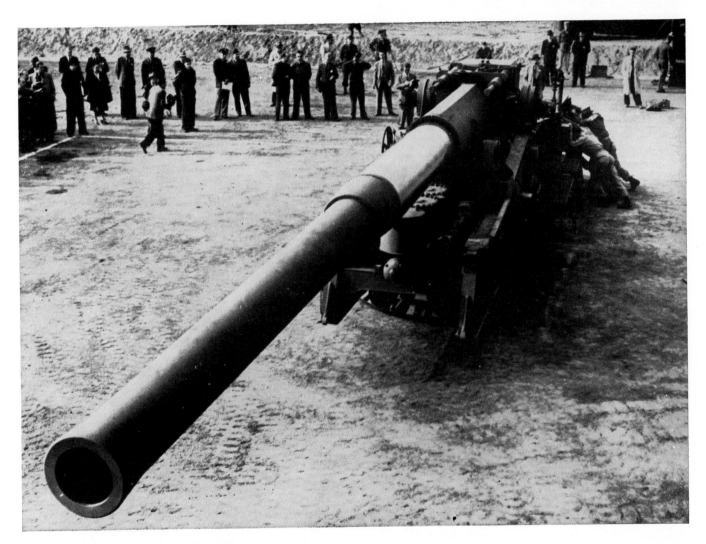

NATO'S SHARPEST TOOTH (*above*) was an 11-inch mobile cannon with a 38.5-foot barrel capable of hurling atomic shells 20 miles. Less devastating than full-size, airborne A-bombs would be (and NATO had plenty of those), such shells would give dire pause to massed ground forces (men, tanks, artillery) as used in the Red school of war.

SECURING SOCIALISM

As the Red armies crunched back westward into Europe (1944-1945), the political commissars who accompanied them at all times were multiplied, to align politically each city and country as it was wrenched from the Germans. Out of the war-plowed ground, like revived mushrooms, sprang the Communist parties of Poland, Bulgaria, Rumania, Albania, Hungary, Czechoslovakia, Yugoslavia, Germany.

Hand-picked by Moscow, the heads of these parties were installed, as soon as feasible, as national dictators subservient to the No. 1 Party Boss in the Kremlin.

Having dissolved the Comintern in 1943 to please the Western allies, Stalin and Zhdanov in early 1947 thought it high time to reassert control over world Communism through a euphemistically named Communist Information Bureau, formed at a secret meeting in a Polish hunting lodge. The object was not only to revamp the machinery for eventual world revolution and to counteract the Marshall Plan, but also to consolidate, through one-party rule, Moscow's hold over the whole new captive area whose wealth and manpower Russia needed to rebuild its own.

Free elections in these countries, for which the West clamored so naively at Yalta and Potsdam, might result in governments obstructive to Moscow's grand design. Moneyed and muscled by Moscow, disciplined through the Cominform, it was difficult to see how established satellite dictators would ever be unhorsed, or why more of them should not be boosted into other saddles. (*Below*): Four Comintern alumni who became charter members of the Cominform. (For another, *see* p. 359)

The Map (*above, left*) shows the Red satellite line-up as it looked at its strongest in early 1948.

CZECHOSLOVAKIA WAS A TOUGH NUT for even the Red juggernaut to crack. Its republic, sired by Thomas Masaryk in 1919, was Central Europe's cradle of parliamentary liberty. As late as March 1948 its Communist party had only 38% power. Three strong minority parties shared the rest, and though Red Klement Gottwald was premier, 15 of his cabinet were non-Communists.

Gottwald's technique for taking over (1945-1948) was simple: he made sure the War Minister feared Moscow, then packed the Prague police with Reds. When the 15 ministers resigned in protest, the police chief screamed, "Plot against the state!" Tommy-guns in his cops' hands restrained objectors while Gottwald forced liberal President Eduard Benes to accept a new all-Red cabinet. Swift and massive purges quickly established one-party rule.

Jan Masaryk, the founder's son, fell, jumped or was pushed from a window in the Czerny Palace, seat of the Foreign Office; but his martyrdom could not restore the people's freedom.

Austria, noting these events, begged the Allied armies of occupation to stay, which they did until 1955 (*see* p. 373) . In Belgrade, too, prudent notice was taken (*see next page*). (*Right*): Rare photo of 1948 Czech purgees upon arrest, including Deputy Prime Minister Jan Ursini (near end, with paper). They got three to 30 years in prison.

RUMANIA'S ANA PAUKER, born in Bucharest, mothered Communism there when it had less than 100 members. She served as a colonel with the Red Army, then as Rumania's foreign minister. (She was purged in 1952 for putting on airs.)

HUNGARY'S MATYAS RAKOSI, one of Bela Kun's commissars in the brief Red dictatorship of 1919, spent long years in prison. Moscow trained him in politics and sabotage. In 1945 he led only one Red faction, dared not attend the Cominform meeting.

BULGARIA'S GEORGI DIMITROV, a Red printer's devil, fled to Berlin, later to Russia. He headed the Comintern (1935-1943), returned to Sofia as Premier. With Tito, he dreamed of a Balkan federation, but the Politburo curbed him. He died in 1949.

CZECHOSLOVAKIA'S KLEMENT GOTTWALD, a Moravian carpenter, was second-fiddle to Rudolf Slansky, the Kremlin's hatchet-man in Prague, until after his 1948 coup. Then he got Slansky. He died of pneumonia contracted at Stalin's funeral.

TITO PULLS OUT

Two months before he attacked Russia in 1941, Hitler blitzed Belgrade and subjugated Yugoslavia — or thought he had. But guerilla bands fought on in the rugged hinterland, some under General Mikhailovic to whom the British sent aid and comfort, some under a tough little mountaineer named Yosip Broz. Long before V-E Day Allied bets were shifted to Broz, even though he was a Communist. For his first press picture (*see left*). When the smoke cleared, Broz emerged as one more Red dictator, now renowned under his nickname, Tito.

In the satellite ring immediately formed by Russia, Tito's star shone brightest of all and he bade fair to dominate a Red Balkan confederacy. But when he found Moscow men spying on his men; when he comprehended Moscow's plan to drain off his strategic metals, to collectivize his peasants, to subordinate and absorb his army — and himself — Tito planted his feet. He defied Stalin's punishment — exile from the Cominform — and struck out alone on his own road to Communism.

Great was Western rejoicing. **"Titoism"** might be Stalinism's downfall if cultivated in Yugoslavia and promoted elsewhere. Western aid for Tito flowed naturally along with Marshall Plan money and later NATO's (though he never joined the latter). Tito was sent funds and flour, planes and plants, tanks and techniques. From 1948 (when he revolted) through 1954, he was lionized wherever he went among Westerners (*below*). He loved it.

And then, in 1955, something else happened to Tito (*see* p. 373).

Flour for Tito (1950).

Tanks for Tito (1952).

Tito in London (1953).

Tito in Athens (1954).

RED STAR OVER CHINA

Ever since the days of Dr. Sun Yat-sen, founder of the Chinese Republic (died 1925), Russia had been trying to sell Communism to sprawling, teeming China. Failure was largely due to the Chinese sense of private property, private enterprise and family ties. A Chinaman put his ancestors and his rice bowl far above politics. Another cause for Russia's failure was Chiang Kai-shek, Dr. Sun's brother-in-law, who had a taste of Communism at its source and wanted no more.

Japan's defeat by the U. S. in 1945 gave Moscow its golden chance. The beaten Japs held all the south and east of China, which now became virtually a politico-military vacuum. The government under Chiang held the southwest corner, the Red revolutionists under Mao Tse-tung held the northeast. Manchuria, bulging with Japanese industries and munitions, fell into Russia's lap when the A-bombs fell on Japan.

While the U. S. palavered about a cease-fire between Chiang and Mao and later faltered about backing up Chiang when Mao failed to play ball, all that Russia had to do was pass the ammunition (mostly Japanese and therefore nice and cheap, since the U. S. had paid to win it) to Mao.

From his cave capital at Yenan above the Yellow River, Mao and General Chu-teh led their bolstered forces into the vacuum. They reached and took Tientsin and Peiping in January, 1949, Shanghai in May, Canton in October. They pushed Chiang off the mainland to Formosa, where with U.S. aid and protection he built a potent economy and a persistent, if hollow, threat to Mao's empire.

Mao consolidated his hold on China by methods made in Moscow: police purges, mass executions and high-sounding "People's" doctrine. In five more short years he had become the eastern pole of a vast Red Axis controlling a billion people. Hundreds of millions more in Southeast Asia, the East Indies and the Indian sub-continent became pawns in the East-West struggle for global supremacy. (*Above, left*): Chu-teh and Mao. (*Left center*): Mao addressing his followers when, like Chiang at Chungking, they were living underground in bombproofs.

"AGRARIAN REFORM" was a Red slogan which never (he said) fooled General George Marshall, whom President Truman sent out to conciliate between Chiang and Mao. Poor peasants did get the lands of rich ones (as in Russia) but awoke to find themselves slaving for the state. (*Below, left*): Marching out to divide up the Good Earth. (*Right*): Staking a claim.

THE RED TIDE flowed to the Yellow Sea in May 1949, producing scenes like the above in Shanghai when non-Communists tried to escape with their belongings.

"INCIDENT" IN KOREA

In the spring of 1948, elections were held in Korea under U. N. sponsorship to unify that country, jointly controlled by the U. S. and the Russians south and north of the 38th Parallel. Agricultural South Korea voted in a Rightist government under President Syngman Rhee. Industrial North Korea boycotted the election, stayed Red under Russian domination. In October, the Chinese Reds took Mukden and domination of North Korea passed from Moscow to Peiping. But when, in June 1950, the well-armed North Koreans struck southward to unify Korea in their own way, their march was paced by Russian-built tanks and guided by Russian advisers. Moscow's finger was still deep in the pie.

President Truman resolved upon a "police action," sanctioned by the U. N. Security Council (with Russia absent). He sent such reinforcements as he could to the skimpy forces (*left*) of General Douglas MacArthur, military regent of Japan, who was put in charge of the explosive "incident." Other U. N. members sent token forces for a show of free-world solidarity to prevent the spread of Communism in the East (*see below*).

After holding at Pusan, MacArthur mounted a brilliant cut-off attack at Inchon, freed Seoul, the South Korean capital, and within six months had pushed the North Koreans all but out of their country at the Yalu River. He

The Canadians brought their tanks.

THE EBB AND FLOW of war in Korea, with G.I.s slogging forward while suffering peasants got pushed around was an old pattern sad enough to behold. But now, over it, hung the menace of atomic weapons if the "incident" should flower into World War III.

Australians were flown in by the U.S.A.F.

362

wanted to go on and smash the North Koreans finally by bombing out their bases and transport in Manchuria, even at risk of all-out war with one or both of their big backers. At this, President Truman hesitated. When Red China threw in its armies and Russian-aided air power, he still forbade MacArthur to strike across the Yalu.

MacArthur chafed publicly at this policy. Truman relieved him of command. He put in General Matt Ridgway to fight a bloody holding campaign that ended in stalemate at the 38th Parallel. Truce negotiations left the Reds in a position to claim moral victory in that they still held North Korea, though they lost much "face" when few Red prisoners taken by U. N. forces chose to return to Communism.

Meantime, Generalissimo Chiang Kai-shek was kept marking time with his rebuilt armies in Formosa, guarded and restrained by U. S. warships, to await settlement of the larger issue: should there be just one China, a Red one, instead of two? As time passed, the likelihood diminished of the Nationalists ever retaking the mainland and cutting off the eastern pole of the new Red Axis.

Admission of Red China to the United Nations continued a No. 1 burning question. Question No. 2 was further Red expansion in Southeast Asia, with Moscow abetting Peiping to keep the latter's attention diverted from Central Asia where rivalry of interests began to take form within the changing Red Axis.

MACARTHUR AND RHEE both felt there was "no substitute for victory." After the truce, determined old Rhee threatened to renew the fighting at any time.

Even some Ethiopians got into the act.

Red Chinese (prisoners) were well winterized.

The Colombians sent a U. S.-built cruiser.

A Red "Welcome Arch" attracted few Red prisoners.

AN EPOCH ENDS

The year 1952 was a quiet one in Russia. Stalin was not feeling well and stayed out of the public eye. Those around him were given a lot of homework. Then, in October, the Communist Party held its **19th Congress,** first one since 1939.

Keynoter was plump and sassy **Georgi Malenkov,** secretary of the Central Committee (*right*). Reviewing the war and postwar periods in the verbose marathon style expected of good Communists, he made these points:

Among the Great Powers of Capitalism, three had been deleted (Germany, Japan, Italy), two sorely weakened (Britain and France). Meantime, Communism had spread westward to the Elbe, eastward to the Yellow Sea.

Industrial growth in the U.S.S.R. was proceeding six times as fast as in Capitalism's fortress, the U. S. And the world was no longer just one market but two: "democratic" and "imperialist." The remaining Capitalist countries must inevitably fight over their shrunken market and split apart. War upon Communism, instigated by the U. S., was Capitalism's only hope to survive even temporarily. Preparing to meet this menace would be the Soviet's prime task, until Europe should turn on the U. S. and save Russia the trouble.

As the Union's leaders the Party, which had grown from 1.58 million in 1939 to 6.01 million members in 1952, must be self-critical; must work harder, more efficiently, with purer zeal.

Joseph Stalin had just published a treatise, *Economic Problems of Socialism in the U.S.S.R.,* which "greatly advanced Marxist-Leninist political economy." Malenkov reviewed this work with fulsome praise. Main points: means of production must have priority in industry; food production must be increasingly nationalized and farm products eventually be exchanged for goods, not money; the working day must be reduced to six, then five hours, and real wages doubled, to ennoble labor, make time for higher education, eradicate the distinctions between town and country, physical and mental work. The Socialist formula: "From each according to his ability, to each according to his labor," might then give way to Communism's formula: ". . . to each according to his needs."

Stalin also addressed the 19th Congress, in what was to be his last important public appearance (*above*). Presently his ailing heart confined him. That winter the Kremlin guard's command was changed and Stalin's staff of doctors got a shake-up. Only the Kremlin shadows knew whether dirty work was done, but on March 5, 1953, Stalin's death was announced. The nation indulged in paroxysms of fashionable grief, but within the month Russia's greatest name dropped out of the official press.

THE GRUESOME TWOSOME in the mausoleum on Red Square is made the more macabre by a widespread belief that only the real heads and hands were preserved for posterity. Of Lenin's remains it is definitely known that an autopsy prevented normal embalming, necessitating a meticulous tattooing process, a cubic centimeter at a time.

XIV. COMPETITIVE CO-EXISTENCE

The death of Stalin left a vacuum too large to be filled by any man still alive in Moscow. Stalin himself had carefully seen to that. Shrewd, plump little Georgi Malenkov, who had maneuvered closer to Stalin than anyone else at the last, was given a brief chance at being Premier, but minus the all-important secretaryship of the Communist Central Committee. Then history's old pattern of oligarchy succeeding autocracy repeated itself, and into Russia in 1954 was ushered an era called Competitive Co-existence. This phrase was coined by Nikita Khrushchev, new strongman of the oligarchs, to describe a new foreign policy for Russia, but it also defined accurately a new attitude of top Red politicians toward each other.

"When the whales do battle, the shrimps will die," says an Oriental proverb. In the shakedown struggle after Stalin's death, most of the dead shrimps were those swimming in the wake of **Lavrenti Beria,** the secret police chief (MVD). His cruelties, as the instrument of Stalin's will, rankled deepest among all the marks left by the dead *Vozhd* (Leader). Even during Stalin's last illness, collective action at the top had begun, and soon after his death the new Plural Leaders took away the independence of the MVD, split its powers, tried Beria and shot him.

Riots in East Germany and open revolt in some slave labor camps precipitated the police reform. The police corps was divided into an MVD concerned only with routine maintenance of law and order, plus supervision of the prison camps and slave labor. Political police functions were vested in a new KGB (internal security corps), smaller and specialized. Its chief was Ivan A. Serov, a man the new Leaders thought they could trust and control. He became bodyguard to the Leaders when they traveled.

Malenkov's error, if he made one, was in stressing prematurely the need for more consumer goods in the Soviet planned economy, at some cost to production of capital goods. To have blamed him publicly for this popular policy would not have gone down well with its beneficiaries, the Russian people. So Malenkov was constrained to plead guilty for failure of the farm program — a sphere of which he could honestly profess deep ignorance. That food production, and its failure, were actually the responsibility of Leader Khrushchev made this maneuver the more useful — and serio-comic. When the team of Khrushchev and Bulganin took over, Khrushchev's still dubious "virgin lands" plan — plowing up multi-millions of acres of semi-arid steppes and sowing them to grain with labor drafted from the cities — was again hailed by all as the formula that would solve Russia's gravest problem: feeding itself properly. It remained to be seen whether full stomachs or vast dust bowls would result. Khrushchev hedged his bet by accenting improved farm technology for acreages of proven productivity — better machinery, better seed (including U. S. hybrid corn), better husbandry (including the U. S. corn-hog cycle and ensilage feeding for other livestock). Even so, in the view of visiting U. S. farm experts, Russia's food problem would last a long, long time.

On other fronts, the Khrushchev-Bulganin team looked better, even to skeptical foreign eyes. From Malenkov's brusque attitude toward the outer world, they switched to a posture of sweet reasonableness, wreathed in smiles and vodka fumes. They resolved the free status of Austria. They made peace with Tito. They made overtures to West Germany. Armed at last with an atom-bomb stock-pile and even some H-bombs of their own, they built up to and in 1955 staged a Big Four conference "at the summit" in Geneva, where the principals tacitly but very solemnly agreed that all-out war in the Nuclear Age was unthinkable.

A subsequent meeting of the Foreign Ministers got nowhere when they tried — with both sides obdurate — to execute the Summit's agenda: disarmament, unification of Germany, closer East-West contacts. But a correspondence between Premier Bulganin and President Eisenhower was generated — which the latter's heart attack of September interrupted only briefly — pointing toward at least a slow-down of the arms race that was becoming so fantastic (intercontinental hydrogen missiles!) and so costly on both sides. Both sides could claim credit if this widely wished-for end were achieved — credit for the strength and wisdom of their behavior up to disarmament (if any). As for Russia, it could not lose by at least debating disarmament, for any breathing spell at all would benefit the fast, disciplined industrial build-up which, begun in late 1945, was impressively far along ten years later (*see table,* p. 369) and which, if continued through 1960, would indeed have hard-headed Red Russia approaching a par with the mighty U. S. A.

Based on that build-up and on their avowed new policy of peace, Leaders Khrushchev and Bulganin, the crude and the suave, spearheaded two astute trade-and-aid drives — modest variants of a lavish U. S. model — into Africa through the Middle East and into Southeast Asia through India and Burma. While holding at the center (Germany) by consolidating the satellite East European armies under Marshal Konev, Moscow was launching what could become vast flanking movements in these new directions. Unrest in the Arab-Israel-Oil area helped them greatly on the one hand. A grateful Red China and India's neutral Nehru helped them greatly on the other. Their advantage over the U. S., Britain and France in these new offensives was manifest. As former colonial powers, the welcome of the last two was worn thin. As the producer and dumper of depressing surpluses, the U. S., even with fistfuls of giveaway cash, was not too popular among raw material exporters like Burma (rice, wheat) and India (cotton). Proof of the new Red puddings would come when Moscow should or should not make good on its promises to purchase, to lend, to build, to advise. Meantime, the political climate should favor the growth of Communist seeds: in deepest jungle guerilla camps; through impoverished farming belts; amid teeming, stinking, starving city populations. Red domination of perhaps one more third of the earth's inhabitants might eventually be brought about thus, with scarcely any more shots being fired. Russia had learned in Korea (1950-1953) about the high price of shooting, and about its fruitlessness. Now the price, and the fruits of shooting, were out of sight.

In February, 1956, the 20th Congress of the Communist Party was convened in the Kremlin. Behind the scenes the new Leaders had painted a brand-new back-drop for all Red activities, foreign and domestic. In a seven-hour keynote oration, Leader Khrushchev lowered this fabric into place for a marveling world to see.

Erased from his all-highest spot in the Soviet firmament was Joseph Stalin, the miracle-worker. In his place sat a "collective" of humbler men, led by Khrushchev, who promised to work together without fear or favor among themselves for the Party's and nation's good. A chorus of affirming speeches by the lesser Leaders was not spoiled by asides, comments or cavalier interruptions from First Leader Khrushchev (*a*) because no outside ear was present to hear them, and (*b*) because the docile delegates understood that, among all men everywhere but especially among Russians, *somebody* has to be the boss; and this risen-from-the-ranks self-made executive, who so long bossed the Moscow and Ukraine party machines, just happened to be a somewhat crude and boisterous fellow, though sharp and sound withal. When it was voted to rewrite Soviet history so as to cut Stalin down to size, and to whitewash the memories of many an Old Bolshevik whom he slaughtered, no one looked for Khrushchev to have himself written in as another demi-god.

Higher but now more distant in the Party's firmament was seen Lenin, as to whose sacred dogma for Communism the new Leaders had decided this: that victory over Capitalism need not inevitably come through violence alone but nowadays (and with war so dangerous) through economic warfare and through political leadership by working people, even by parliamentary means. An invitation was thus extended to Socialists everywhere, however divergent from Communists, to join and persist in world revolution, resorting to force only where Capitalism should strike the first blow and bring war upon itself. (A world Socialist congress held soon afterward in Switzerland was left cold by this appeal, but Red leaders from France, Germany and elsewhere took the message home with stars in their eyes.)

Leader Khrushchev and the rest also articulated one more Five-Year Plan (1955-1960) for upsurging Russia. The new goals, in the light of 1940-1955 accomplishments, were less incredible than usual. Most welcome to the ears of workers and peasants alike were promises of shorter hours, higher pay, better pensions, more food and clothes and shoes and even synthetic stockings! Continued emphasis on education, particularly the training of "specialists" (engineers) sounded good to all young, ambitious citizens and to their long-suffering parents.

Finally, in assurance that Collective Leadership, while more lenient at home, would not be weak abroad, the number of professional soldiers on the Central Committee was doubled (to eight) and one (Marshal Zhukov, the War Minister) was even added as an alternate to the ruling Presidium.

The 20th Congress adjourned amid thunderous cheers. Khrushchev and Bulganin returned to their business of building and selling a "reasonable" Russia to the world. Scheduled were state visits to Great Britain and Scandinavia. Bulganin even cracked that he would visit Washington if he didn't have to be finger-printed to get in there.

The third anniversary of Stalin's death was curious on the Red Square. From his tomb, the Russians stayed away by the hundreds of millions. Police shooed off the few stragglers who did show up, but let them leave flowers. "By evening," reported the watchful *New York Times*, "there were six bouquets. . . ."

INSIDE THE KREMLIN after Stalin's death, the state and Party life of Russia continued super-secret as before. But now there was a trembling of the "monolithic" structure while the little giants of the Party wrestled over the dead big giant's mantle of one-man power. To conceal this ominous atmosphere, to dispel some of the grimness of the Stalin regime, the man momentarily on top, Malenkov, let down the Kremlin's bars a little. The dark citadel was popularized by postcards and posters of the interior and by lending its name to a candy bar. Tourists were admitted, and even cameras. At Christmas time, 1953, a party was pitched within its walls for visiting U. S. students (*below*).

WITH ZHDANOV DEAD, the way was clear in 1953 for fat but sharp Georgi Malenkov to succeed Stalin as Premier. He proceeded to streamline the Government, relax some Stalinist tensions, talk tough to the West and rid himself of his next main rival, Lavrenti Beria of the MVD, who is seen beside Malenkov (*left*) saluting with the wrong hand at the Fat One's first review. Anastas Mikoyan, the trade chief, used the right hand and continued to survive.

It is improbable that Malenkov did away with Beria single-handed. The rest of the power-group had a hand in it, and all shared a deep-seated reason: Stalin's and Beria's truly authentic unpopularity. But while long-range planning went on, Malenkov was left out in front — to take whatever raps might come from popular reaction. It even seems he was promised compensation: being allowed to appear as boss of Russia's atomic energy program.

EXPLOSIONS among the most put-upon sufferers under the Stalin regime resulted when relief from Malenkov was slow in coming, and rumors of Kremlin dissension reached the masses. Chief focus of riot and rebellion was East Berlin, where anti-Communists burned a Red office building on the Potsdamer Platz (*below*). The insurrection spread to Magdeburg and other factory towns but the worst occurred when echoes reached the forced and slave labor camps. In Arctic Russia, a 100,000-man, two-week strike was staged at the slave-dug Vorkuta coal mines.

Tanks and troops quelled East Berlin and 1,200 MVD tommy-gunners blood-bathed Vorkuta. But these uprisings hastened the betterment of forced and slave labor conditions, which were becoming too obviously inefficient. Money and food, as inducements, were found (surprisingly enough) to get more and better work out of the burden-beasts than brutality and starvation had done. East Germany was now given "sovereignty" — but the Red troops remained with the auxiliary "People's" Army under the command of Marshal Konev.

Out of the rubble that was Stalingrad, out of the twisted ruins in other cities that had been steel mills, hydro-electric stations, gun factories, tractor plants, the Soviets doggedly rebuilt their living places and their means of livelihood, beginning with the heaviest first. Women as well as men were used in the work. (*Left*): Women sorting and piling bricks for reconstruction of a gutted shell in Stalingrad.

Where voluntary labor was lacking, slave or forced labor was provided by the MVD, which contracted to supply so many thousands of hands to do and die. Then it went out and made the necessary arrests. Slave labor was employed mostly in the mines, in the forests and on rough work like digging and revetting waterways. The atrocious conditions imposed on the slaves became an international scandal. Diminishing returns from such labor eventually led to slight reforms as to food and clothing.

The ability of educated Russians as engineers was matched, on voluntary projects, by a stolid durability in the working masses, to labor slowly and awkwardly but long and steadily in every kind of weather.

(*Below, left*): Restoration (1947) of the Zaporozhstal iron and steel works on the Dnieper, Ukraine. This plant was the auto industry's sole prewar source of thin steel sheets. (*Below, right*): Unfinished before the war, a huge new hydro-electric plant at Kuibyshev had to be started all over again. In 1955 a forest of cranes was still at work, basing and erecting six monster turbine-generators.

NEW CONSTRUCTION must go forward also under the Five-Year Plans, at the same time as rebuilding. (*Above*): Panorama (1955) of the Kakhova hydro-electric project, one of the many assigned to the MVD. Bombing out the just-finished Dnieper Dam was one of the Hitlerites' proudest accomplishments in 1941. The scale of the rebuilding job is visible in the photo (*left*). And a new dam and power station were started in 1953 near Dubossary, the first on the Dniester (*below, left*).

THE U.S.S.R.'S
EXPANDING ECONOMY

	1940	1955	1967	1970 Plan
Steel	18,300,000 tons*	45,000,000 tons	102,200,000 tons	124,000,000 tons
Oil	31,000,000 "	71,000,000 "	288,000,000 "	350,000,000 "
Coal	166,000,000 "	390,000,000 "	595,000,000 "	670,000,000 "
Grain	100,000,000 "	120,000,000 "	147,600,000 "	178,000,000 "
Cotton	2,240,000 "	3,880,000 "	6,000,000 "	6,000,000 "
Electricity	48.3 billion kw.h.	170 billion kw.h.	589 billion kw.h.	801 billion kw.h.
Motor vehicles	147,000	445,000	728,800	1,360,000
Railways	66,000 mi.	75,000 mi.	80,700 mi.	85,050
Cattle	55,000,000	67,000,000	97,100,000	(unstated)
Hogs	27,000,000	52,000,000	50,800,000	(unstated)
Population	194,100,000	194,400,000	234,396,000	?

(* tons are metric)

LIFE IN RUSSIA

TO WESTERN EYES the scene above of a "model" housing development on the outskirts of Moscow, with the stucco coming unstuck, suggests an existence drab indeed for the inmates, who are above-average people as to means, intelligence and culture. To Russian eyes, however, it represents Progress with a capital P, for even in 1940, after two decades of their Revolution, the Russian people as a mass remained among the world's Have-Nots. Except at the very top they enjoyed a level of creature comforts somewhere between the modest amenities of lower-class Europeans and the abject squalor of the Asian masses.

In trying to follow the contortions and contrivances of the ruling Russian politicos, Westerners should never forget that besides the Communist Party and its captive "government"

there is a Soviet people, some 238,000,000 of them (to lump all races and nationalities) controlled by government and Party, of which only some 13,000,000 are members. Long-drawn and painful though the process was, little improvement in living conditions could be pointed to at most levels since the days of the Tsars.

"Happiness" being a comparative state, it can be said that all but those millions who were *actively* persecuted politically enjoyed some degree of progress in Russia if only as to education and health. Shutting the masses off from all bases of comparison with Western living standards was a dire necessity for a regime which, due not only to a savage war but also to the inherent inefficiencies of a clumsy, suspicion-ridden bureaucracy, would have improved the well-being of the masses only at a snail's pace in any case.

CONTRASTS abound in Russia, as in any young, crude, growing country. Two pairs of women, snapped candidly on the streets of Kiev (*above, left*) and of Odessa (*above, right center*) epitomize a kind of contrast discoverable in any coun-

try, but weighted heavily, in Russia, on the side of the rags and felt boots. The same may be said of the two shots (*above*) of urban lambkins and provincial urchins. All four pictures shown here were shot by a U. S. traveler in 1954.

370

EVERYDAY LIFE
IN THE U.S.S.R.

Because of political and other factors it is impossible to equate the daily life of, say, a worker in a Soviet auto factory with that of a worker in Detroit or of a small U. S. farmer and a member of a U.S.S.R. collective farm. The synopsis below does, however, furnish some inkling as to how life is for the Soviet masses, urban and rural, of whom the two groups (*above* — workers in a tool shop and young members of a collective) are typical.

	FACTORY WORKER	PEASANT
Monthly wage	$114 (U.S., at official rate of exchange)	$66, plus food
Work week	41 hours	48 hours
Tools	Few but good	Few and crude
Off-season occupation	No off-season, few layoffs or strikes	Handicrafts
Housing	One or two rooms, two persons per room	Two-room hut
Transportation	Crowded streetcar or bus	Motor truck or one-horse cart
Food	Black bread, herring, potatoes, tea, vegetable soup, meat twice a week	Same, but with more meat, much milk
Clothes	One street suit, one work suit, one all-weather overcoat, one pair shoes	Same, but of poorer quality
Radio	Small short-wave receiver	None, except in farm club
Television	Sometimes	None
Utilities	Running water, electricity, sometimes gas	Pump or well water, sometimes electricity
Newspaper	Six-sheet *Pravda* or four-sheet city paper, daily	One-sheet district paper, twice weekly
Magazines, books	Cheap and plentiful, mostly technical or Marxist	Few, mostly agricultural
Recreation	Spectator sports, parks, theatre, circus, movies, room parties, saloons	Folk dancing and singing, drinking
Social centers	Factory or professional club, with many attractions	One-croom hut club, pretty bare
Educational opportunities	Good factory and night schools for adults	Village grammar school; technical classes in winter
Freedom to change job	Loses some fringe benefits by changing jobs	Permission required, easy to get
Chance for advancement	Unlimited, through ability and effort	Can rise into farm administration
Family life	Upset by lack of housing privacy	Upset by shortage of men
Marriage	Cheap and easy	Same
Divorce	Expensive and difficult	Same
Birth rate	Declining, because of crowded housing	Declining, because of shortage of men
Medical care	Free and good, in crowded clinics and hospitals	Poorly equipped country doctor
Garden	None	One or two acres
Livestock	Dog or cat	One cow, one calf, a few pigs and goats, a flock of poultry
Pension	$33 to $100 per month, after age 60	Less than $20 per month
Vacation	Two or three weeks, with pay, by law	Winter

WITH THE RUSSIANS AS PEOPLE, no one could quarrel. They are friendly, curious, warmhearted, gregarious, sensitive, humorous, generous — when they can be their primitive selves. Their reception of a world-touring U. S. company of *Porgy and Bess* was enthusiastic. Moses LaMarr of the *Porgy* troupe was seen (*right*) singing "Little David, play on your harp" to an impromptu audience in Gorki Garden, Leningrad. One of his colleagues summed up the Red phenomenon in one classic line: "It's crazy here, but the people are warm."

ENTER: THE H-BOMB

THE MOST AWFUL FACT of life (thus far) was proven by U.S. nuclear scientists at Eniwetok in the Marshall Islands in November 1952 but not made public until March 1954. This fact was that the explosive energy released by *fusing* nascent hydrogen (a reaction triggered by an A-bomb) is vastly more powerful than what you get by *fissioning* Uranium 235. So monstrous is their power, in the range of millions of tons of TNT, that H-bombs, to which there is no limit in size, might have diameters of destruction into the hundreds instead of just tens of miles. And this area would be increased still more through the "fall-out" of the bomb's ash, by encasing the explosive in a substance such as cobalt whose heavy particles would long remain radioactive.

Some luckless Japanese fishermen in the distant path of the Eniwetok bomb's "fall-out" were badly burned. The tuna in their boat were found to be dangerously radioactive (*below, left*), raising speculation as to what might happen to all foodstuffs as well as human beings in an H-war.

Still the arms race went on, and before long Russia blandly announced that it, too, had exploded an H-bomb, which few doubted.

Aghast at what had been done with his basic equations on the conversion of mass into energy, physicist Albert Einstein (*below, right*) shortly before his death went on the air to call the U. S. and the U.S.S.R. "hysterical." Their arms race, he said, "beckons annihilation. The first problem is to do away with fear and mistrust." But that problem, for the time being, defied even Einstein.

"NEW LOOK"

February 1955 brought the peculiar spectacle of sly, shrewd Georgi Malenkov abjectly apologizing for the failure of Russia's current farm program (with which he had little to do) and resigning the Premiership. His real "crime" had been favoring consumer-goods production at some cost to heavy industry — but this could not well be admitted to the consumers.

To the fore stepped Viacheslav Molotov, stolid workhorse of the Foreign Office; Marshal Nikolai Bulganin, bearded banker, industrialist, political soldier, now Premier; and hearty, hard-drinking, baggy-panted Nikita Khrushchev, boss of the Party. It was his "virgin soil" program for exploiting vast areas of pastureland, with labor conscripted from the cities, that had flopped dismally. For taking this rap, Malenkov was retained in the ruling Presidium though demoted to Minister of Electric Power Stations. Minister of War was aging but durable Marshal Zhukov. Troubleshooter was seasoned Lazar Kaganovich as First Vice Premier. He also became the new tsar of Labor and Pay.

That this cast of characters was out to give Russia a "new look" became quickly apparent. If Malenkov had put aside some of Stalinism's grimness, these men tried to erase it entirely, with grins and jollity (*above*). Malenkov had been caustic toward the West, especially the U. S. These now acted relaxed, even cordial. Zhukov wrote a letter to President Eisenhower which began: "My dear old comrade in arms. . . ."

A peace treaty with Austria, so long delayed, was now quickly whipped up and Chancellor Raab (*below*) was feted in Moscow to discuss it. For fat reparations in kind, Russia would return Austria's factories and oil fields, withdraw its troops, return deportees and P.O.W.'s. The Western Allies approved all this and withdrew their troops also. When Molotov went to Vienna to sign the treaty, Foreign Minister Figl said, "Now you arrive as a *real* liberator."

Bulganin and Khrushchev next went to Belgrade, apologized to Tito for past indignities, agreed that Communism might be reached by more roads than one. Tito beamed (*below*).

TITO GAVE A PARTY for his polite guests, invited U. S. Ambassador James Riddleberger (*above, left*), who took Khrushchev aback by explaining that, yes, he did too know about workingmen because he used to be a house-painter and bricklayer. Khrushchev got high and *ad lib* invited U. S. newsmen to visit Russia, which that summer (1955) a lot of them proceeded to do.

373

"THE SUMMIT"

Carefully nurtured by Russia, a blissful atmosphere pervaded Geneva, Switzerland, when in late July 1955 the chiefs of Russia, the U. S., France and Britain gathered at "the summit" to try once more for lasting peace. All agreed at once that World War III would be world suicide.

On disarmament, President Eisenhower proposed that, besides inspection teams (Russian proposal), budget publication (French proposal) and radar screens inside each other's territory (British proposal), the nations permit reciprocal air photography to spot any treacherous rearming. The chiefs adjourned after agreeing on a three-point agenda for their foreign ministers later on. At Geneva, nothing but fragrance remained.

Then Bulganin wrote to Eisenhower that air photography would prove little: both sides had too much space in which to hide wickedness if they wished. And when the foreign ministers met to argue (1) disarmament, (2) unification of Germany and (3) improved West-Red contacts, Geneva's fragrance had vanished.

Russia wanted all nuclear weapons dropped, which the West wouldn't do without all inspection controls, including air photos. Having taken West Germany into NATO, the West wanted a unifying election which would probably bring in East Germany as well. This Russia could not tolerate. On contacts, little tangible was said or done.

When the ministers broke up they were all moving in different directions and the "Spirit of Geneva" was a thing of the past. (*Below*): Pinay, Dulles, Molotov, Macmillan.

KONRAD ADENAUER of free, independent West Germany, delayed accepting an invitation to Moscow like the one tendered Austria in the spring, until after the "Summit" sessions. When he did go, he prayed pointedly in the city's one Roman Catholic church, St. Louis' Cathedral (*above*). Apparently, heaven told him he could, with impunity, exchange diplomatic recognition and open trade relations with the Reds. But he sent an emissary to the West to implore continued insistence there on all Germany's being made one — and free. This aim was quite as paramount for the West as for the aging Adenauer.

NEW OFFENSIVES

As the spirit of Geneva evaporated, vast new non-violent offensives were unveiled by Moscow. Back in the spring Great Britain, which had been ousted from Suez by pressure from Egypt and was having trouble holding Cyprus, negotiated at Baghdad a mutual defense arrangement with the Middle East's "northern tier" — Turkey, Iraq, Iran, Pakistan. The Reds now leapfrogged this barrier by selling, for cotton and rice, a store of arms (tanks, jets, guns) to Egypt, some more to Syria. Further, they offered to help finance and engineer Egypt's great proposed device for national survival: the High Dam at Aswan. While France's dependencies in North Africa boiled with Moslem nationalism and America's foster-child, Israel, screamed about Arab hostility, Russia could thus be seen positioning herself to exploit a southern flank while holding at the center (Germany).

Next, Messrs Khrushchev and Bulganin junketed through South Asia exuding smiles and promises of economic aid and technology. Wreathed in flowers (*above*), they jollied India's Prime Minister Nehru about Western imperialism, disavowed interest in Indian politics. In Burma (*right*) they assured beaming Prime Minister U Nu that Moscow would buy his surplus rice and give him a technological institute to boot. In Afghanistan, gateway to India, their song was the same, their reception cooler.

Moscow's "Joy Boys" did not visit pro-Western Pakistan but sent word there that economic aid would be forthcoming if Pakistan would withdraw from the Southeast Asia Treaty Organization, a defense set-up fostered by Washington and celebrated by war games off Bangkok. Pakistan forthwith snubbed SEATO'S games, but stayed relatively pro-Western.

A WILLING COLLABORATOR in Moscow's plans for the Middle East was General Gamal Abdel Nasser, self-made dictator of Egypt, and apparently a dedicated patriot. Professing fear of Israel, and displeasure with Britain and the U. S. for not helping him, Nasser (*left, center*) set out to weld the Arab states into an alliance which, he openly said, Moscow would back if the West didn't. As bold as he was foxy, he thus staked his and Egypt's future on the gamble that Moscow and the West would not indulge in, or permit, a shooting war in the explosive Middle East.

While this pot boiled, a trade fair staged by Red China was welcomed in the heart of Cairo, and the next thing the West knew, Moscow's influence and instigations were popping up everywhere. The situation got so threatening that the U. N. sent its Secretary-General out to demand peace between Egypt and Israel. Moscow seconded this move but with tongue in clever cheek.

MORE NEW OFFENSIVES

FRENCH REMNANTS leaving Dien Bien Phu as prisoners after its siege and capture by Red rebels (May, 1954).

MOSCOW'S WEAPONS for its new push into Southeast Asia were purchases, promises, pride and peace. Surpluses of rice, jute, cotton, rubber, etc. the Reds could buy gladly and freely for industrial machinery and technical assistance, of which they had enough to export for propaganda purposes. Promises of further trade and aid, and of peace, were cheap to give and pleasant to receive. Pride was easily appealed to as all Asians marked the passing of colonialism in India, Ceylon, Burma, Indo-China, Malaya, Indonesia.

The splitting away of northern Viet Nam after Red guerillas, backed by Peiping, took Dien Bien Phu from the French, dramatized anti-colonialism more vividly than did a slower guerrilla campaign in Malaya, whence Britain was about to withdraw, leaving the natives to work out their own destiny.

(*Above*): **PRESIDENT HO CHI MINH** of North Viet Nam embraces Premier Bulganin in Moscow the year after Dien Bien Phu.

AT BANDUNG, Java, in 1955, 29 Asian and African nations got together for a conference on security and trade. India's Prime Minister Nehru voted with China's Chou En-lai (*above*) in denying Ceylon's charges that Russia's domination of its European satellites constituted "Soviet colonialism." The stage for closer Sino-Russian understanding and propagandizing like this had been set by a 1954 visit of Khrushchev and Bulganin to Mao in Peiping (*right*).

The march of Moscow into Southeast Asia posed a whole new set of geopolitical questions for the future, not without rays of hope for the West. What if a maturing China resented intrusion into its sphere by its older partner in the Red Axis? Might not that axis someday crack in the center if the West helped accentuate the natural strains? Observers concluded, as of 1956, that for the long pull the struggle would be won in the rice fields, not on any battlefield.

NEW "PEOPLE'S" ARMIES

In May 1955 the Russians summoned their satellites to Warsaw, had them sign an eight-power mutual defense "treaty," in answer to NATO, and merged their armies. In charge of the unified command was put Marshal Ivan Konev (*left*), who led Zhukov's left wing in the Battle for Germany. The usual title of "People's" armies was given to these captive forces whose ranks would be filled by conscription, their politics policed by the MVD.

HITLERITE UNIFORMS were designed for the East German "People's" army (*right*) in an obvious effort to revive a nationalistic (within limits) spirit competitive with West Germany, whose new military uniforms showed a strong American influence.

"FACTORY FIGHTING GROUPS" (conscripted) were formed among East German plant and office workers, armed with new tommy-guns and carbines (*above*). Former members of the *Wehrmacht* were, of course, given preference, but an "Organization for Sport and Technics," 10,000 strong and armed with rifles, included many young girls.

"THE FOUNTAIN" was the title of the massed calisthenic display (*above*) by a Byelorussian group at one of the great stadia. It seems to express the all-out nature of the Union's huge sports program, source and fountain of health and striving among the Red masses.

In 1934 the rulers of Soviet Russia awakened to the enormous potential of excellence in sports — for world prestige and otherwise. All athletics would be good basic training for a nation that might have to fight. And soccer, for example, the favorite spectator sport of the West European workingman, had high propaganda value all over the world. Sports clubs, stadia and training programs were ordered wholesale throughout the Union. A sports committee of the Council of Ministers was made directly responsible to the Central Committee of the omnipotent Party.

War interrupted fruition of the sports program, but in 1948 came word from on high: train the year round; go all-out to win "world supremacy" in all sports, especially the Western ones. Nicolai Romanov (no kin) a cultured amateur, was subordinated to hard-boiled Col. Gen. Apollonov of the MVD as sports tsar. High rewards and drastic punishments were provided for success or failure.

In 1950, the first Red Russian track and field team appeared in the European Championships at Paris. They took two gold medals, sixth place. Two years later, at Bern and Brussels, they swept the field, with teams from satellite Hungary and Czechoslovakia close behind. At Helsinki the same year they placed in the Olympic Games second only to the U. S., after sitting out the Winter Olympics at Oslo which, they said, they could have won had they "chosen to enter." At Helsinki, the U. S. took five boxing medals, the Russians none. This precipitated a crash program to produce Red boxers.

The Soviets next proceeded to beat some of Britain's best at soccer, and the world at rowing (Henley Regatta), the Canadians at hockey and

AT THE HENLEY REGATTA (July 1954), in their first appearance, Russian oarsmen (*above*) carried off the Grand Challenge Cup. Russian strong women, like shot-putters **Tyshkavich** (*far left*) and **Sybina** (*left*) may look funny, but they know their business, state-dictated.

"WORLD SUPREMACY"

all the other contenders at rifle-shooting in world matches held at Caracas.

It was understood that the Russians would compete only in events which they figured to win. Figurers were the argus-eyed MVD, whose Dynamo sport clubs enrolled and subsidized 500,000 athletes. Spartak and TsDSA, enrolling millions each, were the sports organs of industry and the Red Army, respectively. Subsidies were supposed to be secret, but all the world knew that the coveted title Master of Sports connoted a full-time job behind each Master's cover job.

This year (1956) preliminary contests marked the Russians as the team to beat in the Winter Olympics at Cortina d'Ampezzo, Italy. True to their rigorous training at Alma Ata and elsewhere, Red skiers and skaters took five gold medals. The amazing Red hockey team then took a sixth gold medal award, once more whipping Canada.

The sports world looked forward ominously to the Olympic Games proper at Melbourne in November-December, which the Russians coldly promised to win. In training they had at least 4,000,000 candidates who would be winnowed at a monster summer Spartakadia (national sports meet) in Moscow, winners to be state-trained intensively for Melbourne in the Caucasus and Central Asia.

Apart from their moot amateurism, which to the Soviets was a point too silly to discuss, competing athletes had this to remark about Soviet athletes and athletics: the former at least had fun, and the latter provided the Soviet masses with something they were otherwise forbidden — an emotional outlet. It was also felt that sport was one area, at least, in which the Iron Curtain could be by-passed.

BEATING THE NORSE and the Finns and all but one super-Austrian (triple winner Toni Sailer) on skis and speed skates were 1956 Red triumphs even greater than the **Red Hockey Team's** over the U. S., Canada and Czechoslovakia. The hockey boys (*above*) had, after all, played together for four years.

Evgenyi Grishin, 500-meter skating champion (*center, left, opposite page*), is nominally an engraver.

Skiers **Lubou Kosireva** (*center, right*) and **Evgeniya Sidorova** (*bottom, right*) were as nimble and courageous as they were good-looking. Jumper **Yuri Moschkin** (*above*) employed a daring belly-whopper style.

20TH PARTY CONGRESS

Only three and one-third years had elapsed since the 19th Party Congress when the 20th was convened in the Great Palace of the Kremlin on February 14, 1956. But during most of that time, Stalin had been dead. The Party bosses — the Central Committee's Presidium — had sat up many a long night figuring how to employ their new freedom, what new "party line" to take.

First spokesman was the Central Committee's bulky, bald First Secretary, **Nikita Khrushchev.** Within the first ten minutes of a seven-hour harangue he made it plain that great changes were in store — at least on paper.

DOWN WAR. After saluting the spread of Communism into a "world system," he observed that Capitalism had not yet fallen apart, as predicted by Lenin. Nor had Lenin been right (said Khrushchev) when he promised that only through war could Communism exterminate Capitalism. There was still much in Capitalism which Communism might profitably study — sciences and techniques — and there were means other than combat through which Capitalist countries could be taken over.

Behind these heretical statements, strong forces could be felt. One, of course, was nuclear energy, which had made any war involving Russians unthinkable even to Red terrorists. The other was Communism's success in areas and under leaderships beyond Moscow's control: in Yugoslavia under Tito, in China under Mao.

Mr. Khrushchev went politely on to say: "It is ridiculous to think that revolutions are made to order [or that Moscow 'exports' revolution].... We have always asserted, and continue to assert, that the establishment of a new social order in any country is the internal affair of its people.... After seeing for themselves the advantages that Communism holds out, all working men and women on earth will sooner or later take to the road of the struggle to build a Socialist society.... It is quite likely that the forms of the transition will become more and more variegated.... There is not a shadow of doubt that for a number of Capitalist countries the overthrow of the bourgeois dictatorship by force, and the connected sharp aggravation of the class struggle is inevitable.... But there are different forms of

social revolution, and the allegation that we recognize force and civil war as the *only* way of transforming society does not correspond to reality.... The political leadership of the working class, headed by its advance detachment, is the indispensable and decisive factor for all the forms of transition to Socialism."

In other words, Moscow would avoid war, would revive its "popular front" efforts over the world and bore from within.

DOWN STALIN. But the best was yet to come. After reviewing Red industrial growth since 1940, applauding his own "virgin soil" plan for agriculture and previewing an ambitious new Five-Year Plan (*see below*), Mr. Khrushchev touched on Stalin's death and the crushing of the Beria "gang," to lead up to his smash finale.

The Central Committee, he said, had now "vigorously condemned the cult of the individual as being alien to the spirit of Marxism-Leninism and making a particular leader the hero and miracle-worker.... The currency of the cult of the individual tended to minimize the role of collective leadership in the Party and at times resulted in serious drawbacks in our work.... The leading core of the party is not a group bound by personal relations or mutual advantage; it is a working collective of leaders whose relations are based on ideas and principles, permitting of neither mutual forgiveness nor personal antagonisms."

So Stalin was really dead. Long live Khrushchev & Co.! The official reporters credited Khrushchev with an "ovation" for his speech, and on succeeding days he was followed on the Grand Palace rostrum by other members of the "leading core" who echoed his sentiments almost verbatim.

Anastas Mikoyan, a Deputy Premier, said: "The cult of personality ... could not but exert an extremely negative influence...." He called for an immediate rewrite of Stalin's *History of the Communist Party, Brief Course* and described Stalin's writings on contemporary Capitalism, so lavishly praised at the 1952 Congress, as unhelpful and incorrect.

Georgi Malenkov, once Stalin's leading sycophant, now only a Deputy Premier, was allowed to say: "The enormous and vitally important significance of the firm course against the cult of personality ... is comprehensible to all."

Viacheslav Molotov, Foreign Minister: "With the support of the entire Party, the Central Committee has firmly dealt with

the cult of the individual. . . ." **Lazar Kaganovich,** another Deputy Premier: "The cult of the individual is harmful. It humiliates the masses and the Party. . . ." **Marshal Nikolai Bulganin,** Premier: "Having vigorously condemned the cult of the individual . . . the Central Committee and its Presidium have been applying the principle of collective leadership in deeds. . . ."

Missing only was the head pig in satirist George Orwell's *Animal Farm* to explain: "All animals are equal, but some are more equal than others."

UP FISTS. Lest anyone think that Russia was incapable of war or unwilling to fight if provoked sufficiently, **Marshal Zhukov,** the War Minister, was detailed to state that if the West's "sly strategists" should launch an atomic attack, the U.S.S.R. would retaliate with "similar and perhaps more power-

ful attacks." Zhukov assured his comrades that Russia now had "diverse atomic and hydrogen weapons, powerful rocket and jet armaments of various kinds, including long range rockets."

In naming their new first team (*see* p. 426) the Party bosses gave it a martial aspect. Military men on the Central Committee were increased from four to eight and Marshal Zhukov was elevated to the Party Presidium as an alternate — the first professional soldier so honored since Frunze.

INNOCENCE ABROAD. In the stormy spring of 1956, the "collective leadership" felt secure enough in its new role of innocence to try a maneuver not dared since the Kremlin first flew the Red flag: a visit to the West. To dress the act, they dissolved the Cominform, waved an olive branch over the hot Middle East. Preceded by Malenkov, who kissed babies and dripped good will, and Serov, Khrushchev and Bulganin sailed to Britain on the cruiser *Ordjonikidze.* Prime Minister Eden met them politely (*above*), but the British public was cool. Their effort to woo Britain away from the U.S., to buy strategic hardware (machine tools, ships), to pose as jolly brokers of peace fell flat. Still, Moscow might have acquired an inkling of civilization, might refrain from hot war indefinitely.

In naming their new first team the Party bosses gave it a martial aspect. Military men on the Central Committee were increased from four to eight and Marshal Zhukov was elevated to the Party Presidium as an alternate — the first professional soldier so honored since Frunze.

MOSCOW UNIVERSITY is the show piece of Russia's educational system, which includes 32 other universities, 180 technical institutes. Here shown illuminated for a big political anniversary, it is a "specialist's" treasure-house of libraries and laboratories, staffed with the pick of the U.S.S.R.'s brains. To gain entrance is to set foot on the ladder to success. So furious is the pace required that many a "specialist" limits himself to four hours' sleep. Married couples live austerely apart. Almost nowhere in the West is there such devotion to self-improvement, nor are the postgraduate rewards so immediate, the political climate so grimly "or else."

381

THE FIRST INTACT MIG 15 to fall into Western hands (*above*) created a minor sensation in early 1953. It was landed on Bornholm by a disillusioned Polish pilot, who had not heard that $100,000 was offered by the U. N. command in Korea for a close look at the 650-m.p.h. Red fighter which had given U.S. Sabre-Jets so much trouble.

FRESCO JETS, new and faster, developed by the Red Navy but also used by the Red Air Force, were unveiled in 1955 (*above*), flying over a sleek new Red destroyer.

THE ARMS RACE between Russia and the West was woefully burdensome to both economies, but on it went. The pay-off parts of it were secret: nuclear weapons and guided missiles. In size, U. S. hydrogen bombs of 20-megaton power (20,000,000 tons of TNT) outweighed the Soviets' two- to four-mega-tonners. In stockpile, the Western lead (1955) was some 5,000 nuclear devices of all types to about 1,000, ready to go.

In ballistic (rocket-type) missiles the Reds were believed ahead, with ranges of 600 to 800 miles as against a 200-mile range for the West. The "ultimate weapon"—an intercontinental missile capable of targeting at 1,500 miles, was probably much nearer reality in the U.S.S.R. than in the U. S., where a hue and cry arose in Congress to close this gap. Apart from the threat to cities, the threat to NATO's forward air bases was obvious. And apart from missiles, the Reds appeared ahead of the West in intercontinental jet bombers.

The whole Red armament was diligently modernized after 1945. The submarine fleet of 400-plus, world's largest, was two-thirds in short-range types, none atom-powered. There were no Red aircraft carriers. Cruisers of the heavy new *Sverdlov* class (*below*) carried only 5.9-inch guns, not aimed by radar.

The bulk of new planes were fast light bombers, fighter types and helicopters for ground-support. Ground transport, historically sparse and poor in the Red Army, was rapidly improving.

In discussing disarmament, which they did loudly and frequently, the Reds sought to ban nuclear weapons without substantially reducing conventional ones. This was natural, with their interior support lines, for any war with the West. Actually, they seemed content to continue the arms race, short of annihilation weapons, since they were satisfied that Capitalism would crack under it before their slave economy would.

XV. THE RISE AND FALL OF KHRUSHCHEV

Nikita Sergeyevich Khrushchev, top Russian ruler from 1957 to 1964, was almost dethroned before his reign began. His open exposure of Stalin's bloody crimes unnerved the entire Soviet society. Puppet rulers in the satellite countries who had been appointed by Stalin now felt insecure. Rank-and-file Communist Party members were in a state of shock, numbed by Khrushchev's revelation that the godlike Stalin had actually been a paranoid killer.

Satellite populations were quick to take advantage of the confusion among their Communist bosses. In mid-1956, workers in the Polish city of Poznan rioted for better living conditions, just as many foreigners were visiting the city's international trade fair. Police crushed the uprising, but the frightened Polish courts meted only short prison sentences to the riot ringleaders. By fall, Poland was seething, and the Polish Communist Party sought salvation by giving leadership to Wladyslaw Gomulka, a Titoist who had been imprisoned by Stalin. Gomulka began granting the Polish people many liberties, which Russia considered dangerous. Khrushchev ordered Soviet troops in Poland to march against Warsaw, while he visited the Polish capital to threaten Gomulka. But the new Polish leader informed Khrushchev that Poland's army would defend Warsaw, whose workers were being armed to fight unto death. Khrushchev backed down, allowing Poland internal freedom if it supported Soviet foreign policy. Soviet troops turned away from Warsaw.

Excited by Poland's bloodless revolution, Hungarian students in Budapest held a street parade demanding mild reforms. When police fired upon the peaceful demonstration, all Hungary erupted into anti-Soviet rebellion. Statues of Stalin were pulled down, and Communist police were burned alive. After some hesitation, Khrushchev ordered a Russian army of 200,000 men and 5,000 tanks to crush the uprising. This took two bloody months.

Blaming the Polish and Hungarian revolts on Khrushchev's de-Stalinization, Russia's collective leaders in 1957 tried to purge him from power. An alliance was formed by the Malenkov liberals and Molotov conservatives, who together expelled Khrushchev from the Party Presidium. But Nikita called a meeting of the Party's Central Committee, where a majority was held by provincial leaders. Khrushchev offered to turn most of Soviet industry over to local governmental administration if the Central Committee would support him, which it did. Malenkov, Molotov, and the other anti-Khrushchevites were fired from the Party Presidium and demoted to minor posts. Khrushchev returned to the Presidium as ruler of the U.S.S.R.

Next to challenge Khrushchev was Marshal Georgi Zhukov, top Soviet military commander during World War II. Zhukov tried to reduce Communist Party control over the Soviet armed forces, but Khrushchev forced him into retirement. Finally in 1958, Khrushchev became U.S.S.R. Premier, replacing Marshal Nikolai Bulganin, who was demoted to minor positions. As head of both the Communist Party and Soviet government, Khrushchev now held the same key positions of power as the late Joseph Stalin.

Already Khrushchev had become (with Bulganin) Russia's travelling salesman, making frequent good-will trips abroad, especially to underdeveloped countries where he would offer lavish Soviet aid. In 1959, securely in power at home, he made the most important tour of his career — to the United States to end the Cold War. Besides conferring with President Eisenhower, Mr. and Mrs. Khrushchev traveled through much of the U.S.A., viewing movie studios, factories and farms, talking with American workers and farmers, and appealing on tele-vision directly to the American public. But all of Khrushchev's charm failed, because he wished to settle the Cold War only on terms advantageous to Russia.

Meanwhile, to show its annoyance at Khrushchev's flirtation with capitalist America, Red China began border skirmishes against India, which Russia was wooing with large-scale technical aid. Angrily Khrushchev stopped almost all Soviet aid to China, which then commenced frontier skirmishes against the U.S.S.R.

In 1960 Khrushchev also got mad at President Eisenhower, because Ike refused to apologize for flying U-2 reconnaissance planes over the U.S.S.R. After walking out of a Paris summit conference (Britain, France, U.S., and U.S.S.R.), Khrushchev again visited America, this time only New York, where he berated the West at the United Nations Assembly. Here he set a new style of diplomacy by pounding his shoe on his desk to interrupt an unfriendly Western speech.

Khrushchev now decided to endanger America militarily. Befriending Castro, Russia placed medium-range (1,000-mile) rockets in Cuba armed with nuclear warheads. Soviet bombers carrying hydrogen bombs were based on Cuban airfields. The new U.S. President, Kennedy, could not allow this military build-up to continue. In 1962, the U.S. Navy blockaded Cuba, stopping the arrival of any further Soviet armament. President Kennedy also mobilized U.S. military reservists. For a few days, Khrushchev threatened to go to war. Then he backed down, agreeing to withdraw the Soviet missiles and bombers if the United States would not invade Cuba.

From then on, Khrushchev's star began to wane. Besides his humiliating retreat in the Cuban crisis, his farm policies were going wrong at home. The new lands of Central Asia, where he had planted 100 million acres of grain, were turning into a dust bowl. His 80 million acres of corn grew poorly in the cold, dry Russian climate. Drought in 1963 resulted in crop failure, and two-fifths of all Soviet hogs had to be slaughtered to save grain for human consumption. Even so, Russia had to import 11 million tons of grain from capitalist countries.

Having learned the hard way that America would not back down in international crises, Khrushchev tried to appease the United States by concluding agreements banning above-ground nuclear tests, and establishing a hot line (direct radio-telegraph) between the Kremlin and the White House. These treaties further angered China, which accused Russia of plotting with America to dominate the world. Albania supported China in the Sino-Soviet dispute, while Rumania was neutral.

By 1964, Khrushchev was in trouble. He admitted that his new lands and corn had largely failed. During early autumn he proposed a new Five-Year Plan stressing consumer goods instead of heavy, war-potential industry. The full text of this speech was never published. In October the Party Presidium decided to remove him. The Party Central Committee was convened, and ordered him to retire. He was neither executed nor imprisoned, but banished to a country home outside Moscow. When interviewed there by foreign newsmen, he seemed broken in spirit, devoting his time to reading and simple garden chores. His study was still filled with expensive gifts received from foreign statesmen in his days of power.

Superficially, Khrushchev would appear to have been a failure. But he was one of Russia's greatest modernizers, like Tsar Peter I or Catherine the Great. By de-Stalinization he discredited mass purging as a method of Soviet rule. His mildness in censorship permitted Russian writers, scholars, and scientists to be more creative. Considerable freedom of discussion appeared in the Soviet press. Many prison camps were closed, new milder law codes were adopted, and much of Stalinist terror disappeared. Soviet daily life became freer and gayer.

Khrushchev also was a great builder. Soviet industry grew by 70 percent during his eight years in power. He fathered the world's first Sputnik, first man in space, first rocket to reach the moon, and first atomic-powered surface ship. His government built the largest airplane, biggest hydrogen bomb, and greatest hydro-electric power station in the world. By his personal suggestion, the U.S.S.R. introduced new fast methods of housing construction, using prefabricated cement sections. The formerly drab Soviet clothing and shoes began to acquire color and style.

Khrushchev opened many holes in the Iron Curtain. No longer was Russia a hermit country with mystic rulers. Tourism and cultural exchange let foreigners see the U.S.S.R. and meet Soviet citizens. By his own travels abroad, Khrushchev learned much about foreign countries, and showed the world that Soviet leaders can be colorful human beings.

Though his successors ridiculed him, modern Russia owes much to Nikita Khrushchev. So too, perhaps, does world comity.

A PEASANT'S GAVEL in barnyard arguments is his boot. During his 1960 appearance at the U.N., a period when he was consuming plenty of vodka, Khrushchev reverted to type by taking off one of his shoes — an elastic-laced loafer for overweight oldsters — and placing it on his desk, handy-by. Photographers who missed him actually hammering with it deny that he did more than bang with his fists. But plenty of others heard and saw the performance, and even Foreign Minister Andrei Gromyko had to grin.

NIKITA KHRUSHCHEV'S IRRESISTIBLE APPEAL TO AMERICANS was that of a hard-nosed, hard-headed, often humorous extrovert — just such a man as many an American conceives himself to be. He was a master of the studied (and unstudied) indiscretion (see shoe-pounding, top of page); of the bombastic boast ("We'll bury you!"); of the folksy aphorism ("When the whales fight, the shrimps whistle"); of the impulsively generous gesture (to the U.S. press, "Come visit me"). His image was vastly enhanced and memorably articulated by his attractive, tireless, boyish shadow, **Interpreter Victor Sukhodrev** (*right,* with pad). Born in Moscow in 1932, Sukhodrev accompanied his mother to England in 1939 when

she went there with the Soviet Trade Mission. He stayed throughout World War II, and later polished the fluent English he then acquired by majoring in it at Moscow's Foreign Language Institute. In the Soviet Foreign Ministry, Sukhodrev has now risen to counselor, but his linguistic talent must long be prized and commandeered by Kremlin bigwigs when they visit America or Great Britain, both of whose accents he has mastered perfectly. He interprets his speakers' ideas, rather than their precise words, instantly and with faithful inflections and emphases, using notes for the longish paragraphs. A charmer personally, he is married to an actress.

POLAND SHAKES LOOSE

Khrushchev's excoriations of Stalin reverberated nowhere more loudly than in Russia's nearest and largest satellite, Poland. There, 30 million proud, spirited, nationalistic people — mostly good Catholics — had never relished their Communist subjugation, and in 1953-56 they seethed over revelations of Russian police controls, which they threw off.

In June 1956, some 50,000 factory workers at Posnan seized the occasion of their city's big trade fair, attended by the world press, to demonstrate riotously for better living and working conditions, and for political autonomy ("Russians, go home!"). They hoisted Poland's old republican flag on the city hall flagstaff (*left*).

The Red regime called out its tanks, which killed 53 and wounded hundreds in restoring order. But deep ground tremor was in motion, and before it ceased Poland had shaken itself largely loose from Moscow's grip. The biggest wigs of the Soviet hierarchy — Khrushchev, Molotov, Kaganovich, Mikoyan — hurried to Warsaw to try to calm things down. So did Marshal Koniev, commander of the Warsaw Treaty powers' unified forces, which "maneuvered" at Poland's borders. A Soviet squadron appeared off Danzig.

But a Polish patriot had arisen at the crucial hour, to endure for many years. He was Wladyslaw Gomulka, one of Poland's earliest and most liberal Communists, a close friend and political emulator of Yugoslavia's Tito, with whom he has shared fair weather and foul (*below*). Long imprisoned by Stalin and Beria for "deviation," Gomulka now in stormy confrontations made the Moscow men accept Poland as mistress of her own destiny within "the camp of Socialism." To their threats of force he retorted that his countrymen, too, had arms. For Poland he won not only political equality but a write-off of war claims, payments for coal, and broad economic aid.

HUNGARY SPRINGS FREE

The spring and summer of 1956 were joyous in Hungary. Following Khrushchev's loud cues and Poland's bold lead, the Hungarians de-Stalinized their government. Tyrannical Matyas Rakosi was forced to resign as the Hungarian Workers' first secretary. Thousands of political prisoners were released from jail. Hungarian independence was in the air.

In October, the Budapest students went full out. They tore down Stalin's towering statue in the capital, breaking it grotesquely forward at the knees (*above*). Though supposedly Red-controlled, the Hungarian army joined in the rebellion instead of suppressing it. The entire western half of the nation was de-Sovietized, with stars, sickles, and other insignia of Moscow everywhere deleted or desecrated. Barbed wire and minefields on the Austrian borders were removed. The secret police were liquidated. In a few short weeks it seemed that this ancient Magyar nation, once the proudest half of a dual empire, had reasserted its historic national autonomy.

IN THE LULL before the 1956 rebellion and its bloody suppression, some young Hungarian officers (*above*), including one of gentle gender, took their ease on a parapet overlooking the Danube. In the offing can be seen the twin cities of Buda and Pest, the former on the river's high right bank (left side of picture), the latter on the low left bank, where visiting traders used to camp from time immemorial.

STUDENTS IN BUDAPEST clamber aboard a Hungarian army tank, waving old-time banners, in the first flush of their October rebellion's early success. But before too long a great many of these same students would be the bloody targets of much bigger, heavier tanks, manned by Muscovite professionals shooting to kill.

BUT THE
JUGGERNAUT
CRUNCHES IN

The Polish and Hungarian crises gave Nikita Khrushchev splendid chances to assert himself among his Kremlin comrades. He took full advantage of the second of these opportunities, to prove himself Russia's undisputed bossman. After some pretense of "negotiation" he arrested the emissaries from Budapest, later deporting their leader (Imre Nagy) to Rumania. He unleashed a juggernaut of 200,000 men with 5,000 tanks, moving inexorably in from the east.

Through the leafy streets of Budapest (*right*) flowed the columns of steel, seeking out "freedom fighters" in their strongholds, many of them centered in and around university buildings. The ensuing carnage (at least 30,000 killed) deeply shocked the Communist parties of other countries. (*The Daily Worker,* voice of Moscow in the U.S.A., never has forgotten or forgiven, to this day.) More important were reactions in nearby Yugoslavia and far-off China. Tito said, in effect, "I told you so — told you too tough policies could only make proud nations rebel." His truce with Moscow soon ended. Red China, on the other hand, while applauding Khrushchev's steel-fistedness, blamed his earlier ineptitude in de-Stalinization, which Peking likened to washing soiled linen in public. It was to mollify Mao that the Kremlin's bull-necked new boss soon arranged for China to be taught the gentle art of nuclear destruction.

PHOTOGRAPHERS WERE NOT welcome, or particularly safe, inside Budapest during Moscow's mop-up (*below*). So one of them contrived this "mood" shot from across the river, showing columns of battle smoke rising from the old city's heart. The blasted bridge in the foreground was a relic of World War II, when the Red Army shot its way into Budapest the first time.

SPUTNIKS

Any blushing that Khrushchev might have done for unhappy Hungary was soon effaced by a scientific spectacular without human precedent. Long proficient with rockets, including huge variants of what they got from the Germans at Peenemünde (see Chapter XIII), Russian scientists blasted one off on October 4, 1957, which hurled aloft a metal globe that did not come back that day or that week. Instead it went whizzing elliptically around and around the earth, from 140 to 560 miles out, and continued doing so every 96.03 minutes for a fortnight. What was more it "beep-beeped" by radio for all the world to hear. It was earth's first man-made satellite and the happy Russians called it "Sputnik," which means "fellow traveler."

At twilight the brightly burnished globule could be picked up by strong binoculars, and even the naked eye could catch occasional gleams from the burned-out last stage of its rocket booster, which coasted along in Sputnik's heavenly wake.

This was the authentic beginning of the Space Age, a solid Soviet achievement for all time. Sputnik I would be followed by hundreds more, of all nationalities, shapes, sizes, and purposes. To their new age the Russians would erect a soaring titanium monolith (*left*) in honor of a long succession of "firsts" in space, and of Sergei P. Korolev (*left*), chief designer of Russia's first spaceships, who died in 1966.

THE ORIGINAL Sputnik I was only 23 inches in diameter, weighing 184.3 lbs. It was fired (as shown *below* in an animation) inside a nose cone, whence it separated and extended its antennae. Sputnik I was soon succeeded by a second weighing 1,120.5 lbs. which carried an instrumented dog named Laika. The whole object of the exercise was, of course, to carry passengers — eventually humans.

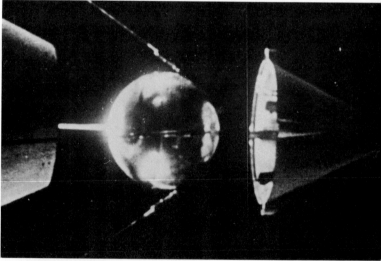

Laika produced some flying puppies (which Mrs. John F. Kennedy begged for and got one. They are shown *below,* with some fellow-travelling mice). So rapidly did space medicine and travel progress that, by 1961 at Vienna, President Kennedy could say to Premier Khrushchev, "Let's go to the moon together."

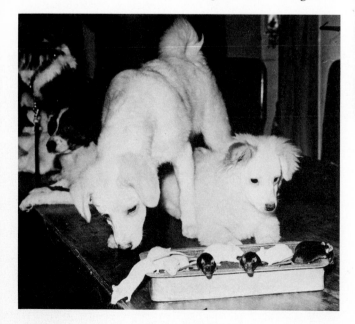

COSMONAUT entered the world's vocabulary from Russia in 1961, when a farm-bred airplane pilot named Yury Gagarin flew around the globe in a 10,400-lb. capsule called "Vostok" (means "eastward") and landed safely after one orbit — the first human ever to do so. When John Glenn of the U.S.A. tripled this feat the next year, he and his mates were called "astronauts."

The U.S.S.R. had paroxysms of grief when Colonel Gagarin was killed in the 1968 crash of a light plane on a routine flight. They buried him in the Kremlin wall. But dozens more Russians had followed Gagarin, including, it was believed, some who failed to return from aloft and may still be up there in

LUNIKS

Less than two years after Sputnik I, on January 2, 1959, a 3,244-lb. vehicle called "Lunik" was shot at the moon by the Russians. It missed, and went into orbit around the sun. But that same September another Lunik landed a pennant on the moon, and then one touched down softly right at the edge of the moon's dark side. This one relayed the first photos ever taken of the moon's rocky, pebbly surface (*above*). This kind of thing was continued apace (by the U.S. also), and in 1966 a Luna 10 was sent into permanent orbit as a man-made moon-moon. For the complicated course arranged for this one, *see left*.

Apart from its pure scientific interest, the moon captured Russian (and American) imaginations as a space target because of its comparative nearness, its potential as a launch pad to the outer universe if not (which all foreswore) as a platform for the military domination of terra firma.

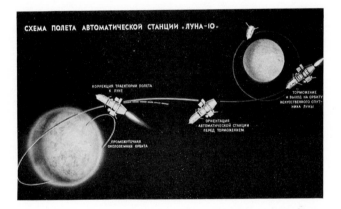

orbiting coffins. In 1963, Valentina Tereshkova became the first female cosmonaut, flying alone in a Vostok two days apart from one containing Valery Bykovsky. This team was paraded by Khrushchev in Red Square (*right*), but more important than her flight survival was Tereshkova's subsequent marriage to yet another cosmonaut by whom she bore healthy children, thus disproving any ill genetic effects of space weightlessness or radiation.

By 1968, Russian (and American) spacemen were travelling in teams, in tandem ships, making rendezvous, "walking" in space, planning space stations and workshops to explore not just the moon but other planets.

"SPIRIT OF CAMP DAVID"

Accompanied by his second wife Nina (*left*) and a large retinue which included his three grown children, Nikita Khrushchev arrived in the U.S. in September 1959 for the first time. His objects were to inspect America, visit with President Eisenhower, address the United Nations, boast about Russia's new space probes, and create an aura of "peaceful co-existence," his personal policy which was under fire at home and from Red China. Widely advertised were friendly talks which the two leaders would have at Camp David in the Catoctin hills, and the entire trip was themed "Spirit of Camp David."

The President put his guests in charge of his handsome and adroit friend Henry Cabot Lodge, Ambassador to the United Nations, for a whirlwind cross-country tour. This proved as entertaining for the American people as for Mr. K., since the chunky extrovert made good copy wherever he went, whatever he did or said, especially with improvisations on his blunt promise, "We'll bury you!"

When they got to the Pacific Coast, there was one hang-up. The visitors had their hearts set on seeing Disneyland, but security considerations supervened. Mr. K. had to settle for watching a girlie show filmed (*Can Can*), at which he turned up his proletarian nose.

IN PITTSBURGH, the former Ukrainian shepherd, miner, and factory hand was an instant hit with steel mill employees, amongst whom he shot the breeze and slapped backs. Many of the Pittsburghers were of Slavic descent, with enough ethnic memory to catch their visitor's wisecracks. But even the Scots and Irishers found him diverting, with Ambassador Lodge (*right*) an ever-genial interlocutor.

AT COON RAPIDS, IOWA, there was commotion in the tall cornfields of Roswell Garst, a prosperous farmer whom Mr. K. had met in Russia when he was there selling seed corn, a product dear to the Premier's heart though it dislikes Russian soil and climate. When some 300 press correspondents traipsed along, Farmer Garst became concerned for his crop and tried to shoo them off, aided by a bellowing Mr. K. Ambassador Lodge had to step lively to protect his polished toes.

Back at Camp David, President Eisenhower kept after the Premier to take the heat off Berlin — to stop threatening a forcible settlement of German reunification on Communist terms. In the end, the Russian promised something vaguely of that sort. At the United Nations he was equally vague about any performance or inspection guarantees for his grandiose proposal that Russia and all other nations scrap all their arms within four years. Before Mr. K. went home, it was understood that he and President Ike would meet at another summit conference in Paris the next year.

DISASTER IN THE URALS

Alas for diplomacy. On May Day 1960 some ack-ack operators (probably rocketeers) near Sverdlovsk in Russia's new Ural industrial complex shot down from extreme altitude a wide-winged U-2 Lockheed reconnaisance plane, flown by Pilot Gary Powers under contract with Washington's C.I.A. (*right*). After some stuttering by the White House to the effect that this was just a weather plane, the State Department admitted what massive evidence made obvious: that this was a spy craft complete with infrared telescopic cameras, radiation detectors, sophisticated radar. Pilot Powers even had a suicide needle in case of capture, a copious assortment of currencies, and "trade goods" such as wristwatches for dealing with any foreigners he might fall in with. His destination was Bodo in far Norway, all the way from Peshawar in Pakistan, straight up across the innermost Soviet heartland.

Pilot Powers was tried, found guilty, jailed — and then released in exchange for Russia's master-spy Rudolf Abel, apprehended in Brooklyn.

Premier Khrushchev used the U-2 episode as excuse to cancel the 1960 summit meeting in Paris. He resumed huffing, puffing, and rattling his rockets about Berlin.

OUT OF CUBA'S SIERRA MAESTRA in 1958 swaggered a bearded revolutionist named Fidel Castro (seen *left* in a re-enactment) who, on January 1, 1959, forced the abdication of Dictator Fulgencio Batista. Counseled by Che Guevara, a professional Red firebrand, this personage soon revealed that his regime would be Communist, Castro style. The Russians were delighted and at once took Cuba underwing for about a million dollars a day, the first Red satellite in the western hemisphere, and right on Washington's doorstep!

In a return engagement at the U.N. in 1960, Nikita Khrushchev warmly embraced his hairy new friend, and backed him when Castro (quite rightly) accused the U.S. of plotting his downfall. The C.I.A.'s ensuing Bay of Pigs debacle did nothing to enhance Washington's credibility abroad.

VIENNA IN JUNE of 1961 was the romantic, but unproductive, scene of confrontation between the two Messrs. K. After each gentleman had posed admiring the other's lady (*right* and *left*), Premier K. handed President K. a 2,000-word memo stating Soviet intentions: to execute an immediate treaty reuniting the two Germanys; failing that, a Soviet treaty with East Germany, which would then throttle West Germany. Any western attempt to break the strangle would, said Premier K., "mean war, and thermonuclear war at that." President K. kept his cool, and the threat came to naught. But within two months, up went the Berlin Wall.

MR. BANG'S BIG BLUFF

People had become quite accustomed to the terrible-tempered Mr. Bang of Moscow — to his loud threats and huffy backdowns — when in 1962 he outdid himself. Freighters plying from Russia to Cuba actually carried, in plain sight on their decks (*left*), what could only be nuclear rockets of medium and intermediate range (600–1800 mi.). Astonished, almost incredulous, the U.S. military flew close reconnaisance on this amazing effrontery, watching where the big crates were landed and where they were taken from the Havana docks. Intelligence pipelines were pumped furiously to discover precisely what Mr. Bang was up to. The findings were fantastic, even nightmarish.

THOUSANDS OF RED TECHNICIANS were being poured into Cuba (*right*), with fleets of trucks and launch facilities, to deploy the big canisters and their lethal warheads where they could do the U.S.A. the least good. Russian bombers and ack-ack were also arriving, being assembled, and parked all over. Despite anguished outcries by anti-Castro exiles, Washington kept its counsel and made no accusation until the threatening picture developed positively, unmistakably. When it had hundreds of photos like the low-level one labeled below, showing dozens of missiles poised and presumably triggered with the potential of destroying not only Key West and Cape Canaveral but cities perhaps as far away as Washington, Pittsburgh, and Detroit, President Kennedy informed the American people of their danger. Then he told Nikita Khrushchev a thing or two.

LAUNCH POSITION

MISSILE-READY TENTS

MISSILE ERECTORS

FROM BANG
TO WHIMPER

After clamping on a naval quarantine to cut off all war munitions from Cuba, and mobilizing an irresistible air-amphibious attack force, President Kennedy informed Premier Khrushchev that he would have to remove all his hideous hardware from Castro's front yard at once — or else. This ultimatum was delivered in a low key consistent with John F. Kennedy's unflappable character. But the power of the U.S. intercontinental nuclear arm, including SAC bombers as well as ICBM's, was well known to the Kremlin. Its wide advantage over the Soviets' long-range striking forces was undisputed. Nikita Khrushchev got the message, and willy-nilly pulled in his horns. Mr. Bang's bluff ended in a whimper. Almost as fast as they had been erected, the Soviet missile sites under the Cuban palms were dismantled, and the long lines of freighters trundled back across the Atlantic, carrying home their perilous cargo. In return, Khrushchev got only Kennedy's promise not to invade Cuba (which was not then intended).

When this reverse maneuver was complete, President Kennedy assured his countrymen that, as near as could be told, the Russians had removed all the hydrogen and other warheads they had brought over, and all means of delivering same. But some Cuban exiles were not so sure. They insisted, and still do, that as part of that 1962 nuclear build-up — which John Hughes of the Defense Department (*left*) is shown pointering long after the event — the Russians

blasted silos deep into the rocky hills of north central and eastern Cuba and there implanted a hard-site hydrogen arsenal which (say the exiles) is still there, with trained Cubans and a few remaining Russians in charge. Against this ugly thought Americans have only the word of their Joint Chiefs of Staff.

MORE FERTILE FIELDS for Russian adventure and influence were offered in other undeveloped countries nearer home than Cuba, notably Egypt. There, America's pull-out from helping to finance the new Aswan High Dam, to add 150 billion cubic meters to Nile irrigation waters and a vast new power source, gave the Soviets an opening into which Khrushchev stepped in 1960 to the tune of 100 million rubles and a large corps of engineers. In 1964 (just before his downfall), he joined Gamel Abdel Nasser (*below*) to watch the first Aswan flood-gates open. Russia also now undertook to arm Egypt against Israel, but here the outcome was less happy.

OIL REPLACES COAL

The economy of Stalin was based on coal, of which Russia had large reserves widely scattered from the Ukraine to Siberia. One result was cities resembling the British Midlands or old-time Pittsburgh — sooty, smelly, and smoggy. Another result was smallish industries burning local fuel, and enormous fuel transportation costs where coal was lacking.

A disguised blessing of the German thrust as far east as the Caspian Sea in 1942 was its threat to the Caucasus oil fields, operated since the 19th century and hitherto deemed suffi-cient for the nation's needs. Geologists were now driven to look for new oil around the Volga and even the Urals. They found it in such vast quantities that within a decade after World War II, Russian oil production was doubled; by 1959, quadrupled; and by 1961, Russia was ahead even of Venezuela, second only to the U.S.A. In 1965 the U.S.S.R. exported 66 million tons of oil (about a quarter-billion barrels), two-thirds of it as crude, one-third in refined products.

AND WITH OIL COMES GAS

With the new oil came natural gas in proportionate quanti-ties, which Khrushchev's engineers quickly learned from the West how to use. So now interminable pipelines carrying both commodities began to lace the broad land, extending from the Volga valley even into the satellite countries of East Europe. A handicap was lack of steel for pipe, which had to be im-ported from West Germany and Japan. But plentiful oil was followed by the dieselization (and electrification) of Russia's railroads, with industrial benefits far to the good on balance. (*Above* and *left*): Trucking and laying some 40-inch gas mains.

FROM BOTH COME PETROCHEMICALS

The Russians' backwardness about oil and gas long retarded their chemical industry, but once they got the hang of petrochemistry, they leapt forward with plants like the one at Polotsk (*above*). Formerly, for example, they had diverted hurtful quantities of food and feed (potatoes and grain) into alcohol for synthetic rubber. They had lacked plastics and artificial fibers for consumer goods. Conversion of natural gas into ammonia and then into nitrogenous fertilizers has more than quadrupled since 1958. By its 50th year (1967), the U.S.S.R. had caught up in these respects with the 20th century.

395

"FROM HUTS TO HIGH RISE"

That apt phrase was applied by Ada Louis E. Huxtable, architecture critic of *The New York Times,* to what happened in Soviet building and architecture during the decade beginning 1957. "It has been," she wrote, "a little like inventing the umbrella."

After the devastation of World War II most Russian urbanites, especially in Moscow and Leningrad, were literally living in slums. As many as six persons had to share one bedroom, and 36 one bath and one kitchen. They slept in shifts, queued up for other functions.

Before Stalin's death, not much was done about living quarters for the masses (*see* p. 370). New power plants, fatcories, and office buildings came first, plus magnificent Moscow University, show-piece of the postwar Soviet Union (*see* p. 381). Even in the early Khrushchev years, when life was supposed to get easier, new apartment buildings were limited to five-story walkups.

But gradually an assault on Russia's housing problem was mounted, and when it got going it was, though crude by Western standards and confined largely to Moscow, one of the most prodigious human habitat efforts ever put forth.

In 1962 apartment buildings rose to nine stories, and in 1964 to 12, with 16's and 17's on the drawing boards. Most novel parts of the procedure were its speed (a new apartment every five working minutes by one Moscow combine) and the streamlined methods employed. There was (is) mass, year-round output from production streams modeled on the good old Henry Ford assembly line. Beginning in the mid-1950's, whole factories were imported from France, and copied, and improved. Bits and pieces of technique were borrowed from Sweden, Denmark, and Finland. The prefabrication of parts, elements, and whole panels was computerized. The world's largest cement and prestressed concrete industry was dreamed and muscled into being. How these house factories extruded the makings of human dwellings, to be whacked together at their sites, is explained in simplest form two pages further on.

Pictured on this page is the march of high-rise office and apartment buildings along Lenin Avenue (*top*) and Kalinin Avenue (*bottom*) during a big push to dress up Moscow for the Union's golden anniversary (1967). (Elsewhere in Russia, huts still predominate, and the rush of peasants into the cities is unstemmed.

Between is a more interesting (if more monotonous) shot of earlier construction in four of Moscow's endless outlying "neighborhoods" — here, the 32nd to 35th on the Southwest Side — capable of sheltering 55,000 persons, about 4 to each 3 cubicles. It is cheering to know that, back of the camera that took this static shot, a dense green forest begins, with a picturesque ravine and sparkling reservoir.

In each of these pictures the questing eye can find the nation's cynosure: ever-present, spired, and inspiring Moscow University.

NEW HOTELS, AND TRADE CENTER. Anything but prefabricated — rather, the last words in slick concrete, steel, and glass — are Leningrad's new Sovetskaya Hotel (*above*) and Moscow's colossal Hotel Rossia (*below*). Both were completed in time for the nation's 50th birthday and can accommodate thousands. The Rossia stands on Moscow's old Chinatown, where Tartar and Mongol merchants used to camp beside the

Moscow River. (Photographer N. Granovsky of Tass had the wit to include in his shot a couple of onions on the old Cathedral of St. Basil.)

Slickest of all (*above, right*), with curved wings, and outside elevators to wash the windows, is the towering Comecon Building, home of the Red bloc's common market.

HOUSE FACTORIES

When the city of Tashkent in remote Turkestan was levelled by earthquake, teams from all over the U.S.S.R., but chiefly from Moscow, were mobilized to rebuild the place instantly. Whole trainloads of prefabricated house parts and of construction machines (chiefly cranes) were shipped in. The standard structure supplied was the five-story "Khrushchev walkup," a homely but efficient job requiring minimum internal fittings (plumbing and stoves but no refrigerators, cabinets, closets, or other frills). Within a year, Tashkent moved into more than a million square meters of new living space.

The pictures on this page afford glimpses of the "combines" (house factories, of which Moscow has three big ones) where such housing is prefabricated. (*Above*): Floor and wall panels coming off the production line to be piled for shipment in carefully sorted lots for quick assembly and erection.

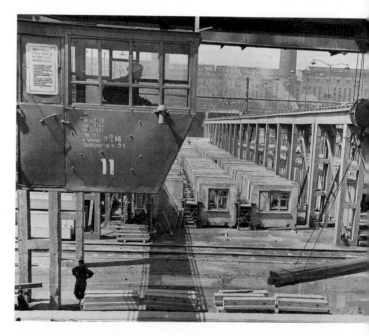

ON THE JOB SITE there are no overnight stockpiles. Parts are swung into place as received and stuck together with black asphalt sealant, which doesn't look pretty but withstands sub-zero weather (for a while). Apartments like these used to be faced with yellowish ceramic tile, but it always peeled off, and was abandoned.

IN ANOTHER AREA of the house factory, windows and doors are inserted into wall segments. The trick of prefabrication is to make elements as large as possible, for fast assembly. The limit is a chunk weighing about 10 tons, though whole rooms have been experimented with, hauled to the job on monster trucks. The norm is now supposed to be 9 sq.m. of living space per person, not counting bath and kitchen.

FUN AND GAMES

As under Stalin (*see* p. 378), athletics in the Khrushchev era were continued on the largest scale as an instrument of national health, international prestige, and popular emotional outlet. With ever-increasing proficiency they continued to be fun for the contestants, who won the Olympic Games of 1956 at Melbourne and of 1960 at Rome. Russian women continued dominant, especially in speed skating (*left*) and weight tossing. Tamara Press (*right*) became the new world queen of shot-put and discus-throw, winning gold medals in each.

As competition intensified, so did scrutiny of the female athletes, whose true sex was checked up on. There could be no question as to buxom Tamara's gender, but one or two of her teammates ducked the official examination and withdrew.

And a curious Red phenomenon began to show. By the mid-1960's, few new young stars were rising. The Russian teams, even in hockey (which Czechoslovakia won in 1968), were becoming dependent on 50 or 60 veterans, who were wearing out. Khrushchev's successor, Leonid Brezhnev, addressed himself to this problem in a harsh fight-talk — a state edict for Soviet child athletes to "get with it."

SIX GOLD MEDALS, two at Squaw Valley (1960) and four at Innsbruck (1964), were the all-time record set by speed-skater Lidia Skoblikova (*above*) — almost as pretty as she was swift. At Grenoble (1968), some of the other girls caught Lidia, but just barely.

MOST GRACEFUL RUSSIAN since the late genius of dance, Vaslav Nijinsky, was Valery Brumel, the high jumper (*below*) who at Tokyo tied much longer-legged John Thomas of the United States at 7 ft. 1⅞ in. Where Thomas grasshoppered, Brumel just soared and floated.

RED SQUARE REVIEWS have always been Russia's spectacular way of warning the world and comforting the home folks about Soviet military strength. As the missiles grew longer and fatter over the years, so did their proclaimed capabilities increase, until at length the Reds announced they could put nuclear warheads into orbit, partial or whole, around the earth high or low, to defeat radar warnings and counterfire.

Agreement not to use space militarily would apparently be violated by such developments, but Russia did not explain or apologize. America's reply was to evolve an "over-the-horizon" radar, using the ionosphere as a reflecting ceiling; and also to put scanning satellites on alert around the clock and the calendar.

ANTI-MISSILE MISSILES like the one shown below operate on the principle of using one nuclear blast to trigger an incoming one prematurely. America's reply to this defense is a system hooking several warheads together on one ballistic omnibus.

The jaw-breaking name for this is Multiple Independently Targetable Re-entry Vehicle — MIRV. It would drop off a string of city busters at a succession of destinations too complex to be predicted or counteracted.

BALANCE OF TERROR

Before he died in 1960, Igor Kurchatov (*right*), the long-whiskered dean of Russian nuclear science and designer of the first Red atom bombs, lived to see a balance of terror struck between his country and the United States. Other names for this insane game were "mutual deterrence" and "massive retaliation," and it was played with ballistic missiles of ever-increasing size. With their much larger rocket engines for lift-off and propulsion, the Russians built and boasted in terms of megatons (equivalents of a million tons of TNT) while the U.S. was content with high kilotonnages (equivalents of thousands). In 1962, after an informal moratorium between the U.S. and U.S.S.R. designed to stop fouling up earth's atmosphere with practice explosions, the Soviets sprang a series of tests which culminated in a 58-megaton blast, undoubtedly the most monstrous man-made explosion ever. Then they signed a test-ban treaty.

The U.S.A. meantime was perfecting the *aim* of its missiles — putting them down in silos out of harm's way and pin-pointing their flight onto Russian launch sites, which were spotted by ceaseless American surveillance. So now began a new game of empyrean target shooting, played by the Russians with anti-missile missiles (*opposite page*). In 1962 they claimed to have shot down two of their own incoming bombs with one A.M.M. of perhaps 20 megatons, exploding the incomers far enough above and short of their targets to render them harmless.

THREATS AFLOAT to match America's missile-firing submarines were added to the Soviet arsenal in the 1960's. Russian submarines like the one pictured at the left had a bombing range of only 1,500 miles (as against 2,500 for Polarises and Poseidons), and the early models had to surface to shoot, but still these threats were real and sobering.

A NEW FACE in Red Square at the military review of May Day 1967 was that of Marshal Andrei A. Grechko, successor to granitic old Rodion Y. Malinovski, who had died just a month before, after nearly 15 years as Minister of Defense.

401

THE NEW RED NAVY

Not since the great days of Peter and Catherine had Russia so aspired to naval power as she did under Stalin just before World War II. The Germans aborted those efforts, and after Stalin's death Khrushchev cancelled the postwar revival of a Russian surface fleet, which he considered obsolete in the Missile Age. But in 1961 the Cuban debacle under the U.S. Navy's guns changed Khrushchev's mind. The huge Red Navy he then ordered, which has now come largely into being, is peculiar to Russia's global spread and strategy; to her notions of how to dominate most widely with the least risk and expense. Light, fast, ubiquitous, it is a surface-and-subsurface fleet designed to defend and intercept rather than to invade or conquer.

A score of **Fast Heavy Cruisers** like the 20,000-ton *Varyag* (*above*) are now armed with potent surface-to-air missiles as well as 6-inchers. They are the showpieces, guardships, and backbone of the new Red Navy, which has no battleships or attack carriers. Historically, the Russians have concentrated on submarines, and so they still do. But now their 360-plus **Pigboats** (*below*) carry more guided missiles than torpedoes, and 55 of them are nuclear powered, with 5 more of that type being added yearly. Main mission of Russia's subsea fleet would be to intercept enemy shipping; second, attack coastal cities.

Supplementing the subs is a tremendous force (nearly 600) of **Fast Torpedo and Missile Craft** (*right*), whose firing range is anywhere from 20 miles for the Styx-bomb **Komar** class up to 200 miles for the **Kresta** and **Kynda** classes of destroyer with missiles designated SS-N-3.

402

PACIFIC OCEAN FLEET
Adm. Amelko - 750 ships
6   50   100   150

Pearl Harbor

Pacific Ocean

Guam

Aleutian Is.
Bering Sea

Petropavlovsk
Sea of Okhotsk

Tokyo

Sea of Japan
(16 surface warships)

Vladivostok

San Francisco

Seattle

San Diego

ALASKA

NORTH KOREA

PHILIPPINES

TAIWAN

CANADA

Arctic Ocean
Ice cap

North ✛ Pole

Summer route
with icebreakers

NORTHERN FLEET
Adm. Lobov
800 ships
3
35
150
60
28 icebreakers

Peking ★

Hong Kong

CHINA

Haiphong
NORTH VIET NAM

Saigon

U. S.

GREENLAND

Severomorsk

Murmansk

Leningrad

U. S. S. R.
Naval HQ, Adm. Gorshkov

Vishakhapatnam

INDIA

SINGAPORE

Washington ★
Cape Kennedy

Havana

CUBA
Panama Canal

BALTIC FLEET
Adm. Mikhailin
750 ships
4
35
70
200

Kaliningrad

Moscow ★

Odessa

Inland waterway

Caspian Sea

Sevastopol
Black Sea

to Australia

Grand Banks

EUROPE

Atlantic Ocean

GIBRALTAR

Mers-el-Kebir

Mediterranean Sea
(40 warships)

Latakia

Port Said

Alexandria
EGYPT

Red Sea

YEMEN

Odessa to Haiphong 16,800 mi.

Indian Ocean

BLACK SEA FLEET
Adm. Chursin - 700 ships
6   50   40   150
2 new helicopter carriers

SOUTH AMERICA

Rio de Janeiro

AFRICA

RUSSIAN SEA POWER

Antarctic whaling fleet
and polar stations

Cape of Good Hope

TIME Map by R. M. Chapin, Jr.

⚓ Fleet HQ & naval base
— Cruisers
Destroyers, frigates
and escorts
Submarines
(nuclear & other)
Patrol boats
(torpedo & missile)
Intelligence
ships (35)
Fishing fleet
— Shipping routes

THE MAP (by Robert Chapin of *Time*) shows how Soviet sea power is deployed around the continents in four main fleets. It also suggests the extent to which Russia's expanding merchant marine is integrated to press such thorns as Cuba and North Vietnam into America's flanks. At least 150 freighters plied regularly to Haiphong in 1966-68. Russia's "fishing fleets" are far-flung, with actual fish only a minor part of what they gather (*see next page*).

403

ADMIRAL SERGEI GEORGIEVICH GORSHKOV (*right*) was the chunky, thumbs-up, 45-year-old hot-shot (now 57) with whom Khrushchev replaced old Admiral Kuznetzov in 1957 to modernize the Red Navy. Khrushchev and other Red Army generals had known Gorshkov during World War II as a brilliant young harasser of the Germans. He welded tank turrets onto fast motor boats and played guerrilla havoc along the Crimean coast and the Don and Danube rivers.

Gorshkov's pet game now is to harass NATO naval forces in the Baltic, and American fleets in Mediterranean and Asian waters. Rigid discipline and physical fitness are his regimen for Russia's naval ratings — no drinks, no women, no nights ashore. His submarine and speed-craft fleets are supplemented by two 25,000-ton helicopter carriers, which carry missiles up front, 'copters aft, and also by about 100 landing craft carrying "naval infantry," a force like the U.S. Marines which can pop ashore with amphibious tanks to seize beachheads. From smallest to largest, all Gorshkov's ships are provided with rockets and guided missiles, including some tactical nuclear ones, in preference to conventional guns.

WHEREVER THE U.S. NAVY OPERATES it can expect to see Soviet snooper crafts — like the one above shadowing a unit of the 6th Fleet in the Mediterranean. For the Israeli-Arab war of 1967, the Red Navy stepped up its Med contingent from a half dozen vessels to 46. It now uses former British anchorages at Port Said and Alexandria, and angles for more such facilities in Malta, Mers-el-Kebir, Aden, India, and Singapore.

In 1968 a Red defector told NATO that Russia's latest atom-powered subs were being equipped with a device, encircling the conning tower, so (literally) shocking that it could emit electric discharges which would completely disable other submarines within a radius of eight miles, knock out guidance and communication systems within 15 miles. The U.S. Navy wondered if this was a clue to the sudden, stark disappearance of its sub *Scorpion* off the Atlantic coast that spring when its ocean-floor ears heard what sounded like the *Scorpion* collapsing and breaking up, soon after some mysterious other sounds that could have been caused by vast jolts of underwater voltage.

IN SEVASTOPOL HARBOR, historically the Russian Navy's main Black base on the Crimean peninsula, some of Admiral Gorshkov's amphibious tanks for his "naval infantry" are seen (*above*) swimming ashore out of the bow of their "LST" during a fleet display.

Anchored in the offing are missile-carrying destroyers and a cruiser. These too go through their paces every Army-Navy Day (February 23).

TRAWLER FLOTILLAS with bulky mother ships, and as much gear for electronic detection and oceanography as for fish harvesting (*above*), have become standard Russian features of the seven seas. They are especially numerous off New England, Cape Kennedy, the Pacific Coast from San Diego to Alaska, Hawaii, the Sea of Japan, and both coasts of Africa. Much of the research that they conduct has to do with abysmal gulfs and snug harbors where, in case of war, Red submarines could lurk, rendezvous, and receive supplies. Their "innocence" is "unquestionable."

XVI. THE BUSINESSMEN TAKE OVER

One chilly morning in mid-October 1964, the Soviet public was stunned by an announcement that Premier Khrushchev had resigned. Few Russians knew much about his successors: Leonid Brezhnev, the new Communist Party chief, and Aleksei Kosygin, the new Premier. Both were dull, colorless men who had been around Khrushchev but seemed always in the shadows. Both had the trim overweight, politeness, self-effacement, and neat dark clothes common among capitalist businessmen. A Western specialist on Soviet affairs groaned: "The clerks have taken over."

But Brezhnev and Kosygin were no common clerks. They were office boys who had slowly, carefully, worked their way up in Kremlin bureaucracy until finally they accumulated enough power to oust their boss.

Undermining one's boss requires courage, patience, and brains, all of which Brezhnev and Kosygin possessed. Both were the first top rulers of Russia since Lenin to be college graduates. Both are the first U.S.S.R. leaders trained in industrial management. (Lenin was a lawyer, Stalin a divinity student, and Khrushchev a school dropout.) For the first time in Soviet history, Brezhnev and Kosygin organized a palace coup which overnight removed a longtime U.S.S.R. leader. (Stalin and Khrushchev achieved power only after several years of bitter Kremlin infighting.) To complete the priorities, Brezhnev and Kosygin were the first dictators of Soviet Russia to be Russians, since Lenin was Mongol-German, Stalin a Georgian, and Khrushchev a Ukrainian. Also the post-Khrushchev team were the first U.S.S.R. leaders to have taken no real part in the 1917 Bolshevik Revolution, since they were children at the time.

Who were these quiet geniuses? Kosygin's career was basically industrial. Born in 1904 of worker parentage, he was a soldier in the Red Army when old enough to fight. For a decade he worked in Soviet co-ops in Siberia. Then he studied textiles, and after graduating from college, in 1935 became a textile engineer in Leningrad. Within three years he was mayor of the city. A year later he was U.S.S.R. Textile Industry Minister, and the following year a Vice Premier of the Soviet Union. Thereafter he was Stalin's expert on consumer goods industry, and after Stalin's death he was the chief economic planner for Khrushchev.

Brezhnev's background was more complex. Born in 1906 in south Russia of worker parentage, he first worked in farmland surveying, becoming assistant head of the Ural agricultural administration. Then he graduated from engineering college, majoring in steel production. Quickly he abandoned engineering to become a provincial Communist Party leader in the Ukraine, where Khrushchev was top local leader. After Stalin's death, Brezhnev served as assistant political chief of the U.S.S.R. armed forces, Party boss of north Central Asia, and then President of the U.S.S.R. By career, Kosygin was a Stalinist, while Brezhnev was a protégé of Khrushchev.

How did these two bureaucrats remove Khrushchev? Very easily. Nikita travelled too much outside Moscow, making clever speeches both at home and abroad. While on the road, Khrushchev had to entrust day-by-day control of the government and Party to Kosygin and Brezhnev, his closest friends. But these friends grew tired of Khrushchevian farm and foreign-policy failures, and the Nikita bluster-blunder style.

Army marshals and police chiefs willingly joined the plot. Both groups had grudges against Khrushchev who had purged the police and prematurely retired many experienced military officers.

With Party, government, army, and police leaders conspiring against him, Khrushchev was finished. He was summoned to Moscow without previous warning, and forced to retire. So quick and secretive was this coup, that Soviet provincial newspapers were still ignorantly praising Khrushchev two days after he lost power.

Then the provincial papers got the message from Moscow: "Forget Khrushchev!" His name disappeared from the Soviet press, and his pictures were taken down from Soviet walls. The Central Asian mountain named after him was hurriedly renamed. The man who had erased Stalin from Soviet history was now himself erased.

De-Khrushchevization was pursued in more than name. Khrushchev had abolished most U.S.S.R. industrial ministries, and placed most factories under the control of newly created regional economic councils. The Brezhnev-Kosygin regime abolished the councils and restored the ministries. Khrushchev had divided regional governments into industrial (ruling cities) and agricultural (bossing the farms). After his dismissal, the provincial governments were reunited. In agriculture Khrushchev had promoted the cultivation of new lands and the growing of corn. Brezhnev and Kosygin downgraded both corn and new lands, instead stressing irrigation, which Khrushchev had neglected. Khrushchev had abolished one of the two U.S.S.R. police ministries, but his successors re-created it. To avoid any comparison with Stalin, Khrushchev called himself "first secretary" of the U.S.S.R. Communist Party rather than use Stalin's title of Secretary-General. After Khrushchev was out, Brezhnev quickly assumed the grander title.

It was soon obvious that de-Khrushchevization meant slow re-Stalinization. First, military museums and memoirs gave Stalin credit for being U.S.S.R. commander-in-chief during World War II. When Stalin's daughter Svetlana defected to the United States, the U.S.S.R. ambassador who let her escape from his embassy was given a high Soviet decoration. In Moscow and other cities, rebellious Soviet writers were given severe prison sentences in rigged court trials similar to the Stalinist purge trials of the late 1930's. Books severely criticizing Stalin were forbidden to be published in the Soviet Union.

While respecting Stalin's memory, Brezhnev and Kosygin undertook big economic reforms, which were more liberal than Stalinist. Peasant private gardens were encouraged, as were private food markets in cities. Taxes on collective farms were cut in half. Collective farmers' pay was doubled to an obligatory minimum equivalent to $66 per month. The peasants responded by working harder, and food supplies to the cities improved.

Under both Stalin and Khrushchev, Soviet factories were rated successful when they fulfilled plans for quantity of production. It did not matter if the products were inferior and unsalable. Borrowing from capitalism, the Brezhnev-Kosygin regime rated factories by profits from sale of products. To sell their production, factories had to concentrate on quality instead of quantity. Many factories manufacturing consumer goods were given no plan but simply produced goods ordered by stores, which knew what the public wanted. Consumer goods immediately improved, and a middle-class Soviet citizen would not appear ill dressed if transplanted to London or New York. Meanwhile these reforms speeded up industrial growth, which had been slowing during the Khrushchev era.

Labor also benefited from the Brezhnev-Kosygin regime. The minimum city wage was raised to the ruble equivalent of $66 per month. More fringe benefits, such as longer paid vacations, were given to workers. And in 1967, the work week was shortened from six days to five, giving Russians a two-day weekend for the first time in Soviet history.

All these economic reforms did not slow the growth of Soviet armament, which the Brezhnev-Kosygin regime constantly increased. By 1967 the U.S.S.R. was building an anti-missile missile defense system, despite a U.S. proposal that neither country construct such costly installations. Russia also claimed to have intercontinental bombers capable of carrying 100-

megaton hydrogen bombs. Meanwhile the U.S.S.R. was catching up with the United States in number of intercontinental rockets. And the Soviet navy was changing from a coast guard to a long-range interceptor fleet sailing the seven seas.

This superarmament was apparently aimed more at Communist China than the U.S.A. Once Khrushchev resigned, Chinese Premier Chou-En-Lai immediately visited Moscow to end the Sino-Soviet dispute. By Peking reasoning, the entire quarrel had been with an incompetent Khrushchev, not the U.S.S.R. as a whole. Chou was surprised to discover that Brezhnev and Kosygin had no intention of making friends with China. Early the next year, 1965, Soviet police even protected the U.S. Embassy in Moscow from an Asian student riot protesting American escalation of the Vietnam war.

Amid mutual accusations by the Soviet and Chinese governments emerged a basic disagreement on how to communize the world. Russia wanted to avoid suicidal nuclear war, and infiltrate undeveloped nations by trade and aid. In Soviet reasoning, the capitalist West could be encircled by an alliance of Communist countries with Africa, Asia, and Latin America. Then the West would either surrender, or be overthrown by internal revolution.

China angrily retorted that the West would surely use nuclear war to save itself. This atomic holocaust should not be feared, because it would end in Communist victory. Also, the leaders of many underdeveloped nations were worthless allies, who pretended to like Communism only because they waxed rich on Soviet aid. Instead of wooing corrupt tropical politicians, Russia should organize revolutions among the oppressed Asian, African, and Latin American peasants.

In rebuttal, Brezhnev and Kosygin quietly encircled China. Soviet aid to North Vietnam increased from $1,000,000 per day to over $2,000,000 — amounts which impoverished China could

not match. Moscow offered to mediate the Vietnam war which China wished to continue. China begged Russia to create a European crisis, so that American troops would not be transferred from West Europe to Vietnam. No crisis came. Kosygin mediated an India-Pakistan undeclared war, stopping China from fishing in muddy southwest Asian waters. Then Russia increased its aid to Pakistan and doubled aid to India. A Soviet-Mongolian military alliance was renewed, obviously aimed against China. Japan, China's longtime enemy, was invited to help develop Russian resources in East Siberia.

To be free to strangle China, Brezhnev and Kosygin had to befriend the West. Turkey was diplomatically disarmed by Soviet aid, and by Russian support of Turkish claims in Cyprus. After being wined and dined in Moscow, French President De Gaulle was the first foreign statesman — Communist or Western — to witness a Soviet rocket launching. France immediately concluded scientific, cultural, and trade agreements with Russia.

Of crucial importance to the Kremlin was to keep America quiet. While the Soviet Embassy in Peking was attacked by Chinese Red Guards, Soviet police again shielded the U.S. Embassy in Moscow from riots by Asian students. In 1967, Russia concluded treaties with the U.S.A. de-militarizing outer space, and allowing Soviet trawlers to fish near Long Island. When Cuba protested against Soviet-American friendship, the U.S.S.R. reduced its aid to Cuba. The United States and the Soviet Union co-operated in stopping the 1967 Israeli-Arab war.

Brezhnev and Kosygin have always looked like businessmen, and have provided Soviet Russia with its most business-like regime. The world future is uncertain; so is the future of the U.S.S.R. (in 1968). But it would appear that Russia and America, the two giant powers, will for some time jointly rule the world.

PICKING OFF PIGEONS, as Premier Kosygin was doing (*above*) when he and Party Chairman Brezhnev entertained Field Marshal Ayub Khan, president of Pakistan, at an estate near Moscow in 1965, just about summarized the Kosygin-Brezhnev foreign policy of 1964-68. Kosygin went hand-shaking, aid-giving, friend-making in country after country, one by one. Besides Pakistan, he cosyed up to Iran, India, and Indonesia, the idea being to encircle China with friends of Russia, as Khrushchev had tried to do. He also made his manners in England, France, and the U.S.A. Everywhere his mousy, almost apologetic manner gave people the impression that, though he was out shooting trouble, the burly fellow at home (Brezhnev) was really the man behind the gun. This impression was strengthened when, after some turmoil among Russia's satellites, Mr. B. called for an all-Communist conclave (*ex* China, of course) to end Red disarray and reassert Moscow's mastery.

MATURE POWER

Following the bold starts made by Stalin at Kuibyshev and Volgograd on the Volga (*see* p. 368), each of which was larger than the 2,000,000 kw. hydro-electric plant at Grand Coulee, America's largest, the U.S.S.R.'s power planners in 1955 mapped a program which, by 1970, would furnish the maturing nation with 1,000 *billion* kilowatts per annum. Some of this output would come from brown Siberian coal burned at the mines, some from oil and gas, some from nuclear fuels. But the most dramatic portion would be churned out by two Siberian rivers.

Most Russian rivers wander leisurely south through the steppes or north through the tundra. But the mighty Yenisei and its tributary, the Angara, rise in the jagged Sayan Mountains of Central Asia and start their courses to the Arctic at headlong speed. The Angara's flow is especially constant since it is the outlet of huge Lake Baikal. Water from the Angara fills the Bratsk reservoir (*right*).

At Krasnoyarsk on the Yenisei and further upstream at Shushenskoye (where in 1897-1900 the exiled Lenin lived and married), plants of 6,000,000 kw. capacity were planned, each with twelve 500,000-kw. generators, the world's largest units. Built in Leningrad, these machines had to be barged in summer to the Kara Sea (below Nova Zemlya) and thence up the Yenisei 1,000 miles from its mouth. But completed before the Yenisei monsters was one at Bratsk on the Angara. At 4,500,000 kw., this station was the world's largest *pro tem*.

BIG BRATSK, when all 20 of its 225,000-kw. generators got rolling (*above*), would produce more electricity than whole countries the size of Austria. Its economists claimed that Bratsk would be the world's most profitable hydro-electric plant since its chief customers would be refineries of light metals (aluminum, magnesium, titanium) used in the aerospace program, and missiles. Many such complexes were being built near the new dam sites, to bring raw materials to raw power instead of the reverse.

Ultimately, however, the Siberian rivers' surplus energy will be transmitted — sub-zero weather notwithstanding (*right*) — clear across the face of Russia and even into the European satellites, where the control switches will govern politics as well as current. Such long-range delivery will be made possible by great Russian strides in direct (instead of alternating) current transmission. An experimental DC line already delivers power at 800,000 volts from the Volga to the Donets Basin, 350 miles west.

SO PRODIGIOUS have Russia's manufacturers of turbines and generators become (for a glimpse of one of their medium-size constructions, *see right*) that when the U.S. Government called for bids on new equipment to enlarge the Grand Coulee, the Russians easily beat a field including West Germany, Japan, and America's top makers. But Washington wanted no part of such virtuosity, and let the contracts elsewhere.

"SOCIALISM PLUS ELECTRIFICATION EQUALS COMMUNISM" was an old Leninism. Seen in application at Bratsk, where an old wooden Cossack fort still stands, the maxim is impressive and convincing. Another plant the same size as Bratsk is already a-building not far down the Angara at Ust-Ulim, an old-time fur station.

NEW HIGHWAYS

Having decided to put more of their people on motorized wheels, and contracted with the Fiat concern of Italy toward that end, it must be supposed that the Kosygin-Brezhnev regime has in mind building a lot of new roads in Russia, which as of 1967 had only 200,000 miles of highway (including gravel) as compared to 2,800,000 paved miles in the U.S.A. Few Russian cities were really joined, and most vehicles, including trucks and buses, operated only locally. *Above* is a brave start in this logistical direction — the intersection of Moscow's "ring road," circling the city's outskirts, with the smooth, well-lighted highway leading to Minsk, 500 miles west.

Climate and soil conditions are all against Russia's road builders, who, except in mountains, have a hard time finding rock under the sand and loam. *Below* can be seen what conditions are like in wintertime, when the permafrost sets in. Sliced through the taiga (forest of conifers between steppe and tundra) is a new work-road aimed at Bratsk on the Angara River, outlet of Lake Baikal, where a vast new power plant (*see* previous page) was finished in time for the nation's 1967 golden anniversary. By November, a gravel-pit like the one in the foreground would be frozen six feet down. In the spring, frost heave wrecks the best of road surfaces.

NEW HEIGHTS

Television was slow arriving in Russia, but by the nation's 50th birthday it had somewhat caught up. Erected at Ostankino near Moscow was a 537-meter tower of steel and concrete (*right*), nearly 290 feet taller than the Empire State Building. This extended the range of the All-Union TV Center from 30 kilometers out to 130 kilometers, and introduced color pictures. Nineteen towns and cities in Siberia and Central Asia also benefited as the Ostankino images were bounced off Molniya 1, an artificial earth satellite. Viewers in Greater Moscow could now dispense with their outdoor antennas, and the quality of their audio was much improved.

THE CREEP CRANE, invented by four engineers in one of Moscow's building combines, improves on previous models, which crawl up inside buildings and erect them, as it were, by bootstrapping. Pictured (*above*) is the new 4.5-ton, two-platform rig, which screw-jacks itself aloft to build towering smokestacks from the *out*side. A boom on the upper platform hoists ferro-concrete ring blocks and sets them in place seriatim. In the picture, the crane is creeping earthward after a job well done.

411

COMMUNISM'S MOST ILLUSTRIOUS ESCAPEE

Berlin's "Wall of Shame" (*below*), ordered built by Nikita Khrushchev in 1961, has become Communism's most conspicuous symbol of repression. Often forgotten is the fact that the Wall is but a small segment of the even more forbidding Marxist Maginot Line (Winston Churchill's "Iron Curtain") which pens in the Soviet's captive populations from the Baltic to Czechoslovakia, 830 miles south. This formidable barrier is a hundred-yard-wide strip of land plowed and harrowed naked to expose escapees, studded with land mines, barbed and electrified wire, and watchtowers bristling with machine guns, searchlights, and ferocious man-catching dogs.

As everyone knows but is prone to forget, this barbaric pentwork was conceived and constructed under steel-fisted Joseph Stalin. It constitutes tangible expression of the strict psychic imprisonment he imposed on the Russians and their satellites, lest they escape to or become infected by Western capitalism. Many a brave Russian has defected, but none more illustrious than the one who in 1967 turned up unexpectedly first in India, then Italy, then Switzerland, and finally in the U.S.A. Amazingly, it was the attractive, thrice-married, disillusioned daughter (*right*) of Dictator Stalin himself.

SVETLANA ALLILUYEVA (*above*), who used her suicide mother's surname rather than her savage father's, eluded confinement by taking the ashes of her Indian third husband to his homeland, visiting his relatives there, and then ducking into the U.S. Embassy, which passed her westward with C.I.A. escorts to final asylum "somewhere in Connecticut" (where Alexander Kerensky also lives). Later she settled in Princeton, N.J. American publishers turned handsprings in bringing out her memoirs, but lost big money on them, for they were — as Moscow perhaps knew or guessed — dull as dishwater. Apart from mewing about old nannies and other servants, and her drunkard brother, and blaming Beria for her father's suspicious, treacherous behavior, Svetlana had little to tell about Russia's darkest years since Ivan the Terrible. Apparently more through naïveté than filial devotion, she glossed over the exiles, tortures, and executions her parent meted out in his heyday. She considered Khrushchev kinder than the Kosygin-Brezhnev regime to sensitive souls like herself.

THE RIGHT TO WRITE

Like everything else in Russia, creative writing is unionized, with the Communist Party in control of the critical machinery. This puts poetical or novelistic whimsey as much at the mercy of the dictatorship's political whimsey as ever it was under imperial censorship. Under Khrushchev, writers who questioned or criticized the regime were treated with much less routine severity than under Stalin: only one or two were sent to prison camps and a few to insane asylums. During the first four years of Kosygin-Brezhnev, however, between 20 and 30 were so disciplined, after purge-like trials.

Of the four writers pictured here, Poets Andrei Vosnesenski and Yevgeny Yevtushenko (*right,* upper and lower) were only harassed as silly egoists, not suppressed as subverters of Soviet youth. But Andrei Sinyavski and Yuri Daniel (*below,* in dock) were sentenced to seven and five years' imprisonment, respectively, at hard labor, for the crime of publishing in the West novels critical of the Soviet system. They argued that their characters protested Stalinism, not later policies, and aimed at improving Communism from within, not damaging it from without. Pavel Litvinov, grandson of the "Old Bolshevik" foreign minister, protested loudly. Nevertheless, to jail they went.

Most remarkably, the all-high Soviet Politburo received an open letter from one Ivan A. Yakhimovich, chairman of a collective farm in Latvia. What happened to Comrade Yakhimovich as a result is unknown, but here in part is what he wrote:

"One must not subvert the confidence of the masses . . . one must not speculate with the honor of the state, even if a certain leader wants to end *samizdat* [underground literature]. . . . I believe that the persecution of young dissenters in a country where more than 50 percent of the population is younger than 30 years of age is an extremely dangerous line in adventurism. It is not toadies, not a public of yes-men . . . not mama's boys, who will determine our future, but rather those very rebels, as the most energetic, brave, and high-principled members of our young generation.

"It is stupid to see in them the enemies of Soviet power, and more than stupid to let them rot in prisons and make mock of them. For the Party such a line is equivalent to self-strangulation. . . ."

MAO'S MAGIC, OR MADNESS

When, after ruthlessly taking over peaceful Tibet, China picked a fight with India over a remote mountain borderline in 1959, Mao Tse-Tung's entirely scrutable purpose was to rebuke and embarrass Nikita Khrushchev, a good friend of Tibet and India, for "going soft on capitalism" and extending a glad hand to the West, especially the U.S.A. "Peaceful co-existence" was translated at Peking into "criminal anti-Marxist revisionism" and other jaw-breaking phrases designating infidelity to Communist world solidarity. As the vituperation continued, and Russian visitors to Peking were vilified, Moscow withdrew all its technicians, engineers, and students, to let fat China stew in its own stupid juice. The Moscow-Peking axis lay in fragments.

This aroused opposition to Mao at home, which he magically subdued by enlisting millions of adolescent Red Guards in a "Cultural Revolution." Each child was armed with a booklet of *Mao's Thoughts,* which they chanted hysterically as they mobbed anti-Mao ministries and officials. Eventually they got so out of hand that the Red Chinese Army under General Lin Piao had to subjugate the Red Guards and send them back to school.

Through all this madness, Mao continued in background command, a bemusing, rotund Buddha, perhaps slightly daffy, perhaps as divinely wise as his idolaters believed; in any case aging steadily (born 1893).

(*Above*) Mao and Lin reviewing a Red Guard parade (1966).

(*Below*) Peking youngsters, each waving his Mao "bible," demonstrate in front of the Russian Embassy against "fascist atrocities" committed in Moscow upon Chinese students and officials — who had merely been deported, unharmed (1967).

RUMORS OF ILLNESS and even death circulated about Mao from time to time, but he always bobbed up smiling in new pictures. Most positive rejoinder was a press release in July 1966 stating that, followed by hordes of the faithful, China's beloved leader, guiding star, soul of wisdom, had swum down the bile-yellow Yangtse-kiang for "about ten miles." (*Above*): Mao's supposed head leads several henchmen's.

THE LARGE AND SMALL OF IT

When Tito Broz of Yugoslavia wrenched loose from Moscow's grip, adjacent little Albania refused to join him and stuck with Moscow. But beginning with the Hungarian atrocity of 1956, on which Albanians frowned even more severely than the Yugoslavs did, the government and party headed by Enver Hoxha became even more anti-Moscow than Tito. When the Moscow-Peking axis broke in the 1960's, Albania shifted its allegiance entirely to Peking. Perhaps distance lent some of the enchantment, or the thought that the smaller you are, the cockier you must be. At all events, Red China's only true friend in Europe has turned out to be world Communism's most minute member — 2,000,000 Albanians tagging along with 800,000,000 Chinese. (*At left*) A Hoxha-Mao popular wingding in the metropolis of Durres (1966).

THE IMPORTANCE OF INDIA

MOST CHIC GUEST at Russia's 50th birthday party on November 7, 1967, was Mrs. Indira Gandhi, be-sabled Prime Minister of India, seen above waving with Premier Kosygin on the balcony of Lenin's mausoleum. The importance of her huge but "backward" nation to Russia's future could scarcely be overestimated. Above all others it has come to loom in Moscow's mind as the bastion (with Pakistan) to contain China north of the Himalayas, out of southwest Asia. Also, Admiral Gorshkov would dearly love entree to an Indian port or two for his growing Red Navy.

Soon after Mr. Kosygin paid Mrs. Gandhi a return visit in January, New Delhi announced that — on top of all the steel mills, power plants, heavy-machinery factories, and military supplies which it had already funded or given to India — Russia had placed "stupendous" new orders with Indian factories; items such as 600,000 tons of steel by 1971, and 40,000 railroad cars by 1975.

(*Right*): A 1958 view of the million-ton steel mill Russia built for India at Bhilai.

415

REMOTE THOUGH IT IS, Red Russia's long trans-Asian border with Red China is her most sensitive frontier and the one most watchfully eyed by the Kosygin-Brezhnev regime. Along it are stationed even more troops than Russia massed opposite Manchuria in the 1930's to keep watch on the Japanese. Opposite Sinkiang Province, where China conducts her nuclear experiments (at Lop Nor), the Kazakh, Kirghiz, and Tadzhik populations are alerted and given air-raid drills. Armed volunteers patrol the border and schoolchildren are trained to detect Chinese spies. Border incidents number about 5,000 a year.

Important government works are in progress on Russia's side of the towering Tien Shan Mountains. *Above* is the site of huge Nurek Reservoir to irrigate 1,200,000 arid hectares near Tashkent and Frunze. On the *right* is a sight which Soviet engineers beheld when they touched off 5,000 tons of trotyl (TNT) and ammonate to form a flood control dam in the highlands above Alma Ata. In the swirling smoke clouds there appeared a bewhiskered Old Man of the Mountains whose features were distinctly and disturbingly Chinese.

GOODWILL AT GLASSBORO

With daughters beside them (*above*), President Lyndon B. Johnson and Premier Alexei N. Kosygin met for the first time at "Holly Bush," home of the president of Glassboro (N.J.) State College in 1967. This unheard-of site was chosen because it was roughly halfway between Washington and Manhattan, where Kosygin was attending U.N. debates on Arab-Israeli peace terms. During that brief but fierce conflict, the Moscow-Washington teletype "hot line" had been kept open and freely used for mutual assurances that neither big power would take any active part. This precaution negated at least one grave error: Egypt's loud Nasser and Jordan's little King Hussein publicly but mistakenly charged that U.S. aircraft from the 6th Fleet had flown cover and even attack missions for the Israelis.

Premier and President conferred for a total of ten hours on two different days. They wound up with a joint statement disavowing any new agreements other than one "reaffirming our common commitment to seek agreement." Nuclear disarmament and nonproliferation were, of course, uppermost in their minds, and the man best fitted to discuss these was on hand to make his pitch (*see below*).

POINT WAS LENT to the Glassboro "summit" meeting by China's explosion, a few days prior, of her first H-bomb. Russia had lately announced the deployment around her major cities of a system of anti-missile missiles, to explode incoming enemy bombs before their arrival. Secretary of Defense Robert S. McNamara stepped up to Premier Kosygin (*right*) and personally begged him to desist from this latest innovation, since it only meant an enormously expensive new competition for both countries, and would accomplish nothing anyway: new offensive weapons are too sophisticated to be screened out. Kosygin, whose whole attitude seemed hesitant and deferential to his colleagues back home, was noncommittal. So the anti-missile movement moved on, and presently — a reluctant McNamara notwithstanding — the U.S. would join it, in a small way at first, vis-à-vis the new threat posed by China.

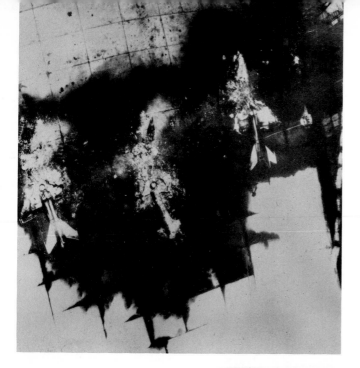

DISASTER IN THE DESERT

The one-week June war between Israel and the United Arab Republic in 1967 was one more classic bungle in the chronically inept record of Russian military intelligence. Having been arming and coaching them for nearly ten years, the Russians mistakenly assumed that Syria, Jordan, and especially Egypt, led by tall-in-the-saddle Col. Gamel Abdel Nasser, could and would fight.

In the upshot, after much loud and bloodthirsty talk by Nasser, who massed his tanks and aircraft in Sinai and the Negev, the Israelis beat him ferociously to the punch. Israeli "Mirage" fighter-bombers, bought from France, flattened scores of expensive Russian-built MIG's on their home fields (*left*). Israeli tanks and armored trucks (U.S. built) shot up the Egyptian armor (Russian-built) almost at will.

From Russia's viewpoint, the worst of it was that, except for Syria's mountain troops and Jordan's artillery, the Arabs did not even stand to make a contest of it. The better trained, highly motivated Israelis slugged them swiftly into flight and captivity.

MITLA PASS, a sandhill bottle-neck on the track back to the Suez Canal from the upper Negev, became a charnel waste when the Israeli jets caught Nasser's retreating columns there and blasted them to charred fragments (*right* and *below*). Refugees from this catastrophe scattered off into the desert to die of thirst and hunger if not rounded up in time as prisoners. Seldom have so many owed their misery to so few.

THE CANAL WAS PLUGGED by the angry Israelis early in the game, for that was much of what the shooting was about: the right of Israeli ships to transit the waterway. Nor would Israel agree to Egypt's unhindered unplugging of the channel until that right was guaranteed. A year after the hostilities, wrecks still littered the canal (*see opposite page*), at a cost in tolls to Egypt of some $250,000,000 per annum.

MOST EXCRUCIATING to Russia were painful pictures published by Israel soon after the fighting of entire anti-aircraft batteries, which the Egyptians abandoned intact, with projectiles still loaded on the launchers (*right*). These surface-to-air missiles (SAM's) were identical with models the Russians were sending the North Vietnamese to fire at American attackers (*see next page*) — with, it could be said, at least cautionary effect. Now the Americans were sure to see and study these weapons and perhaps learn to neutralize their heat-seeking nose cones. It was also likely that, in the next Arab-Israeli go-round, these same SAM's would be shooting down nice new Russian-built aircraft.

MOST SURPRISING was the speed with which Russian bigwigs, led by President Podgorny, hastened to Egypt to console President Nasser, to promise him (and quickly deliver) a brand-new arsenal and continued moral support, including this time much sterner training for his officers and men. Also promised: an $800-million steel complex at Halfa on the Nile. The reason, of course, was that Britain's pull-out from east of Suez — indeed, from east of Malta and Gibraltar — left a major vacuum which Russia could scarcely fail to fill. The whole oil-rich Arab world was Moscow's oyster, not even for the asking but just the taking, albeit politely. Even Turkey, a NATO member, could be lulled with gifts into giving the Red Navy free passage through the Bosporus to make the eastern Mediterranean into a Soviet lake, with the Russian ships snug-harbored in Egyptian and Red Sea ports. Premier Kosygin visited Iran and India to broaden and strengthen this whole strategic concept.

RUSSIAN ARMS FOR HO

From the very first, Russia supported North Vietnam and the Viet Cong in their attempted conquest of South Vietnam, if only to outdo and supplant China, whom all Vietnamese historically detest. A lot of Soviet munitions crept across China by rail to Hanoi, but more went by sea. A steady stream of freighters from Soviet ports puffed into Haiphong, where the U.S. hesitated to bomb them lest World War III be triggered. Pictured (*left, below,* and *opposite*) are some of Russia's contributions to the Communist cause. They totted up to more than $2 billion per year by 1968, but that was less than 10 percent of what the war was costing the U.S., to say nothing of nuisance value.

BIGGEST CACHE of imported Red arms for the Viet Cong was taken by the International Control Commission's officers from a coastal ship sunk off Tuy Hoa in February 1965 (*above* and *right*). Included were quantities of Russian-made rifles, machine guns, and ammunition.

THE 140-MM. ROCKET and launcher, another Russian weapon, did not show until 1967. The 43-in., 90-lb. projectile had a range exceeding five miles, raised hell with airfields and ammo dumps.

GUIDANCE ELEMENT for a Russian SAM like the one pictured top opposite is examined by U.S. personnel (*right*) specially detailed to retrieve it.

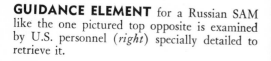

RUSSIA'S SAM'S (*above*), plentifully sprinkled over North Vietnam around the Americans' prime targets, were regarded with respect but did not make the Yank pilots say "uncle." You could see them coming, like flying phone poles, and either evade or shoot them down. Much worse was the conventional ack-ack, most of it Russian-made, which was if anything heavier and deadlier than the German flak of WW II.

HO CHI MINH (*far right, below*) **AND HENCHMEN** (*from left*) Le Duan, Truong Chinh, Vo Nguyn Giap ranked in Russia's book (and the world's) among the top warriors and dedicated Communists. Until old Ho had enough, Moscow would back him all the way, including standing behind him at the peace table.

DECLINE OF SOVIET EMPIRE

All empires in human history have eventually lost their colonies, but the Soviet empire is setting a new world record in speed of collapse. Hardly had the Soviet orbit been formed, when Yugoslavia pulled out. During Emperor Khrushchev's gay reign, the pull-outs became a rush. Poland got half-free in 1956, China began insulting Russia in 1959, Albania declared independence in 1960, and Rumania defied the U.S.S.R. soon after. By 1968, even meek Czechoslovakia was going its own way, while Cuba's temperamental Castro was quarreling with both Russia and China. The Brezhnev-Kosygin regime inherited a Soviet bloc splitting at the seams.

Cartoonist Behrendt of Amsterdam's *Algemeen Handelsblad* masterfully pictured Brezhnev's imperial headaches (*left*). Let's add a few words already spoken by rebellious satellite leaders.

Mao is probably writing: "Give back the Chinese lands Russia stole in the past!" Albania needs no words. Naughty Cuba is arguing: "Rich Communist countries should give more help to poor Communist nations." Yugoslav's Tito is asking Poland's Gomulka: "Why don't you support Czech liberalization like I do?" Rumania has no time to speak. It's too busy walking out of Moscow-sponsored international Communist conferences. Even Russia's home front is boiling, as Soviet students demand: "Free the imprisoned writers!"

No wonder Lenin is shocked, and Brezhnev pictures Stalin tearing his hair. Communist unity is gone, probably forever. If someone says he believes in Communism, a sensible question is: "Which one?"

PRAGUE IN THE NUTCRACKER. Twenty years after its forcible conversion from an industrious, happy little republic to a stagnant Communist slave state, Czechoslovakia stirred with a ferment for un-Communistic freedoms — of thought, speech, press, and economic life. Chief agent of the unrest was a gangling, cheerful, persuasive Slovak named Alexander Dubcek (*right*) who, early in 1968, eased out hardboiled Antonin Novotny, the Red bossman since Stalin's time. Dubcek did away entirely with the secret police and partisan thought-control. Prague and its people were euphoric.

Among leaders of the hardline Warsaw Pact powers — East Germany, Poland, Bulgaria, and Hungary — and among hawks in the Kremlin, the nutcracker treatment for Prague seemed indicated, à la Budapest in 1956. So Russian and other forces "maneuvered" in and around Czechoslovakia, and Dubcek was summoned to the Kremlin.

He not only declined to go, but obliged the mighty Politburo to visit *him,* in a body, at the border hamlet of Cierna. Then he had the hard-line leaders all come to Bratislava (again, in his country) to ratify what the Politburo had granted: liberties for the Czechs within reasonable Red bounds. Tito flew up from Belgrade to congratulate Dubcek, his emulator. So did Ceaucescu of Rumania, evoking memories of the old-time Little Entente.

Grim old Walter Ulbrecht of East Germany was furious, because terrified. He feared a Czech rapprochement with West Germany, which might undermine the whole Soviet system. He harangued and won over the Politburo's hawks, and one August midnight 200,000 Russian troops surged into Czechoslovakia by plane, tank, and lorry, accompanied by token forces of the Warsaw hardliners to make this second rape of Czechoslovakia technically a gang job, not another Russian solo. The Kremlin's clumsy lie was that occupation had been "asked for," to subdue a "revolution."

Dubcek and his colleagues were interned, but not before telling their countrymen to resist passively, bloodlessly, and to have faith. Under the invaders' noses, 1,200 of Dubcek's liberal followers held a secret Communist congress in a big factory,

disguised as workmen. When the Russians looked for prominent quislings to form a new government, none could be found.

The populace hooted the foreign soldiers, who scarcely knew where they were, what with most road and street signs removed. There was little shooting, partly because 125,000 Czech forces stood by, intact and fully armed; the Kremlin knew well how they could fight, and one more blood bath was not desired for Russian history.

Into this impasse stepped venerable Ludvik Svoboda (*above*), the country's lately elected, nonpartisan President, highly respected by Moscow as a Hero of the Soviet Union. He negotiated the reinstatement of Dubcek & Co., though not without iron-clad — that is, Red Army enforced — guarantees of "correct" behavior, especially in print, and of the West German border. In effect, Czechoslovakia was back at Russia's heel after a few heady moments of escape.

But the Czechs were not the only losers. Free World revulsion at Moscow's cynical tyranny was shared and voiced by the Communist parties of almost all but Russia's accomplice countries. The Soviet Empire, though momentarily patched, was shakier than ever. Even home liberals fumed, like Andrei Sakharov, renowned "father" of Russia's H-bomb, who said publicly: "There can be no doubt we should support their [the Czechs'] bold initiative . . . so valuable for the future of socialism, and of all mankind."

"THE MOTHERLAND"

Observing, and often shuddering at, the contorted behavior of the U.S.S.R's ruling bureaucracy, with its manic-suppressive codes for mass existence rather than individual life, Russia-watchers should never lose sight of the underlying biological reality: a population of some 228,-000,000, whose human aspirations are re-awakened and fortified every time they find out about an atrocity, like Budapest or Prague, wreaked by their Communist masters. In the long run they must react as the Russians did when brought to final bay at Stalingrad by the brute forces of Adolf Hitler.

Magnificent expression was given to those aspirations, to that racial vitality, in a statue (*right*) called "The Motherland," by Sculptor Yevgeni Vuchetich. It was erected in 1967 on historic Mamayev Hill, site of the great siege's climax, as a feature of the U.S.S.R.'s 50th birthday celebration. The colossal supernal figure, exhorting Russians to fight for their dear lives, towers 83 meters aloft, nearly 90 feet higher than the Statue of Liberty. Perhaps the tiny people creeping antlike around the feet of "The Motherland" suggest how insignificant is the individual compared to the State, and doubtless that was the metaphor intended by the Kremlin oligarchs. Nevertheless, it was people, not politicians, who actually created the statue as an image of their statehood — people who breathe and live and feel and think as no statue can ever do. Woe to witless oligarchs who ever forget this.

HOW RUSSIA IS RULED

For more than 50 years a Communist dictatorship has ruled Russia. At first, Soviet Russia stood alone as the sole Marxist state in the world. Today (1968) there are 14 Communist countries, containing one-third of the world's population. In all these countries Communist rule was established by force of arms or the threat thereof. The Communist world is an armed camp. Its combined armies total more than 8,000,000 men, and its economy is geared to fast, forced construction of war-potential industry. While talking peace to neutrals and to the West, the post-Khrushchev leaders of the U.S.S.R. openly pledge their devotion to world revolution and endanger world peace by atomic armament. The U.S.S.R. is equally hard boiled about extending Communist influence into non-Communist nations.

Moscow puzzles and worries the West. For most Americans and West Europeans, the Soviet system is a strange, foreign, secretive regime entrenched behind an Iron Curtain. Clarifying and useful is an objective examination of the actual workings of the Soviet system.

During its first five decades, the Soviet Union has been in a state of emergency, including the equivalent of martial law and suppression of civil liberties. Isolation from the outside world was attempted. Education was channeled along lines furthering Communism and criticizing foreign ideas and opinions. All information was presented through the Red lens of Marxism-Leninism. The effect of the coloration is clear: the Soviet population received a largely subjective view of the outside world. Westerners, having a free press, need not remain similarly subjective about the Soviets.

Though the "Union" and "Republic" parts of the "Union of Soviet Socialist Republics" sound familiar to Americans, the two central words are foreign indeed: *Soviet* and *Socialist*.

"Soviet" means a governmental legislature.

"Socialist" means the way of life imposed upon the U.S.S.R. by the Communist leadership.

Taking these terms in order, this page and the next offer further clarification.

"SOVIET"

In theory, the highest authority in the U.S.S.R. under the present Constitution is the legislature — the Supreme Soviet — elected for a four-year term by one-ticket elections. All members are either Communists or nonparty Bolsheviks (non-Communists who, voluntarily or otherwise, echo the Communist party line). The Supreme Soviet consists of two chambers:

The Soviet of the Union (corresponding to the U.S. House of Representatives). Delegates are elected on the basis of one delegate to every 300,000 of population.

The Soviet of Nationalities (corresponding to the U.S. Senate). These delegates are elected on the basis of 32 deputies from each Union Republic, 11 from each Autonomous Republic, five from each Autonomous Region, and one from each National District. Delegates are not required to belong to the majority nationality of these racial subdivisions of the U.S.S.R., but the general aim is a chamber representing the more important nationalities. The two chambers have equal rights, and a simple majority vote in both passes a law. Joint sessions of the two chambers appoint the U.S.S.R. Supreme Court, the Supreme Soviet Presidium, and the Council of Ministers.

In practice, the Supreme Soviet issues few laws, because it meets only twice a year, and then only for a few days. Many more laws are passed by the **Supreme Soviet Presidium** of 33 members, who are always in session. This Presidium also appoints high diplomatic and military officials, and even government ministers when the Supreme Soviet is not meeting. In addition, the Presidium ratifies and denounces treaties, proclaims martial law, declares war, and revokes laws that are held unconstitutional. Its powers are roughly equivalent to those of the U.S. Senate and Supreme Court combined. The President

of the Presidium (in 1968, Nikolai Podgorny) performs the duties of titular head of state; hence he is often called the President of the Soviet Union.

The most powerful of all governmental bodies is the U.S.S.R. **Council of Ministers** (cabinet). It is not only the chief executive, but also the chief legislator, issuing more laws each year than the Supreme Soviet and Presidium taken together. The Council consists of approximately 65 ministries (mostly economic), 15 republic premiers, and about 10 U.S.S.R. vice-premiers. The Premier (in 1968, Aleksei Kosygin) is the most powerful official in the U.S.S.R. Government and the real chief of the Soviet state.

This is the central governmental structure, which (except for the bicameral feature) is duplicated in all 15 Union Republics, and to a lesser extent further down the line in the autonomous republics, territories, regions, and districts.

"SOCIALIST"

The Communist Party is the only organized political party permitted by law in the U.S.S.R. Through this privilege it absolutely controls the country's constitutional structure and governmental personnel. Through its members, the Party — a self-appointed, self-perpetuating trusteeship — maintains the Communist dictatorship. The membership serve as watchdogs throughout the factories, railways, collective farms, co-operatives, schools, and armed forces. In local Soviets the Communists are sometimes in a minority, but as one goes up the governmental ladder the percentage of Communists increases. All top positions in the government, the economy, the police, and the armed forces are held by Party members. Thus in 1968, about 13,000,000 Party members completely dominated the 238,000,000 inhabitants of the Soviet Union.

The Party is best described as a "dictatorship within a dictatorship." From the lowest level, the Party is a pyramid of committees, each selected by the party conference or congress at its level and headed by one or more secretaries. (Party officers are always secretaries; there are no committee presidents or premiers.) The highest legislature is the U.S.S.R. Party Congress, which meets every four years. Highest committee is the Central Committee, which has an executive secretariat and several bureaus, of which the most important is the Politburo (formerly Party Presidium). This Politburo is the "brain trust" formulating all major Soviet policies, and in practice is the real supreme legislature of the U.S.S.R. After Khrushchev's removal in 1964, the Central Committee secretariat (chief Party executive) was headed by Leonid Brezhnev.

In appearance, the Party organizational framework is democratic. However, all elections are indirect, the Party conferences

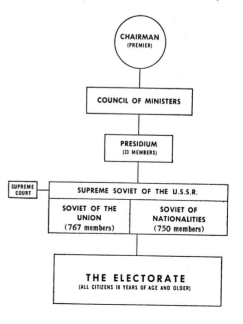

and congresses rarely meet, and even the committees are not in constant session. Local and regional Party organizations are ruled by their secretaries, who in turn are nominated (i.e. appointed) by the Politburo and Central Committee Secretariat. Hence the handful of men composing the Politburo (which includes the head of the Secretariat) are the real rulers of the U.S.S.R. Among the Politburo members are the chairman of the Supreme Soviet Presidium, and the Premier of the Council of Ministers, thus interlocking Party and government at the highest level.

It is not easy to become a Party member. Candidates must convincingly profess to believe in Marxism-Leninism, be faithful followers of the Kremlin leaders, and prove in practice an ability to further the cause of Communism. Most members are skilled in administration, and hold administrative rather than proletarian positions. Wherever things do not go right, a Communist is usually sent in to set them straight. The Party runs the country; the Politburo runs the Party.

"THE PARTY LINE"

The Party Line, or basic strategy of the Communist Party, has its bible in the voluminous writings of Lenin, which are carefully reinterpreted by the high priests of Communism (the Politburo). The line is flexible, and varies with new U.S.S.R. leaders and new situations. Agitprop (Agitation and Propaganda Administration of the Party Secretariat) serves as a doctrinal ministry issuing the day-by-day changes in the Party line. Current emphasis of the Party line is published in *Pravda* (Truth), the Party newspaper, and *Izvestia* (News), the official governmental daily. Whenever propaganda fails to persuade the Soviet people, compulsion is applied by two police ministries, MOOP and KGB, the successors to the old OGPU, NKVD, and MVD.

LABOR

Labor. Of the 83,000,000 manual and office workers employed by the U.S.S.R. government in 1968, over 81,000,000 were members of the Soviet trade unions. These unionists were organized on an industrial basis (like the American C.I.O.) in some 20 nationwide unions. All 20, in turn, were united under the All-Union Central Council of Trade Unions (AUCCTU), which was headed by high-ranking Communists.

In the early years of the Soviet regime, the trade unions were independent and wielded great authority. Lenin broke the political power of the unions at the start of the 1920's. Stalin deprived them of the right to strike and bargain at the beginning of the 1930's. Since then, the Soviet trade unions have become very similar to the old American company unions, but with the government as the company.

Soviet unions protect the worker's health and safety, handle his social insurance, operate the factory club, and serve as a channel for worker complaints. But on vital problems like wages, work-norms and hours, the unions never oppose the government. Unions prevent rather than encourage strikes, though local wildcat walkouts still occur.

The by-laws of the AUCCTU state that the main union task is: "To organize the socialist competition of workers and officials for the fulfillment and overfulfillment of State Plans, for the raising of labor productivity, improvement in the quality of production and the lowering of its cost."

THE POWER WEB

The U.S.S.R. is a land of mass organizations, which Lenin called the "transmission belts" between the Communist Party leadership (the motor) and the nonparty masses (the obedient machine). Membership in most of these transmission belts is not compulsory, but a member receives more privileges than do nonmembers. So most Soviet citizens join the organization appropriate for their age and profession, starting at the age of seven with membership in a Communist youth society, the Octobrists. Many adults are members of two or three transmission belts simultaneously. Thus a peasant usually holds membership in both a collective farm and a consumer cooperative.

Each of these mass organizations is national, and very undemocratic, with strict control from the top. The leaders of all these organizations are closely united by holding membership in the Communist Party's Central Committee, which, in turn, is dominated by the Politburo. At the Soviet summit, dual jobholding in two or more mass organizations is quite common, thus meshing the organizational web into a tight power nucleus. At the republic, regional, and lower levels, each organization has its separate local boss. By this "divide and rule" system, the summit ensures that no local tyrant will emerge.

To make Politburo rule doubly sure, at each level from national to village the local Party secretary watches all non-Party organizations, and with the aid of local Party members and informers makes them toe the Party line. The control is thus not only vertical from top to bottom, but also horizontal, creating a web effect. Meanwhile, the police break up any clandestine revolutionary cells before they can grow into organisms that might upset the power web. With no organization to fight the interlocking web (*see below*) the masses are politically helpless.

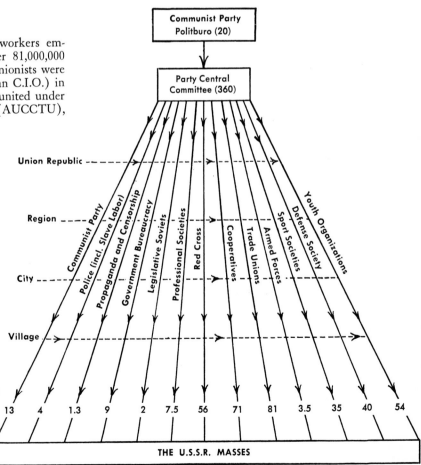

THE EVER CHANGING COLLECTIVE LEADERSHIP

Members of the Party Presidium (Politburo):

in 1953 after Stalin's death,

in 1957 when Khrushchev seized power,

in 1968 during the Brezhnev regime.

(Being a Soviet leader is a hazardous profession. None of Stalin's immediate successors in 1953 were still in power by 1968. Even most of the 1957 leadership had been purged or retired. In the following table, the names of survivors from the previous Presidium are given in italics.)

1953 Party Presidium

Full Members

Lavrenti Beria
Nikolai Bulganin
Lazar Kaganovich
Nikita Khrushchev
Georgi Malenkov
Anastas Mikoyan
Vyacheslav Molotov
Kliment Voroshilov

Candidate Members

Mikhail Pervukhin
Panteleimon Ponomarenko
Maksim Saburov
Nikolai Shvernik

1957 Party Presidium

Full Members

Averki Aristov
Nikolai Belyaiev
Leonid Brezhnev
Nikolai Bulganin
Yekaterina Furtseva
Nikolai Ignatov
Nikita Khrushchev
Aleksei Kirichenko
Frol Kozlov
Otto Kuusinen
Anastas Mikoyan
Nikolai Shvernik
Mikhail Suslov
Kliment Voroshilov
Georgi Zhukov

Candidate Members

Janis Kalnberzins
Andrei Kirilenko
Demyan Korotchenko
Aleksei Kosygin
Kiril Mazurov
Nuritdin Mukhitdinov
Vasili Mzhavanadze
Mikhail Pervukhin
Pyotr Pospelov

May 1968 Politburo

Full Members

Leonid Brezhnev
Andrei Kirilenko
Aleksei Kosygin
Kiril Mazurov
Arvid Pelshe
Nikolai Podgorny
Dmitri Polyanski
Aleksandr Shelepin
Pyotr Shelest
Mikhail Suslov
Gennady Voronov

Candidate Members

Yuri Andropov
Pyotr Demichev
Viktor Grishin
Dinmerkhamed Kunayev
Pyotr Masherov
Vasili Mzhavanadze
Sharaf Rashidov
Vladimir Shcherbitski
Dmitri Ustinov

CHRONOLOGY

RUSSIAN RULERS

862 to 879	**Rurik**	of Novgorod, a Viking or Russ from the North; took command of the Slavs at Novgorod. His family ruled for 700 years.	

DUKES OF KIEV

879 to 912	**Oleg** *cousin of Rurik*	conquered Kiev. Took 900 ships to Byzantium; returned with first treaty. Died of a snake-bite.
912 to 945	**Igor** *son of Rurik*	invaded Thrace (941), defeated by "Greek Fire." With Pechenegs (944) invaded Byzantium. Made treaty with Romanus I, deputy emperor.
945 to 957	**Olga** *widow of Rurik*	Scandinavian (Helga) of Pskov; wise and energetic. Baptized (955) at Byzantium. Tried to introduce Christianity.
957 to 972	**Svyatoslav,** *son of Olga*	a pagan. Invaded Bulgaria (986). Defeated by Emperor John Zimisces after invasion of Thrace. Killed by Pechenegs at rapids of Dnieper. Divided kingdom among three sons.
972 to 980	**Yaropolk,** *son of Svyatoslav*	the eldest, had his brother Oleg killed. Yaropolk reunited the kingdom from Kiev. His brother, Vladimir, supported by Novgorod, attacked and killed him.
980 to 1015	**Vladimir,** *brother of Yaropolk*	a pagan who, on his marriage to Ann, princess of Byzantium, became Christian and enforced baptism on his subjects. Encouraged laws and learning. Divided kingdom among twelve sons.
1015 to 1019	**Svyatopolk,** *son of Yaropolk, adopted by Vladimir*	the "Accursed." Had Ann's son Gleb and Boris slain. Aided by father-in-law Boleslav, reunited kingdom. Died in flight from Yaroslav.

CONTEMPORARY

860 Donald McAlpin crowned King of Scotland.
866 Ethelred succeeded Ethelbert as King of England.
867 Basil I became Emperor at Byzantium. He recovered southern Italy from Arabs.
871 Alfred the Great crowned King of England.
875 Charles II ("The Bald") crowned Emperor of Rome.

885 Normans besieged Paris, defended by Odo.
896 Arnulf crowned Emperor of Rome.
901 Edward the Elder crowned King of England.
907 Epoch of Five Dynasties in China began.
929 Arabs expelled from northern Italy.
929 King Henry I of Germany defeated Slavs at Havel.
930 Vikings established first parliament in Iceland.
935 Wang Chien established central mnoarchy in China.
940 Burning of Library at Alexandria, Egypt.
945 Scots, under Malcolm, took Cumberland and Westmoreland.
946 Edred succeeded Edmund, his brother, as King of England.
951 (to 960) Hou Chou Dynasty in China.
955 Otto I of Germany defeated Slavs at Mecklenburg.
959 Dunstan became Archbishop of Canterbury.
960 (to 1280) Sung Dynasty in China.
962 Otto I of Germany crowned Emperor of Rome.
965 Harold Bluetooth of Denmark baptized.
973 Edgar crowned King of England at Bath.
973 Otto II became Emperor of Rome.
978 Lothair sacked Aix-la-Chapelle.
980 Vikings attacked Chester, Southampton and Thanet.
982 Eric the Red began to colonize Greenland.
955 Olaf Tryggveson, King of Norway, introduced Christianity.
1000 Leif Ericsson, son of Eric the Red, discovered America.
1015 Olaf II (the "Saint") crowned King of Norway.
1016 Norman knights arrived in South Italy.
1017 Canute crowned King of England.
1018 Assembly of Oxford; Danes and English accepted English law.
1019 Synod of Goslar decided against marriage of priests.

1019 to 1054	**Yaroslav** son of Vladimir	enlarged the kingdom and introduced many reforms. Caused Greek works to be translated into Slav. Ordered compilation of first law code (*Russkaya Pravda*). Left a will calling for progression by seniority for his four sons.
1054 to 1078	**Isaslav** *1st son of Yaroslav*	was expelled when Kiev was invaded by the Polovtsy, successors of the Pechenegs. Svyatoslav of Chernigov took over at Kiev. At his death, Vsevold, Yaroslav's favorite son, ruled in Kiev until deposed by Isaslav, aided by the Poles.
1078 to 1093	**Vsevold** *3rd son of Yaroslav*	of Chernigov, returned to rule ably in Kiev. Married daughter of Greek Emperor Monomachus. At his death Kiev wished his son Vladimir to rule, but he adhered to seniority and appointed his nephew.
1093 to 1113	**Svyatopolk II** *son of Isaslav*	Weak and cruel. All during his reign his cousin Vladimir was the outstanding hero, uniting his family and leading them against the Polovtsy in 1101 and 1111. At Svyatopolk's death, Kiev insisted on the rule of Vladimir.
1113 to 1125	**Vladimir II (Monomach)** *son of Vsevold*	After having stepped aside in favor of the senior line of Chernigov, he gave to Kiev a high-minded and able government. He has been called "Alfred the Great" of Russia.
1125 to 1132	**Mstislav** *1st son of Vladimir*	ruled ably and held the family united. His death marked the decay of Kiev as a power. The town was jealous of its rights, the *veche* or public assembly wanted to control the Duke. The boyars looked for greater recognition.
1132 to 1139	**Yaropolk II** *2nd son of Vladimir*	proved an able defender against the Polovtsy, whose raids against Kiev were constantly increasing.
1139 to 1146	**Vsevold II** *grandson of Yaroslav*	a Chernigov prince, claimed the throne on seniority rights according to Yaroslav's will. His attempt to secure a permanent succession for Chernigov was resisted by Kiev and the town chose his successor.
1146 to 1154	**Isaslav II** *son of Mstislav* **AND Vyacheslav** *3rd son of Vladimir*	To offset the jealousy of his uncle Yury, Vladimir's youngest son, Isaslav, called his uncle Vyacheslav to rule with him jointly.
1154 to 1157	**Yury (Longarm)** *5th son of Vladimir*	Emerging from the family's conflicts, Yury, with the aid of his son Andrew, was strong enough to take and hold the throne.

GRAND DUKES OF VLADIMIR

1157 to 1175	**Andrew I (Bogolubsky)** *2nd son of Yury I*	Seeing the land around Kiev being deserted because of raids of the Polovtsy, who were also destroying trade on the Dnieper, he secured himself in Vladimir.
1169 to 1175	**Gleb** (in Kiev) *3rd son of Yury I*	After storming Kiev in 1169 Andrew incorporated it with Suzdal and placed his brother Gleb in charge as deputy.
1175 to 1176	**Michael I** *4th son of Yury I*	Vladimir (town), resisting the conspirators of Suzdal and Rostov, who had slain Andrew, placed his younger brother Michael on the throne.
1176 to 1212	**Vsevold III** *5th son of Yury I*	followed the policy of Andrew and continued to increase his power over a larger domain.
1212 to 1216	**Yury II** *2nd son of Vsevold*	Vsevold had supplanted his eldest son Constantine as heir in favor of Yury, who after ruling four years, was deposed in favor of the eldest son.
1216 to 1219	**Constantine** *1st son of Vsevold III*	Family feuds and jealousies flourished as they had formerly in Kiev, cut short Constantine's rule.
1219 to 1238	**Yury II** *2nd son of Vsevold*	Restored to throne. The 2nd Tartar invasion in 1236 led by Batu attacked Vladimir first. Yury, seeking help, was overtaken and slain north of the Volga.

1040 Duncan slain by Macbeth who became King of Scotland.
1042 Hardicanute died, succeeded by Edward the Confessor, son of Ethelred.
1042 Constantine Monomachus became Eastern Emperor.
1053 Normans defeated and captured Leo IX at Civitate.
1054 Malcolm defeated Macbeth at Dunsinane.
1066 Harold succeeded Edward the Confessor, King of England.
1066 William defeated Harold at Hastings.
1072 Commune formed at Le Mans.
1073 Gregory VII (Hildebrand) made Pope.
1081 Bishop Gundulf built Tower of London.
1084 Henry IV crowned Emperor by Clement III.
1084 Normans sacked Rome, Gregory VII fled to Salerno.
1086 Doomsday Book compiled.
1096 1st Crusade. Peter the Hermit died.
1099 Crusaders took Jerusalem.
1099 The Cid died. Moors recovered Valencia.
1103 Magnus III, King of Norway, invaded Ireland.
1115 State of Chin established in Northern China.
1117 Henry V crowned Emperor of West.
1118 Order of Templars founded.
1120 Concordat at Worms.
1123 Omar Khayyam said to have died.
1126 (to 1137) Alfonso VII became King of Castile and León.
1128 Abbey of Holyrood founded by David I.
1130 Henry I gave Charter to London.
1131 Fulk of Anjou became King of Jerusalem.
1133 Lothair crowned Emperor of Rome.
1134 Western facade of Chartres Cathedral built.
1134 Moors defeated and killed Alfonso of Aragon at Fraga.
1138 Stephen defeated David I at Battle of the Standards.
1139 Matilda landed at Arundel — civil war.
1142 China made tributary to Chin.
1143 Portugal made kingdom with Papal consent.
1143 Foundation of Lübeck.
1147 Geoffrey of Monmouth wrote *Historia Regum Britanniae*.
1147 2nd Crusade joined by Louis VII and Conrad III.
1147 (to 1148) Crusaders perished in Asia Minor and before Damascus.
1148 Normans captured Tunis and Tripoli.

1154 Thomas à Becket made chancellor by King Henry II of England.
1155 Frederick I (Barbarossa) became Emperor of Rome.
1155 Hadrian IV bestowed Ireland upon Henry II.
1156 Hungary recognized Byzantium as overlord.
1157 Eric of Sweden conquered Finland.

1159 Henry II accepted *scutage* (shield money) in place of military service.
1160 Normans expelled from North Africa.
1165 Byzantium allied with Venice against Frederick I.
1166 Assize of Clarendon established Grand Jury.
1167 Oxford University founded.
1169 Norman nobles began conquest of Ireland.
1170 Thomas à Becket murdered by four Norman nobles.
1171 Henry II acknowledged as Lord of Ireland.
1171 Saladin conquered Egypt.
1172 Irish clergy brought under authority of Rome.
1173 Sons of Henry II rebel; allied with Scotland and France.
1176 Scottish bishops asserted the independence of York.
1176 Saladin conquered Syria.
1176 Assize of Northampton; organization of judicial districts.
1176 London Bridge built.
1187 Saladin captured Jerusalem.
1189 Richard I succeeded Henry II; joined Philip in 3rd Crusade.
1199 Richard I died. John became King of England.
1208 Godfrey of Strassburg wrote *Tristan and Isolde*.
1212 Kings of Navarre, Castile & Aragon defeated Moors at Navas de Tolosa.
1212 Children's Crusade.
1215 John sealed Magna Carta at Runnymede.
1215 Pope annulled Magna Carta in favor of John. Barons started civil war.
1216 King John died. Henry III crowned at Gloucester.
1218 Amiens Cathedral begun.
1219 Genghis Khan conquered Samarkand and Persia.
1221 Tartars invaded sultanate of Delhi.
1226 Francis of Assisi died; his church built at Assisi.
1229 Carmelites (White Friars) came to England.
1231 Gregory IX issued new laws against heretics.
1237 Teutonic Order and Knights of Sword united in Livonia.

427

GRAND PRINCES

1238 Yaroslav II Batu with 300,000 Tartars smashed all Russian resistance.
to *3rd son of* Swept down through Poland. Stopped in the west by Vaclav,
1246 *Vsevold III* the Czech. Batu retired to lower Volga, where Yaroslav was
poisoned.

1246 Alexander at Yaroslav's death, was made Grand Prince by Batu. In
to **(Nevsky)** 1236 he routed Jarl Birger on the Neva. Defeated the Teu-
1263 *2nd son of* tonic Knights in 1242. Died returning from his 4th visit to
Yaroslav II the Golden Horde.

1263 Yaroslav III His reign was beset with the intrigues of Novgorod. That
to *3rd son of* city, irked by tribute for the Tartars, was restive under the
1272 *Yaroslav II* rule of the Grand Prince.

1272 Basil The Khan balanced the power of Moscow by appointing
to **Kostroma** Basil from Tver.
1276 *4th son of*
Yaroslav II

1276 Dmitry I Forty years after its destruction by the Tartars, Moscow was
to *1st son of* weathering many difficulties: succession at the will of the
1294 *Alex. Nevsky* Khan; Tartar tribute; family feuds.

1294 Andrew III Family rivalry glowed during this period. Novgorod sup-
to *2nd son of* ported Yaroslav's son Michael, to supplant Alexander's sons.
1304 *Alexander*

1304 Michael I Called to the Horde for an accounting, Michael was met by
to *son of* his rival Yury, who murdered him.
1319 *Yaroslav III*

1319 Yury III Though shocked by Michael's murder, the Khan gave the
to *son of* rule to Yury, who was in turn slain by Michael's son Dmitry.
1326 *Daniel of* In 1320 Gedimir of Lithuania conquered Kiev.
Moscow;
grandson of
Alexander

1326 Alexander Prince of Tver. Because a cousin of Uzbek, the ruling Khan,
to **II** was slain while collecting tribute in Tver, Ivan of Moscow
1328 *son of* asked for and was given an army of 50,000 Tartars with
Michael; which he crushed Tver's resistance. Alexander fled to Pskov.
grandson of
Yaroslav III

GRAND DUKES OF MOSCOW

1328 Ivan I His astuteness in gaining the Khan's support by collecting
to **(Kalita)** tribute from the other princes, gave him great power which
1340 *2nd son of* he ably used as an administrator.
Daniel of
Moscow

1340 Simeon With Tartar power back of him, Simeon kept the peace of
to *son of* his father and further unified and satisfied the family. He
1353 *Ivan I* died of Black Death.

1353 Ivan II The Gentle. To Ivan II the Khan gave great power, the right
to *son of* of justice over the other princes, which he never abused.
1359 *Simeon*

1359 Dmitry To satisfy Moscow, 11-year-old Dmitry was appointed ruler
to *great* by Khan Murad, thus superseding the Prince of Suzdal, who
1363 *grandson of* had previously been made ruler by a rival khan, Abdul.
Yaroslav III

1363 Dmitry Moscow was now united and the Horde was splitting into
to **(Donskoi)** factions. Raids by the Tartars led to the battle of Kulikovo
1384 *son of* on the Don where the Horde was defeated. Later Moscow
Ivan II valiantly defended itself.

1384 Basil I Tamerlane, overthrowing the Khan Tokhta-Mysh, marched
to *son of* through Russia nearly to Moscow but did not attack. In
1425 *Dmitry* 1405 Edegei, the Vizier, did the same. Basil invaded Lith-
Donskoi uania when Smolensk was taken by his father-in-law, Vitout.

1239 Alexander II opposed extension of Papal jurisdiction to Scotland.
1241 Mongols defeated Germans at Liegnitz, Silesia.
1244 Jerusalem taken by Egyptian Khwarazmi.
1244 Innocent IV fled to Lyons from Emperor Frederick II.
1248 (to 1252) 6th Crusade to Egypt led by Louis IX (St. Louis).
1250 Frederick II died, succeeded by Conrad IV.
1250 *The Harrowing of Hell,* earliest extant English play.
1252 (to 1255) William of Rubruque's journey to Central Asia; learned
use of gunpowder.
1257 Robert de Sorbon, chaplain of Louis IX, founded the Sorbonne.
1265 Dante Alighieri born in Florence.
1265 Parliament, representing shires, cities, boroughs, summoned by
Simon de Monfort.
1266 Roger Bacon: *Opus Maius.*
1272 Richard of Cornwall, King of Romans, died; Rudolf of Hapsburg
succeeded him.
1272 Henry III died, succeeded by Edward I, who instituted House of
Commons.
1274 Kublai Khan failed to conquer Japan.
1274 Thomas Aquinas died.
1275 (to 1292) Marco Polo in service of Kublai Khan.
1276 1st Welsh war against Llywelyn ap Gruffyd, Prince of Wales.
1282 Andronicus II repealed union of Eastern and Western churches.
1283 Teutonic Order completed subjugation of Prussia.
1288 Osman I, son of Ertogrul, founded Ottoman Empire.
1290 Jews expelled from England.
1291 Mamelukes conquered Acre; end of Christian rule in East.
1293 1st Christian missionaries in China.
1296 Scottish coronation stone removed from Scone to Westminster.
1299 (to 1301) Palazzo Vecchio, Florence, built.
1301 Edward I's son created Prince of Wales.
1306 Philip IV expelled Jews from France.
1306 Robert Bruce crowned King of Scotland.
1310 (to 1340) Palace of the Doges built at Venice.
1314 Robert Bruce defeated Edward at Bannockburn.
1321 Dante Alighieri died, having completed *La Divina Commedia.*
1322 Master John finished choir of Cologne Cathedral.
1324 Burgos Cathedral consecrated.
1327 Edward II resigned throne; succeeded by Edward III.
1328 Mortimer, who captured Edward II, made Earl of March.
1328 Anglo-Scot treaty recognized Robert Bruce as King of Scotland.
1328 Charles IV, last of Capets, died; succeeded by Philip VI.
1332 (to 1391) Zenith of Arabic civilization in Granada. Yusuf I and
Muhammad V.
1333 Moors recaptured Gibraltar from Castile.
1335 Edward III claimed French crown; start of 100 Years War.
1337 Edward III invaded Scotland.
1339 Edward III invaded France from Flanders.
1341 Petrarch crowned poet in Rome.
1346 Edward defeated French at Crécy; Darby took Poitiers.
1347 "Black Death" (bubonic plague) swept Europe.
1349 Edward III established Order of the Garter.
1349 Great persecution of Jews in Germany.
1354 Turks took Gallipoli, their first European foothold.
1356 Black Prince defeated French at Maupertius; captured King John II.
1356 Charles IV issued Golden Bull at Metz.
1358 Revolt of French peasants; their leader, Marcel, killed.
1360 Final peace of Calais; Edward III and Philip of Burgundy.
1360 (to 1402) Alcazar of Seville built.
1361 "Black Death" reappeared in Europe.
1362 Disbanded English companies defeated French army at Brignais.
1362 English tongue superseded French in Parliament and law courts.
1363 Tamerlane began conquest of Asia.
1369 Mongol Yuan dynasty overthrown by Ming in China.
1371 Robert (II) Stuart became King of Scotland.
1375 Giovanni Boccaccio died near Florence.
1377 Gregory XI entered Rome: end of "Babylonian Captivity."
1377 Edward III died; succeeded by grandson, Richard II.
1387 (to 1400) Geoffrey Chaucer: *Canterbury Tales.*
1388 Scots defeated English at Otterburn (Chevy Chase).
1399 Henry IV dethroned Richard III.
1402 Tamerlane defeated Bajazet I, Emir of Turks.
1403 Henry IV defeated the Percys at Shrewsbury, subdued Northumber-
land.

| 1425 to 1462 | **Basil II (the Sightless)** *son of Basil I* | Civil war raged when Basil was unseated by his uncle Yury. Rulers on the throne changed five times. A unified Moscow and the church fixed the succession from father to son. In 150 years Moscow had grown from 500 sq.mi. to 15,000 sq.mi. and had become a nation. |

TSARS OF MUSCOVY

1462 to 1505	**Ivan III (the Great)** *son of Basil II*	First to assume autocratic rule. Married Zoë (Sophia), Princess of Constantinople. Gained Novgorod and made Kazan tributary. Siberia was explored in 1499. Had Basil (Zoë's son) crowned as co-regent.
1505 to 1533	**Basil III** *son of Ivan III*	Even more formal and autocratic than his father. He recovered Smolensk, annexed Ryazan, gained full power over Pskov. His rule extended from Chernigov to Gulf of Finland, to White Sea, to Urals.
1533 to 1584	**Ivan IV (the Terrible)** *son of Basil III*	A cruel but great ruler, he believed in divine right and was irate at opposition. His father died when Ivan was 3. At 16 he demanded the crown and married Anastasia Romanoff. Invited trade with Germany and England. 300 years of Tartar tribute ended when Ivan captured Kazan in 1552.
1584 to 1598	**Fedor I** *son of Ivan IV*	Weak in mind and body, he was aided in ruling by state council. Nikita Romanoff, his uncle and regent, died, and his brother-in-law, Boris Godunov became regent. Fedor died, perhaps of poison. He was last of the "House of Rurik."
1598 to 1605	**Boris Godunov**	A boyar. Banishment of rivals gave security to his rule which promised well until famine reduced the peasants to robbery and pillage. In 1604 a pretender, calling himself "Dmitry, half-brother of Fedor I," invaded Russia from Poland. A year later Godunov died.
1605 to 1606	**Demetrius (the "False")** *the 1st Pretender*	The desperate peasants, joined by the Cossacks, welcomed "a born Tsarevich" to the throne. The boyars, led by Shuisky, were successful in a plot to destroy Demetrius and his ashes were shot from a cannon back toward Poland.
1606 to 1610	**Basil V (Ivanovich Shuisky)**	The "Time of Troubles." Although a descendant of Rurik, Basil was a poor specimen. All over Russia loyalty and patriotism were smothered by rivalries, treacheries, pretenders and Poles. In 1613 the Cossacks chose for tsar Michael Romanoff; the church and people accepted him.
1613 to 1645	**Michael (Fedorovich Romanoff)** *son of Philaret*	A grandson of Ivan IV's brother-in-law. A Zemsky Sobor (general assembly) met at Moscow and elected Michael unanimously. The people acclaimed him in the Red Square. His father, Philaret, returned from captivity in Poland to act as regent.
1645 to 1676	**Alexis** *son of Michael*	Labor had been roving since the famines of 1601–1604. To re-establish order, a new code of laws (1646) fixed the serf to the land by registration. Riots over taxation spread through the towns. For five years a band of piratical Cossacks, led by Stepan Razin, ran amok.
1676 to 1682	**Fedor III** *son of Alexis*	Tutored by an able scholar, Simon Polotsky, Fedor saw the great need for education. He founded the first college in Moscow to develop and train students for the Orthodox Church. He abolished the old rule of precedence of the nobles which had been predicated on both birth and service.
1682 to 1725	**Peter (the Great)** AND **Ivan V** *sons of Alexis*	A ruthless tyrant in the cause of Russia's advancement, Peter's dynamic urgency promised to push the nation forward centuries in development. He founded the future Russia and left it permanent access to the Baltic. Peter assented to the execution of Alexis, his son by his 1st wife, Eudoxia, when Alexis was balky. Ivan V, older half-brother of Peter, sat with him jointly when they were boys, until Ivan's early death.
1725 to 1727	**Catherine I (Skavronsky)** *2nd wife of Peter I*	In 1721 Peter issued a decree giving to the ruler the right to choose his successor, then failed to use this power. Menshikov and the Guards officers cowed the Senate into having Catherine crowned.
1727 to 1730	**Peter II** *grandson of Peter I*	Only 12 when he was crowned, Peter II died on the day set for his marriage to Prince Dolgoruky's daughter. He moved the court from St. Petersburg back to Moscow.
1730 to 1740	**Anne (of Courland)** *2nd daughter of Ivan V*	Vulgar and harsh, she filled her court at St. Petersburg with wanton, spendthrift Germans who exploited and abused the Russian people, already suffering from fires, epidemics, war and famine. She chose as her successor, Ivan, the infant son of her niece.

1429 Jeanne d'Arc raised siege of Orleans. Charles VII crowned at Reims.
1431 Jeanne burnt at Rouen. Henry VI crowned at Westminster.
1440 Gutenberg invented printing by movable type.
1442 Eton founded by Henry VI.
1445 York excluded from council; start of War of the Roses.
1453 Turks captured Constantinople: Emperor Constantine killed on walls.

1463 François Villon died.
1476 Caxton established printing press at Westminster.
1485 Richard III defeated and killed at Bosworth. Henry VI King of England.
1492 Columbus discovered San Salvador. Spanish conquered Granada.
1498 Savonarola burnt at Florence. Thomas de Torquemada died.

1509 Henry VII succeeded by Henry VIII.
1513 Scots allied with France, defeated at Flodden. James IV killed, succeeded by James V.
1513 Balboa crossed Isthmus of Panama to the Pacific.
1519 (to 1520) Conquest of Mexico by Cortes.
1532 (to 1534) Pizarro conquered Peru.

1535 Ignatius Loyala founded Order of Jesuits.
1547 Henry VIII died; succeeded by Edward VI.
1556 Archbishop Cranmer burnt.
1558 Mary died; succeeded by Elizabeth.

1562 Massacre of Protestants at Vassy; outbreak of Huguenot wars.
1582 Pope Gregory XIII reformed Julian calendar.
1584 Raleigh discovered and annexed Virginia.
1588 Defeat of the Spanish Armada.
1589 Catherine de Medici died. Henry III murdered.
1590 Henry IV (Navarre) defeated League at Ivry.
1597 Chinese expelled Japs from Korea after 5 years' occupation.

1598 Spaniards settled Santa Fe.
1600 Amsterdam bank founded. 1st endorsed bill of exchange at Naples.
1603 Elizabeth died; James VI of Scotland now James I of England.
1603 Champlain's first voyage up St. Lawrence.
1604 1st English dictionary (Cowdry). French settled Nova Scotia.

1605 Gunpowder Plot discovered.
1605 Cervantes: *Don Quixote*. (English translation 1612).
1605 Bacon: *Advancement of Learning*.
1605 Shakespeare: *King Lear* and *Macbeth*.

1607 Ulster estates confiscated, given to English and Scottish families.
1608 Holland gained independence; allied with France and England.
1609 Henry Hudson sailed into New York Harbor.
1609 Galileo perfected the telescope (thermometer and sector, 1597).
1609 Moors expelled from Spain.

1616 Death of Shakespeare at Stratford; Cervantes at Madrid.
1618 Raleigh beheaded. 30 Years War begun.
1643 Louis XIV, King of France; Anne of Austria regent till 1654.
1644 End of Ming, beginning of Manchu dynasty in China.

1649 Charles I beheaded; Commonwealth declared.
1653 Cromwell made Lord Protector, with Council of State.
1660 English Crown restored: Charles II.
1665 Great Plague in London.
1667 Milton: *Paradise Lost*.

1677 Spinoza died, having completed *Ethica*.
1678 Bunyan: *Pilgrim's Progress*.
1679 Habeas Corpus Act passed. Party names "Whig" and "Tory" in use.
1680 Comédie Française established. Samuel Butler died.

1685 Charles II died, succeeded by James II.
1689 Mary II & William III (of Orange) called to English throne.
1702 William III died, succeeded by Queen Anne.
1714 Queen Anne died, succeeded by George Louis as George I.
1722 Louis XIV died, succeeded by Louis XV, his great-grandson.

1725 Louis XV married Maria Leszinska of Poland.
1726 Swift: *Gulliver's Travels*.
1727 George I died, succeeded by George II.

1728 John Gay: *Beggar's Opera*.
1729 Treaty of Seville between England and Spain; France and Holland joined.
1729 Baltimore founded.

1732 James Oglethorpe founded colony of Georgia.
1733 Conscription introduced into Prussia.
1735 Zenger case (New York) established freedom of press.
1738 First spinning machine patented in England.

Year	Ruler	Description

1740 to 1741 — **Ivan VI** *great grandson of Ivan V* — The gentry, incensed at the rule of foreigners, had the regent, Biron, whisked to Siberia, the infant Ivan put in prison, thus clearing the way for Peter the Great's daughter, Elizabeth.

1741 to 1762 — **Elizabeth** *daughter of Peter I* — She wished to follow her father's policies but her mother's peasant blood showed in extravagance and carelessness. Suvorov aided her in bringing back Russian customs, and increased education, founding the first university at Moscow. Russia joined France and Austria to check Frederick the Great's rising power.

1762 to 1762 — **Peter III** *grandson of Peter the Great* — Son of Peter I's slain son Alexis, and heir to his Aunt Elizabeth, who had him married to an Anhalt princess, Catherine. Hare-brained, Peter insulted and antagonized many people. He was slain by Catherine's supporters.

1762 to 1796 — **Catherine II** *daughter of Prince of Anhalt-Zerbst; widow of Peter III* — Although the usurper of a crown gained by murder, she proved an able and adroit ruler, and shone as sovereign in the first brilliant court of Russia. Plots and pretenders rose about her; these she patiently subdued.

1796 to 1801 — **Paul** *son of Peter III and Catherine II* — He showed a weak intellect, reversing all his mother's policies. He sent an army against France; later backed Napoleon. He was murdered in his bed-chamber by Russian nobles.

1801 to 1825 — **Alexander** *son of Paul* — Liberal in thought, handsome and dramatic, he connived to do good. Deserting his allies in 1807 he made peace with Bonaparte. In 1812 Bonaparte was defeated in his retreat from Moscow. In 1813 Alexander led his army out of Russia and freed Europe.

1825 to 1855 — **Nicholas I** *3rd son of Paul* — The Decembrist revolt marred his coronation. Tall and dignified, he accepted his office as a duty. Though laws were codified and made accessible, bureaucracy grew. Reform was halted by checks, proofs, verifications; initiative was dead. The widespread revolts of 1848 shocked the Tsar. The Crimean War against England, France, Austria and Turkey was being lost when he died.

1855 to 1881 — **Alexander II** *son of Nicholas I* — The Tsars, since Catherine's time, wished to free the serfs but found it too difficult. Alexander spent six years getting a plan from the gentry before granting freedom in 1861. Universities grew and censorship relaxed. Marx was translated into Russian in 1872. This Tsar was murdered in 1881.

1881 to 1894 — **Alexander III** *son of Alexander II* — Of powerful physique with limited outlook and strong convictions. Anti-liberal, with faith in autocracy, he rounded up the plotters of his father's assassination and destroyed them. Education and the press were checked to restrain the radicals. A protective tariff and gold standard built up industry.

1894 to 1917 — **Nicholas II** *son of Alexander III* — A man of good will and pleasant charm but lacking any firmness to resist the importunate. In 1898 he sponsored the Hague Convention to limit armaments. His lack of policy in the East led to war with Japan in 1904, which Russia lost. In the war of 1914 his inertia gave the neurotic Empress control of affairs, which culminated in his downfall and death.

1917 — **Provisional Government** (Mar. 16 to Nov. 7) — Nicholas II abdicated March 15 in response to a demand by the Duma, which was dismayed by food riots and the war's mismanagement. A Provisional Government was headed first by Prince Lvov, later by Alexander Kerensky, a Socialist Revolutionary. Universal suffrage was granted, a Constituent Assembly planned. Russia continued losing the war with Germany. Her armies were being undermined by Bolshevik defeatist propaganda.

1917 to 1923 — **Bolshevik Government** — Vladimir Ilyitch Lenin (Ulyanov) and his Bolshevik group overpowered the Provisional Government on November 7 through their control of the armed forces. They abolished suffrage, exercising power through their Party organization and a terrorist police force. They accepted harsh peace terms from Germany and beat off repeated attempts by the Allied powers to intervene. After winning their civil war, they retreated somewhat from pure Marxism. In 1923 they formed the Union of Soviet Socialist Republics. Lenin retired in 1922, died in 1924.

1740 (to 1786) Frederick II, the Great, King of Prussia.
1740 Charles VI, last Hapsburg Emperor, died; succeeded by his daughter, Maria Theresa.
1741 Handel wrote *The Messiah*.
1741 Frederick II defeated Austria, conquered Silesia.
1746 Battle of Culloden; Charles, the young pretender, defeated.
1753 British Museum founded.
1757 Clive took Calcutta.
1758 Washington took Fort Duquesne.
1760 *Public Ledger* published, first English daily newspaper.

1762 English took St. Vincent, Grenada; Martinique, Havana and Philippine Islands.

1769 (to 1770) Cook's first voyage around the world.
1770 The French Dauphin married Marie Antoinette, daughter of Maria Theresa.
1771 First edition of *Encyclopaedia Britannica*.
1776 American Declaration of Independence.
1776 Benjamin Franklin made Ambassador to France.
1789 George Washington inaugurated 1st President, U. S. A.
1793 Louis XVI executed — Reign of Terror — religion abolished.

1797 Jervis and Nelson defeated the French off St. Vincent.
1798 Battle of the Pyramids. Nelson destroyed French fleet off Aboukir.
1799 Bonaparte defeated the Austrians at Marengo.
1801 Jefferson became third President of the U. S. A.

1804 Napoleon crowned Emperor of France.
1805 Nelson destroyed French-Spanish fleet off Trafalgar.
1807 Fulton navigated his steamship on the Hudson River.
1823 President Monroe promulgated the Monroe Doctrine.

1837 William IV died; succeeded by Queen Victoria (d. 1901).
1848 Louis Napoleon elected President of France (Emperor in 1852).
1848 Revolts all over Europe.
1849 Garibaldi entered Rome.
1854. U. S. A. made first treaty with Japan.

1860 Lincoln elected President, U. S. A.
1862 Lincoln decrees all slaves free.
1862 Bismarck appointed Prussian Premier.
1864 Geneva convention: Red Cross begun.
1865 Lee surrendered at Appomatox. Lincoln assassinated 5 days later.
1870 Siege of Paris. (Capitulated 1871.)
1881 President Garfield shot; succeeded by Chester A. Arthur.

1885 Mahdi took Khartoum; Gordon died.
1888 William II became Emperor of Germany.
1888 First railroad built in China.
1889 Treaty of Constantinople internationalized Suez Canal.

1901 President McKinley assassinated; succeeded by Theodore Roosevelt.
1904 Panama Canal begun (completed 1914).
1912 Woodrow Wilson elected President U. S. A.
1914 Germany declared war on Russia (Aug. 1) starting World War I.
1914 Britain declared war on Germany (Aug. 4) and Austria (Aug. 12).
1914 President Wilson announced U. S. neutrality.
1914 First battle of the Marne (Sept. 9).
1914 Great Britain declared war on Turkey (Nov. 5).
1915 The *Lusitania* torpedoed (May 7).

1917 Germany announced unrestricted submarine war (Jan. 31).
1917 United States declared war on Germany (April 6).
1917 Canadians took Vimy Ridge (April 10).
1917 Congress passed Selective Service Act.
1917 First American troops arrived in France (June 26).
1917 General Allenby took Jerusalem (Dec. 9).

1918 Woodrow Wilson announced 14 Points for Armistice (Jan. 8).
1918 Marshal Foch made Generalissimo of Allied Armies.
1918 U. S. Marines victorious at Belleau Wood (June 11).
1918 Germany signed the Armistice (Nov. 11).
1919 Peace Conference started in Paris (Jan. 18).
1919 Mussolini founded the Fascist Party (Feb. 23).
1920 Prohibition became law in the United States.
1920 League of Nations held first meeting: London, Feb. 11.
1920 Warren G. Harding elected President, U. S. A.
1922 Mussolini and his Fascists marched on Rome.

1923 to 1956	**U.S.S.R**	Joseph Vissarionovich Stalin (Djugashvilli) succeeded Lenin as head of the Party, which changed its name to Communist. By purges and "liquidations" he consolidated the country, collectivizing agriculture, nationalizing industry. Five-Year Plans were pushed through to reconstruct Russia's economy. A new Constitution (1936) gave his dictatorship a democratic front. The Red Army was forged to meet Germany's threat. A treaty was made with Germany (1939) which was followed shortly by the Nazi invasion of Poland and the partition of Poland between Germany and the U.S.S.R. But in 1941 Germany attacked the U.S.S.R., which fought gallantly though suffering great setbacks. But with the aid of Britain and the U.S., Germany was finally defeated (May 8, 1945). Three months later, Russia entered the war against Japan and invaded Manchuria. This event added to the impact of the Atomic Bomb quickly brought Japan to her knees and peace was signed Sept. 2, 1945. After World War II, the U.S.S.R. took advantage of Axis defeat and Allied apathy to communize or help communize nine nations: Poland, East Germany, Czechoslovakia, Hungary, Rumania, Bulgaria, Albania, North Korea, and finally, China. Russia rebuilt its ruined cities and industries, then embarked upon fast industrial expansion which soon made the U.S.S.R. second in economic potential only to the United States. The first Soviet atom bomb was exploded in 1949, first hydrogen bomb in 1953. After Stalin's death Russia's new leaders made the dictatorship a little milder, opened the Iron Curtain a little, wooed the Arab world and free Asia with flattery, gifts, loans, profitable trade. Stalin's successors revived the cult of Lenin minus insistence on the inevitability of war with Capitalism. Their new line: Competitive Co-existence."
1956 to 1968	**U.S.S.R.**	In 1956, riots in Poland loosened Russia's control there, but when Hungary revolted the Soviets cracked down bloodily. By 1958, Nikita Khrushchev had bulled to sole leadership, past Malenkov and Bulganin. He took credit for the 1957 Sputnik launchings and subsequent space feats, as well as for Russia's nuclear ICBM arsenal. In 1959 he toured the U.S., visited President Eisenhower at Camp David, talked peace at the U.N. The U-2 episode cancelled a visit to Russia by Ike and a 1960 "Summit" at Paris. Khrushchev ranted at the U.N. about disarmament, and took Cuba's Castro under his wing. He met President Kennedy at Vienna in 1961, talked more war, and built the Berlin Wall. The next year he based missiles in Cuba, but took them out again when President Kennedy became adamant. A Moscow–Washington "hot line" was installed to help safeguard peace. China accused Russia of abandoning world Communism, and a deep rift ensued, all the more serious because Russia had taught China nuclear science. In 1964, Khrushchev was suddenly removed from office and replaced by his underlings Kosygin and Brezhnev. They continued cold toward China, polite toward most other nations. Great advances in space flight and military rocketry continued. In 1967, the 50th anniversary of the Bolshevik Revolution, Russia backed the losers of a six-day Arab-Israeli war. Kosygin visited the U.N. to talk peace, and then, while still supplying North Vietnam with munitions, met President Johnson at Glassboro, New Jersey, to exchange pleasantries. In 1968, Russia rearmed Egypt, deployed its growing navy in the Mediterranean, and courted India as a foil to China. Czechoslovakia, led by Alexander Dubcek (and abetted by Tito), tried to shake off Kremlin disciplines, only to get itself invaded by 200,000 Russian and hardline Warsaw Pact troops, many of whom stayed on as a garrison after Dubcek and Company were reinstated.

1923	President Harding died (Aug. 2); succeeded by Calvin Coolidge.
1927	Washington Disarmament Conference.
1927	Lindbergh flew alone across the Atlantic (May 20, 21).
1928	Herbert Hoover elected President, U.S.A.
1929	Stockmarket crash (Oct. 29); start of U.S. depression.
1933	U.S. banks closed: moratorium.
1933	Franklin D. Roosevelt took office as U.S. President Jan. 20.
1933	Hitler took office as Chancellor of Germany Jan. 30.
1936	Edward VIII of England abdicated; succeeded by brother George VI.
1939	Germany invaded Poland, starting World War II.
1940	Germany conquered all western Europe, with Italy chiming in.
1941	Japan attacked Pearl Harbor, bringing U.S. into war.
1942	Allied armies under Eisenhower landed in Africa (Nov.).
1943	Italy surrendered to U.S. and Britain (Sept.).
1944	Allies landed in Normandy (June) and southern France (Aug.).
1945	President Roosevelt died (April 12); succeeded by Harry S. Truman.
1945	Atomic bombs dropped on Hiroshima and Nagasaki (Aug. 6, 9), bringing Japan's surrender (Aug. 14).
1947	Truman Doctrine opposed further Red expansion westward.
1947	UNRRA succeeded by Marshall Plan to revive Europe's economy.
1947	Peace treaties signed for Italy, Rumania, Bulgaria, Hungary, Finland, but not for Austria and Germany.
1948	U.N. atomic control vetoed by Russia.
1949	North Atlantic Treaty Organization formed.
1950	Aggression by Reds. North Koreans, backed by Red China and Russia, halted by U.N. forces. Red China intervened and hostilities continued.
1950	Eisenhower put in charge of NATO forces.
1952	George VI died (Feb. 6), succeeded by Elizabeth II.
1952	Eisenhower succeeded Truman as U.S. President.
1953	Armistice in Korea after 24 months of truce talks.
1954	West Germany granted sovereignty, admitted to NATO.
1955	Churchill retired, succeeded by Anthony Eden.
1955	Conference "at the summit" in Geneva by Big Four powers.
1955	President Eisenhower recovered from a heart attack.
1956	Egypt seized the Suez Canal. Nasser denounced withdrawal of Western funds for the Aswan High Dam.
1957	First British H bomb fired.
1958	Castro overthrew Batista in Cuba.
1959	Eisenhower, Macmillan, De Gaulle, and Adenauer met in Paris, and invited Khrushchev to join them there next year.
1960	John F. Kennedy elected President of the U.S.
1961	"Bay of Pigs" fiasco.
1962	John H. Glenn tripled Russia's earth-orbiting feat and started a parade of U.S. astronauts.
1963	A treaty banning nuclear tests aboveground signed by the U.S., U.K., and U.S.S.R., but not China or France.
1963	President Kennedy assassinated, succeeded by Lyndon B. Johnson.
1964	President Johnson reelected.
1965	U.S. troops, ships, and aircraft go into action against North Vietnam in an undeclared war.
1965	U.S. space technology overtook Russia's.
1967	Treaty banning nuclear weapons in space, and celestial bodies as war bases, signed by the U.S., U.S.S.R., and many other nations, but denounced by China, which now had A and H bombs.
1968	U.S. continued fighting North Vietnam, but peace talks at last began in Paris.
1968	President Johnson "abdicated." France's first H-bomb fired, in South Pacific.
1968	Senator Robert F. Kennedy was assassinated.

435

DATE DUE

OCT 22 70		

GAYLORD

PRINTED IN U.S.A.